AMERICAN ABOLITIONISM

A Nation Divided: Studies in the Civil War Era
ORVILLE VERNON BURTON AND ELIZABETH R. VARON, *EDITORS*

AMERICAN ABOLITIONISM

*Its Direct Political Impact from
Colonial Times into Reconstruction*

STANLEY HARROLD

UNIVERSITY OF VIRGINIA PRESS
Charlottesville and London

University of Virginia Press
© 2019 by the Rector and Visitors of the University of Virginia
All rights reserved
Printed in the United States of America on acid-free paper

First published 2019

1 3 5 7 9 8 6 4 2

Library of Congress Cataloging-in-Publication Data
Names: Harrold, Stanley, author.
Title: American Abolitionism : Its Direct Political Impact from
Colonial Times into Reconstruction / Stanley Harrold.
Description: Charlottesville : University of Virginia Press, 2019. | Series: A Nation
Divided: Studies in the Civil War Era | Includes bibliographical references and index.
Identifiers: LCCN 2018051832 | ISBN 9780813942292
(cloth : alk. paper) | ISBN 9780813942308 (ebook)
Subjects: LCSH: Antislavery movements—United States—History. |
Abolitionists—United States—History. | Slavery—Political aspects—
United States—History. | United States—Politics and government—
1783–1865. Classification: LCC E441 .H36 2019 | DDC 326.80973—dc23
LC record available at *https://lccn.loc.gov/2018051832*

Cover art: Details of "A Scene in the Hall of Representatives,"
Illustrated London News, April 6, 1861. (Stuart A. Rose Manuscript
Archives and Rare Book Library, Emory University)

For Judy and Emily

Contents

AMERICAN ABOLITIONISM

Introduction

On January 1, 1863, midway through the American Civil War, President Abraham Lincoln signed the Final Emancipation Proclamation. Henceforth the U.S. military would fight to abolish slavery in areas under Confederate control. Nearly two years later, following Union victory in the war, ratification of the Thirteenth Amendment outlawed slavery throughout the country. The Fourteenth Amendment, designed to protect black civil rights, and the Fifteenth Amendment, granting black men the right to vote, followed in 1868 and 1870. As became clear, these amendments did not guarantee black freedom and equality before the law. But if, as Prussian military thinker Carl von Clausewitz wrote in 1832, "war is . . . a continuation of political activity by other means," political power had ended legal slavery throughout the United States and provided a constitutional foundation for black citizenship rights.[1]

A century and a half earlier, an American movement to abolish slavery had begun in the British North American colonies. This book focuses on the movement's leaders' *direct* impact on and interaction with American politics, politicians, and government from about 1700 down to the movement's end during the years following the Civil War. The book utilizes primary sources and historical studies produced since the late nineteenth century to better understand continuity and change in abolitionist political tactics and their results during successive eras. The goal is to develop a precise understanding of to what degree abolitionists, who belonged to a variety of factions, contributed directly, over an extended period of time, to the momentous but incomplete victory over slavery. Throughout, the book acknowledges that factors beyond organized abolitionism had a major role in determining the course of events that led to the Thirteenth, Fourteenth, and Fifteenth Amendments.

The story is as complicated as it is long. This is because the abolition movement changed over time in scope, short-term goals, personnel, leadership, organization, demeanor, and rhetoric. A gradualist approach and state-level action dominated the movement into the early 1800s. Demands for abolishing slavery more quickly within a national framework emerged during the 1820s. In regard to leadership, white men dominated the movement's major organizations throughout. But beginning during the 1830s, African American men and women of both races gained prominence. Pietistic and evangelical Christian as well as Enlightenment values remained at the movement's core. By the 1830s, interracialism had joined them. And as time passed, the movement's direct engagement with politics and government increased. This engagement occurred within a context established by the American Revolution, transatlantic antislavery interaction, the northern market revolution, slave unrest, and a growing white southern commitment to slave labor and its expansion. Apparent slaveholder, or Slave Power, control of the U.S. government and the emergence of a northern free-labor ideology also had roles.[2]

Achieving an understanding of a direct abolitionist impact on politics and government is further complicated by varying definitions of who the abolitionists were and often vague understandings of their relationships to other movements. These other movements included a broader, far less radical political *antislavery* movement. Unlike abolitionists, most antislavery politicians, including those associated with the Federalist, Whig, Free Soil, and Republican Parties, rarely advocated general emancipation throughout the United States or black rights. Although there were significant exceptions that reflected abolitionist influence, most such politicians concentrated on blocking slavery expansion and defeating Slave Power in order to protect white northern interests. The other movements also included slave resistance, northward slave escape, and black efforts to achieve legal and social equality in the North. Despite proslavery claims to the contrary, and despite increasing abolitionist involvement, the great majority of African Americans who resisted slavery and escaped from it acted on their own. Black civil rights efforts in the North often involved abolitionists. But such efforts transcended the abolition movement.

Therefore, to avoid confusion, this book employs the precise definition of abolitionists that historian James M. McPherson presents in *The Struggle for Equality: Abolitionists and the Negro in the Civil War and Reconstruction* (1964). McPherson makes the point that historians err when they employ "the word 'abolitionist' to describe adherents of the whole spectrum of antislavery sentiment," which included nonabolitionist politicians and journalists.[3] In contrast, McPherson describes abolitionists as members of radical societies, churches, missionary organizations, and tiny political parties dedicated to ending slavery quickly throughout the United States. None of these organizations, except for the tiny parties, claimed to be political. Even leaders of the tiny abolitionist parties refused to make the compromises of principle required to gain elective office. However, throughout the abolition movement's existence, the leaders of its organizations sought directly to impact politics and government. They initiated petitioning campaigns designed to influence in turn colonial, state, and national governmental bodies. They lobbied legislatures, on occasion addressed legislatures, and developed personal relationships with antislavery politicians. Other abolitionists undertook physical action against slavery in the South and thereby had a direct impact on politicians, legislative bodies, and sectional politics.

Throughout the movement's existence, abolitionists also sought *indirectly* to shape political dialogue and government policy. They did so by preaching, holding public meetings, and circulating antislavery propaganda in attempts to shape popular opinion. Historians sometimes portray abolitionist petitioning campaigns as aimed primarily at popular opinion. But as mentioned above, forces beyond abolitionism influenced how people, North and South, perceived slavery and opposition to it. Therefore gauging the strength of abolitionist impact on popular opinion in comparison to the strength of such nonabolitionist forces is an impressionistic enterprise. So is evaluating the impact of popular opinion on politics and government. Such problems constitute the main reason why this book concentrates on *direct* abolitionist impact on colonial, state, and national governments. Through such tactics as petitioning, lobbying, and personal contacts with politicians, abolitionists demonstratively influenced broader, less principled, less comprehensive, and far less radical political antislavery efforts. These direct political tactics also influenced southern journalists and politicians who regarded them as threats to the expansion and perpetuation of slavery.

Direct abolitionist efforts to influence politics and government developed in several stages. First came Quaker abolitionists who lived in the Pennsylvania colony during the late seventeenth and early eighteenth centuries.[4] They used their sectarian government, which overlapped with the colony's civil government, to push coreligionists toward freeing slaves. Second, from the 1750s through the early national period, northeastern abolitionists, including Quakers, evangelicals, and African Americans, petitioned and lobbied colonial and then state legislatures. During this phase some prominent northern politicians joined the newly formed abolition societies and became abolitionists. Third, beginning with the U.S. Constitutional Convention in 1787 and the convening of the First Congress in 1789, abolitionists expanded their direct efforts to include influencing the national government.

During the second decade of the nineteenth century, about twenty years after the third stage began, the abolition movement struggled to maintain its political influence.[5] Its influence resurged in 1819 with the controversy over Missouri Territory's application to join the Union as a slave-labor state. The resurgence continued during the early 1820s with a debate over slavery within the state of Illinois. And it reached a peak in 1829 as abolitionists pressed Congress to end slavery in the District of Columbia. During the early 1830s, after a more doctrinaire movement for *immediate* general emancipation arose, abolitionists expanded their petitioning, lobbying, and personal contacts with antislavery politicians. In response proslavery politicians became even more defensive.

In 1840 three issues prompted immediate abolitionists to divide into four factions. The first issue concerned the role of women in abolitionist organizations. The second was the question of whether or not abolitionists should remain in churches that communed with slaveholders. The third (and most relevant for this book) consisted of disagreement over whether abolitionists should independently engage in *electoral* politics under the U.S. Constitution. The first faction to emerge as a result of these issues consisted of William Lloyd Garrison and his associates. Known as *Garrisonian,* this faction endorsed participation of women, rejected remaining in what its members regarded as proslavery churches, and refused to participate in elections under what they regarded as a proslavery Constitution. The second faction consisted of evangelical or church-oriented abolitionists. Its members usually opposed the participation of women, favored working within the churches, and split in regard to electoral politics. The third faction was similar to the second except that all its members favored voting. They asserted that under the Constitution the U.S. government had power to abolish slavery throughout the country, including in the southern states. They led in forming the Liberty Party—the first antislavery political party.

The fourth faction was more moderate and more numerous than the others. Its members endorsed a conventional interpretation of the U.S. Constitution, which denied that the U.S. government had power to abolish slavery in states. Leaders of this faction joined in forming the Liberty Party, soon ceased to be abolitionists, and became antislavery politicians. As a result, by the mid-1840s, the remaining abolitionist factions sought directly to influence the moderate Liberty leaders along with politicians affiliated with the major parties. In 1848 the moderate Liberty leaders joined with those Whig and Democratic politicians who opposed slavery expansion to form the Free Soil Party. The remaining abolitionists then sought to influence Free Soil politicians.

When, six years later, the Republican Party formed in response to the Kansas-Nebraska Act, the abolitionist relationship to antislavery politics and politicians became more complex. Abolitionists sought to shape the party's platform and, especially, the Radical Republican faction. Meanwhile abolitionist physical action against slavery and in defense of fugitive slaves also directly impacted politics and government. That influence peaked with John Brown's raid on Harpers Ferry in 1859. This raid forced Republican leaders to address the issue of violent action against slavery. It affected abolitionist efforts to shape both Republican policies during the election of 1860 and the secession winter of 1860–61, and proslavery characterizations of the Republican Party. Thereafter abolitionists directly influenced Abraham Lincoln's Civil War presidential administration and Republican leaders in Congress.

The degree of abolitionist impact, direct and indirect, on politics and government throughout the controversy over slavery is at the center of a long debate. On one side are those who contend that abolitionists succeeded in pushing politicians to take more radical stands against slavery than they otherwise would have. In this view abolitionists collaborated with antislavery politicians and in many instances *were* antislavery politicians. Both abolitionists and proslavery advocates originated this contention. From the 1780s through the Civil War, abolitionists often portrayed their politician allies as promising opponents of slavery who responded positively to praise and censure. Meanwhile proslavery politicians and journalists portrayed abolitionist influence on politicians as a threat to slavery and white southern interests.[6]

On the other side are those who argue that a great gap separated abolitionists from even the most dedicated antislavery politicians. Abolitionists often expressed this view during the 1830s and thereafter, even as they sought directly to influence such politicians. They held that, unlike themselves, antislavery politicians placed party loyalty, economic interests, devotion to the Union, and personal ambition ahead of Christian morality, natural rights doctrines, national welfare, and ending African American suffering in bondage. Abolitionists noted that politicians who opposed the expansion of slavery into U.S. territories failed to advocate emancipation in the southern states and District of Columbia. They charged correctly that such politicians upheld the legality of the interstate slave trade and the fugitive slave laws.

When antislavery politicians went a step further to advocate "freedom national," abolitionists reacted similarly. Freedom national, or *denationalization,* meant ending slavery in the national domain and ending U.S. government support for slavery. Those Free Soil and Republican politicians who advocated this approach presented it as a means of indirectly forcing emancipation in the southern states. But abolitionists regarded it as a gradualist approach that would permit slavery's indefinite continuation.[7] Conversely antislavery politicians often dismissed abolitionists as extreme, irrational, irresponsible, divisive, and dangerous fanatics who hindered progress toward eventual emancipation.

For nearly a century following the Civil War the first view, holding that abolitionists exercised a profound influence on politics and government, predominated. As aging abolitionists and their children looked back, they placed either themselves or their parents at the center of a political struggle over slavery. They asserted that the abolition movement had—for the sake of the enslaved, Christian morality, and the nation's welfare—brought about the Civil War in 1861 and universal emancipation in 1865.[8]

Historian James Ford Rhodes in the first volume of his *History of the United States from the Compromise of 1850* (1894) refines this interpretation by portraying a powerful but *indirect* abolitionist influence on politics. The movement, he contends, through its impact on northern public opinion brought about the formation of the Republican Party, Lincoln's election to the presidency, and defeat of the slaveholders' threat to the Union. Rhodes writes, "By stirring the national conscience . . . [abolitionists] made possible the formation of a political party, whose cardinal principle was opposition to the extension of slavery, and whose reason for existence lay in the belief of its adherents that slavery in the South was wrong."[9]

Albert Bushnell Hart in *Slavery and Abolition* (1906), the first monographic study of the abolition movement, further refines the argument that abolitionists profoundly influenced American politics. He concentrates on the 1830s and differentiates between religiously motivated abolitionists who were "bent on persuading or coercing the master to give up his authority" and northern antislavery politicians. The latter, he writes, acted "not so much out of sympathy with the oppressed negro, as from the belief that slavery was an injury to their own neighbors and constituents and that the influence of the slave power in national affairs was harmful." Nevertheless Hart links abolitionists to politics. "As time went on," he maintains, "the [political] anti-slavery and [morally based] abolition movements in the north came closer together and sometimes joined forces, partly through the appearance of political abolitionists . . . and partly by the warming-up of the anti-slavery people . . . to a belief that abolition might, after all, be the only way to stop the advance of slavery."[10]

The reactionary, pro-southern scholars who dominated Civil War–era historiography from the 1920s into the 1940s agree with Rhodes and Hart that abolitionists had a major political role in the sectional struggle that led to what the pro-southern historians regard as an unnecessary war. Frank L. Owsley contends that, although "genuine abolitionists were few in number in the beginning," they influenced the northern masses, intellectuals, preachers, and politicians. According to Owsley, "In time the average Northerner accepted in whole or in part the abolitionist picture of the southern [white] people." Avery O. Craven claims, "Abolition[ists] threatened to produce a race problem which had in large part been solved by the institution of slavery, and caused a move for [southern] independence." James G. Randall asserts that abolitionists introduced "the avenging force of puritanism in politics," which became "a major cause of the [sectional] conflict."[11]

Gilbert H. Barnes and his University of Michigan colleague Dwight L. Dumond, who provide a far more positive view of the abolition movement than do Owsley, Craven, and Randall, agree with the pro-southern scholars and with earlier historians that the movement had a major impact on American politics. But Barnes's *Antislavery Impulse* (1933) and Dumond's *Antislavery Origins of the Civil War in the United States* (1939) portray the abolitionist role in antislavery politics as foundational rather than continuing. Barnes asserts, "From the [eighteen] forties to the sixties, the doctrine of the [political] anti-slavery host . . . continued in the moral tenets of the original anti-slavery [abolitionist] creed . . . until 1860, when, county by county, the antislavery areas gave Abraham Lincoln the votes which made him President." Dumond declares that antislavery politician Lincoln "was thoroughly sound on the fundamental principles of abolition doctrine."[12]

During the late 1950s and early 1960s, the civil rights movement and the Civil War centennial encouraged historians to pursue further the view that abolitionist arguments, developed during the 1830s, shaped antislavery politics during the 1840s and 1850s. Merton L. Dillon in "The Failure of the American Abolitionists" (1959) argues that although "the work of the abolitionists as moral reformers had practically ended by 1844," they had by then helped create a broad political antislavery movement. Dillon adds that the abolitionists also encouraged a white southern intransigence that made sectional compromise "unlikely if not impossible." Betty Fladeland in "Who Were the Abolitionists?" (1964) links the abolitionists of the 1830s with those who engaged in antislavery politics during the 1840s and 1850s. According to Fladeland, "Many of the 'moral suasionists' of the '30s simply . . . shift[ed] their strategy to political action. They were still abolitionists." Kenneth M. Stampp in *The Causes of the Civil War* (1965) observes, "During the 1830s, abolitionism . . . became a permanently significant political force."[13]

In *Ballots for Freedom* (1976), Richard H. Sewell summarizes this interpretation. "Because attitudes toward slavery were susceptible to nearly infinite variations and permutations," he declares, "too rigid a dichotomy between 'abolition' and 'antislavery' risks distorting reality." But by 1976, most historians of the abolition movement had come to deny that it had significant political influence. Decades earlier Charles A. and Mary R. Beard had presented the antebellum sectional conflict *not* as one influenced by abolitionist concerns regarding oppression and morality. Instead the Beards perceived a gap between the abolition movement and politics that abolitionists themselves had sometimes emphasized. The Beards' *The Rise of American Civilization* (1927) describes the sectional conflict as a *class* conflict that pitted aristocratic southern slaveholders against the "capitalists, laborers, and farmers of the North and West." "Slavery," the book asserts, "was not the fundamental issue."[14]

During the 1960s, increasing numbers of historians came to agree with the Beards that the abolition movement had no significant influence on the sectional conflict. In "The Northern Response to Slavery" (1965), Martin B. Duberman declares, "The abolitionist movement never became a major channel of Northern antislavery sentiment. It remained in 1860 what it had been in 1830: the small but not still voice of radical reform." In "Slavery and the Slave Power" (1969), Larry Gara traces the origins of the Republican Party to northern fear of southern political dominance "rather [than] to any growth of pure antislavery sentiment or humanitarian consideration for the slave as an oppressed human being."[15]

During the 1970s, the trend toward questioning the abolitionists' political impact continued. Dillon's *The Abolitionists: The Growth of a Dissenting Minority* (1974) and James Brewer Stewart's *Holy Warriors: The Abolitionists and American Slavery* (1976) recognize an abolitionist role in the sectional politics of the 1850s. The two historians nevertheless question whether the movement contributed to emancipation in 1865. Dillon observes, "The relationship between the end of slavery and the long crusade of abolitionists was anything but clear and direct. . . . Emancipation, far from being the result of a morally transformed America . . . served . . . to justify prevailing values and to reinforce the dominion of the ruling order." Stewart writes, "[Immediate] abolitionists could not really claim that their thirty-year movement had led directly to the destruction of slavery." Instead "warfare between irreconcilable cultures, not [abolitionist] moral suasion, had intervened between master and his slave."[16]

In *Free Hearts and Free Homes* (2003), Michael D. Pierson credits abolitionists with establishing "the parameters of debate" in the sectional conflict. But he also argues that abolitionists did not go beyond evangelical moral suasion. Pierson contends, "Abolitionists . . . usually dismissed politics, hoping to persuade individuals to voluntarily give up slavery as a means to religious and personal redemption." Writing two years after Pierson, Frederick J. Blue suggests that those "who led the nation to emancipation" through "the political process" were distinct from less than practical abolitionists.[17]

Other historians go further in separating abolitionists from major events in nineteenth-century sectional politics. They describe abolitionism as an attempt at social control in the North using slavery and the South as negative reference points. In *The Antislavery Appeal* (1976), Ronald G. Walters writes, "Abolitionism . . . reflected a desire to impose moral order upon broad economic and social change." In "Abolition as a Sacred Vocation" (1979), Donald M. Scott describes immediate abolitionism as a surrogate religion. He writes, "Immediatism was less a program of what to do about slavery than . . . a sign of whether or not a person was a saved Christian." In "'Historical Topics Sometimes Run Dry'" (1981), Lawrence J. Friedman declares, "Sectional conflict, Civil War, and legal emancipation would probably have occurred even if there had been no active abolition movement."[18]

Historians have recently used abolitionist writings as sources for understanding race and gender in antebellum northern society without reference to politics or political issues. In 2006 Timothy Patrick McCarthy and John Stauffer presented a collection of essays as the "first major reexamination of American abolitionism in more than a generation." The essays in the collection do not address the movement's impact on the sectional political conflict that led to the Civil War. This led Stewart to comment, "Our current . . . abolitionist scholarship has deeply illuminated the movement's . . . strategies, tactics, and cultural productions. But it has not demonstrated its wider political impact. . . . It has not explained how their [abolitionists'] interventions might actually have changed Northern politics." Recent scholarship expands understanding of how gender, race, religion, economics, and international (especially British) influences shaped American abolitionism.[19] But, as Stewart indicates, there is little parallel expansion of understanding of how the movement directly impacted American politics and government.

It is true that during the past two decades several historians have focused on the short-lived, initially abolitionist Liberty Party and its impact on the larger Free Soil Party. Douglas M. Strong's *Perfectionist Politics: Abolitionism and the Religious Tensions of American Democracy* (1999) is an excellent study of the Liberty Party as it existed in New York. But the book deals more with the relationship between that party and religion than with its impact on politics and government. And Strong argues that New York Liberty leaders burned out by the early 1850s with many of them turning "toward inner-directed personal pursuits." Jonathan H. Earle in *Jacksonian Antislavery and the Politics of Free*

Soil, 1824–1854 (2004) investigates the relationship of Liberty leaders to the Free Soil Party. But Earle centers on the convergence of Jacksonian democracy and antislavery politics and does not include events after 1854. Similarly Bruce Laurie in *Beyond Garrison: Antislavery and Social Reform* (2005) describes abolitionists engaged in antislavery electoral politics. But, except for an epilogue devoted to social issues and nativism, he ends with the "unraveling of the [Free Soil] coalition in 1853."[20]

More recently Corey M. Brooks's *Liberty Power: Antislavery Third Parties and the Transformation of American Politics* (2016) analyzes an abolitionist role in northern party politics between the late 1830s and mid-1850s. Brooks notes the importance of abolitionist petitioning and lobbying. He portrays the Republican Party during the late 1850s and Civil War years as a Liberty legacy. But he defines the term "political abolitionist" loosely and concentrates on politicians who advocated denationalization of slavery rather than immediate emancipation in the South. As Brooks gets to the mid-1840s, he virtually ignores the Garrisonian and church-oriented abolitionists' impact on antislavery politics. In effect Brooks supports the view of abolitionists as progenitors of antislavery politics rather than as an independent force interacting with and continuing to influence that politics.[21]

In contrast to Strong's, Earle's, Laurie's, and Brooks's narrowly focused books, Manisha Sinha's impressive *The Slave's Cause: A History of Abolition* (2016) places abolitionist engagement with American political systems (colonial, state, and national) in a wide context, both chronologically and geographically. Sinha also goes well beyond abolitionist political engagement to cover a variety of topics, including transatlantic exchanges among abolitionists; the role of nonabolitionist African Americans, free and enslaved; the struggle for black rights in the northern states; and the role of abolitionist women. Sinha emphasizes "continuity rather than rupture" in the movement. However she places relatively little emphasis on the differences among the various abolitionist factions. While she at points distinguishes between "political abolitionists" and "antislavery politicians," she allows for a great deal of overlap, which leads to a lack of precision. And she does not cover the Civil War years.[22]

That the abolition movement continues to be the subject of scholarly debate a century and a half after it ended testifies to its importance as well as to the difficulty involved in understanding its significance. The movement had many facets, existed for a long time, and changed over time. It produced a great deal of written material and interacted with other movements and forces. While this book recognizes the broad context within which American abolitionists acted, it centers precisely on the movement's leaders' long engagement with politics and government. It emphasizes rupture as well as continuity. It carefully differentiates between abolitionists and the antislavery politicians they engaged. It clarifies not only the impact of abolitionists on politics and government but the impact that politics and government had on abolitionists.

1

Direct Abolitionist Engagement
in Politics, 1688–1807

When Abraham Lincoln issued the Emancipation Proclamation, the United States was a mighty nation divided against itself in a brutal war. The country's northern section had the most extensive railroad system in the world. Its degree of industrialization rivaled that of Western European counties. Its modern values encouraged individual freedom, initiative, and antislavery politics. The United States' southern section trailed the North in industry. The South's premodern values subordinated individuals. And its agricultural economy sustained its barbaric labor system. Even so the South surpassed most of the world in transportation and production. Before the Civil War, northern and European economies depended on the South for raw cotton and other staples to maintain production and employment.

Two centuries earlier, as race-based chattel slavery emerged on the east coast of North America, no comparatively large, powerful independent nation existed on the continent. Neither did abolitionists or antislavery politics. North America lay on the edge of a European imperialism that had begun during the fifteenth century. Spain, England, and France each claimed portions of the continent, while American Indian nations controlled its interior. In the English colonies servitude remained ill-defined during the seventeenth century. This was in part because England had no law for slavery, in part because of the dispersed rural character of colonial society, and in part because of the slow court-based development of law. Most colonial laborers (American Indian, black, and white) were to varying degrees unfree. The condition, legal status, and length of servitude for white and American Indian servants overlapped with those of Africans. They all faced overwork, brutal punishment, poor living conditions, sexual exploitation, and social disgrace.[1]

Multiple factors changed these circumstances. First, as tobacco cultivation became central to Virginia's and Maryland's economies, plantation owners, courts, colonial assemblies, and public opinion (based on racial prejudice and economic self-interest) assigned an especially disadvantaged status to people of African descent. By the 1640s, aspects of chattel slavery had emerged. Judges and legislatures required black people to serve for life and their children to inherit their status. White people assumed that black people were unfree unless they could prove otherwise. During the late seventeenth and early eighteenth centuries, a similar evolution occurred in the Carolinas, Georgia, and East Florida.[2]

Second, although American Indian slavery persisted through the eighteenth century, disease and westward migration promoted its decline. Third, in 1676 a short-lived rebellion among poor white Virginians led by Nathaniel Bacon frightened Virginia planters away from reliance on unfree white labor. Fourth, English dominance of the Atlantic slave trade by the early eighteenth century lowered the price of black slaves in the colonies. By 1700 black slave labor had become the dominant form of labor in Virginia and Maryland. As slave imports from Africa and the Caribbean increased, plantations replaced small farms as the predominant loci of agricultural production.[3]

Black servitude began in the Northeast as early as in Virginia and Maryland. It existed in New England by 1624. In 1626 the Dutch West India Company brought enslaved Africans to New Amsterdam (later New York City). In 1664 New Jersey provided large parcels of land to those who imported Africans. In 1687, three years after the founding of Pennsylvania, 150 slaves worked there clearing land. And as bondage grew rigid in the South, it did so in the Northeast. Slaves became common, and masters interfered in black family life, independence, and property. Northeastern colonial governments joined those in the South in curtailing manumission and attempting to control free African Americans. Yet slavery took a different form in the northeastern colonies than it did in the South because of varying climate, soil, economics, and demographics. Plantation slavery rarely existed in the Northeast, black slaves there did not lose all their customary rights, and they continued to interact with white people. Forces for freedom had greater strength in the Northeast than in the South.[4]

Slavery's relative weakness north of the Mason-Dixon Line has encouraged assumptions about its eventual peaceful abolition there. A cooler climate, absence of cash crops, large numbers of European immigrants, economic diversification, fewer powerful slaveholders, and a small black population may have predestined slavery's demise.[5] Even so emancipation did not come easily in the Northeast. Slavery brought profits to masters, many white residents regarded black bondage as key to avoiding interracial strife, New England merchants engaged in the Atlantic slave trade, and proslavery interests had political power.

Black resistance, escape, and self-purchase over many years had a major role in undermining slavery in the North. And, as this chapter emphasizes, so did

organized abolitionist encouragement of colonial legislatures and later state legislatures to act against slavery and the slave trade. Such encouragement had consequences beyond individual colonies and later states. This was because decisions
made by northern assemblies and legislatures regarding emancipation during the
late eighteenth century and the first years of the nineteenth century produced
North-South sectionalism. That sectionalism, however, did not lead northern
white majorities to favor ending slavery in the South or advocate equal rights
for African Americans. Instead it inclined white northeasterners, on the basis of
political and economic self-interest, to resist slavery expansion and to tolerate
to various degrees the spread of abolitionism.[6]

Two movements shaped the patterns of thought and action within which
eighteenth-century American abolitionism operated. The first of these, the
Enlightenment, began in Western Europe during the late seventeenth century. Transatlantic commerce, expanding American port cities, the rise of a
merchant class in the Northeast, and a corresponding rise of a master class in
the South helped this intellectual revolution spread to the England's North
American colonies. The Enlightenment's emphasis on perceptions as sources
of knowledge (sensibility), human reasoning (rationalism), and scientific en-
quiry led colonists to establish colleges, publish newspapers, create libraries, and appreciate the value of literate and responsible employees. Sensibility
and rationalism also encouraged criticism of the Atlantic slave trade's brutality and of the violence, degradation, and ignorance associated with slavery.
English philosopher John Locke's *Essay Concerning Human Understanding*
(1690) and his *Two Treatises of Government* (1689) reflected this outlook. His
assertion that all human beings had a natural right to life, liberty, and property
suggested the injustice of slavery.[7]

Four decades later, the second movement, a transatlantic, evangelistic
religious revival known in America as the Great Awakening, began. It grew
out of dissatisfaction with a deterministic and formalistic Protestantism that
seemed to deny most people a chance for salvation. Evangelicals emphasized
emotion rather than reason, and they subordinated logic to enthusiasm. They
challenged social orthodoxy and encouraged believers to demonstrate their
state of grace by providing material aid to the downtrodden. George Whitefield led English evangelicals during the eighteenth century and cofounded
the Methodist Church. During his seven visits to the colonies, beginning
in 1738, he preached that all who believed in God could gain salvation regardless of their social standing. Although Whitefield supported slavery,
he and other evangelicals addressed racially integrated audiences. God,

evangelists said, valued all people regardless of their wealth, education, or race. During the Great Awakening, the great majority of African Americans became Christians. Particularly in the Northeast and in the Chesapeake, this conversion narrowed the cultural gap between black and white Americans. It helped encourage some white Americans to regard African Americans as proper objects of benevolence. It enabled African Americans to create a church-based institutional framework for abolitionist activism. The Great Awakening also profoundly influenced how abolitionists approached politics and government.[8]

For most of the eighteenth century, however, Quakers, few of whom were black and none of whom were evangelicals, led American efforts against slavery. Belief that a God-given inner light united all humans and that violence directed toward any human violated God's law shaped the Quakers' pietistic faith. Black unrest led Quakers to fear that God's wrath in the form of slave revolt awaited those who forced servitude on others. And Quaker merchants, influenced by rationalism, sought to expand flexible, educated workforces based on wage labor. Consequently Quaker abolitionists called on their coreligionists, many of whom owned slaves, to renounce slaveholding and the slave trade. Later they called on non-Quakers to do the same. Most important for this book, Quaker abolitionists pioneered antislavery politics. They had their greatest impact in New Jersey, New York, and Pennsylvania, the last of which Quakers governed from its founding into the 1750s.[9]

Quaker abolitionists were the first to utilize petitioning, a political tactic entrenched in English constitutionalism, to affect government policy regarding slavery. Since before the Magna Carta, English kings had received petitions as a function of their sovereignty. As Parliament developed during the thirteenth century into England's legislature, inhabitants petitioned that body for relief of grievances. By the seventeenth century, in the colonies as well as in England, petitions had become the first step in the legislative process. Colonial assemblies received petitions, considered them, and either passed appropriate legislation or formally refused to do so. Petitions had to be respectfully addressed to an assembly, "state a grievance," and "pray for relief." But anyone, including women, American Indians, African Americans, and children, could petition. No one during the late seventeenth and entire eighteenth centuries doubted the political nature of petitioning.[10]

At first Quaker abolitionists used petitions to influence the yearly meetings that constituted the highest authority within the Society of Friends. In 1688 Dutch and German Quakers in Germantown, Pennsylvania, petitioned

Quaker abolitionist John Woolman (1720–1772) undertook quasi-political action during the 1750s that anticipated later abolitionist tactics regarding state legislatures. (Historical Society of Pennsylvania)

Philadelphia's yearly meeting in opposition to the slave trade. They cited the golden rule and asserted that an oppressed black population posed a violent threat to white society. In 1693 Philadelphia Quaker George Keith's *An Exhortation and Caution to Friends Concerning Buying and Keeping of Negroes* furthered these themes. Keith warned, "He that stealeth a Man and selleth him . . . shall surely be put to Death." Because the Philadelphia Yearly Meeting exercised quasi-government power in early Pennsylvania, the Germantown Quakers worked in a context that mixed religion and politics when they petitioned the meeting. Within a few decades some Quakers began to petition colonial legislatures. Pamphleteer William Southeby had earlier called on Quakers to free their slaves. In 1712, after a New York City slave revolt caused widespread fear, he petitioned the Pennsylvania legislature for general emancipation and prohibition of the importation of slaves. The Quaker controlled assembly rejected both petitions but subsequently discouraged the trade by taxing it.[11]

Other eighteenth-century Quaker abolitionists continued to work through their church's semi-governmental yearly meetings. Benjamin Lay, a merchant who had owned slaves on Barbados before moving to the Philadelphia area in 1731, wrote and spoke against slavery. At the Philadelphia Yearly Meeting, held at Burlington, New Jersey, in 1738, he denounced the hypocrisy of Quaker slaveholding. When the meeting disowned him, it encouraged other

Quakers, including John Woolman and Anthony Benezet to become abolitionists. Woolman, an itinerant preacher who traveled through New Jersey, Pennsylvania, New England, Maryland, and Virginia, advocated gradual abolition among his coreligionists. Benezet, an English Quaker of French descent, beginning during the 1740s conducted an African American school in Philadelphia and wrote against the Atlantic slave trade.[12]

In 1758 Woolman and Benezet gained control of the Philadelphia meeting, using it to condemn Quaker slaveholders. Subsequent yearly meetings in Maryland (1768), New England (1770), and New York (1774) banned Quaker participation in the slave trade. In 1772 New England Quakers led in expelling slaveholders from their meetings. The Philadelphia meeting followed in 1776 and the New York meeting a year later. Local meetings in Pennsylvania and New Jersey took much longer.[13] These quasi-political actions anticipated abolitionist efforts aimed at state legislatures.

Despite progress among Quakers, the divergent forces encouraging abolitionism initially produced a weak, fragmented movement. Many Quaker abolitionists preferred to work only with coreligionists. Quakers living in rural areas lagged behind those in Philadelphia, and Quaker abolitionists did not admit African Americans to their organizations. While some abolitionist sentiment existed in New England, theological and physical distance separated that sentiment from Quakers centered in Pennsylvania and New Jersey. Economic considerations, fear of slave revolt, and desire to limit black populations, rather than moral antipathy, often inspired early abolitionist effort. And although slaves resisted and escaped (often with help from African Americans), free black populations did not provide coordinated assistance until the 1780s. Yet by the 1760s, humanitarian sentiment, evangelicalism, and growing free black communities spread abolitionism. Quakers began to exercise greater influence beyond their meetings, and the Great Awakening's evangelical impulse surged.[14] Most importantly increasing numbers of Americans embraced the Enlightenment's natural rights doctrines as the conclusion of the French and Indian War in 1763 intensified long-existing tensions between their colonies and the British Empire.

As those white Americans who later called themselves Patriots charged that British policies regarding trade and taxation reduced them to slaves, they could not avoid the question of responsibility for black slavery. That question in turn encouraged abolitionist political action. In 1761 an abolitionist petition calling on Pennsylvania's legislature to "prevent or discourage" slave imports led the legislature once again to tax such imports. In 1765 Worcester, Massachusetts,

residents instructed their representative in the state legislature to "use his influence" to pass a law to "end" slavery in the colony. After Boston citizens sent
similar instructions in 1766, the legislature considered and defeated a bill to
end slavery and the slave trade.[15]

As American resistance to British policies escalated into armed conflict and
revolution, Patriot leaders in April 1775 formed the Continental Congress as a
provisional national government. Between June 1775 and July 1776, the leaders
formed state governments in each of the former thirteen colonies. These governments usually had strong bicameral legislatures, consisting of an assembly
and a council, and a weak governor. In 1778 the Continental Congress passed
the Articles of Confederation, which, after being ratified by the states in 1781,
provided a weak central government until the U.S. Constitution superseded
it in 1789.[16] All of these developments allowed abolitionists to increase their
political engagement.

The American Revolution also influenced slaves. Following the Declaration
of Independence's endorsement of universal human rights in 1776, many slaves
left their masters. Others joined British or Patriot armies, and their actions
raised issues related to emancipation. Nevertheless abolitionist politics faced
major impediments. In South Carolina and Georgia planters steadfastly defended slavery. A widespread negative reaction to Quaker pacifism during the
War for Independence diminished their influence. Nearly all northern politicians feared that a too rapid advance toward emancipation would disrupt
the North-South unity required to prevail over Britain. Therefore the new
northern state assemblies tended to discuss abolitionist legislation but take only
peripheral steps against slavery.[17]

Even so abolitionist groups had political impact. In 1775 Quakers, evangelicals, and African Americans began an effort to make the Pennsylvania legislature the first "to pass a law for the gradual emancipation of slaves." In April
of that year, Quakers, led by Anthony Benezet, organized at Philadelphia's Sun
Tavern the world's first abolition society. Although the society suspended operations after just four meetings, it began a new era. In 1784 the society reorganized
as the Pennsylvania Society for Promoting the Abolition of Slavery, which
became known as the Pennsylvania Abolition Society (PAS). As historian
Richard S. Newman notes, members of this organization "never doubted government's power to gradually destroy bondage." They "viewed government as
a critical ally" and "as the vehicle for killing slavery."[18]

Soon after the society's initial organization, the revolutionary Chester County
committee of correspondence petitioned the Pennsylvania state assembly seeking a gradual abolition law. When a year later Philadelphia residents made a

similar appeal, George Bryan, a Presbyterian merchant and gradual abolition-ist who served as vice president of Pennsylvania's executive council, endorsed it. Continued petitioning led Bryan to present gradual abolition bills in 1776, 1778, and 1779. As these bills suffered defeat and delay, the legislature (perhaps led by Quaker William Lewis) prepared another bill, and Benezet lobbied every member of the assembly on its behalf. Despite opposition from Germans, Scots, and Scots-Irish Presbyterians, and delays caused by the war, the assembly passed the gradual abolition act on March 31, 1780, by a vote of 34–21. Technically it freed slaves born after that month but kept them in indentured servitude until age twenty-eight. It freed immediately those slaves who masters failed to regis-ter by November 1780 (later extended to January 1782). The law also ended a separate legal system for African Americans, permitted interracial marriage, and allowed free African Americans to testify in court against white people.[19]

Benezet was not the first abolition lobbyist. In 1700 Massachusetts residents had visited that colony's legislature to urge members to pass a tariff designed to discourage slave imports. Five years later the legislature complied. Most likely the term "lobbying" derives from medieval English efforts to influence members of Parliament as they stood in the physical lobbies of the House of Commons and House of Lords. In the United States, the term did not come into use until the congressional debates of 1819 and 1820 concerning the admission of the slaveholding territory of Missouri to the Union. Historians and journalists often portray lobbying as an unsavory political tactic used by special interests to pres-sure legislatures and executives. In contrast American abolitionists demonstrated increasing skill in using it for noble purposes.[20]

While Pennsylvania abolitionists pursued political tactics that succeeded in 1780, abolitionists in New England expanded their attempts to influence gov-ernment. As in Pennsylvania, the New Englanders' actions did not prevent delay and half-hearted measures. But they did lead to essential, if not universal, prog-ress toward their goals.

Three years before the signing of the Declaration of Independence, several Massachusetts towns petitioned the colony's assembly to end the slave trade and adopt gradual abolition. Meanwhile black abolitionists, led by Felix Hol-brook of Boston, acted politically in the colony. In about 1750 Holbrook, who had been born in Africa, came to Boston as a slave and received an edu-cation from his schoolteacher master. In January 1773 Holbrook petitioned Royal Governor Thomas Hutchinson and the colonial legislature's upper and lower houses for the emancipation of all slaves in Massachusetts. The legislature created a committee to study the issue but refused to act. Two months later

Holbrook joined three other Boston slaves (Peter Bestes, Sambo Freeman, and Chester Joie) to petition the lower house for gradual abolition and grants of land to former slaves. As the committee assigned to study the proposal delayed consideration until the next session, the petitioners turned to Hutchinson, who refused to intervene on their behalf. About a year later another black group sent a third petition. In response the lower house drafted an abolition bill and then tabled it.[21]

In January 1777, shortly after George Washington's Continental Army won battles over the British at Trenton and Princeton, black abolitionists led by Prince Hall resumed the Massachusetts petitioning effort, which they directed at what had become the state legislature. Hall was a former slave, Boston shop owner, Patriot, orator, and local black community leader. According to traditional accounts, Hall's petition influenced discussion of black rights at the 1778 Massachusetts constitutional convention, which led to the insertion of a declaration of rights in the state's 1780 constitution. This provision underlay the Massachusetts supreme court's decision in 1783 to abolish slavery within its jurisdiction.[22]

In Connecticut several white abolitionist groups had by 1777 petitioned the new state legislature. That body, like its counterparts in other states, took the petitions seriously and sent them to a committee, which drafted a plan for gradual abolition. Although the plan failed to pass, a bill designed to make manumission easier became law that fall. Also, as in Massachusetts, some black abolitionists in Connecticut sought political influence. In 1779 and 1780, groups of black men in Salem, Stratford, Fairfield, and Hartford petitioned the legislature to end slavery. In response the upper house passed a bill for gradual abolition, and (although the lower house refused to go along) the black abolitionists gained support from several white ministers. Among them was Jonathan Edwards Jr., son of the great Congregational theologian and a gradual abolitionist since 1773. After continued abolitionist political efforts, including a petition to the legislature from nineteen slaves in 1779, Connecticut in January 1784 passed a gradual emancipation act.[23]

In Rhode Island, Newport abolitionists, led by evangelical schoolteacher Sarah Osborn, had during the 1760s concentrated on black education and community development in what had become a major slave-trading center. Then, during the early 1770s, Samuel Hopkins, a former slaveholder who served as pastor of the city's First Congregational Church, redirected abolitionists toward politics. In 1774 the Newport Quaker Yearly Meeting joined Hopkins's effort by appointing a committee to lobby the legislature "for an abolition law." Within this context, the Providence town meeting instructed its representative to introduce legislation to terminate the slave trade and initiate gradual abolition. Because slave traders and local vegetable farmers, who employed slaver labor, resisted, the resulting legislation was ineffective.[24]

Rhode Island abolitionists, like those in Massachusetts, did not give up. The turning point came in December 1783, as the United States won its war for independence and slave resistance, escapes, and masters' sales of slaves to out-of-state buyers increased due to that resistance and increased numbers of escapes. Quakers, led by recent convert Moses Brown of Providence, petitioned for gradual abolition. Brown, a retired industrialist and merchant, had freed the last of his slaves in 1773. Antislavery representatives responded to his petition with a bill designed to achieve its goal. A Quaker committee attended the session to lobby, and the bill passed on March 1, 1784.[25]

In Vermont and New Hampshire, abolitionists had less impact on emancipation. Vermont, which did not have an organized abolition movement, used its 1777 bill of rights to abolish slavery. How slavery ended in New Hampshire is unclear. Abolitionists there engaged in state politics, and in late 1779 nineteen African-born slaves, led by Nero Brewster of Portsmouth, petitioned the state legislature for freedom and legal equality based on natural rights doctrines. In the process Brewster arranged for a lawyer to argue his and the other Africans' case before that legislature, which (in a manner similar to that of its counterparts in other northeastern states) took the petition seriously. In April 1780 the legislature had the petition published in at least two newspapers, so that "persons" might support or oppose it. Then the legislature indefinitely postponed action on it. Four years later, however, the state adopted a constitution containing a bill of rights, which, like Massachusetts's, declared, "All men are born equally free and independent." By 1790 only 158 slaves resided in New Hampshire. Whether black abolitionist action, the bill of rights, and court rulings led to emancipation in the state or whether slavery simply withered away is debatable.[26]

Abolitionists in New York and New Jersey faced more entrenched, widespread, and profitable slave systems than existed in the rest of the Northeast. No other states in that region had such large enslaved populations. (According to the 1790 U.S. Census, there were 21,193 slaves in New York and 11,423 in New Jersey.) In both states slave labor had an important role on farms, as well as in towns and cities. Slaveholders had more political power than elsewhere in the Northeast, and white fear of creating a large free-black class had proslavery impact.[27] Therefore abolitionist political tactics succeeded in these states much more slowly than in other northeastern states during the revolutionary era.

In 1778 Quaker lawyer Samuel Allinson of Burlington, New Jersey (the state's abolition center), urged Governor William Livingston, himself an abolitionist, to use his influence in what became an unsuccessful effort to convince the state legislature to end slavery. Two years later other New Jersey abolitionists, inspired by success in Pennsylvania, sent three petitions to the legislature. These prompted a heated though inconclusive newspaper debate between antislavery and proslavery political leaders. In November 1785 abolitionist politician David Cooper, who resided in Woodbury, located not far from Burlington, led a group of twelve Quakers that delivered a gradual emancipation petition to the state's legislature, then located in Elizabeth. The group also lobbied on the petition's behalf, once again without success. After eight years of effort, the New Jersey abolitionists' sole political victory came in February 1786 when the assembly passed a weak bill banning the importation of slaves and encouraging manumission.[28]

Unlike New Jersey, New York had during the 1770s no abolitionists who petitioned and lobbied. But as in New Jersey, some New York Patriot politicians, such as John Jay and Gouverneur Morris, were abolitionists. Jay, a wealthy New York City lawyer, served as president of the Continental Congress during the late 1770s. Morris, like Jay a wealthy New York City lawyer, also served in that Congress. At the state's constitutional convention in 1777, Morris gained overwhelming support for a nonbinding resolution in favor of abolition while failing to achieve a constitutional provision to that effect. Within the next four years, the New York legislature freed only slaves who had served in Patriot armies.[29]

The relationship between abolitionists and government in New York became more similar to that in most northeastern states with the formation in 1785 of the New York Manumission Society (NYMS). As with the PAS, Quakers had the major role in organizing this society. But five prominent non-Quaker abolitionist politicians helped. They included Jay, George Clinton (governor of New York, 1777–95), James Duane (mayor of New York City, 1784–89), Alexander Hamilton (U.S. secretary of the treasury, 1789–95), and Melancton Smith (member of the Continental Congress, 1785–87).[30]

As soon as it organized, the NYMS petitioned the state legislature for a gradual emancipation bill. Elderly state senator Ephraim Paine, a former member of the Continental Congress who died later in 1785, introduced such a bill in the state senate, and a group of Quakers traveled to the state capital, Albany, to lobby for its passage. Another Quaker petition led a committee in the legislature's lower house to produce (by a vote of 32–10) a similar bill. But when young and ambitious New York City representative Aaron Burr offered an amendment calling for immediate emancipation, proslavery forces rallied. They characterized emancipation as dangerous and a threat to the state's economy. They charged Quakers with disloyalty during the War for Independence. This proslavery resistance led to legislative deadlock over amendments designed to limit black voting and civil rights—and defeat for the entire measure.[31]

Despite the natural rights rhetoric in the Declaration of Independence and the great blows struck against slavery in the Northeast, daunting obstacles stood in the way of further progress. The failure of New Jersey and New York to pass emancipatory legislation coincided with the end of an era in American politics. Black unrest, democratic movements on behalf of poorer white men, a rebellion among farmers in western Massachusetts, and the inability of the weak central government under the Articles of Confederation to protect the wealthy elite's property interests caused political reaction. In 1787 delegates meeting at Philadelphia produced a U.S. Constitution that supported slavery. The Constitution guaranteed continuation of the external slave trade for twenty years. It denied that slaves who escaped from one state to another became free. It allowed Congress to pass a law aimed at helping masters recover such individuals. And it permitted southern states to count three-fifths of their slave populations toward representation in the House of Representatives and the Electoral College.[32]

Meanwhile race replaced class as the major divider in American society. In the South slaveholders appealed to race unity to convince white nonslaveholders to support slavery and oppose black rights. In the Northeast poorer white people who had shared a similar class interest with African Americans began to interpret social status in racial terms. Many sought to restrict black access to schools, churches, politics, and employment. By the 1780s Thomas Jefferson's assertion that African Americans were inherently "inferior to whites in the endowments of both body and mind" went without challenge among the great majority of white Americans regardless of section.[33]

Yet abolitionist optimism and political impact persisted. New societies organized in Rhode Island in 1786, New Jersey in 1786, and Connecticut in 1790. Quaker abolitionism resurged, and other religious groups, including Congregationalists, Methodists, and some Presbyterians, cooperated on behalf of emancipation. In several states prominent politicians followed the New Jersey and New York examples in becoming abolitionists.[34] And abolitionists continued to shape antislavery legislation in most of the northeastern states.

The New England Friends' Yearly Meeting coordinated efforts among Quaker, African American, and Congregationalist abolitionists in that region. This coalition concentrated on the slave trade because Newport, Rhode Island, had remained a national center for the trade despite the state's gradual aboli-tion act of 1784. Therefore, during the summer of 1787, as the U.S. Consti-tutional Convention met in Philadelphia, the New England Yearly Meeting, held in Newport, endorsed a petition, written by Moses Brown, on the sub-ject. That October Brown and Samuel Hopkins presented the petition to the state assembly. When the assembly responded by banning the trade, Hopkins praised it (incorrectly) as the "first Legislature on this globe" to do so. By January 1789 Rhode Island slave traders had shifted their operations to New Hampshire. To stifle this tactic, Brown organized the Providence Society for Abolition of the Slave Trade. Former Confederation congressman and Rhode Island Supreme Court justice David Howell served as the organization's first president.[35]

In 1788 Brown and other Quakers had brought their anti-slave-trade petition to the Massachusetts assembly. By coincidence, the February 1788 kidnapping of three black men from Boston into slavery in the West Indies led to the circu-lation of two other such petitions in the state. The first of these, championed by Prince Hall, circulated among African Americans. The second, written by Con-gregational minister and historian Jeremy Belknap of Boston, sought signatures from white clergy. In response to these efforts, the Massachusetts legislature on March 26, 1788, banned the slave trade and strengthened the commonwealth's law against kidnapping.[36]

Rhode Island, Massachusetts, and New York Quaker abolitionists also in-fluenced antislavery politics in Connecticut. Together with Connecticut Con-gregationalists led by ministers Jonathan Edwards Jr. and Levi Hart (who had favored gradual abolition in 1775 and had ties to Samuel Hopkins), Brown and his coadjutors petitioned that state's legislature requesting that it ban the slave trade. The legislature did so in September 1788. Four years later, petitions from the Connecticut Society for the Promotion of Freedom and Relief of Persons Unlawfully Holden in Bondage led the same legislature to ban transporting slaves out of state for sale. This record of success in Connecticut ended during the spring of 1789 as the society, supported by twenty-five-year-old Hartford attorney Theodore Dwight, fell short in a petitioning campaign on behalf of immediate, total abolition. The state legislature's lower house passed a bill to free all Connecticut slaves by April 1, 1795, but the upper house narrowly defeated it. Dwight went on to a distinguished career in support of the Federalist Party and continued to link abolitionism and politics.[37]

Similar abolitionist direct political action against the slave trade took place in Pennsylvania, as the PAS sought to protect and expand the 1780 gradual abo-lition law's accomplishments. During the winter of 1787–88, the organization's members petitioned the state legislature to stop slave traders from using Philadelphia as a base of operations. On January 1, 1788, Philadelphia resident Benjamin Rush, who pursued careers as a politician, physician, and abolitionist, addressed the legislature on the issue. Prominent Quakers lobbied. The resulting legislation, which passed that March, stopped the Philadelphia slave trade, freed slaves brought into Pennsylvania by masters who intended to reside there, and strengthened an existing law that placed a six-month limit on bringing slaves temporarily into the state.[38]

In contrast to their Pennsylvania and New England counterparts, New York and New Jersey abolitionists achieved bans on the slave trade *before* their states passed emancipatory legislation. The same 1785 session of the New York legislature that had defeated general emancipation banned importation of slaves into the state for sale and allowed masters to manumit slaves without posting a bond for their support. This limited victory encouraged the NYMS to redouble its activities in 1786. In conjunction with newspaper articles and appeals to masters, the society petitioned the legislature to prevent slave sales to southerners. The upper house passed the resulting bill, and the lower house defeated it. But continued abolitionist pressure led the legislature in 1788 to end the slave trade entirely, further ease manumission requirements, allow jury trials for slaves, ban brutal punishments, and place slaves under the same legal code as free people.[39]

The NYMS suffered setbacks in 1792 when Jay's abolitionism contributed to his failure to gain election as governor, and the society suspended petitioning for gradual emancipation. Then, after Jay won the 1795 gubernatorial election, the society renewed and expanded its petitioning. In January 1796 James Watson, who represented New York City in the state's lower house and had ties to Jay, introduced a gradual abolition bill. This bill languished in committee because proslavery assemblymen amended it to provide for compensation to masters. Thereafter abolitionist petitioning gained momentum. In 1798 the lower house (but not the upper house) approved an abolitionist-sponsored gradual emancipation bill that did not provide for compensating masters. Finally, under continued NYMS prompting, both houses in 1799 passed a similar bill. It freed all children born to enslaved parents starting on July 4, 1799, while requiring technically emancipated young men to serve their masters until age twenty-eight and young women to serve until age twenty-five. The bill also allowed masters to abandon such children a year after birth, with the state assuming responsibility for raising them.[40]

The struggle proceeded similarly, albeit more slowly, in New Jersey. After the state legislature in 1785 defeated gradual emancipation, abolitionists continued their efforts to influence government policy. In 1788 the Society of Friends and citizens of Princeton each petitioned for gradual abolition and strengthening the law against "the negro trade." Abolitionist David Cooper, backed once again by Governor William Livingston, addressed the legislature on behalf of these initiatives. The legislature reacted by defeating gradual abolition while strengthening the law against importing slaves and banning exports unless a master moved out of state with his slaves. The legislature also banned special punishments for slave offenses and ended the separate justice system for slaves. But New Jersey abolitionists still faced political obstacles. In 1790 a legislative committee, contending that slavery would disappear on its own, refused to act on a petition in favor of gradual abolition from "certain inhabitants of Essex and Morris counties." During its 1794 and 1795 sessions, as abolitionists continued to petition, the assembly defeated gradual abolition by one vote.[41]

As it turned out, formation of an abolition society was required to achieve gradual abolition in New Jersey. In 1786 Elias Boudinot, who resided in Elizabeth, and Joseph Bloomfield, of Burlington, had established what became the New Jersey Society for Promoting the Abolition of Slavery (NJSPAS). Both men had careers that mixed law, politics, and organized benevolence. Boudinot served as president of the Second Continental Congress in 1782–83 and as a member of the U.S. Congress from 1789 to 1795. Bloomfield served as the state attorney general from 1783 to 1792, governor from 1803 to 1812, and member of Congress from 1817 to 1821.[42]

The NJSPAS did not become active until 1793, and it lacked the size and organization of abolition societies in other northeastern states. Nevertheless, in 1797 Bloomfield, who had freed his fourteen slaves in 1783, led the society in presenting a gradual emancipation plan similar to New York's to the New Jersey legislature. After that effort fell short, the society succeeded in February 1804 when a similar petition prompted the legislature to approve a gradual abolition bill. The resulting law freed enslaved children born after July 4, 1804, while requiring technically free young men to serve as indentured servants until age twenty-five and technically free young women to age twenty-one.[43]

New Jersey's adoption of gradual abolition successfully ended the abolitionist struggle, begun twenty-four years earlier, to bring about slavery's effective demise in all states north of the Mason-Dixon Line. Well before this major achievement, abolitionists had extended their political efforts beyond the Northeast.

In 1767 American Quakers petitioned George III and Parliament in opposition to the Atlantic slave trade. In 1773 Anthony Benezet unsuccessfully urged the Pennsylvania assembly to beg King George to end the trade. The following year Benezet lobbied the Continental Congress, which met in his hometown of Philadelphia, to ban slave imports. In 1776 Samuel Hopkins sent a pamphlet to the Second Continental Congress calling on it to establish "universal liberty to white and black."[44]

Similar efforts had continued during the Confederation. In 1783 the Philadelphia Yearly Meeting and Warner Mifflin, a very active Delaware Quaker abolitionist who had freed his slaves, petitioned the Confederation Congress to end the Atlantic slave trade. Congress responded accurately that it had no power over commerce of any sort. Four years later the PAS prepared (but did not deliver) a memorial, signed by its president, renowned American statesman Benjamin Franklin, calling on the U.S. Constitutional Convention to act against the trade. Instead, as mentioned above, the convention produced a constitution that, among other proslavery provisions, prohibited Congress from abolishing the external slave trade until 1808.[45]

Following ratification of the Constitution, as the new U.S. government began to function in December 1789, abolitionists remained active at the national political level. In February 1790 Mifflin and John Pemberton, a Philadelphia Quaker whose brother James became the PAS president that year, led an eleven-member delegation to New York City to lobby the first Congress on behalf of three abolition petitions. Pemberton had requested that Quaker abolitionists in Pennsylvania, New Jersey, Delaware, Maryland, and Virginia jointly produce one of these petitions. New York Quakers and the PAS separately submitted the other two.[46]

Some historians characterize these actions as too moderate, religious, and intermittent to be effective. But they were *abolitionist,* Congress took them seriously, and they contributed to sectional tensions. The two Quaker petitions called for legislation against the external slave trade. Citing the golden rule, they denounced the trade for its "licentious wickedness," "inhuman tyranny," and undermining of American "virtue." The PAS petition, signed by Franklin, called for action against the trade *and* slavery throughout the United States. It asked Congress to "restore liberty to those unhappy men, who alone in this land of freedom are degraded into perpetual bondage." It endorsed spreading liberty's blessings "without distinction of color." It implicitly raised the issue of congressional authority over slavery in the states.[47]

Lower South congressmen, anticipating their nineteenth-century successors, overreacted. Fiery duelist James Jackson of Georgia declared defensively, "Never was a Government on the face of the earth, but what permitted slavery." William Smith of South Carolina added that abolition "was a subject of a nature to excite the alarms of the Sothern members." He claimed emancipation would "stain the blood of the whites by a mixture of races." Smith and Jackson argued that constitutional protection of the slave trade until 1808 prohibited *all* federal interference with slavery. They charged that abolitionists encouraged slave revolt. Smith's South Carolina colleague Thomas Tucker added that, if Congress attempted "unconstitutional" emancipation, it would give slaves false hope and require masters to treat them with more "severity." In part because southern threats frightened many northerners, the Senate broke with state-level precedents by taking no action on the petitions.[48]

Nevertheless a few northern congressmen supported the petitioners. Thomas Scott, an at-large representative from Pennsylvania who lived in the southwestern portion of the state, suggested that Congress could tax the trade. Elbridge Gerry, a perennial political power in Massachusetts, held that the proceeds from western land sales might pay for a program of compensated emancipation. Neither Scott nor Gerry had abolitionist ties. Elias Boudinot of New Jersey did, although he often acted cautiously. He joined Gerry in defending the right to petition "for redress of grievances," and praised the Quakers' and Franklin's character. Like abolitionists from his time to the Civil War, Boudinot emphasized that slavery went against "the uniform tenor of the Gospel" and violated the equal rights principles of the Declaration of Independence. He suggested that God would deliver American slaves as he had the "children of Israel." But, as a politician, Boudinot recognized that Congress could not constitutionally act against the external slave trade before 1808. He called only for *gradual* abolition of slavery itself.[49]

Following the 1790 debate, the House voted 43–11 to create a "special committee" to consider the Quaker and PAS petitions. Abiel Foster, a New Hampshire representative who did not oppose slavery, chaired the committee. Quaker abolitionists, mainly from Philadelphia, testified before the committee and distributed pamphlets among its members. On March 5 it reported that Congress could not terminate the external slave trade or emancipate slaves within the United States but could "regulate" the African slave trade when "carried on by citizens of the United States for supplying foreigners." Congress could also "make provisions for the humane treatment of slaves." More controversially the committee suggested that, while Congress could not emancipate slaves prior to 1808, it might do so thereafter. This assertion produced another angry outburst from South Carolinians and Georgians that resulted in an amendment to the report prepared by James Madison of Virginia and adopted on March 23. This amendment asserted that "Congress have no authority to interfere in the emancipation of slaves, or treatment of them." The fact that Scott, Gerry, and Boudinot voted for this amendment indicates the limits of abolitionist influence on antislavery politicians. And Madison's amendment became the standard interpretation, which prevailed through the Civil War, of Congress's power regarding slavery in the states.[50]

Congressional resistance to abolitionist initiatives stiffened in December 1791 when the societies sent memorials that went beyond the Foster Committee report in calling for action against the external trade. In a manner similar to the Senate's disregard of colonial and state-level precedents for dealing with petitions (and in anticipation of the future), a House committee refused to report on the memorials and thereby avoided debate. On February 22, 1793, the House tabled a similar memorial from the Providence Society for Promoting the Abolition of Slavery. A few days earlier Congress had passed its first Fugitive Slave Act.[51]

These setbacks in Congress led to enhanced abolitionist organization. In January 1794 representatives of nine state abolition societies met in Philadelphia to form a national organization known as the American Convention of Abolition Societies (AC). By then the first American party system had emerged out of a disagreement among politicians regarding the strength and purpose of the central government. Led by George Washington's first secretary of state, Thomas Jefferson, those who favored a weak central government and agrarianism formed the Republican Party. Led by Washington's first secretary of the treasury, Alexander Hamilton, those who favored a strong central government and commercial development formed the Federalist Party. The abolitionist centers of the Northeast fell within the main region of Federalist strength, and, as previously noted, such Federalist politicians as Hamilton and Jay were also abolitionists.[52]

Within this new political context the AC, with Joseph Bloomfield presiding, sent more petitions to Congress calling for banning American involvement in the Atlantic slave trade before 1808. In February and March 1794, an AC delegation headed by Moses Brown lobbied House leader James Madison, President Washington, and others for such a measure. Soon thereafter Congress passed a bill to "prohibit the carrying on the slave trade from the United States to any foreign place or country." Abolitionist organizations then petitioned state legislatures and Congress for a constitutional amendment to ban the entire trade before 1808. This effort failed, and it took an initiative by slaveholding U.S. president Thomas Jefferson in December 1806 to produce a law in 1807 that made the external trade illegal beginning in 1808. As might be expected, the most outspoken support in Congress for the measure came from Pennsylvania, New Jersey, and Massachusetts members in whose states abolitionist organizations had the greatest influence.[53]

Congress's hyperbolic sectional debates and restrictions on the external slave trade during the 1790s, followed by abolition victories in New York and New Jersey, demonstrate the level of abolitionist impact on American politics and government at the end of the eighteenth century and start of the nineteenth. Thereafter, historian Arthur Zilversmit contends, abolitionists, having achieved their major goal in the Northeast, "increasingly focused on the South."[54]

Historians disagree however regarding the intensity of that focus and the viability of abolitionist organizations at the turn of the nineteenth century. Some contend that the abolitionists, having achieved emancipation in the North and progress against the external slave trade, assumed they had won the struggle and lost interest in achieving "total abolition." According to James D. Essig, abolitionists thought they had finished their work and "saw little need for sustained political activity at a national level." Therefore, Essig claims, when antebellum abolitionists "wrestled with the problem of political action," they had little guidance from what their eighteenth-century and early nineteenth-century predecessors had done. Yet Manisha Sinha, in her comprehensive study of abolitionism before 1860, finds continuity in abolitionist petitioning efforts between the 1790s and 1830s. Phillip S. Foner portrays northern abolition societies as gaining vigor as a result of their 1794 achievement of the "first national act against the slave trade." The AC, Foner contends, committed itself to "gradual abolition [in the South] . . . immediately begun." It advocated preparation of African Americans "through education for a life of citizenship in the United States." Foner holds that the AC encouraged British abolitionism and contemplated indigenous abolitionist organization in the South.[55]

Foner concedes that this contemplation turned out to be "naïve." The Haitian Revolution, begun in 1791 and ending in black victory in 1804, frightened white Americans and hurt the prospects for peaceful abolition in the South. Eli Whitney's invention of the cotton gin in 1793, which made slavery appear essential to southern prosperity, also hurt the abolitionist cause. So did the failed Virginia insurrection plot directed by the slave Gabriel near Richmond in 1800, as it reinforced white fears that a black rebellion similar to Haiti's could happen in the American South. Southern slavery became numerically stronger during the early 1800s than it had been during the 1790s, and abolitionism in the South "never fully got underway." Yet several historians agree with Zilversmit's observation in 1967 that the state-level emancipation process begun in Pennsylvania and concluded in New Jersey encompassed "the point at which the sections began to tread diverging paths, the point at which the nation became a house divided against itself."

William W. Freehling correctly notes that by 1830, slavery "had been made a *peculiar institution,* retained alone in the southern states."[56] This would not have been the case without the pioneering political tactics of Quaker abolitionists and without northern abolitionist engagement in antislavery politics at the state and national levels during the revolutionary and early national periods.

2

Continuity and Transition, 1807–1830

Historians have long debated the nature and effectiveness of the American abolition movement during the first three decades of the nineteenth century. All recognize that the movement changed. But they disagree concerning the degree of change, the movement's effectiveness during these years, and its relationship to the more radical movement for *immediate* emancipation that emerged during the late 1820s. In order to understand the abolitionists' relationship to state and national politics during these years, this chapter begins with a review of the historians' perspectives. It notes that the political party system also changed during this period. Most importantly it analyzes in depth abolitionists' continued engagement in politics between 1819 and 1829, the impact of that engagement on the sectional struggle, and its influence on abolitionist political efforts during and after the 1830s.

Historian Mary Staughton Locke in *Antislavery in America* (1901) describes the abolition movement during what she defines as its second period. This period, she contends, stretched from Congress's abolition of the external slave trade in 1807 to William Lloyd Garrison's initiation of the *Liberator* in 1831. She describes the period as a time of transition, which she divides into two subperiods.

Just as James D. Essig has more recently described a decline in abolitionists' political action at the turn of the nineteenth century (see chapter 1), Locke portrays her first subperiod, lasting from 1808 to 1815, as a "pause" in the movement. According to Locke, the pause resulted from emancipation in the northeastern states, passage of the Northwest Ordinance in 1787 banning slavery in that region, manumissions in the Border South, and the ban of the external slave trade, which led abolitionists to believe slavery would "die a natural death." Then, according to Locke, during her second subperiod, lasting from 1816 to 1831, abolitionists revived their activities within a context of increased North-South political sectionalism and a renewal of evangelical revivalism during the

Second Great Awakening. The number of abolitionist newspapers increased, surviving abolition societies revived, new societies emerged in the Border and Middle South, and the American Convention (AC) provided a degree of coordination. Petitioning of state legislatures and Congress expanded. And slavery again became "a political issue." Locke characterizes this second subperiod as a "prelude" to demands for immediate emancipation in the South during abolitionism's third and final period that began in 1831.[1]

Alice Dana Adams's *The Neglected Period of Anti-Slavery in America* (1908), in contrast to Locke's *Antislavery,* portrays the entire period from 1808 to 1831 as a time of widespread abolitionist activity "in the North and South." Adams presents an enormous amount of material to illustrate abundant abolitionist "sentiment" during the 1810s and 1820s. Yet, also in contrast to Locke, Adams questions the impact of abolitionism during the latter decade. "It is difficult," she writes, "to calculate the effective strength of that movement, or to determine how far it was a preparation for the livelier anti-slavery era after 1831."[2]

Most of the more recent historians of American abolitionism who focus on the years between 1808 and 1831 agree with Locke's view that the movement changed during those years. They usually, however, do not endorse her subperiods or accept her emphasis on ties between abolitionism and politics. They reject her suggestion that continuity existed between the second and third periods of abolitionist activity. Most historians who have written general histories of the movement since the 1960s also go beyond Adams's equivocation to assert that the second period provided little or no preparation for the third period. Merton L. Dillon in *The Abolitionists* (1974) acknowledges "occasional [abolitionist] success" between 1816 and 1830. But he emphasizes the movement's weakness during the second period. Slave labor spread westward with cotton cultivation. White racial prejudice against African Americans increased. The American Colonization Society (ACS), which had been organized in 1816, enjoyed support in both the northern states and border slave-labor states. It advocated very gradual emancipation *and* deporting free black Americans to Africa. Also many white Americans continued to believe slavery would end on its own. That all of this discouraged organized abolitionism is reflected in the AC's 1819 report, which noted, "very little either of a general or local nature, within our immediate sphere has occurred."[3]

Dillon contends that an increasingly proslavery climate of opinion (assisted by white racism) kept advocates of abolition from wielding political influence during much of the 1820s. He also argues that Second Great Awakening evangelicalism had a greater impact on the course of abolitionism toward the more radical immediatism of the 1830s than the revival of politically oriented abolitionist organizations. Writing a few years after Dillon, James Brewer Stewart makes a similar point and adds that black action against slavery, outside the second subperiod's abolitionist organizations, shaped the movement's future. More recently Richard S. Newman and Manisha Sinha have in more detail than Stewart emphasized that black opposition to the ACS, rather than formal abolitionist organizations, created, in Newman's words, a "new strategy of radical racial vindication." Some historians discuss antislavery politics as it existed during the 1820s without mentioning abolitionists.[4]

Yet abolitionist attempts to influence politics and government did not cease during this era. In many respects the proslavery climate of opinion encouraged such attempts. Although the removal of the U.S. capital in 1800 from Philadelphia to Washington, D.C., for a time made abolitionist lobbying in Congress more difficult, abolitionist petitioning, lobbying, and personal contacts with politicians remained significant tactics at both the state and national levels of government. And, at least in regard to abolitionist political engagement, continuity *did* characterize the movement from the late 1810s through the 1830s. This was because immediate abolitionists followed their predecessors in seeking to influence government policy. Contrary to some immediatist claims during the late 1830s, an emphasis on politics at that time was not "a new departure." Conversely abolitionists during the 1820s, like their successors during the 1830s, understood that they had to change people's minds before "successful political antislavery action could be taken." From the late 1810s through the 1820s, the AC and the societies affiliated with it often combined working through the political system with appeals to moral sentiment. They addressed "free people of color," slaveholders, religious groups, and "the nation" as part of their (sometimes ineffective) campaigns to influence government.[5]

So apparent progress against slavery between the 1780s and 1807 did not lull northern abolitionists into complacency throughout the period between 1808 and 1830. Fugitive slave renditions and kidnapping of free African Americans kept them vigilant. The westward spread of slavery added to that vigilance. Especially from the late 1810s through the 1820s, abolitionists used political means to confront proslavery strategies, abolish slavery where they could, and weaken slavery in the South.

As American abolitionists continued their political engagement during the 1810s and 1820s, the party system within which they worked changed. The elitist and nationalist Federalist Party, which included some abolitionists, had begun to dissolve during the 1800 presidential election in which sitting Federalist president John Adams lost to Republican Party candidate Thomas

Jefferson. The Federalist decline accelerated during the War of 1812 between the United States and Great Britain as New England Federalists, who dominated the party, opposed the war. During the same years, a wartime drop in imports stimulated northeastern manufacturing, and a growing network of canals and macadamized roads transformed the North's economy. These developments widened class divisions in the North and intensified North-South sectional strains. The class divisions and sectional strains in turn led to the breakup of the Republican Party, beginning during the 1824 presidential election campaign, and the formation of the National Republican and Democratic Republican Parties.

The National Republicans, led by John Quincy Adams and Henry Clay, followed the Federalists in advocating U.S. government aid to manufacturing and transportation. As a result their main political strength lay in the North. By the 1830s most of the National Republicans had become Whigs. Meanwhile the Second Great Awakening led, beginning during the 1810s, to formation of northern benevolent organizations designed to encourage conversions and help the downtrodden. These organizations tended to favor the National Republicans and Whigs. The Democratic Republicans, who drew support from a coalition of northeastern working men, southern and western farmers, and most slaveholders, opposed federal government support for industry and commerce. With important exceptions in the Northeast, most Democratic-Republican politicians supported westward expansion of slavery, which helped them among southern voters. Beginning with Andrew Jackson in 1828, the Democratic-Republican Party (which took the name "Democratic Party" by the early 1830s) elected proslavery presidents.[6]

Continued abolitionist political influence during this period of party realignment is clear in the Missouri crisis, the first major sectional clash over slavery expansion. The crisis began in 1818 when slaveholding Missouri Territory, located beyond the Ohio River boundary that had divided free-labor and slave-labor states, prepared to enter the Union. In April of that year, a House of Representatives committee reported enabling legislation to admit Missouri. Immediately Arthur Livermore, a Republican from New Hampshire who had abolitionist sympathies (and like abolitionists regarded slaveholding to be a sin), proposed a constitutional amendment to ban new slave-labor states.[7]

The following December (several days before Speaker Henry Clay, a Kentucky slaveholder, addressed the Missouri issue in the House), a special AC meeting at Philadelphia appointed a committee, chaired by Theodore Dwight of the New York Manumission Society (NYMS), to petition Congress. In 1817

Dwight had moved from Connecticut to New York City to become publisher and editor of the *Daily Advertiser.* The petition his committee produced begged Congress to adopt "such provisions, as will exclude slavery from the limits of such territorial governments as may hereafter be established within our country." The petition also called for preventing "any such future territory from being erected into a state, unless slavery shall be prohibited by the constitution thereof."[8]

On February 15, 1819, the House of Representatives began considering a bill that would admit Missouri to the Union as a slave-labor state. Livermore spoke on behalf of the NYMS petition and went beyond it. He said he wanted "to show what slavery is, and to mention a few of the many evils which follow in its train." He charged that southern states, in preventing slave literacy and in not allowing slaves "to hear the Gospel preached," sought to keep them "more easily bowed down to servitude." He denounced the domestic slave trade's disruption of black families. The children, he said, "wring their little hands and expire in agonies of grief, while the bereft mothers commit suicide." In his speech Livermore also anticipated immediate abolitionist portrayals of a sinful, proslavery U.S. Constitution, a similarly proslavery colonization society, and proslavery religious organizations. If slavery were allowed to remain in Missouri, he said, "let us at least be consistent, and declare that our Constitution was made to impose slavery, and not to establish liberty." He declared, "Let us no longer tell idle tales about the gradual abolition of slavery; away with colonization societies, if their design is only to rid us of free blacks and turbulent slaves; have done with bible societies . . . while they overlook the deplorable condition of their sable brethren within our own borders."[9]

A day after Livermore spoke, James Tallmadge Jr., a Republican lawyer from Poughkeepsie, New York, presented an amendment to the Missouri bill. It would prevent "the further introduction of slavery" into Missouri and provide for the gradual emancipation of slaves already there. A few months earlier Tallmadge had unsuccessfully opposed admitting Illinois to the Union because he believed its constitution did not adequately ban slavery. On that occasion he declared, "It had often been cast as a reproach on this nation, that we, who boast of our freedom . . . yet hold our fellow-beings in service." He portrayed Americans "with one hand exhibiting the declaration of independence, and with the other brandishing the lash of despotism." Two years later Tallmadge, as a delegate to the 1821 New York state constitutional convention, urged (once again unsuccessfully) a provision that would absolutely end slavery in New York by 1827. He vowed, "The oppressed people . . . shall receive my support, in every place, and every situation where I may . . . introduce it."[10]

Based on these proposals, one historian refers to Tallmadge as an abolitionist "before there really was an abolition movement." This is not true, because an abolition movement existed well before Talmadge's speech and the movement influenced the speech. It *is* true, however, that Tallmadge's words influenced abolitionists. The influence is clearest in regard to his remarks on his proposed amendment to the Missouri bill. These remarks, even more than Livermore's earlier ones, foreshadowed the immediatists' fierce morality. In reply to Georgia representative Thomas W. Cobb's claim that an attempt to end slavery in Missouri threatened disunion and civil war, Tallmadge declared, "If a dissolution of the Union must take place, *let it be so!* If civil war, which gentlemen so much threaten must come, I can only say, *let it come!*" Tallmadge continued, "I know the will of my constituents. . . . I will proclaim their hatred to slavery, in every shape . . . till this Union, with the Constitution of my country which supports it, shall sink beneath me." Tallmadge called slavery "this monstrous scourge of the human race" and "this bane of man, this abomination of heaven." He told white southerners they had a "canker" in their breast that would drive African Americans "to accomplish your destruction."[11]

Like abolitionists before and after him, Tallmadge's observation of the slave trade in Washington, D.C., contributed to his moral indignation. He noted that "a slave driver, a trafficker in human flesh," with a coffle of fifteen slaves had recently "passed the door of the Capitol." The trader had "torn [the slaves] from every relation, and from every tie which the human heart can hold dear." Tallmadge went on to denounce southern states for "prescribing by law, penalties against the man that dares to teach a negro to read." Anticipating words John Brown would speak four decades later, Tallmadge exclaimed, "Here is the stain! Here is the stigma! which . . . all the waters of the ocean cannot wash out; which seas of blood can only take away."[12]

Livermore's and Tallmadge's confrontational approach set them apart from their northern Republican colleagues. In the House John W. Taylor of Saratoga, New York, and Timothy Fuller of Cambridge, Massachusetts, spoke on behalf of Tallmadge's amendment. But they confined themselves largely to constitutional issues, northern self-interest, and the negative impact of slavery on free labor. In the Senate Federalist Rufus King of New York, who had in 1816 run unsuccessfully as his party's last presidential candidate, acted similarly. Although King lamented the breakup of black families caused by the domestic slave trade, he refused to raise moral issues. To do so, he feared, would "call up feelings . . . which would disturb, if not defeat, the impartial consideration of the subject." Like Taylor and Fuller, King emphasized economics, domestic security, and politics as reasons for banning slavery in Missouri and the West generally. The following November, King denied being an abolitionist.[13]

The NYMS supported the Tallmadge Amendment and the congressmen who spoke on its behalf. In his *Daily Advertiser*, "Ultra-Federalist" Dwight encouraged Republican Tallmadge. Dwight also published articles written by Isaac M. Ely, a New York lawyer and leader of the NYMS and AC, which supported Tallmadge. On February 24, Ely, his NYMS colleagues Hiram Ketchum (another lawyer), and George Newbold (a Quaker born in Burlington, New Jersey) sent Tallmadge and Taylor copies of resolutions adopted by a special meeting of the society held the day before. The resolutions praised the congressmen for their "manly and persevering efforts in Congress, to prevent the further extension of the evils of slavery." According to the society, Tallmadge and Taylor had "elevated the character of the state of New York." The congressmen responded "that the very humane and benevolent objects of your association, may ultimately receive their full accomplishment, is our constant desire and ardent prayer." The congressmen pledged that their "best exertions on all occasions will be faithfully directed to the promotion of the same grand design." That November Richard Peters of Philadelphia, who was president of the AC and a federal district judge, sent a similar letter to King and James Burrill Jr., a Federalist senator from Rhode Island. Peters praised their speeches in "the cause of their country and of humanity" and offered to publish them.[14]

Abolitionist Benjamin Lundy also encouraged Tallmadge, who in turn influenced Lundy. A Quaker journalist who lived in Mount Pleasant, Ohio, Lundy had helped edit the *Philanthropist* newspaper and in 1815 helped organize a local abolition society. Following Tallmadge's speech, Lundy referred to the congressman as "this American Wilberforce," after British abolitionist William Wilberforce. Lundy and his wife also named their first son Charles Tallmadge Lundy. Later in 1819 mobile Lundy moved to Herculaneum, Missouri, where he naively and futilely hoped to organize antislavery political action against admitting more slaves to the territory. Although this effort failed, Lundy became one of the more influential abolitionist leaders during the 1820s and 1830s.[15]

On February 16, 1819, the House of Representatives adopted Tallmadge's amendment. Its first clause, banning the "further introduction of slavery" into Missouri, passed 87–76 by an almost entirely sectional vote. The second clause, providing for the gradual emancipation of slaves already in the territory, passed 82–78. The next day the Senate struck out both clauses by less sectional votes of 22–16 and 31–7, respectively. On March 2 the Senate passed the Missouri statehood bill without restriction regarding slavery. Congress adjourned shortly thereafter, leaving the issue unresolved.[16]

As historian Glover Moore notes, "a carefully organized barrage of propaganda and a series of mass meetings" arranged by "those who favored restriction" followed. Although Republicans had led the struggle for the Tallmadge Amendment in Congress, Federalists dominated this campaign to shape northern political action. What historians have not perceived concerning the anti-Missouri meetings is the key influence abolitionists exercised in organizing and conducting them.[17]

The series began on August 30, 1819, at Burlington, which remained the center of New Jersey abolitionism. Pennsylvania Abolition Society (PAS) member Elias Boudinot chaired the Burlington gathering, and many assumed he organized it. As mentioned in chapter 1, Boudinot had political experience as president of the Continental Congress and as a Federalist congressman. He had belonged to the PAS since 1790 and helped create the American Bible Society. But Boudinot, at nearly eighty, was too old to have initiated the Burlington meeting. There were also mistaken claims that Joseph Hopkinson, a prominent Philadelphia attorney who in 1797 wrote the patriotic song *Hail Columbia,* organized the meeting. Like Boudinot, Hopkinson mixed experience in politics and benevolence. He joined the PAS in 1799, and he had as a Federalist congressman supported Tallmadge's amendment.[18]

In fact Quaker abolitionist William Newbold prepared the way for the Burlington meeting. Newbold, closely related to George Newbold of the NYMS, had been a member of the New Jersey Society for Promoting the Abolition of Slavery (NJSPAS), which disbanded in 1817. His "benevolent mind deeply sympathized with the wrongs and afflictions of the much injured African race." Another Quaker abolitionist and Burlington resident, Samuel Emlen Jr., assisted Newbold. Emlin had been a PAS member at least since 1789. His father had worked with John Woolman, and his wife came from an abolitionist family. His 1837 bequest established the Emlen Institute to benefit black and American Indian children.[19]

The Burlington meeting is significant because of this abolitionist role in it. It is also significant because of its call for a larger gathering, which took place at the New Jersey State House in Trenton on October 29. There, in the presence of the governor and many state legislators, Federalists, Republicans, and abolitionists gathered "in a great Assemblage of persons," which (strikingly for the time) included women. Those attending concentrated on the Missouri issue but went beyond it to endorse emancipation throughout the United States and "prevention of the importation of slaves into it." Boudinot's declining health prevented him from attending, but other Burlington leaders did. William Griffith, a Federalist lawyer and former president of the NJSPAS, served as secretary.[20]

These two New Jersey meetings set an example for a similar gathering in New York City on November 16, 1819. Planning for this meeting began early that month, with Dwight guiding and publicizing it. Nonabolitionists John T. Irving, a Republican lawyer, and John B. Coles, a merchant and local politician, headed the effort. But when the two thousand participants gathered at Broadway's City Hotel, abolitionists constituted nearly half of those on the podium. Several of them belonged to the NYMS. Peter Augustus Jay, son of former NYMS president John Jay and himself an NYMS member, provided an "Address to the American People." In the course of his remarks, Jay denounced slavery for its "injustice and inhumanity, its immoral and irreligious character," while emphasizing the political threat of slavery expansion to northern interests.[21]

A week later a Philadelphia meeting proceeded similarly. And abolitionists dominated its leadership more thoroughly than had been the case in Burlington, Trenton, and New York. The Philadelphia chairman Jared Ingersoll Jr., secretary Robert Ralston, and principal speaker Horace Binney either belonged to abolitionist organizations or assisted in their activities. Attorney Ingersoll, the Federalist vice presidential candidate in 1812, had in 1798 represented the PAS before Pennsylvania's High Court of Errors and Appeals in arguing for total abolition in the state. Ralston worked with black abolitionist Richard Allen to establish the African Methodist Episcopal Church. Binney, who had studied in Ingersoll's law office, later served as a counselor for the AC and attended its annual meetings between1824 and 1827. In his address to those assembled, Binney called on Congress to "prohibit the extension of slavery to new states," and stressed "the inhumanity, impolicy, and injustice of slavery generally." As had been the case with the earlier meetings, the Philadelphia gathering mixed moral and political arguments, and petitioned Congress.[22]

Circulars sent from Trenton and New York resulted in a meeting in Boston on December 3. In contrast to the other gatherings, only a single identifiable abolitionist, John Gallison, helped lead this one. Federalist politicians Daniel Webster and Josiah Quincy and Republican politicians George Black and James H. Austin dominated. And only in Boston did a participant deny the constitutionality of slavery restriction. Yet the meeting produced an abolitionist-style report that declared "the extirpation of slavery . . . to be . . . a measure deeply concerning the honor and safety of the United States." The report claimed that the Constitution favored gradual abolition, rather than "nourishing the evil." It called for planning slavery's end in "the states where it chiefly exists." Gallison, who died a year later at age thirty-two, joined Webster, Quincy, Black, and Austin in communicating the meeting's views to Massachusetts congressmen.[23]

As these meetings transpired, Pennsylvania abolitionists took additional action designed to influence Congress in regard to Missouri. Initially the AC, meeting in Philadelphia during October 1819, had considered the "expediency of sending a committee or delegation to attend the next session of Congress." Instead William Rawle, a Philadelphia Quaker who a year earlier had become president of the Maryland Society for the Abolition of Slavery, prepared a "memorial and remonstrance" to submit to Congress. On December 15 Pennsylvania senator Jonathan Roberts presented this AC petition to the U.S Senate. Roberts, a Republican, had, despite his Quaker background, only moderately antislavery convictions and wavered over slavery restriction. He feared Federalists would take advantage of the Missouri issue to elect Rufus King to the presidency in 1820. He therefore presented the petition only because he wanted to represent his abolitionist constituents. In contrast to Roberts, Philadelphia congressman John Sergeant consistently reflected abolitionist influence. The day after Roberts introduced the AC's views in the Senate, Sergeant, a longtime Federalist politician and a PAS officer since 1815, did so in the House. The following February, as debate on Missouri continued in the House, Sergeant said of slavery, "It is an evil to the slave; it is an evil founded on wrong, and its injustice is not the less because it is advantageous to some one else." He warned of slave revolt and civil war.[24]

Sergeant praised gradual abolition in Pennsylvania as "removing, as much as possible the sorrows of those who have lived in undeserved bondage." He hoped to apply abolitionist tactics "whenever the question presents itself." Appropriately, considering the Missouri issue at hand, Sergeant devoted much of his speech to defending Congress's power to ban slavery in territories and new states. But he had a broader abolitionist perspective. Uphold slavery in a new state such as Missouri, he warned, "and the constitution becomes stained with the sin of having originated a state of slavery." In contrast to Tallmadge, and in anticipation of radical political abolitionists during the 1840s, Sergeant suggested that slavery in the existing states violated the spirit of the U.S. Constitution.[25]

During the early months of 1820, other restrictionist petitions reached Congress. They came from such cities as New Haven, Providence, Newport, and Hartford, and such states as New York, Ohio, and Delaware. One presented by Senator Benjamin Ruggles, an Ohio Republican, declared, "The existence of slavery in our country must be considered a national calamity, as well as a great moral and political evil." Others did not go so far. But they all reflected abolitionist influence.[26]

On March 2, in what became known as the Missouri Compromise, the Senate and House of Representatives agreed to admit Missouri without restriction regarding slavery, ban slavery north of the 36° 30' line of latitude in the remaining territories, and admit Maine as a free-labor state. In response abolitionists tried to rally opposition. Dwight called on Congress "to wipe off the deep stain . . . fixed upon our national character, by the vote on the Missouri bill." On April 5 Philadelphia's *National Gazette and Literary Messenger* (financed by a group headed by PAS leader Roberts Vaux and edited by Robert Walsh Jr.) advocated northern efforts to derail the compromise. On April 13 the PAS, claiming that the United States had been founded "on the abhorrence of slavery in every form," called on Congress to refuse to seat members from Missouri so long as the new state did not ban slavery in its constitution. These statements failed to have a positive impact on Congress. Nevertheless the *Richmond Enquirer* accused abolitionists of "sport[ing] upon the edge of the barrel of gunpowder with the torch in their hands."[27]

Some historians contend that Congress's refusal to end slavery in Missouri "frustrated and demoralized" abolitionists during the 1820s. On passage of the compromise, Elihu Embree, a Quaker abolitionist who lived in Tennessee, declared, "Hell is about to enlarge her borders and tyranny her dominion." Most abolitionists, however, drew encouragement from their political engagement. Lundy commended Tallmadge, Taylor, Sergeant, and others, who had "stepped forth so boldly, and pled the cause of liberty so manfully." The AC published the speeches of Tallmadge, Taylor, and King along with a letter from John Jay. Lundy and the PAS recognized that antislavery politicians had succeeded in banning territorial slavery north of the 36° 30' line. And by stimulating antislavery rhetoric and action in Congress, abolitionists had placed slaveholders on defense.[28]

The Missouri crisis also prepared abolitionists for other political struggles during the 1820s. Two of them occurred in northern states: Illinois and Pennsylvania. In regard to Illinois, PAS members during 1823 and 1824 helped the state's governor, Edward Coles, as he led an assortment of local abolitionists and antislavery politicians in opposition to an effort to legalize slavery in his state.[29]

Coles, a well-connected Virginian, became a gradual abolitionist in 1814 and in 1818 moved to Illinois to free his ten slaves. During the latter year Illinois entered the Union, over James Tallmadge's objection, with a constitution recognizing existing slavery within its jurisdiction and providing for black indentured servitude. Encouraged by the Missouri debates, local proslavery advocates then called for a state constitutional convention to insert clauses that would fully legalize slavery. Whether or not to call such a convention became the major issue in Illinois's 1822 gubernatorial election, which Coles (running as an antislavery candidate) narrowly won. In his inaugural address that December, he called on the state legislature to formulate "just and equitable provisions . . . for the abrogation of slavery." A heated and often violent struggle followed, as proslavery forces sought to hold a convention and those who favored abolishing slavery in the state opposed doing so.[30]

In March 1823 (if not earlier), Illinois abolitionists, composed mainly of Baptists, Quakers, journalists, and politicians, began organizing county societies dedicated to "the prevention of slavery in the State of Illinois." With Coles's help, they published pamphlets, purchased a newspaper, and sought outside abolitionist support. As part of this effort, Benjamin Lundy, who had begun publishing his *Genius of Universal Emancipation* at Mount Pleasant, Ohio, in 1821 and moved it to Jonesboro, Tennessee, in 1823, provided articles to Hooper Warren, who edited the *Edwardsville* (Illinois) *Spectator.*[31]

In April Coles called on Nicholas Biddle (who was *not* an abolitionist), Coles's Philadelphia friend and president of the Second Bank of the United States, to solicit help from Biddle's fellow Philadelphian and PAS leader Roberts Vaux. In Biddle's words Vaux, a Quaker involved in a variety of reform organizations, "perceived the deep importance of defeating this first effort to extend to the north-western country the misfortune of the slave population." Because of "hostility" to the PAS in Illinois, Vaux and several other society members discretely aided the antislavery cause in that state by sending six thousand antislavery pamphlets to the governor for "gratuitous distribution."[32]

Coles praised Pennsylvania abolitionists for promoting "the cause of humanity" in a struggle against "the oppression and abject slavery of their fellow creatures." A year later Vaux returned the compliment by commending Coles's efforts on behalf of "the rights of mankind." Vaux wrote that Coles had upheld "justice and mercy toward a degraded and oppressed portion of our fellow beings." After Illinois voters in August 1824 refused by a substantial margin to hold a convention, Coles called for "speedy . . . abolition" in the state and for "severe penalties" for anyone convicted of kidnapping free African Americans into slavery. But as would always be the case with politicians, Coles had accepted abolitionist help on *his* terms. It was he who urged Vaux to be discreet in the aid Vaux provided lest proslavery leaders in Illinois charge the anticonventionists with fanaticism. Coles and his allies emphasized slavery's threat to white rights and interests. Even as he predicted antislavery victory, he complained of "the indiscretions of the advocates of freedom out of the State."[33]

In regard to slavery in the South, Coles acted even more conservatively. In 1823 he favored "very stiff" laws in that section to control African Americans slave and free. In 1826 he agreed with the ACS in rejecting "speedy [southern] emancipation" and supporting removal "of free negroes from the country." He based his agreement with the ACS on what he and many others considered to be the incompatibility of black and white people. As some northern colonizationists became immediate abolitionists during the 1820s and 1830s, Coles continued to support removal of free African Americans.[34] Coles's 1823–24 alliance with abolitionists nevertheless achieved significant results that fundamentally shaped the sectional conflict.

Two years after the victory in Illinois, PAS lobbyists in Pennsylvania shaped a bill initiated by proslavery Marylanders into what historian William R. Leslie calls "the first to interfere with the administration of national legislation for the recovery . . . of property in fugitive slaves."[35] Many years earlier Pennsylvania abolitionists had produced gradual emancipation. Now their efforts heightened North-South political tensions. They also set an example for other northern states in designing laws to protect fugitive slaves against recapture and defend other African Americans against kidnapping into slavery.

On February 2, 1826, a delegation of Maryland legislators arrived in Harrisburg, Pennsylvania's capital city. They carried draft legislation designed to expedite in Pennsylvania renditions of fugitive slaves by their masters or agents thereof. Forewarned by Robert Walsh's *National Gazette,* abolitionist groups (including the PAS, Quakers, and African Americans) mobilized. Philadelphia Quaker Thomas Shipley, Vaux, and other PAS members met on February 10. They prepared a memorial and sent letters to assembly leader William M. Meredith, who had charge of the Marylanders' bill. Anticipating later abolitionist letters to antislavery politicians, Vaux's advised Meredith, "As one of your constituents—as one of your friends—I pray you to pause upon this matter, & employ your gifts & intelligence, in preserving Penna. from so *black a deed* as this black bill proposes. . . . You will pardon my zeal—it is honest, it is fearless."[36]

Shipley and Vaux then traveled to Harrisburg to "become acquainted with the most prominent members of the House" during the legislative session. Their lobbying mission aimed "to remove any erroneous information which may be found to exist in the minds of the delegation from Maryland & . . . to afford the Legislature such facts & other information connected with this subject as in the possession of the Society." According to historian Leslie, Shipley and Vaux hoped to "nullify [in Pennsylvania] the fugitive slave clause of the Constitution and the federal fugitive slave act of 1793."[37]

By influencing Meredith and Jacob F. Heston in the assembly, as well as Stephen Duncan in the senate, Shipley and Vaux achieved their objective. One amendment to the Marylanders' bill repealed a section of an earlier law requiring Pennsylvanians to aid masters who sought fugitive slaves. Another banned claimant oaths as evidence in rendition cases. After some disagreement between the assembly and the senate, the amended bill became law on March 25. In effect it ended in Pennsylvania the right of recaption under the fugitive slave clause of the U.S. Constitution. Abolitionists, and at least some of the Marylanders, realized that the new law (even without a jury requirement in rendition cases) made recovery of escaped slaves in Pennsylvania difficult. A PAS committee called the law "a manifest improvement upon the previously existing laws." The PAS, Quakers, and Harrisburg African Americans urged the legislature to pass no additional laws on the subject.[38]

The abolitionist efforts in Illinois in 1823–24 and in Pennsylvania in 1826 joined those in regard to the Missouri crisis in having national political impact. So did an abolitionist campaign during the first three decades of the nineteenth century against slavery and the slave trade in the District of Columbia. This campaign contributed to sectional animosity, spread antislavery sentiment, directly impacted national politics, and anticipated abolitionist political strategy during the 1830s and 1840s.

In 1805 James Sloan, a Republican congressman from Gloucester County, New Jersey, raised the first serious challenge to slavery in the national capital when he introduced resolutions calling for gradual emancipation there. Sloan, a former Quaker, had over ten years earlier joined the Gloucester Society for Promoting the Abolition of Slavery and had served as its delegate to an AC meeting in Philadelphia. Cantankerous and not a party regular, Sloan convinced thirty other congressmen to support his failed effort.[39]

In 1816 eccentric Virginia slaveholder John Randolph's quixotic demand for a congressional investigation into the district slave trade gained more notoriety than Sloan's resolution. Randolph's initiative, Philadelphia abolitionist Jesse Torrey's 1817 pamphlet on the same subject, and a December 1817 PAS call for "advocates of humanity" to focus on the district inspired an intense political effort that reached a peak in 1829. This coordinated effort to pressure lawmakers took time to reach full strength because kidnapping of free African Americans, slavery expansion, and the illegal foreign slave trade vied for abolitionist attention.[40]

In 1818 the AC sent to each house of Congress a "request" for "gradual but certain termination" of slavery in the district, as part of a more comprehensive petition campaign. Slavery, the organization charged, should not exist in the capital of a nation "whose constitution proclaims that all men are born equally free." The petition lamented that "children of the same Almighty Father" were "doomed for a difference of complexion . . . to hopeless bondage." Although the AC failed to follow up this initiative in 1819 and 1820, it did so in December 1821. And in early 1822, the Manumission Society of Tennessee, under Benjamin Lundy's leadership, sent a similar petition to Congress.[41]

The AC again stopped its petitioning effort during 1822 and 1823, as its leaders feared sectional animosity intensified by the Missouri crisis made continuing the effort "inexpedient." Not until early 1824, when Lundy took the lead, did the effort gain consistency. The AC began sending more petitions and advised other abolitionist organizations that "by petitions to Congress . . . slavery may be wholly abolished in the District of Columbia." The AC also called on state legislatures to instruct senators to oppose slavery or the slave trade in Washington.[42]

Two arrivals in the Washington vicinity helped the effort. First Lundy during the summer of 1824 moved from Tennessee to Baltimore and in October began publishing the *Genius of Universal Emancipation* there. Lundy declared, "In my view, the subject of universal emancipation is a *political* one, in the most emphatic sense of the word." Second, in March 1825, Charles Miner of West Chester, Pennsylvania, began his brief career in the House of Representatives. Miner, an attorney and journalist, had become a PAS member in 1820 and part of what historian Richard S. Newman calls the organization's "lawyerly contingent." Elected in November 1824 as a Republican supporter of John Quincy Adams, Miner had favored gradual abolition and colonization of former slaves. A visit to Washington Jail in early 1826 to investigate conditions under which slaves languished pending removal south by traders led him to take action in favor of the former. He challenged the existence of slavery in the district, and did so more adamantly than had anyone before.[43]

Abolitionists soon began helping Miner. Led by Daniel Raymond of Baltimore, the AC in October 1825 called for electing more congressmen who favored abolition in the district. Raymond, a Connecticut native, presided over the Maryland Anti-Slavery Society and ran that fall as the society's candidate for the state's general assembly. In December Lundy circulated a petition among district residents favoring "prohibition" of the slave trade. In early March 1826 the *Genius* "respectfully suggest[ed]" to Miner "the propriety of offering a resolution for the *abolition of slavery in the District of Columbia.*" Two months later, during a session unrecorded in the *Register of Debates in Congress,* Miner asked the Committee on the District of Columbia to report a "bill for the gradual abolition of slavery . . . and such restrictions upon the slave-trade therein as shall be just and proper." Several southern congressmen objected, and "an apparently large majority" refused to consider the subject. When the following December Miner again raised the issue of emancipation in the district, proslavery representative Charles A. Wickliffe of Kentucky reacted with a threat. He declared that "discussion of the subject, as presented by the gentleman's resolutions, was calculated to rouse feelings and produce an excitement which it would be difficult to repress."[44]

Abolitionists, aware that such threats helped their cause, pressed on. The NYMS urged Miner to renew his effort when Congress reconvened. The arrest that August in Washington of New York citizen Gilbert Horton as a fugitive slave, and the chance that he might be sold into slavery to pay his jail fees, added momentum. William Jay, another son of John Jay, and other New York abolitionists organized a meeting at Newcastle in Westchester County, New York. On August 30 the meeting called on New York governor DeWitt Clinton to demand Horton's release. The meeting also authorized Jay to circulate "a petition to Congress for the *immediate* abolition of slavery in the District of Columbia."[45]

In response to a message from Clinton, sympathetic president John Quincy Adams (acting through Secretary of State Henry Clay) secured Horton's freedom. Simultaneously Jay alerted Miner to the New York petitioning campaign, emphasized a need for publicity, and drafted the "Westchester Memorial" to Congress. In Philadelphia the AC called on other "Anti-Slavery and Abolition Societies" to "forward petitions to Congress, praying that body to take immediate and efficient measures for the final abolition of slavery in the District of Columbia."[46]

At the end of 1826, Westchester County's congressman, Aaron Ward, another northern Republican but not an abolitionist, requested on the House floor that the Committee on the District of Columbia investigate whether Horton had been legally jailed and, if so, "inquire into the expediency of repealing" the law under which he had been arrested. During the heated discussion that followed, southern congressmen charged those who pushed the Horton case with seeking "to excite angry debate and irrational feelings." And although a modified version of Ward's request passed, the committee reported the following July that free black men could be treated in Washington as Horton had been. According to Jay, this decision proved that only abolition could solve the problems associated with slavery, and that the effort in the district should be "the first necessary step in a campaign against slavery itself."[47]

As 1827 began Lundy and Raymond circulated in Baltimore a petition supporting Miner's call on Congress to provide for gradual abolition in the district. Like Jay's memorial, this petition described such an achievement as a step toward ending slavery throughout the country. On February 10 John Barney, who represented Baltimore in the House, presented a resolution based on the petition, which "sundry citizens" of the city had signed. In a manner similar to Ward, Barney was an Adams Republican but not an abolitionist. When several of his colleagues sought to table the resolution, he acquiesced. "Agitation of this question," he asserted, was "premature, impolitic . . . and not calculated to produce any beneficial results." Clement Dorsey, another Adams Republican who represented Baltimore, went further in opposing action in regard to the resolution because, he said, it "breathed the spirit of general emancipation."[48]

Despite, or perhaps because of, proslavery resistance, abolitionist determination to concentrate on the national capital intensified. When the AC met in October 1827, Lundy chaired a committee entrusted with the task of requesting "the several Abolition and Manumission Societies" to continue petitioning Congress for "the abolition of slavery in the District of Columbia." A letter from the NYMS called for action on behalf of either "immediate or gradual abolition" in the district. Anticipating a late 1830s immediate abolitionist initiative, the NYMS suggested employing "a respectable and intelligent agent" to lobby on behalf of this goal.[49]

Shortly after the AC met, Miner, in cooperation with Lundy, compiled more "information respecting slavery and the slave trade" in the district. Miner then circulated a "Memorial of the Inhabitants of the District of Columbia, praying for the gradual abolition of slavery in the District of Columbia." District "property holders" provided many of the thousand signatures. Miner presented the petition to the House on March 24, 1828. It denounced the sale of free African Americans into slavery and "the rapacity of slave traders." Slavery, it charged, hurt black character, white morals, and respect for "honest labor." Without debate the House referred the petition to the Committee on the District of Columbia, from which it never emerged.[50]

To highlight the district slavery issue, the AC met in Baltimore in November 1828. The delegates, convened for the first time in a slaveholding city, prepared another petition to send to Congress. Once again they urged other abolitionist organizations to do likewise. They also authorized publication of an "Address to Citizens of the United States" on the issue. And they predicted optimistically that members of Congress would soon respond to the petitions. The address declared that AC members acted "on behalf of the sufferings, the privations, and the unmerited degradation of their fellow men—the colored people of

America." The petition called for "the immediate enactment of such laws as will ensure the abolition of slavery within the District of Columbia, at the earliest period that may be deemed safe and expedient."[51]

PAS leaders, several of whom also led the AC, engaged in related activities during the final weeks of 1828 and the first of 1829. They successfully encouraged the Pennsylvania legislature to instruct the state's U.S. senators and advise the state's representatives to vote against slavery in the district. A similar effort in the New York legislature failed during February 1829 after a heated debate. In both cases abolitionists did not expect Congress at that time to act against slavery and the slave trade. Instead they again sought to support Miner so that he, in PAS leader William Rawle's words, might press "an opening wedge" for future action by his "successors."[52]

On January 6 and 7, 1829, when Miner introduced a preamble and two resolutions into the House of Representatives, he emphasized support from the Pennsylvania legislature and the "numerous petitions" he had received. The preamble and resolutions called for the immediate abolition of the slave trade in the district and suggested that "measures should be adopted to effect the abolition of slavery here gradually." In his lengthy remarks Miner recalled his 1826 visit to slave traders' prisons. There were in the district, he charged, "instances of injustice and cruelty, scarcely exceeded on the coast of Africa." Such instances, he maintained, violated America's republican and Christian principles. Yet, unlike the PAS, Miner dealt in racial stereotypes, characterizing African Americans (rather than slavery) as threats to prosperity and security. Gradual abolition, he predicted, would "protect the District from being over-run by free negroes."[53]

Miner's remarks again elicited a strong southern reaction. Representative John Crompton Weems, a Maryland slaveholder, angrily defended slavery and the slave trade. He portrayed the latter as moral and beneficial to those traded. He accused Miner of violating separation of church and state, and then he delivered a biblical defense of slavery! He also claimed Miner aimed to "drive out" African Americans "as we do the poor Indians."[54]

Two days later the House voted 141–37 to reject Miner's preamble. Then, in what appeared to some to be an antislavery victory, the same body voted 120–59 to have its Committee on the District of Columbia consider Miner's anti-slave-trade resolution and voted 114–66 to have the committee consider his antislavery resolution. The result a few weeks later was that the committee, dominated by slaveholders from Maryland and Virginia, denounced the resolutions. The committee's report, likely written by Weems, described the Washington slave trade as "one way of gradually diminishing the evil [slavery] complained of here." In what became a major argument against abolition in the district, the committee added that recognizing the power of Congress to end slavery would violate "the rights of property" secured to citizens of the states that had ceded the land for the district. The committee urged Congress "not to disturb [slavery], but to leave it where it now rests, with the laws, and the humanity of those who are interested in protecting . . . this species of property." The committee predicted that, were slavery abolished within the district, it would become a haven for fugitive slaves. The committee warned, "This constant [abolitionist] agitation must sooner or later be productive of serious mischief, if not danger, to the peace and harmony of the Union." Abolitionists risked arousing "false hopes of liberty" among slaves and making them "restless."[55]

The following December the AC met in Washington literally to press home preparation of yet another petition "for the gradual abolition of slavery in the District of Columbia." Inspired by Miner's resolutions, and indicating their broader agenda, the delegates declared "that the existence of slavery within the United States is a great evil and one for which an adequate remedy is . . . the most to be desired." The delegates also recognized the Pennsylvania legislature's resolutions and sent memorials to other state legislatures requesting similar action. But they noted "much censure" had been "cast upon" abolitionists and advised that they "must indeed expect that the[ir] object can only be obtained by very gradual means."[56]

Direct abolitionist efforts to influence politics and government during the 1810s and 1820s had mixed results. They did not prevent Missouri from entering the Union as a slave-labor state. But their efforts to prevent it impacted sectional debate in Congress and encouraged the introduction into that body of moral opposition to slavery. In Illinois, abolitionists played an important role in defeating a proslavery effort that, if successful, could have changed the sectional balance of power. In Pennsylvania abolitionists led the state legislature to take action against state enforcement of the Fugitive Slave Law. The abolitionists' decade-long campaign to encourage their allies among politicians to take action in regard to slavery and the slave trade in the District of Columbia did not succeed. But even more than the abolitionist experiences in regard to Missouri and Illinois, it led them to believe they must over time encourage broader political pressure. "This object [of emancipation in the district]," the AC delegates asserted, "cannot be obtained except perhaps at a distance of time now invisible, unless the wishes of the states with regard to it are audibly expressed." And although the abolitionist drive against slavery and slave trading in the District of Columbia lost momentum after 1829, it remained to be reinvigorated by a younger abolitionist generation.[57]

3

Escalation, 1831–1840

The publication on January 1, 1831, of the first issue of William Lloyd Garrison's *Liberator* is a symbolic occasion in the nation's struggle over slavery. Garrison represented a younger generation that took control of the abolition movement and transferred its center from Philadelphia to Boston. More emphatically than elements within the American Convention (AC), Garrison and his comrades rejected gradualism. They demanded immediate, peaceful measures on behalf of black freedom and natural rights.[1]

Garrison's contemporaries called this more insistent approach "modern abolitionism," and historians call it "immediatism." It reflected black demands for racial justice, Great Britain's progress toward emancipation within its empire, and an increased awareness of slavery's brutality. In addition evangelicalism associated with the Second Great Awakening had a stronger impact on the younger abolitionists than on their predecessors. Therefore Garrison and his associates appealed more consistently to individual conscience, personal responsibility for social evils, commitment to suppress all sin, and universal redemption. Compared to their predecessors, they more fervently embraced moral absolutism and rejected compromise. Increased involvement of women in the movement had a role in this transformation. Abolitionist women formed "female" antislavery societies and assumed major responsibility in circulating petitions.[2]

Political change also affected the abolition movement during the 1830s. As the Democratic Party led by President Andrew Jackson aligned increasingly with proslavery interests, two new political parties emerged. First, in 1828, evangelical fervor in western New York's Burned-Over District encouraged formation of the short-lived, narrowly based Anti-Masonic Party. This party, whose influence spread throughout the Northeast, charged that secretive Masonic lodges posed an elitist threat to republican government. The party attracted abolitionists, and several prominent Anti-Masons embraced abolitionist criticism of the

William Lloyd Garrison (1805–1879) led
the American Anti-Slavery Society from the
1830s through the Civil War. (Library of
Congress Prints and Photographs Division)

slaveholding elite. Second, in 1834, the much more widely based Whig Party
replaced the National Republican Party in the national two-party system. The
Whig Party in the South at first attracted extreme proslavery advocates. But in
the North, business interests, evangelicals, former Anti-Masons, and moral reformers (including abolitionists) found it to be attractive.[3]

Within this changing political context, Garrison epitomized abolitionism.
Born at Newburyport, Massachusetts, to a poor family and self-educated, he
became a reform journalist who initially identified with the Federalist Party and
supported the American Colonization Society (ACS) during much of the 1820s.
It took contacts with black abolitionists and observation of slavery in Baltimore
to radicalize his outlook. He had gone to Baltimore in September 1829 to join
Benjamin Lundy as coeditor of the *Genius of Universal Emancipation*. After a
brief imprisonment in the city, based on charges that he had slandered a slave
trader, Garrison returned to Massachusetts in late 1830 to begin the *Liberator*.
Nat Turner's slave revolt in southeastern Virginia the following August convinced Garrison and the few who agreed with him that peaceful, immediate
emancipation alone could keep God from punishing the American nation. In
December 1833 Garrison led in forming the American Anti-Slavery Society
(AASS), dedicated to using appeals to Christian conscience (known as moral
suasion) to achieve prompt emancipation and equal rights for African Americans throughout the United States.[4]

Some historians claim that abolitionists during the early 1830s did not "direct . . . much energy into political channels." These scholars portray apparent abolitionist engagement with politics and government, including petitioning, as *primarily* designed to shape northern popular opinion and build community support. The evangelical reform culture that had emerged in the North as a result of the Second Great Awakening certainly encouraged abolitionists to proselytize. The immediatists' more intense moral fervor did not, however, change abolitionists' *political* tactics. According to Merton L. Dillon, "Neither the antislavery arguments [immediate] abolitionists used nor the measures they employed differed fundamentally from those of previous years." Russell B. Nye adds that Garrison and his associates sought "political advantages" in Congress.[5] And, as immediatists continued their predecessors' direct efforts to influence northern politicians, they also continued to encourage a southern proslavery political reaction.

Abolitionist petitioning of Congress, which had reached a peak with Benjamin Lundy and Charles Miner in 1829, continued during the 1830s. Garrison in 1828 and 1829 had written "petitions and circulated them to New England postmasters." During the latter year, he sent a petition with 2,352 signatures to his congressman. Two years later Garrison devoted much of the *Liberator*'s first front page to a Boston petition calling on Congress to abolish (immediately or gradually) slavery and the slave trade in the District of Columbia. Embracing this political tactic, Garrison declared, "It is certainly time that a vigorous and systematic effort should be made, from one end of the country to the other, to take down that national monument of oppression which towers up in the District."[6] During the 1830s other immediatists, including Quakers, evangelicals, and former evangelicals, unrelentingly interacted with sympathetic politicians. In addition to petitions, they used correspondence, publications, meetings, and private visits to press their political agenda.

A few weeks after Garrison endorsed the Boston petition in the *Liberator,* Congressman Benjamin Gorham, an "Anti-Jacksonian from Boston" (and later a Whig), presented it in the House of Representatives. Although the petition died in committee, Garrison, who by then identified with no political party, portrayed petitioning as a political measure that would "ultimately succeed" in regard to slavery in the district. That June he wrote, "We rejoice at this [petitioning] movement." He called for expanding it and asserted his faith in government action. Once abolitionists expressed their sentiments "to their representatives in Congress," he over-optimistically predicted, slavery would end in the nation's capital "with ease and expedition." That fall former Democrat

George Henry Evans, who helped lead an ephemeral New York City Working-man's Party, endorsed Garrison's call for a more vigorous petitioning campaign.[7]

In December Garrison urged abolitionists to send "petitions to Congress for the abolition of Slavery in the District of Columbia without delay." He reported an increase of petitioning in Massachusetts, Ohio, and New York. He approved a *Hudson* (Ohio) *Observer and Telegraph* editorial arguing that southern fears stemming from Turner's rebellion might enhance the impact of abolition in the national capital. Reflecting what had since the late 1820s become an abolition-ist mantra *and* a proslavery accusation, the *Observer and Telegraph* asked, "Who can tell, but the abolition of Slavery in the District of Columbia, may lead the way to the adoption of a system of universal emancipation." A few months earlier William Jay had linked Turner's revolt with emancipation in the district and throughout the South. The "slaves," Jay predicted, "will either receive their freedom as a boon, or they will rest it by force."[8]

Abolitionist emphasis on congressional action continued even though, for a few years after Charles Miner retired in early 1829, the movement lacked rep-resentatives supportive of its petitions. When moralistic former U.S. president John Quincy Adams gained election to Congress from Massachusetts in 1830, abolitionists mistakenly assumed he would immediately replace Miner, and go beyond him, in supporting their cause. The son of founder John Adams, ex-traordinarily well-educated, and verbally agile, John Quincy Adams appeared to be decidedly opposed to slavery. During the Missouri debates of 1819 and 1820, he had described slavery as an evil. Yet he supported the Missouri Com-promise as a means of achieving sectional harmony. As president between 1825 and 1829, he avoided the slavery issue. And shortly after he entered the House in December 1831, he shocked slavery's strongest opponents.[9]

In the course of presenting fifteen petitions from Pennsylvania Quakers praying Congress to abolish slavery and the slave trade in the district, Adams announced his opposition to abolition there. Congressional consideration of the issue, he said, intensified sectional animosity. An astonished Garrison de-clared, "This is not a time for northern dough-faces to trifle with the sympathies and petitions of their constituents." Philadelphia's Quaker *Advocate of Truth,* incorrectly characterizing Adams as "an advocate of abolition from his youth," accused him of deserting the cause to aid its enemies.[10] As it turned out Adams's negativity *encouraged* abolitionist petitioning. This in turn drew Adams by mid-decade into a sectionally divisive debate he had sought to avoid.

In the interim immediatists found a congressman more willing than Adams to support their petitioning. This was William Hiester, an Anti-Mason from Lancaster County, Pennsylvania. In 1832 an abolitionist effort in that state had produced seven petitions, with a total of one thousand signatures, calling for abolition of slavery in the District of Columbia. The following February Hiester presented the petitions in the House of Representatives and drew a proslavery reaction.[11]

Overlap between abolitionism and Anti-Masonry is clear in Hiester's brief remarks regarding the petitions. He denounced "the gross inconsistency" that allowed "the most abject slavery in this boasted land of liberty . . . at the very portals of your hall of legislation." He praised the character of the petitioners. He agreed with them that "the whole nation is deeply involved in the contin-uation of slavery and the slave trade in this District." Hiester did not ask to have the petitions read, only that they be referred (as usual) to the Commit-tee on the District of Columbia. Nevertheless proslavery members bristled. As had other proslavery congressmen (as well as abolitionists) before him, Virginia Democrat John Y. Mason characterized emancipation in the district as "but the commencement of a series of measures" tending to general emancipation. Only cautionary words from Adams and Mason's fellow Virginia Democrat Robert Craig prevented what Adams believed would have been "a very unpleas-ant debate."[12]

In 1833 and 1834 John G. Whittier in Massachusetts and Theodore Dwight Weld in Ohio encouraged immediatist organizations such as the AASS to initi-ate more petition drives. Quaker poet Whittier began his abolitionist career as one of Garrison's closest associates and as an advocate of direct political engage-ment. During the 1830s he lectured across the North, wrote to and met with politicians he deemed likely to support the cause, and lobbied. Weld, an evan-gelical preacher named after Theodore Dwight, advocated manual labor and temperance as well as immediate emancipation. He aligned with wealthy fellow evangelicals Arthur and Lewis Tappan of New York City and helped organize the movement in Ohio.[13]

At the spring 1834 Garrisonian-controlled New England Anti-Slavery Society meeting, Whittier suggested forming a central committee to encourage aboli-tionists in each northern town to send petitions to Congress favoring abolition in the District of Columbia. That December the AASS moved toward complying with Whittier's proposal by printing petition forms and requesting regional affil-iates to distribute them. In January 1835 Garrison, who was away from Boston, urged his *Liberator* partner Isaac Knapp to give preference to stories about the petition debate in Congress.[14]

Historians often portray December 1835 as the time when a more conse-quential North-South congressional clash over abolitionist petitions began. But escalation of the long-existing sectional debate in Congress started nearly a year

John G. Whittier (1807–1892), who became a major American poet, worked closely with antislavery politicians throughout his abolitionist career. (Engraving by Stephen Alonzo Schoff, The Miriam and Ira D. Wallach Division of Art, Prints and Photographs: Print Collection, The New York Public Library)

earlier with a February 2 speech in the House of Representatives by John Dickson. An Anti-Mason from western New York, Dickson had graduated from Middlebury College and practiced law. In his speech Dickson presented "several petitions and memorials," including one "signed by more than eight hundred ladies from the city of New York."[15]

Dickson understood that he had joined a longstanding, abolitionist-inspired political effort. "For more than thirty years," he observed in his speech, "hundreds of thousands" of "citizens of the country have petitioned Congress to abolish slavery and the slave trade in this District." He defended the right of women, as well as men, to petition government, and he referred to the 1829 congressional debate Miner had sparked. Dickson summarized the petitioners' charges against the inhumanity of slavery, denial of black rights, kidnapping of free African Americans into slavery, and horrors of the district's slave trade. Because he recognized that the Committee on the District of Columbia would not act, he supported the petitioners' request for "a select committee" to consider their prayer. Like abolitionists, he denounced slavery as "unchristian, unholy," and he promised to oppose its "existence . . . in every form, and in every land."[16]

When Dickson finished talking, Joseph W. Chinn, a Virginia Democrat who chaired the Committee on the District, had the petitions tabled by a 117–77 vote. Two weeks later, when Dickson, George Evans of Maine, and Stephen C. Phillips of Massachusetts presented additional petitions for abolition in the district, they provoked a heated debate. Most of the southerners who participated warned (as had their counterparts during the first Congress) that discussing antislavery petitions could lead to disunion. They condemned northern imprudence, fanaticism, firebrands, and interference in southern institutions. Clement C. Clay, an Alabama Democrat, linked "the Garrisons" and "the Tappans" to this dangerous interference. Volatile Henry A. Wise, a slaveholding Virginia Whig, declared that continued abolitionist petitioning would unite the white South in defense of slavery. Regardless of political affiliation, white southerners would "all [be] united on the subject—ready, ripe for revolution, if worst come to worst!"[17]

As they had with Hiester, immediatists used Dickson, his allies, and the southern reaction to them to encourage additional petitioning as a means of influencing national politics. Garrison published Dickson's speech and the following congressional debate. He praised Dickson as "sound and fearless" and condemned Clay and Wise as "imprudent and ferocious." Garrison did not regard petitions merely as a means of influencing northern opinion. Rather he remained over-optimistic regarding political action, claiming that petitioning could produce results "at the next session of Congress." He wrote that "an effort will be made on the part of the people to effect the abolition of slavery and the slave trade in the District of Columbia that will overwhelm all opposition." Anticipating later tactics among what became known as "political abolitionists," Garrison in early March called on voters to "send abolition representatives to Congress" to support the petitions. That May the AASS "warmly eulogized" Dickson. And when Congress's actions did not match Garrison's hopes, he got the outpouring of petitions he sought. A proslavery House committee reported it had received during the 1835–36 session 176 petitions with 34,000 signatures, "nearly 15,000 of whom were [signed by] females."[18]

William Slade, a congressman from Vermont, had a central role in this petition increase. A Middlebury graduate, lawyer, and Anti-Mason like Dickson, Slade had been a journalist, Vermont secretary of state, county judge, and clerk in the U.S. State Department. He had entered the House of Representatives in 1834 and became a Whig in 1836. His reciprocal relationship with immediate abolitionists was similar to that between some earlier politicians and abolitionists, and it foreshadowed later such relationships. Less able than John Quincy Adams as a speaker, taciturn Slade initially shared Adams's caution and moderation in regard to slavery. During the mid-1830s Slade worked against slavery in the District of Columbia, while, as a member of the ACS, he endorsed deporting

African Americans.[19] Nevertheless when Slade, Adams, and others presented moderately worded abolitionist petitions, they affected national politics because slaveholders continued to respond viciously.

When on December 16, 1835, Slade first spoke in the House on behalf of the petitioners and their goals, he distinguished himself and the petitioners from abolitionists. In urging the House to print a petition presented by Congressman John Fairfield, a Maine Democrat, Slade portrayed the petitioners as "less connected with the efforts for general and immediate abolition of slavery in the southern States than was commonly believed." Then, according to late nineteenth- and early twentieth-century political scientist and historian John W. Burgess, Slade delivered "an antislavery speech . . . such as had never been heard upon the floor of Congress." This is not true, but Slade, by referring to slavery as "this foul blot" and calling for its abolition in the district, certainly aroused slaveholders' "fury." James Garland of Virginia, Thomas Glascock of Georgia, and John C. Calhoun, James H. Hammond, and Waddy Thompson, all of South Carolina, responded to Slade by denouncing fanatics. They warned that such remarks would cause slave revolt. They threatened disunion and vowed to kill abolitionists.[20]

Historian Russell B. Nye suggests that Slade, in differentiating between petitioners and abolitionists, sought to avoid this sort of reaction. Shortly after Slade spoke, Adams took a similarly moderate stance while revealing abolitionist influences on him. He warned southerners that an effort to block the petitions would produce more sectional clashes in Congress, spread antislavery sentiment in the North, and lead to the election of congressmen more adamantly opposed to slavery. He also advised southerners and their northern allies not to suppress freedom of speech, press, petition, and religion. Opposition to slavery, he contended, was a "religious question." The petitioners "act[ed] under what they believe[d] to be a sense of duty to their God." A few months later Adams stated privately that he had, for the sake of sectional harmony, not mentioned *his* beliefs, based on "the law of God and of nature," regarding slavery.[21]

Despite Slade's and Adams's restraint, the flood of petitions led to the socalled Pinckney Gag, introduced by South Carolina congressman Henry Laurens Pinckney in February 1836 and enacted as a House rule on May 26, 1836. It became the first of a series of proslavery maneuvers in Congress designed to block petitions "relating in any way . . . to the subject of slavery or the abolition of slavery." Pinckney denied Congress had constitutional power "to interfere, in any way, with the institution of slavery in any of the states." For Congress to act against slavery in the District of Columbia, he added, "would be a violation of public faith . . . and dangerous to the Union." Taking the gag as a challenge, the AASS, with Garrison's support, called for more petitioning, particularly among women.[22]

At the AASS's May 1836 annual meeting, evangelical Elizur Wright Jr., then residing in New York City as one of the organization's leaders, stressed national politics. He acknowledged that changing "public sentiment . . . must be the direct and principal object of our [abolitionist] labors." But he believed influencing public sentiment had a political goal. "Our success," he declared, "[will] show itself in the question of abolition in the District." Abolitionist encouragement of a "spirit of tyranny" in Congress, he predicted, would produce a "tenfold" increase in petitions during the coming year.[23]

Several scholars characterize the motivation of congressmen who opposed the gag rule as a desire to uphold a white right to petition rather than a black right to freedom. According to biographer Samuel Flagg Bemis, John Quincy Adams subordinated "antislavery agitation" to defending northern rights against slaveholding politicians' attempts to limit those rights. Similarly historian James Brewer Stewart emphasizes white northerners' selfish fear that proslavery actions in response to petitions threatened *their* civil rights and *their* domestic tranquility." Such fears, Stewart notes, coexisted with northern white "race prejudice" and suspicion of abolitionists. Nevertheless historians recognize the political impact of the petitioning campaign. John W. Burgess contends that "the struggle in Congress over the abolition petitions" determined "the whole course of the national history of the United States from 1836 to 1861." Russell B. Nye asserts that the expanding petition controversy "gave abolition its *first* open wedge into national politics." Bruce Laurie, noting that petitioning was a "traditional form of politicking," observes that it served the abolitionists' purpose "beyond anyone's expectations." Edward Magdol, who centers on what petitions reveal concerning "abolitionists' grass roots," remarks that petitions became "serious instruments of political action."[24]

By December 1836 the number of antislavery petitions to Congress had increased. As a result slaveholding Speaker of the House James K. Polk of Tennessee prevented William Slade and others who supported the petitioners from taking the floor. This led to Adams's emergence as petitioning's leading defender. He had the knowledge of House rules and verbal dexterity to challenge parliamentary attempts to silence him. He mainly defended white northerners' rights. His devotion to the Union continued to dispose him toward moderation. As late as April 1836 he favored quieting the petition controversy. But in February 1837, he went so far as to advocate the right of southern free black women and slaves to petition Congress.[25]

In response to Adams's defense of petitioning, the Massachusetts Anti-Slavery Society (MASS) in January 1837 commended him for defending "the unrestricted right of THE PEOPLE to petition" for abolition in the District of Columbia. The organization then called on the Massachusetts legislature to request the state's congressmen to act against the gag rule and for emancipation in the district.[26]

On behalf of this political effort, Henry B. Stanton on February 23 and 24, 1837, addressed that legislature for five and a half hours. In his speech Stanton (like Wright an evangelical who helped lead the AASS) denounced slavery as an oppressive system that robbed African Americans of their rights. Slavery was, he told the legislators, "a system at war with natural justice and moral equity . . . a political and moral wrong, a sin against man and God." But like Adams, Stanton appealed to northern self-interest as he described the restrictions on "freedom of speech, of debate, and the press" slavery's defenders had imposed. And he lamented the negative impact slavery in Washington had on America's international reputation.[27]

In this manner abolitionism, state politics, and national politics interacted and fed on each other. By May 1837 the AASS's centrally directed petitioning effort, led by Stanton, Weld, Whittier, and Wright, had become, in historian Barnes's words, "a prodigious undertaking." In support of the AASS effort, Weld wrote *The Power of Congress over the District of Columbia*. And encouraged by the AASS central committee, local abolitionist organizations throughout the North sustained the campaign. The result, according to historian Dwight L. Dumond, was that northern representatives presented 1,496 petitions during the 1837–38 session.[28]

Meanwhile Slade and Adams welcomed two new congressional allies. The first of these, Thomas Morris, unlike other congressmen who came to sympathize with abolitionists during the 1830s, was a hard-money, states' rights Democrat. He began life in northeastern Pennsylvania in 1776, grew up on a farm in western Virginia, and settled east of Cincinnati in 1797. He began practicing law in 1802, after serving time in a debtors' prison. He gained a seat in the Ohio legislature in 1806, and in 1832 that body elected him to the U.S. Senate, where he served one term. He was large, rough-hewn, and not usually noted for eloquence.[29]

In contrast to the House of Representatives, antislavery petitions in the Senate had usually gone without debate to its Committee on the District. Morris during his first three years in the Senate neither questioned this nor spoke in regard to slavery. Then in January 1836, abolitionist petitioners from Ohio prompted him to defend them against a barrage of criticism from John C. Calhoun. In a successful attempt to reject petitioners' memorials favoring abolition in the District of Columbia, which Morris had presented, Calhoun, like others before him, claimed that raising the issue could spark slave revolt. Proslavery Pennsylvania Democrat James Buchanan supported Calhoun, characterizing Morris and the petitioners as "fanatics . . . scattering fire-brands." Morris replied with defenses of Congress's power to legislate for the district and of the right to petition. He went on to praise the character of abolitionists who signed the petition. "The feelings . . . which prompted these petitioners," Morris asserted, "were the deepest rooted of any in the human breast; they were excited by a high sense of *religious duty.*" He called the petitioners "upright, conscientious, patriotic citizens . . . [who] had a right to be heard."[30]

In early 1838 Morris advanced from defender to supporter of abolitionists. As he presented a petition from Brown County, Ohio (home to some militant abolitionists and located just north of the Ohio River), he described slavery as a moral and political evil. During a second clash with Calhoun, he advised, "The friends of humanity . . . *be not discouraged.* . . . The light in the Temple of Liberty is not yet quite extinguished; though your members are few, and yourselves at present a despised class; yet your cause is just, strong and powerful. . . . *Your final triumph is . . . certain.*" Even more remarkably, Morris defended the right of African Americans to petition Congress. Those, he maintained, who objected to black petitioners, "begin and end with the assertion that a negro has no constitutional right to petition, because he has not the right of voting . . . because he has no political rights." Displaying knowledge of eighteenth-century petitioning, Morris declared denial of a black right to petition to be a "gross injustice, and high-handed despotism." According to Morris, those who denied African Americans the right to petition were "lovers of negro slavery in its worst form; tyrants in heart, and enemies of the human race."[31]

William Slade's and John Quincy Adams's second new ally, Joshua R. Giddings, like Morris, had been born in northeastern Pennsylvania. When he was eleven, Giddings's family moved to Ashtabula County in Ohio's Western Reserve. By the 1820s that county had become a center of evangelical Protestantism and Anti-Masonry. By the 1830s abolitionists constituted a significant portion of its population. Therefore, in contrast to abolitionist relationships with Slade, Adams, and Morris, the movement influenced Giddings for several years before he entered Congress. During a tour of the Western Reserve in 1835, Theodore Dwight Weld boarded at Giddings's Jefferson, Ohio, home. In 1836 Giddings served as the Ohio Anti-Slavery Society's "manager" for Ashtabula County. He continued to do so in 1837.[32]

As a result, when Giddings entered Congress as a Whig in December 1838, he arrived prepared to foster an antislavery agenda. Slade's influence, and the two men's observation on January 30, 1839, of a slave coffle composed of fifty "chained and handcuffed" men, women, and children as it passed by the Capitol, provided additional motivation. But abolitionist petitions and proslavery attempts to block them prompted Giddings antislavery actions in Congress, as they had with his predecessors.[33]

Like other antislavery congressmen before him, Giddings initially favored a moderate course designed to conciliate slaveholders. He recognized that Adams's vow not "to vote for abolition in the District of Columbia" had a favorable impact on southern representatives. When that February Slade proposed to ask Adams to explain this vow, Giddings dissuaded Slade from doing so. Shortly thereafter, however, an anti-slave-trade petition from Giddings's constituents and an anti-abolitionist speech by Whig leader Henry Clay led Giddings to speak on behalf of abolitionist petitioners. They were, he said, "the voice of American freemen in favor of liberty." As Giddings went on to advocate moving the national capital to a location without slavery, he faced constant southern interruption. Even so, politician Giddings tried to appear conciliatory. He noted that he directed his remarks only to the slave trade in the District of Columbia. Slavery itself was "another subject." He said, "Let no man accuse me of now saying anything in regard to his right of holding his fellow man as property."[34]

As southern representatives and senators became even more extreme in their rhetoric and tactics regarding abolitionist petitions and those who presented them, the southerners continued to help expand abolitionist political influence. When on December 20, 1837, Slade attempted to speak on behalf of petitioners requesting abolition in the district, he faced a barrage of southern interruptions. When he turned to discussing slavery's evil nature, interruptions increased. Hugh S. Legare of South Carolina charged that Slade's words endangered southern "homes and firesides" and "begged" Slade to stop. After many southerners walked out, Speaker James Polk silenced Slade. A few days later the Democratic *Ohio Statesman* compared Slade to leading abolitionists, and a *Baltimore Patriot* correspondent complained that Slade had thrown "'abolitionism' . . . into the House of Representatives." In April 1839, a few months after he and Giddings had observed the slave coffle, Slade presented a resolution against such coffles in Washington. Immediately a South Carolina representative approached Slade, brandished "his fist menacingly, [and] cried out, '*Offer those resolutions* IF YOU DARE . . . !'" Throughout the late 1830s abolitionists praised Slade for "the firmness with which he stood the shock of bullying and brow-beating of the slaveholders." They urged other northern congressmen to imitate the "fearlessness" of Slade, Adams, Morris, and Giddings. Giddings called Slade "the greatest Abolitionist in the House."[35]

As had been the case earlier, ties between abolitionists and sympathetic officeholders during the 1830s went beyond petitioning. Abolitionists corresponded with and visited Slade, Adams, Morris, and Giddings. Abolitionists presented arguments to these politicians, appealed to their consciences, and flattered them. Abolitionists provided the politicians with documents and invited them to antislavery meetings. They encouraged politicians to advocate immediate emancipation. Abolitionists also monitored the politicians' progress toward that goal and criticized the politicians if they moved too slowly or appeared to backslide. In the process abolitionists often became either too optimistic or too exacting in their evaluations of such politicians. Overall they had more success with Slade, Morris, and Giddings than with Adams. But even with Adams, they began to have a major, if not determining, political impact.

Contacts with abolitionists and their organizations account for Slade's increasing radicalism. But it took time for him to *become* an abolitionist. In March 1836, in response to a resolution from the Young Men's Anti-Slavery Society of Philadelphia approving his actions in Congress, Slade, who still belonged to the ACS, emphasized patience and moderation. As late as October 1837, the Vermont Colonization Society elected Slade to serve as a delegate to the ACS national convention. And he portrayed himself as being more restrained than abolitionists. He recognized the right of slaves to petition Congress while contending they should not exercise that right and instead remain quiet, patient, and obedient to their masters. Even so Slade praised the abolitionists' goals of emancipation and "elevation [of African Americans] to the rights of men."[36]

It was as Slade corresponded with prominent abolitionists, including Garrison's friend and associate Francis Jackson and evangelical Joshua Leavitt, that he began to identify with them. The process of conversion culminated in August 1838 when Slade announced that American abolitionists James A. Thome's and J. Horace Kimball's recently published *Emancipation in the West Indies* "completely answered every objection against immediate emancipation." Although Thome and Kimball's book described gradual and compensated emancipation on the British islands of Antigua, Barbados, and Jamaica, Slade henceforth regarded immediate emancipation as "safe for the community" and "advantageous" for the slaves.[37]

Slade began to denounce the district slave trade in moralistic terms. Referring to the trade's victims, he advised Leavitt, "These people are, without their consent torn from their homes; husband and wife are frequently separated and sold to distant parts; children are taken from their parents." In regard to children in the slave coffle he and Giddings had seen, Slade declared, "Oh, that every father and mother at the North could have seen these children." Such a sight, he declared, should lead parents to urge their congressman to "go to the *very verge* of your constitutional power" to clear Washington "from the curse of slavery." In December 1838 Slade presented a resolution calling on the United States to recognize the black Republic of Haiti. He subscribed to the abolitionist *Colored American* and read it "with deep interest." He engaged in attempts to purchase freedom, and throughout the rest of his congressional career participated in abolitionist gatherings. He urged white people to overcome "prejudices of *caste,*" so as to "regard the black man as a BROTHER, entitled to the same respect for his rights and feelings as the white man." He joined abolitionists in calling on white Americans to "remember those in bonds, *as bound* with them."[38]

Contacts with abolitionists also influenced Thomas Morris, although during the late 1830s such contacts had a less direct and decisive impact on him than on Slade. With Congress not in session during the summer of 1836, Morris stayed at his Clermont County, Ohio, home. There his proximity to Cincinnati helped draw him toward the abolition movement as proslavery mobs attacked James G. Birney's *Philanthropist* newspaper office. That November Morris attended the initial meeting of the Clermont County Anti-Slavery Society. Although he did not "formally join," he supported the society's goal of ending slavery in the United States. In early 1837 Birney worked with Henry B. Stanton in an unsuccessful attempt to have Morris attend the AASS annual meeting in New York City. The Ohio Anti-Slavery Society praised Morris along with John Quincy Adams for pro-petitioning efforts. And in January 1838 Philadelphia abolitionists invited Morris to speak on May 14 at the dedication of Pennsylvania Hall, built on behalf of free speech.[39]

When illness and business in Washington prevented Morris from attending the Pennsylvania Hall event, he wrote a letter to be read there. Much of the letter urged northerners to defend their freedom of speech against the "slaveholding power"—the slaveholders' political influence on the U.S. government. But reflecting an emerging radical view among a minority of abolitionists who favored independent participation in electoral politics, Morris also declared that law could never convert "men into property" or "into a thing." He held that courts could not "rightfully adjudge that a negro slave is property, BECAUSE HE IS NOT A THING."[40]

In a failed attempt during the fall of 1838 to retain his Senate seat, Morris appealed to Ohio Democratic leaders in a manner that calls into question the sincerity of his expressions of commitment to emancipation and black rights. In an open letter to "the Legislature and People of Ohio," Morris recognized slavery's constitutionality in the states. He declared, "I consider . . . that the Negro has no claim in our country to the enjoyment of equal, social, or political privileges, with the white race."[41]

Nevertheless, in February 1839, Morris strongly defended abolitionists, this time in response to Henry Clay's Senate speech linking them and anti-slavery petitions to disunion. Morris once again concentrated on opposition to the "slaveholding power." But he also said abolitionists acted on conscience peacefully to help enslaved human beings. He defended abolitionists' right to take political action against slavery. He denounced the inhumanity of the Washington, D.C., slave trade and the interstate slave trade. He portrayed "prejudice against color [as] the strong ground of the slaveholder's hope," and declared, "The NEGRO will yet be set free." In 1840 Morris helped establish the American and Foreign Anti-Slavery Society (AFASS). During the following years, he stood out as a radical in the moderate Ohio Liberty Party. He served as the national Liberty Party's vice presidential candidate in 1844 and died in December of that year.[42]

In contrast to Slade and Morris, Joshua Giddings's closest abolitionist ties during the late 1830s were with moderate Ohio immediatist Gamaliel Bailey of Cincinnati. Bailey was a physician who had been born in southern New Jersey and briefly lived in Baltimore. He succeeded Birney as editor of the *Philanthropist* in 1837 when Birney moved to New York City to help administer the AASS. In February 1839 Giddings wrote to Bailey seeking support for his plan to present the petition from his constituents calling for abolition of the district slave trade. Giddings had feared that Bailey would demand direct action against slavery in the southern states. Instead Bailey advised Giddings, "Assault, if you please, the slave trade first. Abolitionists will help you. . . . What we all wish is *action now.* Do something, only make a *beginning*—it is only by *aggression* that we can put a stop to further encroachment of slavery and work its final over-throw." Bailey pointed out that southern congressmen and journalists reacted "as furiously" to opposition to the slave trade in the district as to slavery itself. He praised Giddings and Slade for their earnestness. And he assured Giddings that he and his congressional colleagues had "the moral sentiment of the world, and more than all, the God of truth" on their side.[43]

Among antislavery congressmen during the 1830s, John Quincy Adams's personal, intellectual, and motivational relationships with abolitionists are the best documented. This makes the Adams-abolitionist ties appear more complex.

Adams's political and intellectual sophistication, his insights into abolitionist morality, sensitivity to sectional relations, and his abiding nationalism also contribute.

Historian James Brewer Stewart portrays Adams as "certainly not an abolitionist." Politician Adams restrained himself from expressing abolitionist views. Unlike Slade, Morris, and Giddings, he never joined an abolition organization and never attended an abolitionist meeting. He characterized abolitionists as naively optimistic, blinded by moral rectitude, and too dismissive of slaveholders' rights. They were, he believed, unrealistic in their hope that slavery could be abolished without bloodshed. Yet Giddings in 1839 believed Adams's "views as stated would compare with those of Abolitionists generally, except that he declared himself not prepared to vote for abolition in the District of Columbia."[44]

When in 1831 Adams had first presented petitions for abolition in the District of Columbia *and* stated his opposition to the abolitionists' goal, Quakers associated with the AC questioned his rationale. Adams responded that abolition in the district by act of Congress would not be fair to slaveholders living there, that discussion of the issue would inflame sectional divisions, and that his constituents opposed meddling with slavery "in the Southern states." In December 1833 Adams informed veteran Rhode Island abolitionist Moses Brown (who was ninety-three years old) that he agreed with abolitionists as to "the nature and Character of Slavery." But, because he believed "the spirit of the age and course of events is tending toward universal emancipation," he doubted the necessity of a radical abolition movement.[45]

Adams became closer to abolitionists as he read their publications, worked with them, and corresponded with them. He gained a far better understanding than other politicians of their policies and what they struggled against. And his words and actions in Congress on behalf of the right of petition furthered their cause. In January 1837, during a heated debate with southern congressmen, Adams described abolitionists (and especially women among them) as "pure and virtuous citizens." He said they favored "the greatest improvement that can possibly be effected in the condition of the human race—the total abolition of slavery on earth." The following May Adams cited Congress's 1808 prohibition of the external slave trade as a precedent for "interference with the institution of slavery in the States" and noted that Congress might also rely on its war power to do so. He went so far as to say that "by war the slave may emancipate himself." But he continued to deny that he was an abolitionist. Instead he placed himself within a nonabolitionist American antislavery tradition stretching back to slaveholders George Washington and Thomas Jefferson.[46]

During the 1830s Adams's closest ties to an abolitionist were with Benjamin Lundy, whose earlier efforts against slavery in the District of Columbia are described in chapter 2. The two men's interaction had a significant impact on the course of the sectional conflict and lasted until Lundy's death in 1839. In April 1836, when slaveholding Americans in Texas defeated a Mexican army and Texas became essentially independent, Lundy published articles in Robert Walsh's *National Gazette* warning the North against annexing that slaveholding republic to the United States. Lundy sent copies of these articles to Adams, who relied on them in an effort that helped delay annexation and perpetuate sectional animosity.[47]

In July 1836 Adams visited Lundy, James and Lucretia Mott (both founders of the AASS), and other Quaker abolitionists in Philadelphia. Adams and these abolitionists spent an evening talking about "slavery, the abolition of slavery, and other topics." During the next two years, as the anti-annexation effort broadened, Lundy continued to prod Adams toward action in Congress. Adams, in turn, continued to rely on Lundy for information "respecting Slaves, Slavery, and the [Atlantic] Slave trade." He asked Lundy to publish letters from abolitionists that accompanied the anti-annexation petitions he had received.[48]

When Adams emerged as the leading congressional presenter of these and other antislavery petitions and defender of the right to petition, other abolitionists contacted him. These abolitionists associated more directly with the AASS than Lundy did. But they followed Lundy in using correspondence and social meetings to engage Adams in debate over antislavery tactics. In January 1837 John G. Whittier, in a private letter to Adams, praised him as "the inflexible opponent of the baneful system of Slavery" and "defender of our right of petition." During the following month, Garrison, wealthy evangelical Gerrit Smith, and Henry B. Stanton each sent Adams packages of petitions to present. In his package Garrison enclosed a statement from MASS, which succeeded the New England Anti-Slavery Society, lauding Adams's course in Congress. Smith praised Adams for showing "the pity of your heart for the enslaved poor." Stanton emphasized that the petitions he sent to Adams included "one from 53 *colored* voters of Boston."[49]

Adams responded to the abolitionists positively *and* negatively. He described the petitioning debate as "merely the *symptom* of a deep seated disease, praying upon the vitals of this Union—and that disease is Slavery." It would, he predicted, "pray till radically healed, or till it shall terminate in death." But he continued to fear that abolitionist agitation risked disharmony, disunion, and war. He asserted that his Massachusetts colleagues in the House were all

Lucretia Mott (1793–1880) was a Quaker abolitionist and Garrisonian who by the 1840s also advocated women's rights. (Library of Congress Prints and Photographs Division)

"Anti Abolitionists" and that the great majority of northerners had "a practical aversion to any movement tending to the *agitation* of the abstract question of slavery." He warned that abolitionists had to subject their "ardent zeal" and "passion" to "somewhat fastidious judgment." He advised his abolitionist correspondents that when they called on Congress to abolish slavery and the slave trade in the District of Columbia, the territories, and other places under its exclusive jurisdiction, they had explicitly to "disclaim the use of force." Before calling slaveholders *"man Stealers,"* they had to consider that the Bible called for putting man stealers to death. Slavery, established by law, he insisted, was not "stealing." Unlike abolitionists, Adams wanted to embrace slaveholders as "our fellow christians, our Countrymen, our fellow servants in the cause of a common master, our kinsmen, neighbors, and friends."[50]

At times direct abolitionist efforts to influence Adams irritated him. In September 1837 Adams met in Philadelphia with Quaker abolitionists Lundy, Samuel Webb of that city, and Arnold Buffum of Providence, Rhode Island. Following the meeting, Adams wrote in his journal, "Lundy. . . . and the abolitionists generally are constantly urging me to indiscreet movements, which would ruin me and weaken not strengthen their cause." Adams's wife and adult children warned him against "all connection with the abolitionists." He believed "the public mind" in his Massachusetts district "convulsed between the slavery and abolition questions." Such "adverse impulses," he claimed, "agitated" his mind "almost to distraction."[51]

Adams nevertheless continued his close relationship with abolitionists. In a July 1839 letter to Leavitt and Stanton, he observed that the AASS sought peacefully to abolish slavery throughout the United States by relying on "moral suasion" directed at masters. He recognized that the organization's declaration of sentiments rejected slave revolt and congressional action against slavery in the states. He endorsed emancipation as a "great and glorious object" that all who believed in "natural equal and unalienable *rights*" wished for.[52]

Interaction with Adams and other antislavery politicians tended to complicate abolitionist understandings of their movement. Some abolitionists doubted the sincerity and reliability of men like Adams, Giddings, Morris, and Slade. The abolitionists worried that the politicians' emphasis on how proslavery gag rules threatened the liberties of white northerners undermined efforts on behalf of black equality. At the same time, abolitionists continued to recognize that the words and actions of antislavery congressmen provoked their proslavery colleagues into saying things that helped spread antislavery sentiment. Slaveholder infringements of civil liberties, demands for spreading slavery westward, and threats of disunion angered nonabolitionist white northerners. Sometimes abolitionists joined antislavery politicians in exploiting such anger while disagreeing among themselves on how best to do so.[53]

Two additional factors further complicated the situation. First, the great majority of Americans did not perceive slavery and black rights as major issues facing the nation. Instead they focused on economics, government policy toward American Indians, westward expansion, presidential power, workingmen's rights, industrialization, transportation, and immigration. That these issues divided Americans by class, ethnicity, religion, as well as region (East-West as well as North-South) perpetuated a national two-party system resistant to sectional division.

Second, waves of anti-abolitionist and anti-black riots swept the North during these years. At Alton, Illinois, in November 1837 a proslavery mob killed abolition journalist Elijah P. Lovejoy. In May 1838, shortly after Morris had been asked to speak there, a similar mob burned Philadelphia's Pennsylvania Hall. Other mobs wrecked abolitionist newspaper presses, disrupted abolitionist meetings, and attacked black neighborhoods. The violence caused abolitionist leaders to doubt the effectiveness of their tactics, to disagree among themselves concerning solutions, and (as mentioned in this book's introduction) to divide into factions.[54]

The Garrisonian faction, centered in New England with outposts in Pennsylvania and Ohio, concluded that American society required cultural and political restructuring well beyond general emancipation. To various degrees members of this faction favored women's rights, denounced mainstream churches as pro-slavery, and advocated an extreme form of pacifism (called "nonresistance") that rejected all government that employed force. They interpreted the U.S. Constitution as intrinsically proslavery and opposed participation in *electoral* politics. When the AASS broke up in 1840, the Garrisonians retained control of a much diminished organization. During the early 1840s they began calling on northern state governments to dissolve the Union as the only way to end their sinful and criminal support of slavery. However Garrisonians did not reject petitioning and lobbying. They continued to seek national political and governmental influence.[55]

A second abolitionist faction formed in and around New York City among black and white evangelicals, including several who had led the AASS during its petitioning campaign. Led by Lewis Tappan, this faction concentrated on working through the churches that Garrisonians denounced. Tappan and other evangelical (or church-oriented) abolitionists held more traditional views than the Garrisonians concerning the role of women in society. They regarded disunionism as abandonment of the slaves to their masters. And they charged Garrisonians with raising issues extraneous to the abolition movement, using repulsive rhetoric, and driving away potential converts. In 1840 these evangelicals organized the AFASS to carry out their program.[56]

A third abolitionist faction formed in intensely evangelical western New York. This faction, led by Gerrit Smith, emphasized "righteous government" and physical action against slavery. Its members, best known as radical political abolitionists (RPAs), advocated independent abolitionist engagement in electoral politics. They led in forming the Liberty Party. The RPAs also regarded the U.S. Constitution as an entirely antislavery document that made slavery illegal throughout the country—including the southern states. Slaves therefore had a right to escape, and other people had a duty to help them do so. Black abolitionists influenced the development of this outlook and often became RPAs.[57]

A fourth, more moderate, but initially abolitionist faction centered in Cincinnati under Gamaliel Bailey's and nonabolitionist Salmon P. Chase's leadership. Chase had been influenced by James G. Birney and the anti-abolitionist, anti-black rioting in Cincinnati. He had also served as an attorney for men and woman accused of being fugitive slaves. In 1840 Bailey, Chase, and other leaders of this faction followed the RPAs into the Liberty Party. But unlike the RPAs and Garrisonians, they relied on a conventional constitutional interpretation. In contrast to the RPAs, the Cincinnatians denied that Congress could abolish slavery in the southern states. In contrast to the Garrisonians, this fourth group

Gerrit Smith (1797–1874) was a wealthy western New York landowner who from the late 1830s into the Civil War years led the radical political abolitionists. (Library of Congress Prints and Photographs Division)

denied that the U.S. Constitution was a wholly proslavery document. Instead the Cincinnatians accepted what historian William M. Wiecek calls the "federal consensus." According to this interpretation of the Constitution, which contributed to the development of the "freedom national" doctrine, Congress could act against slavery only in the national domain. Therefore, unlike RPAs and like Garrisonians, the moderate Cincinnati faction proposed to rely on moral suasion alone to affect slavery in the southern states.[58]

During the 1830s abolitionist petitioning, lobbying, and personal contacts with sympathetic congressmen affected national politics. They encouraged a small number of northern politicians to criticize slavery in speeches delivered in the U.S House of Representatives and Senate. Although the politicians to varying degrees questioned the practicality and rationality of abolitionist tactics, Joshua G. Giddings, Thomas Morris, William Slade, and to a lesser degree John Quincy Adams recognized the value of abolitionist support. They appreciated the prominence they gained in the North as a result of their defense of petitioning and freedom of debate. And, after relatively brief attempts at moderation, they embraced sectional confrontation. This in turn encouraged bitter and sectionally divisive rhetoric among southern politicians, worsening sectional conflict and increasing anti-abolitionist violence in the North. This violence in particular had a major role in causing abolitionists to split into factions. The dedication of two of these factions to independent participation in elections significantly influenced the movement's relationship to American politics and government during the following decades.

But the most important development affecting abolitionism and sectional politics during the late 1830s lay outside the movement, electoral politics, and Congress. This was the increase in northward slave escapes that began during the late 1830s. The harsh white southern response to Nat Turner's revolt, increased sales of Border South slaves to the Lower South, improved transportation, and a growing willingness among black and some white northerners to help fugitive slaves all contributed to the upsurge in escapes.[59] This in turn contributed to a North-South fugitive slave issue that rivaled the slavery expansion issue in further dividing the nation. Within this altered context, abolitionists intensified their role in national politics by creating a semi-permanent abolitionist lobby in Washington, D.C.

4

The Rise and Fall of the
Abolition Lobby, 1836–1845

Joshua Leavitt was a Congregational minister who edited the abolitionist *Emancipator,* first in New York and later in Boston, and during the early to mid-1840s traveled frequently to Washington, D.C. There he reported on Congress and lobbied members of the House of Representatives on behalf of the abolition movement. In August 1842, when Congress was not in session, Leavitt, in response to a letter from Joshua R. Giddings, compared what became known as the abolition lobby to a railroad train. "It is a lobby," Leavitt wrote, "able to carry double or triple, or by the dozen, & it behooves every man who wishes to ride, to jump on where he can find a place, and then *hold on.* . . . Look out for the locomotive when the bell rings."[1]

This comparison reflects Leavitt's time. Construction of a branch of the Baltimore and Ohio Railroad connecting the Northeast to Washington allowed him to get to the capital inexpensively and quickly. Therefore railroads, for Leavitt and others, symbolized progress, mobility, and freedom. It followed that as slave escape networks expanded during late 1830s, they became known as the underground railroad. Abolitionists regarded such networks as progress toward black freedom, while white southerners regarded them as threats to slavery's existence in the Border South. Meanwhile government support for building railroads divided the country's major political parties. The Whig Party included railroads in its nationalist program in favor of internal improvements, industrialization, and a national bank. In contrast the Democratic Party opposed a national economic program that, its leaders argued, favored northern capitalists at the expense of planters, farmers, and workers. Also contributing to party differences was another type of mobility—territorial expansion. As mentioned in chapter 3, following Texas's successful war for independence in 1836, pressure grew, especially in the South, to annex the huge slaveholding republic to the United States.[2]

Despite slavery's role in these developments, most northerners during the late 1830s and early 1840s did not regard slavery itself to be a major political issue. They hoped Congress would settle North-South disagreements through negotiation. Even antislavery congressmen shared much of this outlook. While they believed slavery *was* America's central political issue, John Quincy Adams, Joshua R. Giddings, William Slade, and their political allies also believed the existing party system could handle it. Many church-oriented abolitionists, who often aligned politically with the Whig Party, agreed. So did William Lloyd Garrison and his associates, even as by 1842 they demanded disunion as the best means of ending northern support for slavery. In contrast, by the late 1830s, Leavitt and many other church-oriented abolitionists had come to believe they had to change the party system by forming what became in 1840 the Liberty Party. These divergences both encouraged formation of an abolition lobby *and* limited its effectiveness.

Other factors contributed to the lobby's formation. First came the tradition, stretching back to colonial times, of abolitionists lobbying during legislative sessions. Second came the petitioning campaign that, since the late 1820s, had produced congressmen, such as Giddings, with whom abolitionists might co-operate. Third came the likelihood that increased abolitionist influence in Congress would lead to more inflammatory statements by southern politicians that could be used to spread antislavery sentiment among northern congressmen and their constituents. Finally there was the completion of the Baltimore and Ohio branch.

Well before that completion, a few abolitionists had come to Washington to observe the city's slave trade. In 1815 Jesse Torrey of Philadelphia stood outside the Capitol door to watch what he described as "a procession of men, women, and children . . . bound together in pairs, with ropes, and *chains.*" Torrey asserted that each year, hundreds of African Americans departed Washington against their will for Lower South cotton and sugar fields. In 1834 Leavitt traveled from New York City to visit Franklin and Armfield's slave prison in Alexandria (then part of the District of Columbia) and to inspect a slave ship as it prepared to sail for the Lower South. With the completion of the Baltimore and Ohio branch, increased numbers of abolitionists could visit Washington, and the city became their outpost in the Border South. They observed slavery and the slave trade, interacted with slaves, attended black church services, and developed relationships with free African Americans. They learned that slaves in and about Washington sought to escape to the North and Canada, and began to assist them.[3] All of this overlapped with the initiation of the abolition lobby.

Historian Gilbert H. Barnes describes this lobby as "one of the strangest . . . in history," because congressmen joined it. In fact the relationship between antislavery congressmen and abolitionists did not amount to a united lobbying effort. Rather it consisted of a congressional antislavery caucus, which Giddings called a "select committee on slavery," and a separate abolition lobby. The caucus predated the lobby by several years. It had had begun in November 1833 when Whig congressmen John Dickson and William Slade visited their fellow congressman John Quincy Adams to discuss partisan political issues as well as abolitionist petitions.[4] Later, as railroads sped travel, abolitionists took steps toward initiating the lobby by approaching members of the growing caucus, delivering anti-slave-trade and antislavery petitions, providing information, and helping to organize legislative opposition to slavery.

Benjamin Lundy took the first such steps. In December 1836 he traveled from Philadelphia to Washington to meet with Adams regarding Texas annexation. During the following year, the still-united American Anti-Slavery Society (AASS) sought to employ Theodore Weld to facilitate the presentation of antislavery petitions in Congress. The organization requested that Weld attend Congress "when the discussion on Slavery shall come up, and remain there as long as he deems it expedient, his salary to be continued and his expenses to be paid." Weld, who was in poor health at the time, could not accept the mission. Then, during September 1837, Whiggish abolition journalist Richard Hildreth of Boston traveled to Washington to report on a special session of Congress called to address the Panic of 1837. He stayed "for a large part of the regular [1837–38] session."[5]

Several other abolitionists joined Hildreth during the session. Henry B. Stanton came "to look after the imperiled right of petition" and met with Adams, who greeted him graciously. An unnamed correspondent for the New York City *Colored American* and the Utica, New York, *Friend of Man* also met with Adams. The correspondent reported that, while Adams criticized abolitionists for "wild measures," he did not oppose them. Garrison's associate J. Miller McKim, who lived in Philadelphia and had helped organize the AASS, came (as had Leavitt before him) to observe slave trading establishments and interview keepers and inmates. Unlike Leavitt in 1834, however, McKim spoke "in the lobbies of the Capitol . . . and in a few instances with proslavery members of Congress."[6]

During Congress's 1838–39 session, abolitionists corresponded with Adams and invited him to their meetings but did not visit Washington. By then the AASS had begun to split into the factions discussed in chapter 3. Most Garrisonians *seemed* to be concentrating on influencing northern popular opinion. Many non-Garrisonians had turned toward independent engagement in electoral politics through what in 1840 became the Liberty Party. As a result support for petitioning Congress and lobbying members of it declined. In August 1839

John G. Whittier, referring to the campaign in favor of congressional action against slavery in the District of Columbia, lamented, "Some of our most active friends . . . are growing lukewarm in this matter." If the decline continued, he worried, "We yield every thing in our cause which commends it to *practical* minds." Henceforth, he warned, abolitionists would deal only with "abstractions."[7]

Whittier need not have worried because a way for more effective abolitionist cooperation with antislavery Whigs in the House of Representative opened that December as the 1839–40 congressional session began. Giddings, Slade, and their new associate Seth M. Gates had rented rooms at Ann Sprigg's boardinghouse, located within two blocks of the Capitol. Born and raised in western New York's Burned-Over District, Gates had become an abolitionist before entering Congress. He had met Weld during the early 1830s, and in September 1835 he helped lead the Le Roy, New York, Anti-Slavery Society. He started in politics as an Anti-Mason and gained election to Congress in 1838 and again in 1840 as a Whig. Usually silent in the House, he wrote for the press and worked with Adams, Giddings, and Slade against slavery and slaveholders. Gates, Giddings, and Slade formed the nucleus of an expanded antislavery caucus on which an abolitionist lobby might focus. Such a lobby might also influence Whigs who did not have direct ties to abolitionist organizations. Among them were Adams and Massachusetts representative William B. Calhoun, who served from 1835 to 1843.[8]

The organization of the Liberty Party negatively impacted the lobby's functioning. Liberty partisans criticized members of the antislavery caucus for supporting proslavery Whig candidates for office. They disliked the emphasis caucus members placed on Whig economic programs, including passing a bankruptcy bill, raising the tariff, and creating a new national bank. Liberty leader Gerrit Smith considered Gates to be "a genuine abolitionist—a sincere friend of the slave." But Smith also characterized Gates as "blinded . . . by political party feeling." And Leavitt's attempts to cajole Gates and the other caucus members into choosing between the Whig Party and consistent opposition to slavery had predictable results. When in December 1839 Gates, Giddings, and Slade (but not Adams) joined a North-South alliance that elected slaveholding Virginia Whig Robert M. T. Hunter as Speaker of the House, Leavitt chastised them. He used Gates's, Giddings's, and Slade's actions to encourage abolitionists to "rally under our own banner" to "put men in Congress who do not care a straw for other questions in comparison with that of slavery." In response Giddings accused Leavitt of nurturing a "wild ultraism" that might destroy antislavery politics. According to Giddings, Leavitt should have been put in a "straight jacket."[9]

Nevertheless Leavitt and other immediatists continued to believe they could influence congressmen. Slade encouraged this belief when, during a speech he delivered in the House on January 18 and 20, 1840, he unequivocally endorsed emancipation. He declared "the deliverance of *men* from the ownership of others, and restoring them to the ownership of themselves" to be "among the noblest of the objects which can engage the efforts of man." He added that, while slaveholders denounced abolitionists as "incendiaries," "knaves," and "vile fanatics," abolitionists in fact represented "the best feelings of the human heart." He agreed with slavery's defenders that abolitionists regarded emancipation in the District of Columbia only as a preliminary step. Their ultimate goal, he said, was "to create such a public sentiment in the South as shall effect the abolition of slavery in the slaveholding States by their own legislation." He warned that the *"permanency"* of slavery could not coexist "with the permanency of the Union."[10]

According to Adams, Slade in this speech "delivered himself of the burden that had been four *[sic]* years swelling in his bosom." Yet, like Adams and other antislavery politicians before and after him, Slade also suggested the limits of the abolition movement's influence by vowing his loyalty to the Whig Party, which included slaveholders among its leaders and favored compromise on sectional issues. Later in 1840 Slade supported Whig presidential candidate William Henry Harrison despite Harrison's ambiguous views concerning slavery. During the campaign Slade advocated placing "abolitionism *entirely out of the question.*" To bring the subject up, he declared, would hurt the antislavery movement.[11]

A week after Slade's speech, Waddy Thompson Jr., a South Carolina Whig, and William Cost Johnson, a Maryland Whig, led the House to pass a permanent gag rule, known as the Johnson Gag. That same day Whittier and two other Quaker abolitionists, Isaac Winslow and Samuel Mifflin, arrived in Washington from Philadelphia, where Whittier edited the *Pennsylvania Freeman.* Like other abolitionists before them, the three men came mainly to visit slave-trading establishments and talk with slaves and traders. But they also lobbied, and Whittier remarked to Adams that the stronger gag "might perhaps be the best thing that could have been done to promote the cause of abolition." In fact the new rule encouraged organization of an expanded abolition lobby that would work with the antislavery caucus.[12]

Two other developments had roles in the development of the lobby as well. They included Democratic control of the 1840–41 winter session of Congress and the poor showing of Liberty presidential nominee James G. Birney in the November 1840 election. These circumstances, along with the new gag rule,

Church-oriented abolitionist Joshua Leavitt (1794–1873) helped lead the Liberty Party during the 1840s but ceased to be active in the movement after 1848. (Massachusetts Historical Society)

encouraged abolitionist concentration on Congress. That December the *Colored American* sent a reporter who used the nom de plume Libertas. In mid-January 1841 the *Emancipator* sent Leavitt, who moved into Sprigg's boardinghouse and began engaging the antislavery Whig congressmen.[13]

Leavitt spent his days in the House taking notes for the *Emancipator* and listening to Adams and Giddings speak. Adams talked about the right of petition, and Giddings addressed the U.S. government's war to remove Seminoles from Florida Territory and recapture escaped slaves. In the course of his remarks, Giddings accused the North of sharing the "sin and guilt" of slavery. Leavitt praised both speeches, and Gates reported to Gerrit Smith, "Mr. Leavitt is here and is doing good of course." In early March Leavitt (who had a law degree) spent a day helping Adams prepare a brief for the Supreme Court on behalf of Africans who had in 1839 violently freed themselves on board the Spanish slaver *Amistad,* been captured by an American vessel off the coast of Long Island, and imprisoned in Connecticut.[14]

Leavitt hoped that by working with antislavery congressmen on such issues, he would draw them into the Liberty Party. Instead the relationship between pious and dogmatic Leavitt and righteous and sensitive Whig politicians grew contentious. Leavitt upbraided the congressmen when they, in his opinion, placed loyalty to the Whig Party above antislavery principles. When Leavitt temporarily left Washington for New York City during April and early May 1841, Slade charged him with publishing "constant" criticism of those who did not support the Liberty Party. Slade defended himself and other Whig congressmen, "who thought there was something else in the world worth considering besides the question of slavery." Shortly thereafter Gates claimed Leavitt meant "to injure . . . those who do not bow to the behest of a third party in all things." In a public letter to Leavitt, Gates asked "in freedom's name" that "the future course of abolitionists . . . be discussed . . . with some respect for the feelings of others who . . . may differ from you . . . [so as] not necessarily to produce deep, and perhaps incurable alienation of feeling among brethren of the same general faith."[15]

While still in New York City, Leavitt further exasperated the congressmen during a special session of Congress (called to produce a bankruptcy bill) that began in late May. At that time Adams, Gates, Giddings, Slade, and a few other northern Whigs refused to vote for John D. White, a slaveholding Kentucky Whig who became Speaker of the House. Gates observed, "Mr. Slade, Giddin[g]s and myself, did all we could in caucus to get a Speaker from a free state nominated. . . . Went and saw father Adams and got him to go with us." Yet Leavitt, in an *Emancipator* editorial, accused the antislavery Whig congressmen of making "no opposition" to White. And because Gates, Giddings, and Slade had voted with other Whigs to ban petitions during the special session so as to concentrate on their party's bankruptcy bill, Leavitt characterized the three as bowing "to the dark spirit of slavery."[16]

Leavitt returned to Washington in mid-June to resume what he called his "seat" in the House. Shortly after he arrived, he met with the three Whigs and momentarily relented in his criticism of them. In a letter published in the *Emancipator* on July 1, he wrote that the three "firmly resisted the gag at great risk to their party objects." Yet even as Leavitt asserted that he hoped to cooperate with the congressmen in the future, he soon returned to denouncing their support for the Whigs' short-term petition ban. Gates, Giddings, and Slade, he contended, compromised "in order to do business." He claimed antislavery congressmen used their disagreement with him "as a reason why they should abandon their principles." Leavitt also defended northern Democrats. "Let them alone," he advised abolitionists. "Let them come in as they may."[17]

The antislavery congressmen responded predictably. Slade asked Leavitt, "Must I be driven to the conclusion that you are predisposed to censure me and my abolition friends in Congress?" Giddings wondered if Leavitt sought "to diminish the influence of the few individuals who are now placed between

Wealthy New York City businessman Lewis Tappan (1788–1873) led the American and Foreign Anti-Slavery Society and the American Missionary Association. (New York Public Library Digital Collection)

you and the common enemy." He charged that Leavitt, as a result of Liberty Party zeal and Democratic bias, "often . . . assailed" members of the antislavery caucus.[18]

Church-oriented abolitionist Lewis Tappan, who also supported the Liberty Party, agreed with Leavitt. Claiming incorrectly that "the Whig party is going to pieces," he advised Giddings to "go with the whole heart . . . for the new [Liberty] party." But Giddings and the other antislavery congressmen continued to resist the third party, in part because they believed its 1840 campaign took away enough votes to defeat some antislavery Whig candidates and thereby hurt, in Gates's words, "the cause of the slave."[19] Rather than ally with the Liberty Party, Giddings, Gates, and their associates had an alternate strategy to achieve their goals: They planned to use their relationship with Adams, the recent election of three more antislavery Whigs to Congress, and slave unrest in and about Washington to influence the nation.

Meanwhile abolitionists acted to keep the lobby going and strengthen the petition campaign. First, in September, Tappan's recently formed American and Foreign Anti-Slavery Society (AFASS) encouraged prominent abolitionists to lobby in Washington "for two or three weeks at the beginning of the [December 1841–March 1842] session." Second, in October, the Massachusetts State Liberty Party Convention pledged two hundred dollars to return Leavitt to the capital. The party believed that, despite the friction between Leavitt and antislavery

Theodore D. Weld (1803–1895) led a band of evangelical abolitionists during the 1830s and had a key role in the abolitionist lobby during the early 1840s. (Library of Congress Prints and Photographs Division)

congressmen, his "presence and abilities at Washington, as a reporter will do more to advance the cause of humanity than any one else we can employ at that price."[20]

Later in October Leavitt (who was about to move the *Emancipator* from New York City to Boston) informed Giddings that he would arrive in Washington in December and remain longer than he had the previous winter. In what historians have incorrectly interpreted as a conciliatory gesture, Leavitt included in his letter to Giddings a condescending characterization of the congressman "as sincerely opposed to the domination of the slave power [not slavery] as myself." According to Leavitt, Giddings, rather than advocate immediate emancipation, preferred to "aim first at specific points of politics, which [he] deem[ed] beneficial to free labor—or rather to the North—as in bank, tariff &c." Leavitt charged that this amounted to "continued toleration of slavery." He advised Giddings that only opposition to slavery itself could unite the North. This sort of negative prodding remained a component of abolitionist political strategy through the Civil War. And, inept as he often was, Leavitt helped shape Giddings's and other antislavery congressmen's course of action.[21]

Early that December Leavitt once again became Gates's, Giddings's, and Slade's messmate at Sprigg's. By then three additional Whig congressmen had joined the antislavery caucus. They had been elected in November 1840 and entered Congress in May 1841. Two of them were undoubtedly abolitionists. Sherlock J. Andrews of Ohio had in 1833 helped lead the Cleveland Anti-Slavery Society and, like Giddings, had hosted Weld during Weld's 1834 speaking tour. Nathaniel Briggs Borden of Fall River, Massachusetts, had in

1834 formed a local antislavery society and from then through the 1850s assisted escaping slaves. The third, John Mattocks of Vermont, described himself as an abolitionist but his connection to the movement is less clear than Andrews's and Briggs's.[22]

As soon as Leavitt arrived in Washington he joined with the AFASS in urging other abolitionists who could "afford" it to come to the capital for "a few days or weeks" to put a "watchful eye" to work. Two who responded were Charles T. Torrey and Theodore Weld. Torrey, a Massachusetts native living in Albany, New York, had, like Leavitt, served as a Congregational minister, journalist, and founder of the Liberty Party. Also like Leavitt, he came to Washington as a newspaper correspondent as well as a lobbyist. Torrey sent his reports to the *New York Evangelist, Worcester* (Massachusetts) *Spy, Emancipator,* and several other newspapers. In Congress he worked with Slade, Borden, and Giddings. He roomed at Frances Padgett's boardinghouse, located not far from Sprigg's. Torrey asserted, "The subject of abolition cannot be kept out of Congress. We shall get it in, in a multitude of forms, before the session closes." Short, slight, tubercular, and fearless, Torrey while in Washington also engaged with the local black community and acted physically against slavery by helping slaves escape.[23]

In contrast to Leavitt, Torrey, and others who came to Washington on behalf of abolitionist publications and organizations, Weld came solely in response to Leavitt's and the antislavery congressmen's invitation. In Weld's words, they wanted him to help them "carry the war in upon the enemy . . . and attack slavery at every point." Weld believed the Johnson Gag had "thoroughly roused" the antislavery congressmen. They planned, he reported, "to bring in bills and introduce resolutions of inquiry, etc., etc., which the gag or any gag which it is possible for Congress to pass cannot touch." They proposed "a series of speeches" dealing with slavery in the District of Columbia and Florida, the domestic slave trade, black rights, Texas, Haiti, and colonization. The congressmen paid for Weld's travel to Washington and his expenses during his stay. His duties, they suggested, would keep him in the Library of Congress "gathering and arranging materials" for antislavery speeches.[24]

Weld had two objectives for the speeches he helped prepare. First, he believed they could contribute to changing northern popular opinion. One such speech in Congress, he advised Tappan, would achieve more through the national press than "what our best [abolitionist] lecturers can do in a year." Second (in contrast to Leavitt and Torrey), Weld hoped the speeches would help reorient immediatists "intoxicated" with the Liberty Party toward effective political action through the Whig Party.[25]

Weld arrived at Sprigg's on December 30, 1841. The next day he became more than a researcher as he, Giddings, and Leavitt attended the New Year presidential levee hosted by John Tyler. Tyler, a radically proslavery Virginia Whig, had risen to the presidency from the vice presidency following William Henry Harrison's death in April 1841. At the levee Weld, Giddings, and Leavitt made a point of *not* shaking Tyler's hand. The three then attended Adams's New Year "saloon," where the former president revealed his admiration for Weld's abolitionist writings. According to Weld, Adams initiated a conversation about the recent slave revolt on the American brig *Creole* in which the slaves took control of the ship as it went south from Virginia, and sailed it to freedom in the British Bahamas. Then the former president discussed a plan developed in the North African country of Tunisia to end slavery there and the prospect of abolition in Cuba. On January 8, 1842, Weld again met with Adams, this time at what Weld called "a genuine abolition gathering." There Adams raised the issue of imprisonment of black sailors in southern port cities and petitions on the sailors' behalf. Of all these topics, the *Creole* became most significant in Congress.[26]

Because of Weld's, Torrey's, and Leavitt's interactions with the antislavery caucus, the abolition lobby's influence peaked during the early months of 1842. In January Weld helped members of the caucus prepare to present petitions and address Congress. That same month Torrey, at caucus members' urging, traveled to Annapolis where a slaveholders' convention seeking a means to end slave escapes had convened. Torrey's note-taking at the convention led municipal authorities to imprison him on several charges, including exciting "discontent among the colored people." Giddings and the Massachusetts congressional delegation then sent a team, including prominent lawyer David A. Simmons of Boston, to represent Torrey. A local judge dismissed the charges, and Torrey returned to Washington on January 17.[27]

In the House of Representatives on Thursday, January 20, with Weld's and Leavitt's assistance and with Torrey looking on, the antislavery Whig representatives along with several allies began a verbal onslaught. Gates presented a petition opposed to the admission of slaveholding Florida to the Union. Slade introduced antislavery resolutions from Vermont's legislature. William Calhoun submitted a petition from Springfield, Massachusetts, calling for American recognition of the Republic of Haiti. Adams took the floor on Friday, January 21. Although old and still denying he was an abolitionist, Adams's charisma exceeded that of his associates. Before he spoke he told Weld he would "present some petitions that would set them [slaveholders] in a blaze."[28]

First, Adams introduced a petition in favor of granting citizenship to "colored" immigrants. When Henry A. Wise of Virginia objected, the House tabled the petition by a 115–68 vote. When Adams regained the floor, he criticized slave trading and slave breeding. Then he presented a petition from Haverhill, Massachusetts, calling for the dissolution of the Union because the South drained resources from the North. As Adams, other antislavery congressmen, and abolition lobbyists anticipated, slaveholders in the House overreacted, with Virginia representative Thomas W. Gilmer moving to censure Adams. During the next two weeks, slaveholders attempted to intimidate Adams by browbeating him and physically surrounding him. Adams, assisted by Leavitt, coached by Weld, and supported by the other antislavery congressmen, used this outrageous conduct to draw other northern Whig congressmen and northern popular opinion to his side. Northern newspapers protested what they regarded as an attack not only on Adams's but also on their section's rights. In his "defense" against censure, Adams presented over two hundred more petitions. With grudging respect, Francis W. Pickens of South Carolina called Adams a "most extraordinary man." And as Weld expected, on Monday, February 7, the House tabled the censure motion by a 106–93 vote.[29]

Adams became an abolitionist hero. Leavitt exclaimed, "It was amazing to see him [Adams] rise up and breast the current and turn it back with gigantic ease. . . . May God give the old man strength to endure the evil. The tide will soon turn if he will not yield." Writing from Massachusetts, Whittier thanked Adams "for thy determined opposition to slavery." Liberty abolitionists hoped the debate would either draw antislavery Whig politicians and abolitionists who voted for Whig candidates into the Liberty Party or split the Whig Party.[30]

Some antislavery Whigs and abolitionists portrayed Adams's victory as a turning point in sectional politics. Giddings wrote, "I entertain not the least doubt that a moral revolution in this nation will take its date from this session of Congress." "The *north,*" he wrote, "has for once triumphed." Theodore Weld declared similarly to his wife, Angelina Grimké Weld, "Triumph is complete. . . . This is the first victory over the slaveholders *in a body* ever yet achieved since the foundation of the *government,* and from this time their downfall *takes its date.*" Historians agree. Adams biographer Samuel Flagg Bemis calls the failure of censure the "greatest triumph" of Adams's career. Weld biographer Benjamin P. Thomas asserts, "Slavery could not stand against free speech." The 1841–42 session of Congress, Thomas writes, "marked a turning point in the battle for freedom." James M. McPherson claims Adams inflicted a "crippling blow" to the "conspiracy of silence" in Congress regarding slavery. Russell B. Nye concludes that "from such blows [as Adams struck] the 'gag rules' never recovered."[31]

Yet a few days after the attempt to censure Adams failed, Weld realized the abolitionist effort in the House had achieved less than he had proclaimed.

Referring to slavery's defenders, Weld commented, "Satan never retreats without a death struggle. . . . Slavery has begun to fall," but "woe to abolitionists if they dream that their work is well nigh done." And Adams's victory did not necessarily mean an abolitionist victory. Weld had influenced Adams, as had other abolition lobbyists and abolitionists generally. Still Adams advocated only "ultimate emancipation." In addition, following his "triumph" over the gag, Adams had no success in derailing slavery's westward expansion or slaveholders' political power.[32]

Earlier in 1842 Weld had investigated international legal aspects of the *Creole* case. He did so as he helped Giddings prepare resolutions on the topic. Giddings based these resolutions on the freedom national doctrine that Weld had helped develop. The doctrine held that slavery could legally exist only under state law. It could not be legal under national jurisdiction or on the high seas. Because this suggested that slaves had a right to revolt on ocean-going vessels, Weld predicted that the resolutions would "produce a tremendous sensation among the slaveholders." This proved to be the case as, when Giddings introduced his resolution on March 22, John Minor Botts, a moderate Virginia Whig, asserted that Giddings had "justified" "mutiny and murder." Botts called on the House to condemn Giddings's "conduct," and after parliamentary maneuvering, the body complied by a 125–69 vote. In response Giddings resigned his seat, returned home, easily gained reelection in late April, and came back to Congress in May.[33]

As they had in regard to Adams's victory over those who sought to censure him, abolitionists portrayed Giddings's forced resignation and resounding reelection as a triumph of antislavery politics in general and the abolition lobby in particular. Whiggish Garrisonian journalist David Lee Child reported to Gates from Massachusetts that "hundreds who never sympathized with the abolitionists come out now and declare themselves abolitionists to the death." Gates in turn predicted, "This will be another instance . . . where the wrath of men will be made to praise God." AFASS leader Amos A. Phelps hoped that as a result of Giddings's victory, "the North will yet make a stand against the domineering encroachments of Slavery."[34]

Historians go further. According to Gilbert H. Barnes, Giddings's reelection "changed the whole aspect of the antislavery agitation in the House" and opened slavery "to direct attack" so that petitions were "no longer essential." McPherson asserts that the reelection presaged the 1852 breakup of the Whig Party, the end of the second American party system, and the election in 1860 of Abraham Lincoln to the presidency. Barnes and McPherson credit abolitionist lobbyists Leavitt and Weld with some or all of these momentous changes. Yet abolitionists in Washington judged Giddings's impact as circumspectly as Weld had Adams's. Torrey regarded the censure as a proslavery "blunder" and predicted Giddings's reelection. But he perceived an escalation of a proslavery threat in Congress from one limited to the right of petition to one against freedom of speech as well. And Torrey noted the failure of some northern Whigs to join in Giddings's defense.[35]

More important for the future of the abolition lobby, southern congressmen soon realized they had gone too far in censuring Giddings and therefore had to change their tactics. As Gates explained, the Adams controversy, the Supreme Court's proslavery decision in *Prigg v. Pennsylvania* denying state authority to counteract the Fugitive Slave Law of 1793, and Secretary of State Daniel Webster's statement that Great Britain must return the *Creole* rebels to their masters had encouraged slaveholders in the House to "over act" in regard to Giddings. They thereby alienated many "Northern Whigs" and aroused northern popular opinion. Gates correctly mistrusted northern Whig claims that their "last tie" with southern Whigs had broken. But he also understood how the southerners had miscalculated.[36]

During the rest of 1842, throughout 1843, and into 1844, slavery's defenders in Congress became less confrontational, more restrained in their pronouncements, and less committed to the Johnson Gag. This change in strategy resulted in less drama that the abolitionist press could publicize. It contributed to disillusionment among abolition lobbyists. And it had a role in attrition among antislavery congressmen. All of these things, plus the resounding Democratic victory in the 1842 national elections, contributed to the decline of the abolition lobby.

Initially, however, following the hyperbolic confrontations launched by proslavery congressmen against Adams and Giddings, the lobby's influence appeared to increase. In April 1842, as Leavitt returned to his reporter's desk in the House after a brief absence, Botts acknowledged the abolitionist journalist's influence by threatening to expel him. Although Botts did not represent proslavery extremists, this threat improved antislavery congressmen's regard for Leavitt. Adams praised him as "this excellent man, who is the salt of the earth." Giddings asked Leavitt to expand the lobby.[37]

Such expansion seemed to be taking place the following December as the 1842–43 congressional session began. David Lee Child came to report on Congress for the *Liberator* and the similarly Garrisonian *National Anti-Slavery Standard*, edited in New York City by David Lee Child's wife, Lydia Maria Child. When Maria Weston Chapman, who was serving as a substitute editor of the

Liberator, learned of David Lee Child's mission, she reminded her Garrisonian readers that "we are not a political party." But she nevertheless described his mission as to provide "lucid expositions of the great congressional game now playing for slaves and the souls of men." She hoped that having another abolitionist correspondent in Washington would "impose a salutary restraint upon southern violence, and administer some deserved rebuke to northern tameness and servility."[38]

David Lee Child stayed in Washington throughout the session. Other abolitionists visited the city briefly during January. Among them Lewis Tappan lobbied in the Senate, and Lucretia Mott of Philadelphia and Jacob Knapp of Baltimore worked in Washington outside Congress to encourage antislavery sentiment. Mott, a Quaker minister and the only woman who spoke at the initial AASS meeting, preached at Washington's Quaker and Unitarian meetinghouses. Knapp, an evangelical Baptist preacher born and raised on the eastern edge of New York's Burned-Over District, attracted "immense crowds" to his antislavery sermons. Weld and others who boarded at Sprigg's attended "every evening." As a result of Mott's and Knapp's activities, Weld declared, "Abolition is talked not only at our table but all over Washington." Leavitt added, "Things are evidently improving here in the Anti-Slavery line, since I first came here alone and uncertain of my reception, less than two years ago." To take advantages of the circumstances, Weld, Leavitt, and the antislavery congressmen they worked with planned to raise the issue of slavery in Florida Territory, present more petitions, advocate legislation to protect black sailors in southern ports, and call for black citizenship.[39]

Weld, who had returned to Washington on December 27, 1842, and consulted with Adams shortly thereafter, understood that slaveholders in Congress believed they had erred in their verbal and procedural assaults on Adams and Giddings during the previous session. On this basis Weld and Adams assumed proslavery congressmen would not "rally" during the 1842–43 session. But Weld and Adams misinterpreted what changed proslavery tactics meant for antislavery.[40] If, as Whittier had observed in February 1840, a more strident proslavery stand aided abolitionists, less aggressive proslavery tactics worked against abolitionists. And mainly because slaveholding congressmen restrained themselves, the session failed to reproduce the sectional drama of a year earlier.

During mid-January 1843 Giddings and Adams (supported by Weld's research) addressed the Florida slavery issue. Lower South representatives replied briefly and moderately. During February Giddings spoke at length against a bill to compensate American slave traders for slaves freed by Britain following a shipwreck. Weld and David Lee Child praised the speech as "a great move upon the slaveholders" and as "manly and impressive." Slavery's defenders again responded mildly. As a result Weld complained that questions he had prepared for did not come up and that there had been little "of interest" in Congress concerning opposition to slavery. Additionally he decided to leave Washington in mid-February, two or three weeks before the session ended, because, he believed, nothing had been done regarding important issues. At this point, for personal as well as political reasons, Weld began to withdraw from organized abolitionism. He also claimed that "all the abolitionists" in Washington agreed that during the rest of the session, it would be "undesirable" to press petition issues. Leavitt too despaired and placed some of the blame for lack of action on Weld, who, according to Leavitt, opposed the Liberty Party as strongly as Garrison, Lewis Tappan, and the Whig abolitionist congressmen. Leavitt had come to believe the congressmen could not be extracted from the Whig Party and described Weld's lobbying as mere "foundation work."[41]

Lack of antislavery progress and abolitionist frustration continued. During late February Adams presented a gigantic petition on behalf of George Latimer, who with his wife had escaped from slavery in Virginia in October 1842 and had recently been arrested in Massachusetts. In response to Adams's petition, the proslavery House leadership avoided confrontation. Rather than invoke the gag, Speaker John White referred the petition to the Judiciary Committee. Southern absences, rather than confrontation, prevented the committee from acting on the petition. Adams kept it on his desk wound about a reel for over a year as an antislavery symbol. But before antislavery caucus member Calhoun had spoken "upon the employment of slaves on the fortifications of the south," Leavitt left Washington.[42]

Historian William Lee Miller best describes the confusing situation in the House of Representatives as the 28th Congress reconvened in December 1843. President Tyler's veto of much of the Whig financial program and a national economic rebound had helped Democrats retake control of Congress in the 1842 elections. Therefore, in December 1843, 142 Democrats confronted 82 Whigs in the House. Northern Whig representatives had always accounted for most votes against the gag rule. Now their strength, and especially that of the antislavery caucus, had declined. The number of boarders at Sprigg's had increased to twenty-five, including new (although elderly) abolitionist congressman Samuel Chandler Crafts of Vermont. But core members of the caucus, including Gates, Slade, Sherlock Andrews, and John Mattocks, did not return. They had either not sought reelection in November 1842 or had lost in their reelection bids. Gates expressed disillusionment with Washington politics and soon joined the Liberty Party. Among caucus members only Adams and Giddings remained. Yet despite these circumstances, Adams's motion on December 4 to repeal the gag lost by only four votes (95–91). Debate over the gag dominated the session until an 88–87 vote on February 28, 1844, saved it.[43]

Meanwhile the abolition lobby weakened along with the antislavery caucus. As Giddings and Leavitt again boarded at "the Sprigg lodging house" during the 1843–44 session, Giddings came to believe that Leavitt's allegiance to the Liberty Party had led him to be not "as friendly and social as formerly." In fact Leavitt, like Slade and Gates, had tired of Washington. He missed his family, and his plan to begin a daily edition of the *Emancipator* required that he be in Boston. Therefore Leavitt departed Washington in late January, well before the session ended. For his part Torrey turned his focus away from Congress and toward helping slaves escape from the Chesapeake region. And Lewis Tappan's offer of financial support and Adams's increased momentum in his effort against the gag failed to revive Weld's commitment to lobbying. "I cannot feel that my *call* is to Washington this winter," Weld declared.[44]

Even so Giddings perceived slaveholders could not keep the gag rule much longer. To take advantage of this he wanted abolitionist support in an effort "to abolish slavery in this district before we adjourn." Invoking ideas Whittier, Tappan, and Leavitt had developed over the past eight years, Giddings in January 1844 begged Weld for "the time and labor of one dozen abolitionists." Giddings wrote, "We want help. We want men here to [go] among the people of the city, get up petitions, hold meetings, prepare the minds of the people here, both Blacks and Whites." Giddings also wanted "men who will visit members in their rooms and talk to them and lead them into the subject." So far, he lamented, "We have been unable to get any body to come here."[45]

Eleven months later, as the House convened in early December 1844, Adams's motion to end the gag rule passed by a 108–80 vote. No abolition lobbyist helped prepare Adams for this apparent victory. No abolition journalist entered the House chamber that day. Torrey had been arrested in June 1844 for helping slaves escape. Leavitt had decided to deliver "a major address" to a Liberty Party meeting in Albany rather than be in Washington when Congress convened. He did not arrive at the capital until two weeks after the gag had been repealed.[46]

As historian Miller shows, factors other than the abolition lobby led to the repeal. The most active and vocal of the gag rule's defenders (like most of its strongest opponents) had left Congress. Among them were Henry Wise, Waddy Thompson, and William Cost Johnson, a Maryland Whig who chaired the committee on the District of Columbia. Also northern Democrats, for various reasons, joined northern Whigs in voting against the gag rule. Some of the Democrats had always believed the rule threatened civil liberties. Others responded to constituent pressure. They all sought revenge against their southern colleagues, who had at the 1844 Democratic national convention passed over former president Martin Van Buren of New York to give the party's presidential nomination to Tennessee slaveholder James K. Polk. Most importantly, as historian William W. Freehling puts it, "Slaveholders had at last learned . . . gag rules deployed too little tyranny to silence antislavery northerners and too much tyranny for antislavery Yankees to tolerate."[47]

For years abolition lobbyists and the antislavery caucus, working together, had used petitions and the gag rule restrictions to influence Congress, the South, and a national debate over slavery. But well before the repeal of the rule, slaveholders in Congress had begun to control themselves. In turn most abolition lobbyists and congressmen had become distracted or disillusioned.

Immediately following repeal Adams wrote in his diary, "Blessed, ever blessed be the name of God." The *Liberator* predicted repeal would encourage more antislavery petitions to be "received *and* referred." Adams biographer Bemis refers to repeal as "a turning point from slavery to freedom." Other historians, however, characterize the entire petition versus gag rule issue as a "sideshow" compared to debate over the nation's economic difficulties and the issue of annexing Texas.[48]

Leavitt had come to regard the gag rule controversy as another sort of sideshow—one to the issue of slavery. "The right of petition is worth defending," he wrote in the *Emancipator*, "but so far as our three millions of enslaved countrymen is concerned, it has long ceased to be of any consequence." Northern Democrats, Leavitt reasoned, joined northern Whigs to end the gag rule in order to deprive abolitionists of a means to raise the slavery issue in Congress. He contended that a majority of the Democrats had concluded that receiving the petitions "and reporting against the prayer" was "the readiest way to kill abolitionism."[49]

Based on this analysis, Leavitt, after years working with Adams, began to criticize him. Leavitt emphasized Adams's opposition to congressional action against slavery in the District of Columbia. He complained that Adams and his allies in Congress had not taken "a practical step towards removing that piece of carrion from under the nostrils of our republicanism." He asserted that only Liberty Party victories in congressional elections could help the enslaved. He naively asserted, "A power is in the field which will hurl them from their seats ere long, unless they do much more." Leavitt realized these remarks would make his Whig associates in Washington "exceedingly bitter," and he did not regret it.

Instead he welcomed their bitterness and coolness because it was "rapidly glazing the fissure" between antislavery Whigs and the Liberty Party, "so as to secure us against all danger of coalition or absorption."[50]

As the 1844–45 congressional session began, Leavitt sat in the gallery and concentrated on reporting debate as the House turned to the issue of whether or not to annex the slaveholding Republic of Texas. Although the great majority of northern Democrats had turned against the gag rule, most of them did not object to slavery expansion. When Congress, on February 28, 1845, passed a joint resolution annexing Texas, Leavitt had already returned to Boston. He had hoped northern Democrats would join northern Whigs to vote against it. But he had not tried to persuade them—the abolition lobby had died. When a new Washington lobby against slavery organized in early 1847, under new leadership, it was *not* an abolition lobby. It had a broader political scope and a more nuanced commitment to ending slavery.[51]

5

Discord, Relationships, and Free Soil, 1840–1848

Well before the abolition lobby ceased to function, a decade of rapid change among abolitionists and their relationship to the American party system had begun. As mentioned previously the American Anti-Slavery Society (AASS) split apart in May 1840. That same month the Liberty Party organized—with an initially abolitionist agenda. Also in 1840 the second American party system, consisting of national Democratic and Whig organizations, reached maturity with the Whigs' first victory in a presidential election. As the decade progressed, a half-dozen largely sectional issues put this party system (including the Liberty Party) under considerable stress. The issues included the white South's perception of an abolitionist threat, slave escapes, northern resistance to rendition, annexation of slaveholding Texas, war against Mexico, and growing northern opposition to slavery expansion. This chapter analyzes the relationships that intertwined the abolitionist factions with these major national issues, politics, and government. There are two major questions: First, how did abolitionists contribute to the formation of a political coalition centered on opposition to slavery expansion rather than on slavery itself? Second, how did that coalition affect abolitionism?

The advent of immediate abolitionism during the late 1820s, initiation of the *Liberator* in 1831, Nat Turner's Virginia slave revolt later that same year, organization of the AASS in 1833, and increasing northward slave escapes intensified the abolitionists' long-existing emotional appeals. Such appeals emphasized slavery's sinfulness, masters' criminality, and a threat of interracial violence in order to influence northern popular opinion. But, as chapter 4 demonstrates, abolitionists during the 1830s and thereafter did not turn away from direct political engagement. Like their predecessors, they relied on petitioning, lobbying, and personal contacts with antislavery politicians to influence government. Despite mutual criticism between the two groups, abolitionists and such politicians often agreed on the nature of an issue and used similar terminology. Abolitionists frequently joined antislavery politicians in calling for protection of wage labor and white civil liberties. As members of the moderate wing of the Liberty Party did so, they moved away from abolitionism. But radical political abolitionists (RPAs) and Garrisonians made similar calls while remaining immediatists. A few antislavery politicians continued to discuss the immorality of slavery and racial oppression.

By 1834 the interaction between abolitionists and antislavery politicians had spread beyond petitioning, lobbying, and personal contacts as abolitionists began to question northern Democratic and Whig candidates for Congress regarding their willingness to present antislavery petitions. Only rarely did the Democrats respond or respond honestly. Therefore, during the 1830s, when abolitionists voted they usually voted for Whig candidates who claimed to stand for Christian morality and antislavery principles. Yet such Whig politicians supported their party's proslavery leaders in Congress and in national elections. As a result some evangelical and Quaker abolitionists in the Northeast had determined to engage directly in electoral politics by organizing the Liberty Party.[1]

RPAs led this effort, and on April 1, 1840, at Albany, New York, the new party nominated James G. Birney for president. During the following months, Joshua Leavitt, Henry B. Stanton, other Massachusetts evangelicals, some abolitionists in the New York City area, and the Cincinnati-centered moderate abolitionist faction joined in support of Birney. But Garrisonians and some non-Garrisonian abolitionists, including Lewis Tappan, Theodore Weld, and John G. Whittier, initially did not. Whittier accepted the principle of independent abolitionist electoral politics. But he also recognized that in 1840, "nine tenths of the voting abolitionists" would support Whig candidate William Henry Harrison against incumbent Democratic president Martin Van Buren.[2]

Birney fared poorly in the election, gaining only 6,225 votes out of 2,408,630 cast. And although an overwhelming majority of abolitionists supported the Liberty Party, it attracted throughout its existence only a tiny portion of the northern electorate. Some historians, beginning with Theodore Roosevelt, describe the party as a mistake and failure. Merton L. Dillon notes that it "attracted only scant support." Reinhard O. Johnson writes that the party had no "national identity," "no national strategy." Lawrence J. Friedman describes Liberty abolitionists moving closer to "more moderate northern antislavery elements" and losing their principles in the process. Other historians question whether the Liberty Party really was a political party. They describe it instead as a "surrogate religious denomination formed by those harboring anti-party attitudes."[3]

In contrast historians who have a positive view of the Liberty Party and up-hold the party's political nature emphasize its practical goals. Alan M. Kraut con-tends that the party succeeded in "propelling the slavery issue onto the national political agenda" and contributed to the breakup of the second American party system. Corey M. Brooks argues that the party contributed an abolitionist ele-ment to the antislavery parties that followed it. James Brewer Stewart insight-fully provides a more balanced approach. He emphasizes the Liberty Party's role in pushing northern Whig politicians toward greater sectionalism. But he notes that such politicians appealed to northern self-interest rather than to concern for enslaved African Americans.[4]

Liberty leaders certainly had ambitious political goals. They included trans-forming northern politics, encouraging emancipatory legislation in the bor-der slave-labor states, and imposing either a moderately or radically antislavery interpretation of the Constitution. For a time a few such as Joshua Leavitt dreamed that the party would elect abolitionists to state and federal office, grow into a major party, take control of the U.S. government, and abolish slavery. Others such as Lewis Tappan, who gradually came to support the Liberty Party, hoped to use it to reunite all abolitionists. But most of the party followed a plan pioneered by the moderate Cincinnati faction to move away from immediate abolitionism in order to facilitate cooperation with sympathetic northern poli-ticians in the major parties.[5]

As early as December 1841, the issue of whether to advocate immediate emancipation by political means divided the party. Its moderate faction, em-phasizing the freedom national doctrine, advocated denationalizing slavery rather than ending it quickly. Its RPA faction, declaring that slavery could never be legal, called for federal government action to end slavery immedi-ately throughout the country. But getting Congress to do so did not appear to be a practical goal. And in June 1845 the moderate faction, at its Southern and Western Convention of the Friends of Constitutional Liberty, did not mention immediate abolition or black rights. Such a stance supported Garri-sonian claims that the Liberty Party sold out abolitionist principles in order to compete for votes within an irrevocably proslavery political system. Garrisoni-ans also contended that the third party reduced abolitionist influence on the Whig and Democratic Parties. According to the Garrisonians, *real* abolitionists had to rely on "the Spirit of Truth . . . the omnipotence of Love," and disunion to end slavery. They characterized abolitionists who supported the Liberty Party as sinful backsliders. And they launched the One Hundred Conventions cam-paign to break immediate abolitionists in New York, Ohio, Indiana, and Penn-sylvania away from that party.[6]

Meanwhile, during the early 1840s, the gap between all abolitionist factions and antislavery politicians widened. A few antislavery congressmen such as Joshua R. Giddings were still abolitionists. Others such as John Quincy Adams had close but ambivalent ties to abolitionists. But by far most antislavery congressmen had no such ties. They opposed only slavery expansion and southern domination of the U.S. government. Even Giddings and Adams remained in a political party controlled by slaveholders. Consequently interactions between abolitionists and antislavery congressmen often became more bitter than Leavitt's strained relationship with members of the congressional antislavery caucus. In 1839 Nathaniel P. Rogers, a nonresistant, anarchistic Garrisonian who edited the *Herald of Freedom* in Concord, New Hampshire, declared that he had "no confidence in any body who goes to Congress." If abolition in the District of Columbia came to a vote, he charged, such antislavery politicians as Thomas Morris, William Slade, and Adams would likely vote against it. In 1844 Ohio Liberty newspapers denounced Giddings for supporting slaveholding duelist Henry Clay for president of the United States. That same year Birney, citing Adams's reluctance to criticize slavery where it existed and endorse immediate emancipation, accused the devout congressman of denying God's "right to reign on earth among men." According to Birney, Adams used "his *quasi* sympathy" with abolitionists "to deaden the awakening sensibilities of our countrymen against the private iniquity and the public disgrace of slavery."[7]

In turn antislavery politicians made harsh comments about abolitionists. In 1842, for example, antislavery Whig Horace Mann objected to abolitionist Samuel Joseph May's involvement in a fugitive slave case and his denunciation of the U.S. Constitution.[8] Yet despite such friction, abolitionist political tactics during the 1840s remained similar to those of the 1830s and earlier. All abolitionists realized they had to interact with antislavery Whig and Democratic politicians.

Garrisonians relied on a variety of strategies to influence political and governmental policy. In December 1841 Quaker Garrisonian Lucretia Mott addressed the Delaware, New Jersey, and Pennsylvania legislatures. A year later she tried, without success, to have Adams arrange for her to address the U.S. House of Representatives. Lydia Maria Child, who in 1842 edited the AASS's *National Anti-Slavery Standard,* wrote of working through the major parties. That fall, as mentioned in chapter 4, William Lloyd Garrison arranged for Child's husband, David Lee Child, to report on Congress for the *Liberator* as well as the *Standard.* In 1845 Samuel Joseph May, who had worked closely with Garrison in Boston and had moved to Syracuse, remarked that reliance on political parties

Garrisonian Samuel Joseph May (1797–1871) increasingly favored abolitionist political action and interaction with antislavery politicians. (Library of Congress Prints and Photographs Division)

amounted to a "loss of confidence in the sufficiency of truth." Yet May soon began attending Liberty meetings and expressed a belief that the RPA version of third-party action would promote black rights.[9]

May's change of mind indicates that mutual respect among the abolitionist factions never entirely disappeared. Neither did mutual respect between abolitionists and those who foreswore immediatism to participate in party politics. Correspondence, private meetings, and joint participation in public gatherings had larger roles in abolitionist-politician interaction during the early and middle 1840s than did antagonism. Salmon P. Chase's close association with abolitionists allowed him to function as an intermediary between them and antislavery politicians. Gamaliel Bailey, of the moderate Liberty faction and editor the *Philanthropist,* had hoped the Liberty Party would draw Chase and others like him into abolitionism.[10] Instead, by the mid-1840s, Bailey and other moderate Liberty leaders had moved away from immediatism and assumed roles similar to Chase's in linking abolitionist goals to nonabolitionist political means. At times, Gerrit Smith, John G. Whittier, and Lewis Tappan, who remained abolitionists, acted similarly.

Abolitionists who sought direct political impact continued to focus on Adams. His conduct during the gag rule controversy helped convince Samuel Joseph May that antislavery politicians could be effective. The Garrisonian Massachusetts Anti-Slavery Society (MASS) praised Adams for his support of petitioning and opposition to the gag. In 1841 Frederick Douglass, at the time a Garrisonian, recalled reading to "fellow slaves" one of Adams's speeches, and "the joy and gladness it produced to know that so great, so good a man was pleading for us." In 1842 Tappan wrote of Adams, "He is wrong headed on some points. . . . Still he accomplishes great things." Leavitt in 1843 went so far as to declare that Adams had more devotion "to the cause of liberty than nine-tenths of our liberty men."[11]

Abolitionists regarded Giddings similarly. In 1840 Tappan acted within a long abolitionist tradition when he urged Giddings and other northern Whigs "honestly and courageously [to] take . . . [abolition] ground." That same year Bailey discouraged nominating a Liberty candidate to challenge Giddings when he ran for reelection to Congress. In 1841 the Ohio Liberty Party and the AASS supported Giddings's post-censure reelection to Congress. As Giddings and other antislavery Ohio Whigs began to portray their party as the true antislavery party and to argue that the Liberty Party divided the antislavery vote, relations deteriorated. Even so Bailey maintained a political friendship with Giddings that contributed to the congressman's desertion of the Whig Party for the Free Soil Party in 1848.[12]

Because by then Bailey and most Liberty leaders had ceased to be abolitionists, Garrisonians became Giddings's most enduring abolitionist partners. Earlier mutual opposition to the Liberty Party had brought the congressman and Garrisonians into a political alliance that had broader foundations. Garrisonians had praised Giddings's February 1841 congressional speech against the Seminole War, declaring it gave "a strong impetus to the anti-slavery cause." Giddings in 1843 hosted a Garrisonian lecture tour. In 1845 he provided lodging in his home to Garrisonian firebrands Abigail Kelly Foster and Stephen Foster. Giddings did these things despite his rejection of disunionism and Garrisonian criticism of him for his devotion to the slaveholder-controlled Whig Party.[13]

Abolitionist ties to Adams and Giddings during the early 1840s are the best documented. But both radical and moderate Liberty Party leaders interacted with other antislavery politicians, including New York's Whig governor, William H. Seward. When in 1840 Seward refused to extradite black New Yorkers accused of aiding fugitive slaves citing "universal laws of civilized countries," he approached RPAs' contention that slavery could never be legalized. He declared slavery to be "the greatest of all crimes" and asserted that all men were born free and equal. Gerrit Smith and Charles T. Torrey responded by providing help to and praise for Seward. Smith and Tappan joined Chase in asking Seward to consider running for president in 1844 as the Liberty candidate. However, to a greater degree than Giddings, Seward defended the Whig Party as the party of "emancipation." He called the party "firm, fearless, resolved." In 1845 Seward, incorrectly believing Chase to be an abolitionist, advised him that, because "emancipation" had become "a political enterprise," abolitionists had to practice "wise and enlightened moderation."[14]

The interactions of abolitionists with Adams, Giddings, and Seward occurred as the abolition movement affected the major American political events of the 1840s. As described in chapters 3 and 4, continued petitioning for emancipation in the District of Columbia intensified sectional tensions in Congress during the first half of that decade. Abolitionist opposition to the annexation of Texas and the war against Mexico that followed, as well as abolitionist aid to escaping slaves, had wider political impact. Conversely annexation, war, and fugitive-slave issues shaped the course of the abolition movement.[15]

Texas annexation became a much larger political issue than the gag rule, in part because abolitionists helped make it so. During the late 1830s the AASS and MASS had opposed Texas's request to be annexed to the United States. Soon petitions to Congress against annexation had joined those for abolition in the District of Columbia. In Vermont, Rhode Island, Ohio, Michigan, and Massachusetts, abolitionists had persuaded legislatures to send anti-annexation resolutions to Congress. Congressman Adams had welcomed these actions. In 1837 he told Birney he needed petitions "from the people." That same year he advised Whittier that abolitionists must act quickly "for the cause of freedom and righteousness." Whittier in turn had written to U.S. Senator Henry Clay in an attempt to convince this slaveholding, anti-abolitionist, professedly anti-slavery Whig leader that he must firmly oppose annexation.[16]

Clay had realized, however, that, at least in the short run, he need not do so. President Andrew Jackson had for diplomatic reasons put off annexation during his final term as president. Jackson's successor as president, Martin Van Buren, had feared that the annexation issue would split the Democratic Party along sectional lines. And Adams, by monopolizing the House floor from June 6 through July 7, 1838, prevented Democratic leaders from bringing an annexation bill to a vote. A few months later Texas withdrew its application for admission to the Union.[17]

Historian William Lee Miller calls this "a kind of victory . . . for the opponents of slavery." For months thereafter abolitionist-inspired anti-annexation petitions continued to pour into Congress. Then the death of moderately pro-slavery Whig president William Henry Harrison in April 1841, and the elevation of staunchly proslavery vice president John Tyler to the presidency, gave annexationists new opportunities. In February 1842 Tyler signaled that a more determined annexation effort had begun by appointing South Carolina slave-holder Waddy Thompson Jr. to be envoy extraordinary and minister plenipotentiary to Mexico. When abolition lobbyist and journalist Torrey learned of this, he precipitously warned, "A desperate effort will be made to involve us in a war with Mexico at once."[18]

In March 1843 antislavery caucus member Seth M. Gates drafted an "Address to the People of the Free States of the Union." It declared annexation to be an unconstitutional attempt to establish "the undue ascendency of the slaveholding power in the Government." Reflecting Garrisonian influence, Gates's address claimed annexation would "not only inevitably . . . result in a dissolution of the Union, but fully justify it." Two months later Lewis Tappan initiated a private transatlantic diplomacy that he hoped would either end slavery in Texas or prevent the republic's annexation to the United States. Tappan (with Leavitt's support) called on the British and Foreign Anti-Slavery Society to ask the British government to encourage the Republic of Texas to abolish slavery. Tappan also worked to make British action regarding Texas an issue at London's World Anti-Slavery Convention scheduled for June. After conferring with Adams at Adams's Braintree, Massachusetts, home, Tappan and Stephen Pearl Andrews (a Massachusetts-born abolitionist who had worked in Texas for emancipation) sailed to England. While there they attended the World Convention. They also "lay before the British Government facts in relation to Texas, with a view to persuade her to interpose in a legitimate way to prevent the annexation of Texas to this country . . . and the extension of slavery over vast tracts."[19]

Tappan's and Andrews's abolitionist diplomacy influenced U.S. government policy. But it did so in a manner opposite from what they intended. British foreign secretary George Hamilton-Gordon, Lord Aberdeen, who met with the two abolitionists, declined to do more than urge the Mexican government to make emancipation a condition for recognizing Texas's independence. When Andrews publicly exaggerated this weak response, Texas's London agent Ashbel Smith used Andrews's words to push the U.S. Congress toward favoring annexation. Smith's efforts led Duff Green of the *United States Telegraph,* Senator John C. Calhoun of South Carolina, and incoming secretary of state Abel P. Upshur of Virginia to demand immediate action to prevent British-inspired emancipation in Texas.[20]

In April 1844 an annexation treaty that Upshur had negotiated with Texas reached the U.S. Senate. Immediately the *Liberator's* Washington correspondent and abolition lobby member David Lee Child predicted the treaty's defeat, which occurred that June. Whittier later reported that Child had supplied Adams with "facts and arguments" for a speech in the House "on the Texas

Question." That fall Child and some other Garrisonians supported Henry Clay, the Whig candidate for president, based on the assumption that a Clay administration would block further annexation attempts.[21]

When pro-annexation Democrat James K. Polk defeated Clay that November, Tyler called on Congress to annex Texas by joint resolution. To pass such a resolution required only a simple majority in both houses, rather than the two-thirds majority required for the Senate to ratify a treaty. The resolution passed on February 28, 1845 (not long after the House ended the gag rule), and at that point nearly all northern Whigs stopped resisting annexation. Some antislavery Whigs blamed the Liberty Party for this proslavery victory, claiming (not improbably) that Liberty votes in New York cost Clay that state and the election. Some Garrisonians agreed with this interpretation, and the white South's annexation victory increased Garrisonian influence among antislavery Whigs. Even more politically significant, annexation drew antislavery Whigs and the moderate wing of the Liberty Party closer together, opening the way for the formation of what became the Free Soil Party.[22]

Whig opposition to annexation had its greatest strength in Ohio's Western Reserve, where Giddings led, and in Massachusetts, where a group of young "Conscience Whig" politicians began cooperating with abolitionists. Prominent Conscience Whigs included Charles Francis Adams, Charles Allen, Ebenezer R. Hoar, Samuel Gridley Howe, George S. Hilliard, John G. Palfrey, Stephen C. Phillips, Henry Wilson, and Charles Sumner. Adams, a son of John Quincy Adams, served in the state assembly in 1841 and state senate during 1844 and 1845. Allen served in the assembly and senate during the 1830s and early 1840s. And Hoar gained election to the state senate in 1846. Howe, who later became an abolitionist, pioneered in educating the blind. Hilliard gained prominence as a legal and literary editor. Palfrey taught at Harvard College. Phillips served in Congress from 1834 to 1838. Wilson served in the state legislature and as secretary of the commonwealth during the early to mid-1840s.[23]

Of all the Conscience Whigs, Sumner, who did not hold a political office during the 1830s and 1840s, had the closest connections with abolitionists. A Boston native, his friendship with Garrisonian leader and orator Wendell Phillips began when they attended Harvard Law School together during the late 1820s. In 1833 Sumner read Lydia Maria Child's *An Appeal in Favor of That Class of Americans Called Africans*. He began subscribing to the *Liberator* in 1835. In 1836 he exclaimed, "We are becoming abolitionists at the North fast." In early 1845, after hearing Garrison speak for the first time, Sumner declared, "He spoke with natural eloquence. . . . His words . . . fell in fiery rain." Sumner recalled that he "listened [to Garrison] . . . with an interest hardly ever excited by any other speaker." Independent Boston abolitionist Theodore Parker's condemnation of slavery's negative impact on American morality, education, prosperity, and destiny also contributed to Sumner's outlook. In turn Sumner's antiwar "True Grandeur of Nations" speech of July 4, 1845, impressed Parker, Garrisonians, and Whittier. Parker informed Sumner, "I just read your oration on the true grandeur of nations, for the second time." Parker regretted that Sumner had to endure "attacks from men of *low morals* who can only swear by their party."[24]

As this suggests, abolitionist interactions with Conscience Whigs did not mean abolitionist dominance. Shortly before Congress annexed Texas, "political gentlemen," including a half-dozen Conscience Whigs and the more prominent and conservative Whig Daniel Webster, had organized a Massachusetts "Anti-Texas Convention." When the convention convened on January 29, 1845, at Boston's Faneuil Hall, abolitionists attended and attempted to direct its course. Garrison, who on entering the hall had been greeted with a "deafening cheer" from abolitionist women seated in the gallery, presented a disunion resolution. Charles Francis Adams feared Garrison would take control. But Conscience Whigs, who constituted the great majority at the convention, defeated Garrison's resolution and a more mild disunion resolution offered by non-Garrisonian abolitionist Joseph C. Lovejoy. The Conscience Whigs, in a manner similar to most Liberty leaders, believed disunion to be too radical a platform for successful electoral politics. They, like most church-oriented abolitionists, also believed disunion would end what influence the North had on the South.[25]

In September abolitionists had more success as Garrison and Phillips spoke against Texas and for disunion to a mostly Whig audience in Concord, Massachusetts. Garrison told those attending, "I am afraid you are not ready to do your duty; and if not, you will be made a laughing-stock by tyrants and their tools; and it ought to be so." Phillips suggested that Whig politicians were too timid. A month later Garrison addressed a similar meeting at Cambridge. With Phillips and Whittier in attendance and Charles Francis Adams as chairman, the meeting passed Garrison's resolution urging the Massachusetts legislature to declare Congress's annexation of Texas "null and void." And when in November Conscience Whigs formed a "State Anti-Texas Committee," Garrison and Whittier served on it. Thirty thousand people signed this committee's petition. In December Conscience Whig Wilson and abolitionist Whittier took the petition to Washington for John Quincy Adams to present in the House of Representatives, which tabled it.[26]

Although Charles Francis Adams believed the State Anti-Texas Committee's abolitionist members caused the committee at times to be "very wild," the Garrisonians had a positive impact. Wilson drew close to Garrison, read the *Liberator,*

Wendell Phillips (1811–1884) was a close associate of William Lloyd Garrison. During the 1850s, he emerged as the North's leading orator. (Library of Congress Prints and Photographs Division)

praised abolitionists, and received Garrison's praise. More importantly cooperation with Garrisonians helped split the Conscience Whigs from their party.[27]

Torrey's prediction that the annexation of Texas would lead to military conflict with Mexico proved to be correct when in May 1846 Congress declared war against that nation. Fourteen northern Whig representatives and two northern Whig senators voted against the declaration. Among them John Quincy Adams, Giddings, Erastus D. Culver of New York, and John Strohm of Pennsylvania had abolitionist ties. But it was Pennsylvania Democrat David Wilmot who led congressmen opposed to allowing slavery to expand as a result of the war. On August 8, 1846, the House of Representatives passed Wilmot's amendment to a war appropriations bill. This amendment, which became known as the Wilmot Proviso, declared that "neither slavery nor involuntary servitude shall ever exist in any part" of territory acquired from Mexico as a result of the war. All northern Whig representatives and all but four northern Democratic representatives voted for the proviso. All southern Democrats and all but two southern Whigs voted against it. On February 15, 1847, the House, by a 115–106 margin, passed a version of the proviso that applied to all future territorial acquisitions. The Senate defeated both versions.[28]

It is important to note that Wilmot and most of the northern Democrats who acted with him were "anti-abolitionists." Even as the House passed the second version of the proviso, Wilmot boasted, "I have stood up at home, and battled, time and again, against the Abolitionists of the North." He said he had no "morbid sympathy for the slave." He had voted for the gag rule, for Texas annexation, and for war against Mexico. But Wilmot and his closest political allies, who belonged to the Van Buren (or Barnburner) wing of the northern Democratic Party, did believe that slavery expansion threatened white northerners' ability to move west. Also, even though Barnburners were aggressively racist in their characterizations of African Americans, they joined antislavery Whigs and abolitionists in opposing slaveholder control of the U.S. government. This made Barnburners politically compatible with the moderate wing of the Liberty Party, which emphasized slavery's threat to all who labored. While rejecting Barnburner racism, most Liberty politicians shared the Barnburners' economically driven demand for free soil and free labor.[29]

As the Wilmot Proviso opened the way for a political antislavery coalition among the Liberty moderates, Conscience Whigs, and Barnburners, the remaining abolitionists reacted with optimism. Garrison interpreted the proviso's "triumph in the House" as "anti-slavery . . . marching forward with irresistible power." His outlook resembled that of the abolitionists who in 1819 had supported government action to prevent the spread of slavery to Missouri. Like them, Garrison assumed that while stopping slavery expansion did not threaten its existence in the southern states, nonextension amounted to a step in the right direction.[30]

However it was Whittier who, despite poor health, led abolitionists in seeking to shape the emerging political coalition against slavery expansion. During the autumn of 1845, he had prodded the still-abolitionist Massachusetts Liberty Party toward what he hoped would be a lasting political coalition with Conscience Whigs. As he explained his motivation to RPA leader Gerrit Smith, Whittier believed that, evil as the Whig and Democratic Parties were, they contained "men with warm hearts" who could be swayed by "truth." Therefore, during early 1846, Whittier promoted a call for an "anti-slavery league." As he envisioned it, such a league would unite abolitionists with northern antislavery politicians and operate on "a broader scale" than earlier cooperative ventures. It would, he hoped, promote "better understanding and a kinder feeling towards each other." This political union, according to Whittier, would oppose voting for slaveholders and all "political fellowship with slaveholders." He regarded it as a step toward the abolition of slavery throughout the country.[31]

The first effective movement toward creating such a political union had come over a year and a half earlier in New Hampshire and focused on Democratic politician John P. Hale. Since 1840 Hale had been influenced by his abolitionist

Unitarian minister, John Parkman. When Hale had entered Congress in December 1843 and joined a growing corps of northern Democrats who voted against the gag rule, other abolitionists exerted additional influence on him. And New Hampshire Garrisonian Parker Pillsbury had praised Hale for his "grand attempt to lift the Democracy of the Granite State from the . . . most base subserviency to the unrighteous slave power of the South."[32]

But Hale at this point expressed only mild, indirect opposition to slavery. In January 1845, when he announced his opposition to Texas annexation, he did not oppose slavery's existence in the southern states. In regard to slavery expansion, he informed his constituents that if annexing slaveholding Texas "would [also] add more free than slave States to the Union," it had his support. Nevertheless, on February 12, 1845, the New Hampshire Democratic Party, led by future U.S. proslavery president Franklin Pierce, replaced Hale with a more proslavery candidate for Congress in the approaching March election. Hale's supporters then organized as Independent Democrats to renominate him. Sounding like abolitionists, they called for "human equality and universal justice," and abolitionists joined in support of Hale. The *Liberator* published Hale's Texas letter and, despite the letter's equivocation regarding slavery expansion, praised it as "a miracle of political independence and uprightness." The MASS sent "four agents" to New Hampshire to work on behalf of Hale's reelection. Whittier, who had introduced himself to Hale in late January 1845, urged the congressman to "do manly and vigorous [political] battle" so that the Democratic Party might "shake off the loathsome embrace of slavery."[33]

Four times between March 1845 and March 1846 New Hampshire voters failed to elect a representative to fill what had been Hale's seat in Congress. During this struggle Whittier in October 1845 called on the Massachusetts Liberty Party to help "anti-Texas" politicians in New Hampshire. In March 1846 Whittier supported a New Hampshire Independent Democrat–Liberty-Whig coalition devised to defeat the Democratic candidate for Hale's seat, elect a Whig governor, gain control of the state legislature, and elect Hale to the U.S. Senate. When the coalition achieved these goals, Whittier declared, "New Hampshire has gone gloriously. I was half tempted . . . to take off my Quaker hat, & 'Harra for Jack Hale!'"[34]

That September the New Hampshire legislature demonstrated continued abolitionist influence when it declared its sympathy for "every just and well-directed effort for the suppression and extermination of . . . human slavery." At the same time, with Whittier, Henry B. Stanton, and Whittier's Quaker abolitionist second cousin Moses A. Cartland in attendance, leaders of the New

Hampshire Liberty and Independent Democratic Parties merged their organizations and called for the extinction of slavery. These two statements, one coming from a government body and one from a political organization, encouraged abolitionists regarding coalition politics. So did Hale, who moved beyond his previously limited opposition to slavery expansion. In a letter to Massachusetts Garrisonian Henry I. Bowditch, Hale called for challenging "the monstrous anomaly that man can hold property in man." Whittier, overestimating the meaning of this statement (as well as Hale's influence), advised Hale to create a party that would make "abolition of slavery the leading and paramount political question."[35]

By 1847 Whittier and others imagined that a Liberty nomination of Hale for U.S. president could be the locus for an 1848 union of Independent Democrats, Conscience Whigs, Giddings's Western Reserve Whigs, and Barnburners. With this goal in mind, during July 1847 a group of northeastern Liberty leaders met in Boston with Hale and his New Hampshire political associates George G. Fogg and Amos Tuck. Abolitionists among those representing the Liberty Party included Whittier, Leavitt, Tappan, Charles D. Cleveland of Philadelphia, and Samuel Fessenden of Maine. But now former abolitionist Stanton, who led in arranging the meeting, had views similar to those of nonabolitionist Salmon P. Chase. Soon Stanton, Hale, Chase, Bailey, and many others who were no longer or never had been abolitionists looked beyond the Liberty Party and Hale for the means of forming a broader political coalition focused on stopping slavery expansion rather than promoting universal emancipation.[36]

At the Liberty Party presidential nominating convention in Buffalo on October 20–21, 1847, Chase and Stanton led those who feared that if the party nominated Hale it would limit coalition options. Therefore they attempted to postpone nominating. On the other extreme, an RPA group led by Gerrit Smith and William Goodell believed Hale and a platform he would run on could not be sufficiently abolitionist. They wanted to nominate an immediatist on a slavery unconstitutional platform. The majority at the convention, however, disregarded both extremes and nominated Hale on a nonabolitionist platform.[37]

Abolitionists reacted to this in ways determined by ideological perspective *and* political calculation. Whittier regarded the candidate and platform as steps toward emancipation. He dismissed Smith's and Goodell's demand for a platform asserting the unconstitutionality of slavery in the states. He advised Hale that "with the Constitution, or without the Constitution, *Slavery must die.*" Leavitt, Tappan, and Cartland joined Whittier in supporting Hale's candidacy while inconsistently insisting that an antislavery political union had to be grounded on an abolition platform.[38]

Garrisonians tended to agree with Whittier, Leavitt, Tappan, and Cartland that the political situation required a broad appeal. Prior to Hale's nomination, Wendell Phillips recalled the Garrisonian prediction seven years earlier that Liberty politicians "would be forced to gain strength by selecting for candidates men not of their party." Now Phillips observed, "The Liberty Party *as such* is dying and merging under other names in other movements." Edmund Quincy, writing in the *Liberator*, congratulated "the Third Party on having got at last a reputable candidate." He added, "We . . . think that the Party did the wisest thing it ever did in merging itself into Mr. Hale's party." But RPA Gerrit Smith continued to demanded more than opposition to slavery expansion. He also objected to political union with Conscience Whigs because they had worked with slaveholders in the Whig Party. Smith's RPA colleagues preferred to support him as their presidential candidate on a platform declaring slavery unconstitutional and illegal throughout the country.[39]

As these complicated events regarding antislavery political coalition transpired, abolitionists affiliated with the Liberty Party launched two other efforts designed to influence Congress and electoral politics. First, in December 1844 at a Liberty meeting in Albany, New York, Tappan had proposed that the party hold a convention in Washington the following winter. Such a convention, he hoped, would "adopt an address to Congress" and an address to the "People of the United States" dealing with the "connection of the General Government with Slavery and the Slave trade." When the Albany meeting failed to endorse this suggestion, Tappan sent it on to James C. Jackson, RPA editor of the *Albany Weekly Patriot*, who proposed to hold such a convention in March 1845. Jackson wanted two or three hundred abolitionists (including *"personal* friends" of congressmen) to attend and rally the North. Southern journalists reacted to these proposals with threats of mob action. The *Constitution*, published in Washington, charged that abolitionists, emboldened by the gag rule's defeat, intended "more disturbing efforts on this deadly subject."[40]

As it turned out lack of interest among abolitionists rather than proslavery threats led Jackson to put off plans for the convention. Then in August 1846 Edwin S. Hamlin, a Giddings Whig from Cleveland, revived the proposal while attending a regional Liberty meeting in Chicago. In contrast to Tappan, nonabolitionist Hamlin wanted a Washington convention that would foster political coalition against slavery *extension*. Therefore Leavitt, who at the time was still an abolitionist, killed the idea. He described the convention proposal as "a cunning trap devised by heartless politicians" to lure abolitionists into helping proslavery major party candidates.[41]

The second Liberty abolitionist political effort involved interrelated proposals to revive the congressional lobby and establish a newspaper in Washington. At the same December 1844 Albany meeting where Tappan had suggested a Washington convention, he announced that RPA William L. Chaplin of Groton, New York, would replace imprisoned Torrey as the *Albany Weekly Patriot*'s Washington correspondent. Tappan also suggested sending eight other abolitionist reporters to Washington to watch over the country's "true interests." A year later Whittier had gone to Washington to deliver a Massachusetts anti-Texas-annexation petition and lobby northern Democratic congressmen to vote against annexation. While Whittier was at the capital city, Jacob Bigelow, a Massachusetts-born congressional reporter, convinced him that an abolitionist newspaper could succeed there. When Tappan learned of this he led a joint effort of the American and Foreign Anti-Slavery Society (AFASS) and a committee appointed by a northwestern Liberty Convention held in Chicago in June 1846 to establish and sustain such a newspaper, which became the *National Era*.[42]

Under Tappan's direction, Bailey, leader of the moderate Cincinnati Liberty faction, became the newspaper's editor in chief. Staunch abolitionists Amos A. Phelps and Whittier became corresponding editors. Limaeus P. Noble, a RPA from Buffalo, became business manager. In November 1846 Leavitt called on "the friends of the slave and of universal liberty" to support the new newspaper. Whittier believed it would be worthy of the "cause of humanity, the Democracy of the New Testament." He hoped it would influence Congress and spread abolitionism into the Border South.[43]

When the *National Era* began publication in January 1847, Bailey acted much as abolition lobbyists Leavitt, Weld, and Torrey had years earlier. He cultivated ties to Washington's black community. He searched for documents to support speeches by antislavery congressmen. He helped to write speeches. And he became a familiar figure in the House of Representatives, caucusing informally with antislavery congressmen. Starting in 1848 Bailey and his wife, Margaret, invited politicians to weekly social gatherings at their large house located not far from the Capitol. On occasion Bailey advocated abolitionist goals, and when in April 1848 he entered the House gallery to hear Giddings speak, William W. Wick, a proslavery Indiana Democrat, declared, "The Abolitionist is among us." Yet Bailey did not fulfill all of Tappan's, Leavitt's, and Whittier's abolitionist desires. Instead, in conducting the *National Era* and in lobbying Congress, Bailey sought to appeal to "the enemies of Slavery of all classes."[44]

Like Chase and Stanton, Bailey (who rarely used the term "abolition") did not believe a viable political coalition could be based on advocating emancipation in the southern states. In his editorials he did not emphasize ending slavery in the District of Columbia or convincing his readers of the moral evil of slavery. Instead he concentrated on uniting northern congressmen in a political party opposed to slavery expansion and slaveholder control of the U.S. government. To reach this goal he went beyond working with John Quincy Adams, Giddings, and other antislavery congressmen to reach out to politicians who had few if any abolitionist ties. Such politicians lacked moral fervor and advocated only the "ultimate extinction of slavery." Among them were such relative conservatives as Whig senator Thomas Corwin of Ohio, Democratic representative John Wentworth of Illinois, and Democratic senator Thomas Hart Benton of Missouri.[45]

Garrison, Frederick Douglass, Gerrit Smith, and other steadfast abolitionists portrayed Bailey as a backslider. But they recognized the value of his work and sought to influence him. Tappan visited Bailey in February 1848, and the *National Era* published letters from Tappan and other abolitionists. Whittier, despite continued poor health, contributed regularly to the newspaper during its early years. And in addition to Tappan and Whittier, such abolitionists as Leavitt, Moncure Conway, and James Freeman Clarke came to Washington to help with Bailey's lobbying, attend his parties, and enjoy his hospitality.[46]

Progress toward a coalition among Liberty moderates, Conscience Whigs, and Barnburners sped up during the spring and early summer of 1848 as the Democratic and Whig Parties rejected or ignored the Wilmot Proviso. On May 22 the Democratic national convention, meeting in Baltimore, nominated conservative Lewis Cass of Michigan for president on a platform allowing settlers to decide the issue of slavery in each territory (popular sovereignty). On June 7 the Whig national convention, meeting in Philadelphia, nominated slaveholder and Mexican War hero Zachary Taylor for president without reference to slavery expansion. In response Chase, on behalf of the moderate Liberty faction, organized a Free Territory Convention, which met in Columbus, Ohio, on June 21. This convention endorsed denationalization rather than abolition and called for "Friends of Freedom, Free Territory, and Free Labor" to gather at Buffalo on August 9. On June 22, Barnburners met in Utica, New York; nominated Van Buren for president; endorsed the Wilmot Proviso; and agreed to meet in Buffalo. On June 28 Conscience Whigs met in Worcester, Massachusetts. With Giddings, some other out-of-state Whigs, and at least one Barnburner in attendance, they too agreed to attend the Buffalo meeting.[47]

At Buffalo, as Hale withdrew, delegates representing the Liberty moderates, Barnburners, and Conscience Whigs nominated Van Buren as the Free Soil Party candidate for president and Conscience Whig Charles Francis Adams for vice president. The new party's platform, drafted principally by Chase, called for "no more slave states and no more slave territories." It pledged "no interference by Congress with slavery within the limits of any state." It suggested that the Fugitive Slave Law of 1793 was unconstitutional but did not call for its repeal. Neither did it call for emancipation in the District of Columbia, an end to the interstate slave trade, or removal of the Constitution's three-fifths clause. At best the Free Soil platform supported denationalization as it declared "the settled policy of the nation [to be] . . . to limit, localize, and discourage slavery." Black abolitionists Frederick Douglass, Henry Bibb, Samuel Ringgold Ward, Henry Highland Garnet, and Charles Remond attended the convention. Douglass and Bibb each briefly addressed those attending, but the platform did not mention black rights.[48]

Some remaining Liberty abolitionists, such as Leavitt and Elizur Wright Jr., embraced the Free Soil platform without qualification. Leavitt declared at the convention, "The Liberty party is not dead, but translated." Shortly thereafter he called Van Buren "our glorious old man," and in effect ceased to be an abolitionist. Wright, who also attended the convention, regarded the limited platform to be practical politics. Although Wright continued thereafter to express abolitionist views, he no longer participated in abolitionist organizations. Whittier too endorsed "Free Soil and Free Labor." But at the end of July, he qualified his endorsement. He would "cheerfully vote" for Van Buren only so long as the former president agreed to run on a platform expressing "opposition to the *continuance* as well as to the extension to Slavery in territories under the exclusive legislation of Congress."[49]

As they had welcomed Hale's presidential nomination a year earlier, Garrisonians now welcomed the Free Soil Party. They regarded it as a major step toward general emancipation and claimed credit for its formation. But, following long-established abolitionist tactics, they also noted the party's shortcomings and, like Whittier, attempted to prod it toward opposing slavery in the South. Edmund Quincy, substituting as *Liberator* editor for an ill Garrison, first stressed the positive. Immediate abolitionist "labors of near twenty years . . . preaching the Gospel of the Wrongs of the Black man and the Guilt of the White man" had, Quincy declared, produced the new party. Its organization, he wrote, amounted to the beginning of the end of the proslavery American party system. Then, turning to the negative, Quincy pointed out that because the Free Soil Party accepted the U.S. Constitution's proslavery principles, it was "only indirectly and by implication an Anti-Slavery party." If the Free Soilers triumphed, "slavery would still be guaranteed in the slaveholding States," the three-fifths clause would still operate, as would the fugitive slave clause: "In case of servile revolution, the military arm of the nation, and if necessary the whole force of the Free States would be put forth to crush it."[50]

Other Garrisonian leaders approached the new party similarly. Samuel Joseph May, who offered a prayer at the start of the Buffalo convention's second day, praised the new party as the first "broadly based political party" founded on "an antislavery principle." Then he urged its leaders to move toward opposing slavery in the states. Frederick Douglass declared, "This grand movement, so long desired and so long maturing, has at last arrived in definite and tangible form, and is now fairly launched forth upon the storm tossed sea of American politics." Douglass denied charges that the Buffalo convention had deliberately overlooked black rights. He urged those who voted, especially black men, to support the Free Soil ticket. But he promised that *he* would not vote for Van Buren.[51]

During the 1848 campaign virtually all Garrisonians stood by disunionism as the only effective strategy for ending slavery in the South. With some exceptions they did not campaign for Free Soil candidates, hold meetings, publish literature, or write letters on the party's behalf. They emphasized the political importance of an *independent* abolition movement. To a greater degree than Quincy, May, and Douglass, most Garrisonians prodded Free Soilers. "Only while the abolitionists persevere," Maria Weston Chapman advised Douglass, "can any such half way political movement proceed." As Garrison put it, "The Abolitionists, who accept the morality and method of the American Anti-Slavery Society, cannot act with the Free Soil party in its organization and at the polls." Rather they had to lead Free Soilers "up to yet loftier heights" by insisting on "NO UNION WITH SLAVE-HOLDERS." Henry C. Wright, at a Ravenna, Ohio, Whig convention, simultaneously praised Free Soil congressional candidate Giddings and sought to convince him to become a disunionist.[52]

RPAs provided less praise and more criticism of the Free Soil Party than did Garrisonians. While Garrisonians portrayed Free Soil as a more useful political force than the Liberty Party had been, RPAs regarded it to be a sellout of Liberty abolitionism. Gerrit Smith classed the Free Soil convention, along with its Whig and Democratic counterparts, as "an anti-abolition Convention." Unlike Douglass, he advised African Americans not to vote for a party that, once in power, would undertake "no effort to deliver them from slavery," that would "acquiesce, and even take part, in the prescription and crushing of your race." William Goodell later observed that the Free Soil Party placed "the claims of liberty on the lowest possible ground, that of the non-extension of slavery."[53]

Frederick Douglass (1818–1895) emerged
as a leading abolitionist during the
early 1840s. At first a Garrisonian, he
became a radical political abolitionist by
1850. (Library of Congress Prints and
Photographs Division)

Black RPA Samuel Ringgold Ward characterized the Free Soil Party as "not
at all an unfavorable union." But, like Smith, he advised black voters not to
support the party because it failed to endorse "Equal and Inalienable Rights of
ALL MEN." Ward pointed out that Free Soilers offered free land in U.S. territories
only to white men and would allow Van Buren, if elected, to maintain slavery in
the District of Columbia. That September a black national convention meeting
in Cleveland and dominated by RPAs praised the Free Soil Party as "calculated"
to help the "down-trodden and oppressed of the land." But those attending rejected a resolution that called on black men who could vote to cast their ballots
for Free Soil candidates. They vowed "to maintain the higher standard and more
liberal views which have characterized us as abolitionists." Meanwhile Tappan
and other AFASS leaders became RPAs. Prior to the Buffalo Convention, the
AFASS had declared, "Non-extension [of slavery] is not abolition." Tappan opposed Liberty participation in the Buffalo Convention and counselled Hale
against withdrawing. He regretted that Leavitt had been "mesmerized into a
full blooded Van Buren man." In the general election Tappan voted for Smith,
who, running on a platform declaring slavery to be unconstitutional and illegal
everywhere, received 2,600 votes.[54]

Compared to most third parties in American history, the Free Soil Party did well in its first campaign. Van Buren failed to carry a single state as Taylor won the presidential election over conservative Democrat Cass by a wide margin in the popular and electoral vote. But the Free Soilers elected respectable numbers of state legislators and nine congressmen. Their campaign pushed northern Democrats and Whigs toward stronger statements against slavery expansion.[55]

Following the election most abolitionists continued to portray the Free Soil Party as a progressive step toward general emancipation, while noting the party's shortcomings and pledging their continued vigilance. In July 1849 Whittier, who had begun to shift his focus from politics to literature, advised Tappan that he was "well satisfied with the result of . . . [the Free Soilers'] labors thus far." He believed the party had abolitionist potential. But he also expected that "the old Liberty men" in the party might "get off the track now and then," and he worried that other Free Soilers might be "drawn into some unworthy compromise." He perceptively predicted that New York Barnburners would leave the Free Soil Party to reunite with their more conservative former colleagues in the Democratic Party. He informed Tappan, "The responsibilities of the cause, never rested heavier on the genuine old fashioned abolitionist than at this time."[56]

As Whittier's words suggest, the antislavery political coalition, like the antislavery newspaper in Washington and the new congressional lobby, did not turn out as the remaining abolitionist leaders wished. Historian James Brewer Stewart contends that "organized abolitionism in politics had expired" with the breakup of the Liberty Party and formation of the Free Soil Party. Yet Garrisonians, members of the AFASS, RPAs, and unaffiliated abolitionists such as Theodore Parker continued to exert political influence. Garrisonians, in particular, cajoled and encouraged sympathetic politicians—especially in Massachusetts and Ohio. Frederick Douglass predicted Garrisonians would continue "to expose the frauds of political parties . . . till slavery be abolished, the Union dissolved, or the sun of this guilty nation must go down in blood."[57]

Antislavery politicians, of course, frequently refused to be influenced by abolitionists. In 1849, when Garrisonians invited Charles Sumner and John G. Palfrey to speak at a commemoration of West Indian emancipation, both declined. Palfrey emphasized his objections to disunionism. Sumner praised the Garrisonians' "sincere devotion to the slave," while invoking a prior commitment. Nevertheless antislavery politicians continued to value abolitionist input and often endorsed abolitionist goals. Hale accepted Parker's help with his early Senate speeches. Chase and Seward subscribed to Douglass's *North Star* newspaper.

Following the 1848 election Sumner commented to Whittier regarding slavery, "We shall have it soon in a state of moral blockade. Then it must fall." In 1850 Chase, by then a U.S. senator, sought Douglass's council concerning the theory that climate would lead African Americans to migrate from the United States.[58] During the 1850s interactions between abolitionists and antislavery politicians would continue. And, as the following chapter indicates, physical abolitionist action—and abolitionist support for actions by slaves—shaped sectional politics and government policy.

6

Physical Action, Fugitive Slave Laws, and the Free Democratic Party, 1845–1852

During the 1840s physical action against slavery, which abolitionists had undertaken in the North and in the Border South since the 1780s, accelerated. To an even greater degree than petitioning and lobbying, efforts to help slaves escape and to prevent kidnapping into slavery encouraged defensiveness among southern politicians. The resulting southern-led attempts to strengthen the Fugitive Slave Law rivaled the slavery expansion issue in causing sectional division in Congress and in electoral politics. Simultaneously physical action positively influenced northern antislavery politicians, who increased their advocacy of various degrees of denationalization. In turn abolitionists used a variety of political means to prod these politicians to go further. As the Free Soil Party decomposed after 1848, radical political abolitionists (RPAs) especially attempted to shape the direction of that party's much smaller successor, the Free Democratic Party. They did so in a manner that anticipated abolitionist tactics regarding the Republican Party.

As is the case regarding abolitionist interactions with politicians and government, the story of their physical action against slavery, and the political impact of that action, is a long one. Historians sometimes portray white southern charges of abolitionist interaction with slaves as either fantasy or propaganda. Unfree African Americans had resisted their masters and escaped on their own since before American chattel slavery had fully developed during the late 1600s. The escapees often found sympathetic black, American Indian, and nonabolitionist white people who provided shelter, food, and transportation. But there is also a long, well-documented history of abolitionist assistance to escaping slaves and to those kidnapped into slavery. This history supports proslavery perceptions of an abolitionist threat to ownership of human property and to social stability in the Border South. These perceptions encouraged proslavery journalists and politicians to demand that the federal and northern state governments pass fugitive slave laws.[1]

Beginning during the 1780s the Pennsylvania Abolition Society (PAS) sent agents into Delaware, Maryland, and the District of Columbia to help black kidnapping victims and attempt to bring their abductors to justice. One of the most politically influential of these abolitionist undertakings began in 1788. During that year the former master of John Davis came to Pennsylvania, where Davis lived, and took him to Virginia as a slave. In response white abolitionists associated with the PAS traveled to Virginia, located Davis, and brought him back to Pennsylvania. When bounty hunters recaptured Davis, the PAS demanded legal action, and Pennsylvania governor Thomas Mifflin in 1791 attempted to extradite the bounty hunters. As a result Congress in 1793 passed what became the nation's first fugitive slave law.[2]

In several respects this law made slave renditions easier. It required northern state governments to help masters or their agents recover escaped slaves. It fined individuals who interfered with recovery efforts. It provided that alleged escapees could not testify on their own behalf, have a lawyer present during hearings, or have a jury trial. However, reliance on northern state officials for support in recovery efforts and on northern state courts to authorize return of alleged fugitives south allowed for legal resistance to masters and agents.[3]

As described in chapter 2, such resistance led the Maryland legislature in 1826 to send a "deputation" to Harrisburg to demand that its Pennsylvania counterpart pass a state-level fugitive slave law. There, under PAS influence, the Pennsylvania legislature responded with the "Law of 1826," which made recapturing fugitive slaves more difficult. Another dispute between Maryland and Pennsylvania that began in 1837 led to more abolitionist influence on northern state legislation. Maryland slave catchers had taken a black woman from Pennsylvania without getting the required permission from a local justice of the peace. The resulting legal case produced the U.S. Supreme Court decision in *Prigg v. Pennsylvania* on March 1, 1842. This decision banned state government interference in slave renditions and relieved state governments of responsibility for enforcing the Fugitive Slave Law of 1793.[4]

During the years preceding the *Prigg* decision, abolitionists had been petitioning northern state legislatures to pass laws, known as personal liberty laws, that authorized procedural protections for people accused of being fugitive slaves. In early 1837 the Massachusetts Anti-Slavery Society (MASS) called for "such laws as will secure to those claimed as slaves . . . a trial by jury." In support John G. Whittier led a group of abolitionists to Boston to lobby at the Massachusetts State House. Regarding this effort Whittier wrote, "We have caucused in season and out of season, threatened and coaxed, plead and scolded." That March he predicted, "We shall get a bill through . . . granting a jury trial for fugitive slaves." In April the legislature by an overwhelming margin passed the bill.[5]

In New York, abolitionists, led by Elizur Wright Jr. and New York Anti-Slavery Society (NYASS) president Alvan Stewart, had initiated a similar effort. When this campaign failed, New York abolitionists in 1838 turned to questioning political office seekers concerning the propriety of such an act. Led by William Jay and Gerrit Smith, they asked Democratic and Whig gubernatorial candidates to express their views concerning jury trials. Neither Democratic candidate William L. Marcy nor Whig candidate William H. Seward responded satisfactorily to the requests. A few months after Seward won the election and became governor in January 1839, the New York legislature failed to pass a bill providing for jury trials in rendition cases. Nevertheless Jay's and Smith's undertaking shaped Seward's decision that July to refuse to extradite three black New York citizens demanded by Virginia for helping slaves escape. The following year the state legislature passed and Seward signed a jury trial law that made slave renditions in New York more difficult. It was this conduct by Seward and his portrayal of slavery as illegal under international law that led Smith and Lewis Tappan to favor nominating Seward as the Liberty presidential candidate in 1844.[6]

Seven months after the *Prigg* decision, the jailing in Boston of a black man named George Latimer, whom a Virginia master claimed as a fugitive slave, prompted William Lloyd Garrison, Edmund Quincy, and Wendell Phillips to lead a series of public gatherings. At the abolitionists' "Grand Latimer Meeting," convened in Faneuil Hall, young Whig politicians Charles Francis Adams and Charles Sumner took their first steps toward becoming Conscience Whigs, as they shared a platform with Phillips and Quincy. Shortly thereafter Adams, emulating his father, John Quincy Adams's introduction of abolitionist petitions in Congress, presented a huge Latimer petition to the Massachusetts House of Representatives. This resulted in the legislature's passage of a stronger personal liberty law. Four years later, the "Joe" fugitive slave case led to another meeting, chaired by the elder Adams. At this meeting a large group of Conscience Whigs joined abolitionists Quincy, Phillips, and Theodore Parker as speakers.[7]

Earlier, as settlement expanded farther west during the first decades of the 1800s, abolitionists' physical actions directly affected political relations between states north and south of the Ohio River. In 1822 Presbyterian minister John Rankin and his family had moved from Tennessee to Ripley, Ohio, located on the north bank of the river. In Ripley Rankin soon began working with African Americans to aid escapees and fight against slave catchers. In 1826 Levi Coffin, a Quaker abolitionist who had moved from North Carolina, led a similar

interracial escape network in southern Indiana. By the late 1830s, as slave escapes increased, John B. Mahan, a founder of the Ohio Anti-Slavery Society and
a Methodist minister, led armed bands in Mason County (located northeast of
Cincinnati) against masters, slave catchers, and kidnappers.[8]

Following Mahan's September 1838 arrest by Kentuckians in Ohio, Kentucky's Whig governor James Clark warned against "the overthrow of all social
intercourse between neighboring states." Seeking reconciliation, Ohio's Whig
governor Joseph Vance upheld the arrest. As a result Ohio abolitionists entered
into an electoral alliance with Democrats, which prevented Vance's reelection
that November. In December, after a Kentucky jury acquitted Mahan because
he had not acted in that state, Kentucky sent two commissioners to Columbus
to consult with the Ohio legislature. The resulting Ohio Fugitive Slave Law
(known as the "Black Law") led abolitionists to rouse opposition among Whig
and Democratic politicians in the state. Whig state senator Benjamin F. Wade,
who represented the Western Reserve, defended the right of Ohioans to help
fugitive slaves avoid recapture. Wade also asserted the right of a fugitive slave
"to turn upon his pursuer, and in defense of his liberty cleave him to the earth."
In 1843, following a spurt of slave catching aggressiveness, the Democratic-
controlled Ohio legislature repealed the Black Law.[9]

The political impact of abolitionist physical action extended beyond Pennsylvania, New York, and Ohio. In 1841 three theology students attending the
abolitionist Mission Institute, located on the east bank of the Mississippi River
at Quincy, Illinois, crossed the river to Palmyra, Missouri, in a failed effort to
entice slaves away from their masters. The arrest and trial of the three students,
Alanson Work, James E. Burr, and George Thompson, amid riotous conditions
attracted national interest. Also in 1841 abolitionists helped former slave Madison Washington return to Virginia from Canada in an attempt to free his wife.
When Virginia authorities recaptured Washington, and his owner shipped him
south on the brig *Creole* for sale in a New Orleans slave market, Washington
orchestrated a successful and well-publicized revolt that led to freedom in the
British Bahamas for all of the slaves on board.[10]

Aid to fugitive slaves, remarks such as Wade's, repeal of the Ohio Black
Law, and physical abolitionist interference with slavery in Missouri and Virginia encouraged proslavery politics in the Border South. In 1839 Virginia
congressman Henry A. Wise threatened, "If violence or intrusion upon our
rights be persisted in and pursued, gentlemen will find . . . the South all
united on the subject.—ready ripe for revolution." In 1840 Thomas Marshall, a member of the Kentucky House of Representatives, declared that slave
states had been "systematically and boldly assaulted." The Washington *Globe*

agreed, arguing that assisted escapes threatened slavery in Maryland, Virginia, Kentucky, and Missouri. And, as mentioned in chapter 5, the *Creole* revolt produced white southern demands for federal action and led to Giddings's expulsion from the House of Representatives because he had defended the right of slaves to revolt at sea.[11]

Abolitionist interaction with slaves in Washington, D.C., most directly encouraged verbal conflict in Congress. In 1835 Washington police had arrested northern abolitionist Reuben Crandall for possessing antislavery publications. In 1839 the police arrested black abolitionist and local hack driver Leonard Grimes for transporting an enslaved woman and her seven children from Virginia to freedom. Both incidents led to southern charges that the ongoing abolitionist petitioning campaign for emancipation in the District of Columbia threatened slavery in neighboring states. Virginia representative Robert Craig argued (with good reason) that emancipation in the District of Columbia would make it a haven for fugitive slaves and those who aided them. If that happened, he warned his fellow congressmen, "Virginia must either emancipate her slaves or 'stand upon her arms.'"[12]

In November 1843 abolitionist journalist and lobbyist Charles T. Torrey and his free black associate Thomas Smallwood barely escaped capture by Washington police as they attempted to help two enslaved families escape northward from the city. When Torrey persisted in daring attempts to help slaves escape from the district, Maryland, and Virginia, he had strategic political as well as humanitarian motives. Slavery in Washington, he wrote, is "a sort of symbol and proof of its control over the government of the country. It is in this point of view, that I regard it as important to make more vigorous assaults than ever upon slavery in this District." Torrey hoped increased escapes might doom slavery in Maryland and the district "in 4 years." Instead Baltimore police arrested Torrey on June 24, 1844. Convicted of helping three slaves escape and sentenced to serve six years in the Maryland State Penitentiary, Torrey died there of tuberculosis in May 1846.[13]

Prior to Torrey's arrest, proslavery politicians feared the impact of his actions on slavery in the District of Columbia and adjacent parts of Maryland and Virginia. They also knew that as an abolition lobbyist, he had ties to Congress's more dedicated antislavery members. In May 1844, as Joshua G. Giddings spoke in the House of Representatives against the annexation of Texas, William Winter Payne of Alabama interrupted to suggest that a "committee ought to be appointed to inquire" into Giddings's involvement with Torrey's efforts to help slaves escape. In February 1845 Edward Black of Georgia "called . . . Giddings a 'slanderer,' a libeler . . . a 'co-laborer of Torrey the thief'" and threatened Gid-dings with a cane.[14] Torrey's and Smallwood's actions also led to Border South state legislation designed to protect slavery, as well as to pressure Congress to pass a stronger fugitive slave law.

In addition to raising white southern concerns regarding slave escape, aggres-sive physical abolitionist action in the South (and allegations of such action) increased fear of slave revolt. No major slave revolts occurred in the United States after Nat Turner's in Southampton County, Virginia, in 1831. But mass slave escape attempts appeared to white southerners to be much like revolts, and because they occurred in the Border South, they impacted political opin-ion throughout the region—especially in the nation's capital city. The first such attempt began in southern Maryland in July 1845 as Bill Wheeler, a free black man, led approximately seventy-five enslaved black men north. The men carried a few pistols, scythes, and other weapons. As they approached Washington, they divided into two groups. The larger group passed through the city's outskirts, with about three hundred "well armed" white men in pursuit, and shortly there-after surrendered to a Rockville, Maryland, posse. Although Wheeler had no known abolitionist ties, a meeting at Port Tobacco, Maryland, accused aboli-tionists of invading the state, taking "property," and risking citizens' lives and rights. In August 1848 a similar mass slave escape attempt occurred in Kentucky, which ended as about 350 white militia recaptured about 58 escapees. Because a white student at Centre College accompanied the slaves, there were more charges against abolitionists.[15]

A mass escape attempt from Washington that *was* planned by an aboli-tionist had a much bigger impact on politics and government than either the Kentucky or Maryland attempts. William L. Chaplin, who replaced Torrey as the *Albany Weekly Patriot's* Washington correspondent, had in 1844 ex-claimed, "I believe that one hundred men like Charles T. Torrey, in courage and devotion to his object, would do more to deliver the slave speedily, than all our paper resolutions, windy speeches, presses, and *votes* into the bargain."[16] Nevertheless, during his first several years in Washington, Chaplin avoided physical tactics as he institutionalized purchases of freedom in the city. Then in early 1848, as expanded sales of slaves south threatened black families, Chaplin allied with Daniel Bell, a free black man, to organize a peaceful mass escape. Chaplin contacted Daniel Drayton, a white boatman from the Phila-delphia area who had experience helping slaves escape. Drayton paid Cap-tain Edward Sayres one hundred dollars to charter the schooner *Pearl*, which reached Washington on April 13, 1848. Two days later the vessel sailed down the Potomac River with Drayton, Sayres, and white crewman Chester English standing on its deck. In its hold were seventy-seven black men, women, and children. Early on April 17 thirty-one heavily armed volunteers on board a steamer overtook the *Pearl*. The volunteers captured the *Pearl*'s crew and passengers without resistance, took them back to Washington, and paraded them through city streets to jail.[17]

In reaction to the *Pearl* escape attempt, Washington's local leaders instigated a mob assault on Gamaliel Bailey's *National Era* office and confronted Bailey at his home. The mob also threatened Congressman Giddings when he visited the city jail to offer legal services to Drayton, Sayres, and English. Shortly thereafter, sounding like a RPA, Giddings declared on the House floor, "The slaves of this District possessed before the universal world and before God himself the right to free themselves by any means God has put into their power." Giddings also introduced resolutions against holding the escapees in the jail. Only actions by city police, city officials, and President James K. Polk saved Bailey, Giddings, and others whom the mob perceived to be abolitionists from physical harm.[18]

The *Pearl* escape attempt also revived extreme southern rhetoric in Congress. Southerners charged Giddings, Senator John P. Hale (who had begun his term in December 1847), and Conscience Whig representative John G. Palfrey with complicity in the escape attempt. In the House of Representatives, Robert Toombs of Georgia, Abraham W. Venable of North Carolina, Robert Barnwell Rhett of South Carolina, and William T. Haskell of Tennessee defended mob action against what they portrayed as an abolitionist-inspired black revolt. Haskell declared that Giddings and other antislavery congressmen "ought to swing as high as Haman." In the Senate, after Hale introduced legislation to protect the *National Era*, southern rhetoric became even more threatening. John C. Calhoun, his South Carolina colleague Andrew P. Butler, Jefferson Davis of Mississippi, and Davis's Mississippi colleague Henry Foote tied the *Pearl* to other sectional issues, including resistance to the Fugitive Slave Law of 1793, threats to abolish slavery in the District of Columbia, and encouragement of slave revolt. Calhoun described slave escape as "the gravest and most vital of all questions to us and the whole Union." Davis called the district "ground upon which the people of this Union may shed blood." Foote accused Hale of instigating "a sort of civil war . . . in behalf of the liberties of . . . the blacks—the slaves of the District of Columbia."[19]

In response to Toombs, Venable, Rhett, and Haskell, Giddings said, "Gentlemen in making such threats appeared to forget they were not now on their plantations, exercising their petty tyranny over slaves." Leading proslavery northern Democratic senator Stephen A. Douglass, in response to the southern senators' rhetoric, warned them that, by their words, they encouraged antislavery politics and abolitionist influence on it. He told the senators that if they had connived "to manufacture abolitionism and abolition votes in the North, they would have fallen upon precisely the same kind of procedure which they have adopted today."[20]

Douglas used the term "abolitionism" loosely as he meant that the non-abolitionist Conscience Whig and Liberty politicians who were then merging into the Free Soil Party would benefit from the extreme southern rhetoric in Congress. Among such politicians, Salmon P. Chase expected the "vehement & coarse vituperation" engaged in by proslavery senators to "do more than anything that has yet occurred to open the eyes of the [northern] people." Another Ohio Liberty politician, Edward Wade of Cleveland, exclaimed, "I . . . cant but think that this great case at the Capitol . . . Presidential election pending . . . was Providential and that a merciful God has yet freedom in store for the slave." Conscience Whig Charles Sumner wrote to Giddings, "Who can doubt that the day will yet come when Torrey & Capt Sayres will be regarded as martyrs of Liberty."[21]

Garrisonians and RPAs joined antislavery politicians in praising the *Pearl* escape attempt. In contrast to the politicians, however, Garrisonians and RPAs criticized Bailey and Hale for not publicly endorsing physical tactics on behalf of slave escape. Frederick Douglass followed the long-established abolitionist policy in combining censure with praise. On the one hand he portrayed Hale as too frightened to defend Drayton and Sayres and uphold black rights. On the other he commended the "noble-hearted Giddings, Palfrey, and Hale." The *Pearl* initiative, combined with the antislavery politicians' words, Douglass asserted, portended slavery's demise in the District of Columbia and throughout the South.[22]

It may be that the increase in slave escapes from the Border South would have destabilized national politics, even without a long history of abolitionist aid to them. And, of course, other factors beyond slave escapes contributed to growing North-South antagonism. Yet physical abolitionist involvement, real and alleged, in slave escapes helped produce the southern demand for federal protection of slavery in the Border South that led to the especially divisive Fugitive Slave Law of 1850. Just days after the hyperbolic *Pearl* debate in Congress, Butler, who chaired the Senate Judiciary Committee, introduced a bill to strengthen the Fugitive Slave Law of 1793. Although his brief on behalf of the bill portrayed it as necessary to counter abolitionist-inspired northern state personal liberty laws restricting renditions, Butler's timing suggests that events in Washington motivated him.[23] When the Senate failed to act during the limited amount of time left in the 1848 session, southern complaints about escapes escalated.

In January 1849 Calhoun asserted that northern resistance to the 1793 law through legislation, judicial decisions, and biracial mobs might force the South to "appeal to arms for redress." One month later a committee appointed by the Virginia House of Delegates called on "the senators and representatives from this state in the congress of the United States" to revive efforts to strengthen the Fugitive Slave Law. In January 1850 Virginia senator James M. Mason complied. He introduced a bill designed to diminish the role of state governments in fugitive slave renditions. The bill provided that masters and their agents, with or without a warrant from a federal judge or commissioner, could seize fugitive slaves. The bill also allowed federal marshals to enforce warrants and command citizens to assist in captures. Anyone who interfered with such a capture or with the return of an alleged escapee could be fined and imprisoned.[24]

Soon the slave escape issue fused into a wider sectional crisis that reshaped antislavery politics, the abolitionist relationship to that politics, and the national political framework. Several weeks before Mason introduced his bill, California Territory, which had been annexed to the United States as a result of the war against Mexico, applied for admission to the Union as a free-labor state. This application revived the issue of slavery in U.S. territories and encouraged demands for a comprehensive sectional compromise to save the Union. As presented by Henry Clay on January 29, 1850, such a compromise would admit California as a free-labor state, allow settlers in New Mexico and Utah territories to permit or disallow slavery, have the U.S. government pay the Texas state debt in return for slaveholding Texas giving up its claim to much of New Mexico, include Mason's fugitive slave bill, and abolish the slave trade (but not slavery) in the District of Columbia.[25]

As these measures advanced slowly through the Senate, slave escapes in the Chesapeake helped supporters of a stronger fugitive slave law defeat attempts to add provisions allowing alleged fugitive slaves access to writs of habeas corpus and jury trials. On August 3 eleven Maryland slaves escaped to a black man's farm located near Shrewsbury, Pennsylvania. There, with a mob's help, the escapees resisted recapture. On August 22 the *Baltimore Sun* reported an escape of between thirty and forty slaves from Maryland's Prince George County during "the last few days." The *Sun* attributed the escape to an "underground railroad." On August 26 the *Sun* noted that a violent confrontation at Harrisburg,

Pennsylvania, between Virginians seeking fugitive slaves and a black mob led to the arrest of the Virginians.[26]

The *Sun* could only assert abolitionist involvement in these events. But abolitionist action encouraged such assertions. On August 8, following a violent confrontation, Washington police had arrested William L. Chaplin (who had not been charged in regard to the *Pearl* escape attempt) as he drove a carriage north through the city with two slaves on board. The fact that Georgia congressman Alexander H. Stephens owned one of the slaves, and Stephens's colleague Robert Toombs owned the other, added to the incident's political impact. So did the Cazenovia, New York, "Fugitive Slave Convention" convened on August 21. Prominent black abolitionists, including Frederick Douglass, Charles B. Ray, and Jermain Wesley Loguen, and prominent white abolitionists, including Gerrit Smith, Samuel Joseph May, and James C. Jackson, participated. So did about forty fugitive slaves, two young women who had been on the *Pearl,* and a large audience including men and women of both races. Those gathered praised Chaplin and issued a "Letter to the American Slaves from those who have fled from American slavery." Written by Smith, the letter urged slaves to escape and promised them assistance.[27]

The Cazenovia Convention angered white southerners and divided them regionally. Senator David L. Yulee of Florida, representing the Lower South, argued in the U.S. Senate on August 23 that the meeting showed how abolitionist influence in the North made *any* fugitive slave law unenforceable. In contrast Border South journalists contended that the multiracial meeting at Cazenovia and its militant message fortified the necessity of passing Mason's bill. The *Sun* declared, "The black and white convention of madmen at Cazenovia" would strengthen northern support for the law. The *Washington Republic* promised the new law would have "a benign and wholesome influence."[28]

With Stephen A. Douglas's leadership, a series of shifting congressional alliances passed all the compromise measures. First came those dealing with slavery in the West. Then came those centering on the North-South sectional line. President Millard Fillmore signed Mason's fugitive slave bill into law on September 18. On September 20 Fillmore signed the bill abolishing the District of Columbia slave trade while maintaining slavery's legality there.[29] Physical abolitionism and advocacy of it, by encouraging proslavery reaction, helped secure the last two measures. But the new Fugitive Slave Law, by expanding slave catching and infringing on state sovereignty, challenged many northerners' conceptions of justice. Northern resistance to enforcement of the law drew abolitionists and antislavery politicians together. And the resistance angered southern politicians, even as conservative Democrats and Whigs, north and south, sought to quell sectional animosity.

Theodore Parker (1810–1860) was a Unitarian minister and independent abolitionist who corresponded with Charles Sumner and other antislavery politicians. (Print Department Collection, Boston Public Library)

To further encourage abolitionist cooperation with antislavery politicians, Samuel Joseph May in May 1850 had referred to the "Higher Law" speech that William H. Seward had delivered in the U.S. Senate during the preceding March in opposition to the extension of slavery. May also referred to a speech Seward had presented in Cleveland in 1848. May noted that in the earlier speech Seward had asked his audience to "extend a cordial welcome to the fugitive who lays his weary limbs at your door, and *defend him as you would your household gods.*" Using the abolitionist rhetorical tactic of combining criticism with praise, May observed that although Seward fell "far short of what to us seems the true and the right . . . he has rendered himself specially obnoxious to the slaveocracy . . . and therefore we ought to uphold him." As violent confrontations occurred throughout the North as a result of the new Fugitive Slave Law, abolitionists used the clashes to encourage other politicians to express sentiments similar to Seward's.[30]

In mid-October a large, racially integrated anti–Fugitive Slave Law meeting at Faneuil Hall in Boston brought abolitionists and politicians together. Henry I. Bowditch, Frederick Douglass, Charles Ingersoll, Theodore Parker, Wendell Phillips, Josiah Quincy, Charles Lenox Remond, and Samuel E. Sewell represented the former. Charles Francis Adams (who presided) John A. Andrew, Thomas Wentworth Higginson, Charles Sumner, and James A. Briggs (who edited the Cleveland

Free Democrat) represented the latter. Douglass, Parker, Phillips, Remond, and Briggs spoke. The *Liberator* referred to what went on at the meeting as "Rocking the Old Cradle of Liberty." Between fall 1850 and spring 1851, similar meetings occurred in Boston, Lynn, and Worcester, Massachusetts.[31]

Cooperation between abolitionists and antislavery politicians continued in Massachusetts because of repeated confrontations over slave renditions within the state. In Boston during February 1851, abolitionist Lewis Hayden led a group of black men who daringly rescued fugitive slave Shadrach Minkins from a courtroom and sent him on to Canada. This incident and abolitionist resistance to the successful rendition of Thomas Sims from Boston to Georgia during April 1851 prompted antislavery politicians Richard Henry Dana and Sumner to urge the Massachusetts legislature to strengthen the state's personal liberty laws. Physical resistance to slave renditions and a sermon by Theodore Parker impressed on Sumner the centrality of the fugitive slave issue as he prepared to enter the U.S. Senate. "No other form of the slavery question," Sumner assured Parker, "not even the Wilmot Proviso . . . offered equal advantages in defeating 'the slave power.'" Meanwhile the Sims case led abolitionists Phillips and Parker to cooperate with Free Soiler Higginson on a vigilance committee. The cooperation in turn led Higginson to become an abolitionist.[32]

Abolitionists in western New York also encouraged antislavery politicians to speak and act against the Fugitive Slave Law. In January 1851 the Garrisonian Western New York Anti-Slavery Society passed a resolution praising Seward, Hale, Chase, Mann, Giddings, Thaddeus Stevens of Pennsylvania, and Charles Durkee of Wisconsin for opposing the law and slavery extension. The society simultaneously criticized these politicians for supporting the "pro-slavery compromises of the Constitution." The following October federal marshals arrested a black man named Jerry (also known as William Henry) in Syracuse as RPAs held a meeting there. Instigated by Samuel Joseph May, Gerrit Smith, Samuel Ringgold Ward, and Jermain W. Loguen, who attended the meeting, a biracial mob freed Jerry from custody. A grand jury then indicted about twenty-five men, not including the instigators, for rioting.[33]

The Jerry rescue and the following indictments influenced Seward, who offered to serve as defense counsel for those indicted. And May sought other antislavery politicians to speak on behalf of the rescuers as a means of promoting integration of abolitionists and antislavery politicians. In January 1852 he invited Mann to come to Syracuse. Later that year May invited Giddings, Chase, Hale, Samuel Lewis (a former Liberty abolitionist from Cincinnati), and Charles Francis Adams to speak at what became an annual series of Jerry Rescue Celebration meetings. None of the politicians accepted May's invitation, but three sent letters to be read at the meeting. Chase in his letter approached RPA rhetoric in declaring that, on the basis of "natural justice and revealed religion," the Fugitive Slave Act was "no law." Lewis in his "rejoice[d]" that Jerry had been rescued "from torture and cruelty more severe than any other land on God's green earth would tolerate." Lewis also expressed a belief that "there are influences at work, which . . . will redeem the land from the blight and curse of slavery . . . at no distant day." Adams in his letter more reservedly deplored that the country had reached a point "when . . . respectable citizens feel justified in rejoicing that a law has been successfully resisted." He hoped that at a "time not long distant," the "cessation of slavery" would prevent the "scandal of further such attempts." In response to an invitation to attend the following year's anniversary, Giddings praised the rescuers and denounced the Fugitive Slave Law as "the most flagrant violation of the Constitution, of God's law and man's inalienable rights."[34]

In contrast to the abolitionists and the politicians they targeted, most northerners endorsed the Compromise of 1850, including the new Fugitive Slave Law. They believed responsible politicians, including Henry Clay, Daniel Webster, and Stephen A. Douglas, had in a struggle against fanatics North and South settled the slavery issue and kept the country united. Patriotic "Union" meetings proliferated, and mob attacks on abolition meetings revived. As suspicion of abolitionism intensified, disintegration of the Free Soil Party, which had begun soon after the 1848 election, accelerated. Residual loyalty among Free Soilers to one or the other of the major parties and the attractiveness of their economic policies had roles in this. So did hope that state-level alliances with one or the other of the major parties could advance black rights. And some Free Soil leaders sought to gain public office with major party assistance. All these factors contributed to the formation of electoral coalitions that by 1851 had gravely weakened the third party.[35]

In Ohio Chase, supported by a large majority of the state's Free Soilers, favored merger with the Democratic Party. In return, during 1849, the Democratic majority in the state legislature passed a bill ending the state's discriminatory black laws. The legislature also elected Chase to the U.S. Senate. In New York most of the Barnburner element of the Free Soil Party embraced the compromise, abandoned the Wilmot Proviso, and returned to the Democratic Party. Although many of these Barnburners retained an antislavery commitment, particularly regarding the Fugitive Slave Law, they did not upon their return to the Democratic Party have the strength to set party policy. In 1852 RPA William Goodell declared the New York Free Soil Party "extinct."[36]

In Massachusetts the Free Soil Party unraveled more slowly. It had emerged from the 1848 state elections stronger than the state's Democratic Party. This led to a coalition of Free Soilers and Democrats against the Massachusetts Whig Party, in which the Free Soilers could make more demands on Democrats than was the case in Ohio. Even so opposition from Whiggish Free Soilers and resistance among Democrats loyal to the compromise made cooperation difficult. The result was that Massachusetts Free Soilers achieved little beyond electing Sumner to the U.S. Senate in April 1851.[37]

As Free Soil mergers with largely proslavery Democrats took place, abolitionist hope for antislavery politics declined. John G. Whittier recognized the threat coalition politics posed to progress against the Fugitive Slave Law and toward universal emancipation. But Whittier's poor health and increased literary production limited his influence. Therefore others better represented abolitionist concerns. The Garrisonian *Anti-Slavery Bugle,* overlooking that Chase had never been an abolitionist, charged that he had "abandoned his principles" to advance his political career. Lewis Tappan added, "Alas! That such a man should, for the sake of office, commit such an act." Frederick Douglass, who had become a RPA, maintained that the Free Soil Party had "perished because it was held together by no imperishable principle." When Congress passed the Compromise of 1850, Douglass wrote that the Free Soil Party had "expired for want of a tangible and definite object."[38]

Similarly the MASS emphasized that the Free Soil Party had not organized on "a vital principle"—not even denationalization. Rather the party only opposed slavery expansion into territories gained from Mexico and did so while accepting a proslavery constitutional framework. The MASS quoted Hale's assertions that he did not wish to threaten "Slavery at the South," and that Free Soilers "should be held responsible to the limit of the Constitutional obligation, for everything that may be required for the support and sustenance of American slavery." Even Giddings had declared that Free Soilers must "observe to the very letter" requirements under the Fugitive Slave Law not to help, defend, or rescue fugitive slaves.[39]

Nevertheless the MASS continued the abolitionist policy of mixing criticism with praise. It distinguished between what constituted principled action for abolitionists and what constituted principled action for those who sought elective office. On that basis, prior to the Free Soil Party's disintegration, the MASS expressed "a high respect for the gentlemen who compose the leadership of the Free Soil Party." The society, along with all abolitionists, understood that Free Soil engagement in state-level coalition politics had led to the election to Congress of a core of outspoken critics of slaveholders. In the Senate there were Chase, Hale, Sumner, Seward, and Benjamin F. Wade. In the House of

Representatives there were Charles Allen of Massachusetts, Amos Tuck of New Hampshire, Giddings and Joseph Root of Ohio, George W. Julian of Indiana, and Charles Durkee of Wisconsin.[40]

Most of these politicians had longstanding abolitionist ties, and Sumner had the closest connection of all. Abolitionists influenced his decision to run for the Senate and supported him in the effort, which required them to compromise their principles. In return abolitionists sought to shape Sumner's course of action. Upon Sumner's election, Theodore Parker urged him to be "in morals, not in politics." Parker warned Sumner, "I expect heroism of the most heroic kind," and "I am not easily pleased." Parker believed, as had abolitionists for decades, that U.S. senators' words and deeds could more effectively influence the nation than those of any moral reformer. Similarly, as Sumner departed Boston for Washington, Whittier urged him to enlist Seward, William Cullen Bryant of the *New York Post,* and Horace Greeley of the *New York Tribune* in counteracting "Union savers."[41]

Once Sumner began his Senate career, Garrisonians monitored his conduct. Early in 1852, when Sumner failed to present a petition seeking to have *Pearl* crew members Drayton and Sayres released from Washington Jail and instead sought a presidential pardon for them, Garrison and Phillips mildly criticized him. When Sumner failed to call for repeal of the Fugitive Slave Law, Phillips warned him that both abolitionists and those who remained Free Soilers were asking, "Do you put trust in C.S.?" Phillips added that when Sumner diverged from Garrisonians' views, he "must bear the burden of a public expression of their discontent." Phillips assured Sumner that he and his colleagues acted not out of personal hostility but in "honest love for a movement which they feel so many sacrifices have been made."[42]

Through July into August 1852 Garrisonian (as well as Whig and Free Soil) criticism of Sumner mounted as proslavery senators blocked his attempts to speak on the Fugitive Slave Law. Parker wrote to Sumner, "I have . . . defended you in your delay of speaking, though *to me* it has seemed unwise & even dangerous to defer it so long." Sumner responded that "nothing but death, or deadly injustice" could keep him "from speaking." And on August 26 Sumner gained the Senate floor to present his "Freedom National; Slavery Sectional" speech, which endorsed denationalizing slavery to encourage gradual emancipation in the South.[43]

As usual abolitionists greeted the speech with praise and criticism. Parker described it as "a grand speech, well researched, well arranged, well written," "masterly," and popular with the "masses." Lydia Maria Child declared the speech to be "magnificent." But William Goodell and Wendell Phillips pointed out that "freedom national" need not free a single slave in the southern states. Sumner had said that once "banished from the National jurisdiction," slavery "may linger in the state as a local institution, but will no longer engender national animosities." Phillips disagreed, contending that slavery "will continue to vex our National politics while it exists." Sumner and other Free Soilers, Phillips observed, only proposed to put slavery "back where it was in 1789." What proof did such politicians have that "if so . . . limited it will behave better?" The MASS declared denationalization to be "far . . . from striking at the root of the evil tree." It noted that while Sumner had described the unconstitutionality of the Fugitive Slave Act of 1850, he did not deny the constitutionality of fugitive slave renditions.[44]

This abolitionist criticism irritated Sumner but did not alienate him. He wrote of Phillips, "He may have criticized me . . . but I know he has said nothing unkind of me." In turn Garrisonians recognized Sumner's right to "form and carry out his own plan," while emphasizing their duty to be "critical." They wanted to treat Sumner no differently than they had "Mr. GIDDINGS, Mr. MANN . . . Mr. HALE, and every Anti-Slavery member of Congress." Phillips informed Sumner that Garrisonians would "mete out to . . . [him] the same measure as they did to erring Whigs and Democrats."[45]

As Massachusetts abolitionists influenced Sumner, New York abolitionists attempted to influence that state's Free Soil remnant, which had adopted the name Free Democratic Party. RPAs Lewis Tappan and Gerrit Smith and ambivalent Garrisonian Samuel May Jr., who was Samuel Joseph May's first cousin, hoped to unite all who opposed slavery, including abolitionists and former Free Soilers in the Free Democratic Party in order to counter pro-compromise conservatism. Simultaneously Free Democratic leaders Giddings and Samuel Lewis hoped to build the party into an organization that could protect the Wilmot Proviso and the principle of denationalization against compromise or obliteration that would result from coalition with, or absorption into, one of the major parties or factions thereof.[46]

When Giddings and Lewis organized a "National Convention of the Friends of Freedom," which met in Cleveland on September 24, 1851, to prepare for an 1852 Free Democratic presidential campaign, several RPA leaders attended. They included Tappan (whom Giddings had invited), Smith, William Goodell, and F. Julius LeMoyne, who presided. Their goal was to have the convention's platform go beyond denationalization to declare slavery illegal everywhere and move toward advocacy of immediate emancipation. But while the convention declared the Fugitive Slave Law of 1850 to be a "violation of the principles of natural and revealed religion," it stood by denationalization. Tappan accepted this as progress and called for a Free Democratic national nominating convention for the 1852 national election to be held in Pittsburgh.[47]

Lewis, who chaired the arrangement committee for the Pittsburgh convention and at times expressed views similar to the RPAs, hoped to hold that convention before the Whig and Democratic national conventions, which were scheduled for June 1852. Meeting early, Lewis believed, would avoid attracting "nominal anti-slavery men" from the major parties who might further weaken the Free Democratic platform. Meeting early would also open the way for RPAs to lead a relatively small gathering and attract abolitionist support by adopting a platform radical enough to preclude cooperation with such Democrats or Whigs. But in December 1851 Free Democratic leaders who advocated exactly such cooperation decided at a meeting in Washington that "no judicious action could be taken by the Free Soil [Free Democratic] men until the field had been fairly opened by the actions of the two other parties." As a result, the Free Democratic convention did not meet until well after the Democrats and Whigs had chosen platforms and presidential candidates. Frederick Douglass predicted that this meant the Free Democrats would keep coalitionist options open by pledging "to denationalize and sectionalize and not to abolish slavery."[48]

The 1852 Whig and Democratic conventions had endorsed the Compromise of 1850 measures as the final solution to sectional discord and opposed further antislavery agitation. Tappan responded by attempting to persuade Free Democratic leaders *not* to adopt a platform designed to attract Whig and Democratic nonextensionists who might be alienated by the major party platforms. He urged "the friends of Liberty to summon high principles, not only against the *extension* but the *existence* of Slavery." But, once again, antislavery coalitionists among Free Democrats did seek to attract former Free Soilers, especially those in the Democratic Party who might not support a pro-compromise platform or that party's proslavery presidential nominee, Franklin Pierce. Therefore Lewis disregarded immediatist advice and issued a call for a Free Democratic national convention that embraced all who had supported the anti-extensionist 1848 Free Soil platform. Tappan, Smith, LeMoyne, Douglass, and other RPAs nevertheless decided to attend the convention to push for resolutions in favor of universal emancipation.[49]

As the convention convened at Pittsburgh in August, Smith and Tappan shared the podium with Giddings and convention chair Henry Wilson. Smith also served on the platform committee. Douglass attended as a delegate from New York, and on August 11 he told a large audience, "I am, of course, for circumscribing and damaging slavery in every way I can. But my motto is extermination. . . . Slavery has no rightful existence anywhere. The slaveholders not only forfeit their right to liberty, but to life itself." This was too much for most of the delegates, who regarded denationalization as the only constitutional and potentially successful political antislavery doctrine. Giddings's majority report for the platform committee called for denationalization. Smith's minority report declared slavery "incapable" of legalization. Former Liberty abolitionist and current Free Democrat Sherman M. Booth of Wisconsin produced a compromise stating that no legislation could make slavery "right." Aimed at vagueness so as to appeal to anti-extensionists and RPAs, Booth's resolution also declared "that Christianity, humanity, and patriotism" demanded "abolition." This became a plank in the platform on which Free Democratic presidential nominee John P. Hale and vice presidential candidate George W. Julian campaigned. Other planks declared the Fugitive Slave Law to be unconstitutional and denied that the compromise could be final.[50]

When the RPAs at Pittsburgh fell short of placing immediate abolitionism in the Free Democratic platform, LeMoyne and Goodell denounced the platform as "too conservative." In September Smith and three other RPAs sent letters to Hale and Julian requesting that the candidates indicate whether they believed in equal rights and that slavery was "a matchless crime . . . which no Constitution nor Legislature, nor Judiciary can afford the least possible shelter." When neither candidate responded, Smith organized the tiny National Liberty Party, which nominated Goodell for president on a slavery illegal everywhere platform.[51]

Douglass reacted more pragmatically to the Free Democratic platform than did LeMoyne, Goodell, and Smith. As Douglass had in regard to the Free Soil Party in 1848, he welcomed this platform as a step in the right direction. In a *Frederick Douglass' Paper* editorial he pledged to support the Free Democratic ticket so long as neither Hale nor Julian wrote compromising letters when they accepted their nomination. In a mid-October speech Douglass predicted that if the Free Democrats received a "strong vote . . . slavery will be checked. . . . Otherwise, slavery may run rampant." Aiming at an audience beyond abolitionists, Douglass wrote, "It is idle and short-sighted to regard this question as merely relating to the liberties of the colored people."[52]

Garrisonians responded to the Free Democrats' presidential ticket and platform in a manner similar to their former colleague. The MASS described denationalization as "a political impossibility to be achieved, and . . . a moral inequity if it could be brought about." But Garrisonians also distinguished between *flawed* Free Democrats and *proslavery* Democrats and Whigs. They praised "such men as Hale, Sumner, Mann, Giddings, and Chase, [for] earnestly endeavoring to resist the encroachments of the Slave Power."

Garrisonians praised the RPA-influenced plank in the Free Democratic platform, which suggested that slavery was always a crime. They also praised the
antislavery (but not necessarily abolitionist) planks that declared the Fugitive
Slave Law of 1850 unconstitutional and denied that the Compromise of 1850
could be final.[53]

If the Free Democratic Party had been more successful in the 1852 elections,
abolitionists might have more uniformly viewed it as a positive step. But the
return of the Barnburners to the Democratic Party, which had opened the Free
Democrats to greater abolitionist influence, also reduced the third party vote.
Many antislavery Whigs preferred their party's presidential candidate, Winfield
Scott, over Hale. And proslavery Democratic candidate Franklin Pierce of New
Hampshire and his party won a decisive victory in the election. Out of nearly
4 million votes cast, Hale received 156,667. In 1848 Free Soilers had elected
nine men to the House of Representatives. In 1852 Free Democrats elected two
(Giddings and his neighbor Edward Wade, a former Liberty abolitionist and
Benjamin Wade's younger brother). RPA Gerrit Smith also gained a seat in the
House.[54]

During Giddings's difficult reelection campaign in a new Western Reserve
district gerrymandered against him, a variety of abolitionists, including Cassius M. Clay, William Jay, Smith, Elizur Wright Jr., and Theodore Parker, provided letters of support. A similarly broad range of abolitionists helped Smith,
who campaigned on an illegality of slavery platform in his western New York
district. Free Democrat Giddings joined abolitionists Douglass and Samuel Joseph May in campaigning for Smith, who became the most radical abolitionist
ever elected to Congress.[55]

Abolitionists drew inspiration from Giddings's and Smith's relatively small
victories. Tappan appraised the election of "ultra abolitionist" Smith as "a significant sign of the times." According to Tappan, Smith's victory meant "the
time is approaching when the great body of the people will . . . overleap
the divisions of party and elect . . . friends of Humanity and freedom." The *Liberator* perceptively noted that "radical of radicals, 'ultra,' 'disorganizer,' 'infidel,'
and 'traitorous'" Smith owed "his election to Whigs and Democrats, who gave
him a strong support, in the face of all his heresies." Continued physical resistance to the Fugitive Slave Law and the popularity of Harriet Beecher Stowe's
great novel *Uncle Tom's Cabin* also inspired abolitionist optimism concerning
the political system.[56]

At the small Free Democratic Pittsburgh convention, RPAs, working with
politicians who regarded themselves as radicals, had performed relatively well.

But the convention was not a major political event. In its 1853 annual report, the MASS gave much greater coverage to resistance to the Fugitive Slave
Law than to electoral politics.[57] In fact abolitionists between 1845 and 1852
had exercised a more profound impact on American politics through physical
action and their relationships with antislavery politicians than through electoral politics.

7

Abolitionists and Republicans, 1852–1860

By the early 1850s abolitionist involvement in antislavery politics had existed for over a century and a half. It spanned the colonial, revolutionary, early national, Jacksonian, and antebellum eras. Ties between *immediate* abolitionists and antislavery politicians had existed since the 1830s. As older generations of abolitionists and politicians passed away, younger men and (among abolitionists) women maintained the ties. As antislavery political parties broke apart, weakened, and ceased to exist, new parties came into existence.

In contrast to generational change and fluctuating political organizations, continuity dominated abolitionist principles and tactics. Radical political abolitionists (RPAs) had since the late 1830s held that slavery could never be legal. They continued to believe so during the 1850s. Garrisonians had since the early 1840s called for disunion. They continued to do so during the 1850s. Abolitionist petitioning of state legislatures and Congress also continued. So did abolitionist circulation of propaganda and public speaking. Abolitionists continued to invite antislavery politicians to their meetings, correspond with such politicians, and develop personal relationships with them. Physical abolitionist action continued to have a political impact.

It is true that during the early 1850s abolitionists worried, for several reasons, about the fate of their movement. Despite widespread northern resistance to the Fugitive Slave Law of 1850, government efforts to enforce it convinced RPA James G. Birney and such black leaders as Henry Highland Garnet and Martin R. Delaney that only black migration to the Caribbean or Africa could establish black rights. In January 1853 Garrisonian Parker Pillsbury reported to the Massachusetts Anti-Slavery Society (MASS) annual meeting that "he had witnessed a great decline of Anti-Slavery interest" in New England. He blamed it on the Free Democratic leaders' "over-cautious policy." Meanwhile abolitionist newspaper circulation and organizations declined. In 1854 the MASS stopped issuing annual reports. In 1855 the American and Foreign Anti-Slavery Society (AFASS) ceased to exist. That same year the American Anti-Slavery Society's (AASS) annual income dropped. And Lydia Maria Child "lost patience with [such] societies as instruments of reform."[1]

Yet well-publicized cases of physical resistance to the Fugitive Slave Law of 1850, along with nonabolitionist Harriet Beecher Stowe's *Uncle Tom's Cabin*, enhanced northern sympathy for escapees and resentment of the Slave Power. These events opened the way for an abolitionist resurgence. So did the likelihood that the Democratic Party victory in the 1852 national election would produce new efforts to expand slavery. And there was the appearance of a younger generation of abolitionist leaders who did not fit into established patterns. Thomas Wentworth Higginson, Samuel Gridley Howe, and George L. Stearns had been Conscience Whigs and Free Soilers. During the 1850s each of these men endorsed violent means against slavery, attended Garrisonian meetings, and continued to identify with nonabolitionist political parties. At the January 1853 MASS meeting, Higginson "spoke in favor of the most thorough agitation . . . on the subject of Slavery . . . according to the principles and methods of this Society," while declaring himself to be a member of the Free Democratic Party. Based on these developments, John G. Whittier advised J. Miller McKim (who led the Pennsylvania Anti-Slavery Society) that, despite setbacks, abolitionists had "brought Freedom and Despotism, Light and Darkness, Christianity and Heathenism, Face to Face" before the nation. Whittier believed they had "hastened the long foreseen crisis" between the North and South.[2]

Abolitionists worked to push the nation's political party system toward such a crisis. They sought a political revolution that would produce a major northern political party favorable to general emancipation. In 1848 Garrisonians and RPAs had vainly hoped to mold the Free Soil Party into such a party. In 1852 RPAs had failed to turn the Free Democratic Party into an abolitionist organization. By 1853 the likelihood that abolitionists could influence the national party system seemed more promising. The previous year's election had resulted in the collapse of the Whig Party south of the border slave-labor states, and a rising nativist movement against foreign immigrants and Roman Catholics had undermined the Whig Party in the North.[3]

Months before the Democratic Party's decisive 1852 electoral victory, Theodore Parker had predicted that such a victory would lead to new two-party system. It would, he wrote, consist of a "Hunker" party, devoted to slavery, and a "Party of Freedom," formed by antislavery Whigs and Free Democrats. An abolitionist identified only as J.T. suggested a similar scenario in an article published in the *Frederick Douglass' Paper*. J.T. predicted that antislavery Whigs and antislavery Democrats would "fall into the embrace of the Free Democracy," while the national Whig and Democratic Parties disintegrated. Shortly after the election Wendell Phillips wrote, "The recent total annihilation of the National Whig Party . . . is, probably, destined to result in the formation very soon of two great parties, Northern & Southern." He believed this would be "the beginning of the end" for slavery. Parker and J.T. between them identified antislavery politicians Salmon P. Chase, Charles Durkee, Horace Greeley, Joshua R. Giddings, John P. Hale, Horace Mann, William H. Seward, Charles Sumner, and Thurlow Weed, plus abolitionist Gerrit Smith, as likely leaders in forming such a northern antislavery party.[4]

In April 1853 Frederick Douglass assured Seward, who had become a U.S. senator, that because "slave holders fear you, I will trust you." Douglass praised Seward's ability "to command and give Shape to the cause of your country, and to the cause of human liberty." He urged Seward to leave the Whig Party and lead "a great party of freedom." The following November Whittier advised Sumner that the Massachusetts Free Democrats, having ended their coalition with the state's Democrats, must return to their "old platform" (denationalization) and "unite all who are sick of the rule of the slave-power."[5]

To help reach such goals, abolitionists continued to interact publicly with antislavery politicians whom they believed they could influence. A striking example of this occurred in May 1853 when William Lloyd Garrison, Kentucky state-level abolitionist Cassius M. Clay (a distant cousin of Henry Clay), and John Jay (abolitionist son of William Jay) attended a Free Democratic dinner in Boston to honor Hale at the end of his first term in the U.S. Senate. With antislavery politicians Hale, Sumner, Palfrey, Mann, Charles Francis Adams, Henry Wilson, Anson Burlingame, and Richard H. Dana Jr. listening, Clay called for "The Union of ALL the opponents of the propaganda of slavery." Garrison declared that despite differing views "as to the best measures to be adopted, or the precise position to be occupied . . . we are all 'Hale fellows.'" When Garrison then asked how many in the hall favored "the immediate and everlasting overthrow of slavery," nearly everyone shouted "Aye!"[6]

Such camaraderie did not prevent abolitionists from maintaining their policy of castigating antislavery politicians for their inconsistency and irresolution. The previous January, at the MASS annual meeting, Parker Pillsbury had claimed that the "Freedom National; Slavery Sectional" speech that Sumner had delivered during August 1852 had more "effect in fastening the chains of the slaves" than Daniel Webster's "Seventh of March" speech in favor of the Compromise of 1850. At the same meeting Stephen S. Foster had criticized Free Democratic politicians, excepting only Giddings, for not engaging their constituents in face-to-face discussions of slavery issues. And Garrison had introduced resolutions upbraiding Sumner for his silence and Hale for his levity in response to the Senate's decision in 1852 to bar them from committee service.[7]

Wendell Phillips capped the MASS meeting with a speech entitled "The Philosophy of the Abolition Movement." In this speech he asserted that abolitionists had created political antislavery and sustained it by provoking slaveholders to "assault" the right of petition, freedom of speech, and freedom of press; to annex Texas; and to pass the Fugitive Slave Law of 1850. "Old-fashioned, fanatical, crazy" abolitionists, Phillips added, had originated "every important argument or idea that has been broached [by politicians] on the Anti-Slavery question from 1830 to the present time." Phillips contended that although Free Democrats mistakenly tried to be moderate and conciliatory to distinguish themselves from abolitionists, they had come to "rely on the same arguments" as their abolitionist mentors. Then Phillips denounced Mann and Sumner for asserting that Free Democrats had "no wish to interfere with Slavery in the States; that they 'consent to let Slavery remain where it is.'" For Phillips, as for Pillsbury and others, denationalization meant forever keeping "the Slave beneath the heel of his master." As had Stephen S. Foster before him, Phillips excepted Giddings from his critique. He described Giddings as "one of the original Abolition party . . . a large contributor to our Anti-Slavery resources."[8]

When antislavery politicians Sumner, Seward, and Mann responded to abolitionists, they revealed a great deal about their relationship to the movement. Shortly after Phillips spoke, Sumner insisted (contrary to abolitionists) that denationalization would break "the backbone of the Slave Power" and allow "Anti-Slavery sentiment . . . [to] find a free course." But Sumner, as usual, also expressed admiration for Phillips and abolitionists generally. He stated that abolitionists influenced his views, and he expressed distrust of his fellow politicians. The following August Sumner's speech at Plymouth, Massachusetts, entitled "Finger-Point from Plymouth Rock," contained the line: "Better to be the despised Pilgrim, a fugitive for freedom, than the halting politician, forgetful of principle, 'with a Senate at his heels.'" That September, in a letter to independent abolitionist Parker, Seward joined Sumner in acknowledging abolitionist influence. He claimed that in developing his antislavery views, he "took [his] latitude and longitude first from Massachusetts." Acknowledging that Parker worked in a "bolder and more energetic way" for abolition than he did, he claimed that they shared "the same great principles." Mann, about to leave politics to become president of Antioch College, reacted differently. He accused Phillips of misrepresenting him. He asserted that reality, not antislavery politicians, kept slavery in existence in the South. And he denied taking rhetorical "weapons from the armory of the abolitionists." He would, he wrote, "never imitate the spirit that arrogates where it cannot create, denounces where it cannot argue, and flies in the face of all the best friends of the cause it professed to cherish."[9]

The difference between Sumner's and Seward's points of view in 1853 and Mann's did not so much represent a split in Free Democrats' outlook as an ambivalence that had long characterized both sides in the relationship between abolitionists and antislavery politicians. Sumner, who had read the *Liberator* since 1835, had written in 1850 regarding that newspaper, "I have never been satisfied with its tone. . . . It has seemed to me often vindictive, bitter & unchristian." Sumner disliked disunionism as much as abolitionists disliked denationalization. As Phillips and Mann exchanged charges in 1853, Sumner declined to participate in what he called "the feud between brothers." But he suggested to Parker that "the position of our pioneer friends [Garrisonians] seems more untenable and less *practical."* Phillips, Sumner observed, would do better to direct his "skill and eloquence . . . not against allies but against Slavery and its enormities—against its influence on our Government." For his part, Seward reminded Parker that politicians could not move far ahead of public opinion.[10]

Strained ties between abolitionists and antislavery politicians did not end. Abolitionists continued to denounce as well as praise and prod. Politicians, restrained by the Constitution, devoted to the Union, and more influenced by racism, continued when it suited them to ignore abolitionists or push back. Even so the relationship between abolitionists and antislavery politicians changed as a result of Stephen A. Douglas's introduction of his Nebraska bill in January 1854. This bill proposed to repeal the Missouri Compromise's prohibition of slavery in territories north of the 36° 30′ line of latitude, divide Nebraska Territory into two territories (Nebraska in the North and Kansas in the South), and allow settlers to legalize or ban slavery in each. Douglas introduced the bill because he wanted to organize Kansas Territory to facilitate building a railroad to the Pacific Coast that would benefit his home state of Illinois and his home city of Chicago. Southern leaders hoped to use Douglas's bill, which became the Kansas-Nebraska Act, to establish slavery in Kansas and thereby protect slavery in Missouri by securing that state's western border against escapes.[11]

Three weeks after Douglas introduced his bill, Chase, Giddings, and Sumner wrote the "Appeal of the Independent Democrats to the People of the United States." They recruited three additional signees (Free Democrats Edward Wade of Ohio and Alexander De Witt of Massachusetts and abolitionist Gerrit Smith) and published the appeal in the *Congressional Globe, National Era,* and *New York Times.* It described the Nebraska bill as part of a plot to extend slavery at the expense of white northerners who wanted to move west. It favored nonextension of slavery rather than abolition or denationalization. It endorsed the Missouri Compromise and accepted the Compromise of 1850's opening of New Mexico and Utah territories to slavery expansion.[12]

Neither the Nebraska bill nor the "Appeal" caused an immediate northern reaction. Even abolitionists took more than a week to recognize the act's significance. Nevertheless Parker's "The Nebraska Question" sermon, presented at Boston's Music Hall on February 12, which concentrated on moral and political opposition to slavery *expansion,* impacted "Anti-Nebraska" politicians. Chase objected to Unitarian minister Parker's denial in the sermon of the "Divine origin of the Bible and the Divine nature of Christ." Chase also found some of Parker's language too harsh. But Chase lauded Parker's "defense of justice, truth, and right against oppression, falsehood, and wrong." Parker's "lofty sentiments," Chase wrote, inspired him "with fresh determination to maintain the right." And Chase called on Parker to encourage anti-Nebraska public meetings and petitions. Parker in turn expressed "admiration" for Chase and claimed that he shared Chase's antislavery political views. In addition to Chase, Parker interacted with Sumner. He praised Sumner's February 21 Senate speech against the Nebraska bill, which (like Parker's sermon) only opposed the further extension of slavery while condemning the institution's barbarism and immorality. Parker suggested to Sumner that abolitionists and antislavery politicians shared the same mission, same struggle for righteousness, and same fate. Parker's prediction that "we shall be beaten—*beaten—beaten* . . . but must fight still" became literally true for Sumner.[13]

Parker also influenced Seward. Since the 1830s several abolitionists had expressed the view that "Freedom and Slavery" were "antagonistic forms" that could not "long continue" to coexist. In a February 17, 1854, Senate speech, Seward came close to this view by portraying the Nebraska bill as an example of an existential conflict "between conservatism and progress, between truth and error, between right and wrong." In early May Parker, having read Seward's speech, wrote to Seward (among others) elaborating on this theme. There were, Parker suggested, three possible trajectories for the United States: the North and South could separate, freedom could "destroy Slavery," or slavery could "destroy Freedom." When on May 22 Seward again spoke against the Nebraska bill, he followed Parker in declaring that "fundamental antagonism [existed] between slavery and freedom," which must lead either to separation or to victory of one over the other. Shortly thereafter Seward acknowledged Parker's influence and urged Parker to continue his efforts to "awaken the [North's] public conscience" as Seward worked in Congress against the Slave Power.[14]

Opposition to the Nebraska bill also brought a new abolition lobbyist to Washington. As congressional debate continued, *Frederick Douglass' Paper* assistant editor Julia Griffiths (an English woman on an extended visit to the United States) arrived in the capital city. She lodged with Gerrit Smith, praised his service in the House, visited both houses of Congress, and attended a presidential levee hosted by Franklin Pierce and his wife. Griffiths judged most senators to be "entirely unequal" to their "vast" responsibilities, and ridiculed "traitor" Stephen A. Douglas. But she had "very pleasant" interviews with Seward and Chase, as well as with Giddings and Gamaliel Bailey. She informed Frederick Douglass that, were he in Washington, he "would sympathize deeply with the little [Senate] band who go for *Freedom,*" even though that band called for action against slavery expansion rather than against slavery itself. Shortly thereafter Douglass wrote to Sumner thanking him for his February 21 speech against the Nebraska bill. Without such speeches, Douglass warned, "this wicked measure will pass." Even *with* such speeches, the bill passed, and President Pierce signed it into law on May 30. Implementation of the Kansas-Nebraska Act led to civil war in Kansas Territory and began a sequence of events that further undermined the Whig Party, splintered the northern wing of the Democratic Party, and encouraged formation of a new major party.[15]

Eleven days before the Kansas-Nebraska Act became law Parker had proposed a July 4 free-labor-state convention to oppose its enforcement. He called on the northern people to "interfere, and take things out of the hands of the politicians." Although Chase, Seward, Sumner, and Hale rejected this strategy, they agreed with Parker's objective. They and other antislavery politicians had already begun holding state-level meetings to create political organizations that would appeal to northern Whigs, antislavery Democrats, and Free Democrats. Some of the meetings, such as that held at Columbus, Ohio, in March 1854, were conservative enough to endorse the Compromise of 1850. But when abolitionists Owen Lovejoy, Zebina Eastman, and Ichabod Codding met with anti-Nebraska politicians at Springfield, Illinois, that October, the result was a stronger anti-extensionist platform that also called for jury trials in fugitive slave cases.[16] As this call for jury trials suggests, abolitionist involvement in resistance to the Fugitive Slave Act of 1850 had a role in the formation of what became the Republican Party.

On May 26, 1854, Parker, Phillips, and Samuel Gridley Howe among others spoke at Faneuil Hall against the arrest by federal marshals two days earlier of fugitive slave Anthony Burns. Their speeches aroused a biracial mob that, under Thomas Wentworth Higginson's leadership, attacked a courthouse and killed one of the marshals in a failed attempt to rescue Burns. As state and federal troops occupied the city, opposition to the Fugitive Slave Law of 1850 spread. A Massachusetts petition begging for repeal of the law gained almost three thousand signatures. On June 12 Sumner assured Parker he would present the petition in the Senate. Instead, on June 22, Massachusetts's other senator, Julius Rockwell, presented it. That did not prevent a debate between proslavery senators and Sumner.[17]

During the debate James C. Jones of Tennessee linked the Massachusetts petition to "such miserable miscreants as Parker, Phillips, and such kindred spirits." Sumner responded by comparing abolitionist "fanaticism" to the role of Boston residents in starting the American Revolution. When South Carolina senator Andrew P. Butler asked Sumner if he would follow the U.S. Constitution in helping to return a fugitive slave to the slave's master, Sumner replied that he would not. On June 29 Sumner submitted another petition calling for the repeal of the Fugitive Slave Law.[18]

Abolitionists Garrison, Parker, Phillips, John Jay, and Whittier welcomed Sumner's words. On June 27 Garrison described the senator "as one who has given his reputation and all he can offer upon the altar of freedom so that not a slave shall be left to clank his chains upon our soil." According to historian W. Caleb McDaniel, Sumner's opposition to helping return fugitive slaves to their masters is what led Garrison that July 4 to burn publicly copies of the Fugitive Slave Law of 1850 and U.S. Constitution. Seeking "to agitate Congress from without," as Sumner had from within, Garrison famously characterized the Constitution as "a covenant with death and an agreement with hell." Whittier perceptively tied Sumner's Senate speeches and actions to the anti-Nebraska meetings that led to Massachusetts's first Republican state convention, held at Worcester in September. Whittier advised Sumner: "Everybody has read the newspaper reports of the [Senate] encounter, and everybody save a few desperate office holders and Hunkers commend thy course in terms of warm admiration."[19]

As the Republican Party grew (in competition with the nativist American Party) throughout the North, much interaction between Garrisonians and members of what became the Republicans' radical wing took place. Civil war in Kansas Territory between Free Staters, who sought to ban slavery there, and proslavery Border Ruffians from Missouri spurred this process, which followed the pattern of convergence mixed with criticism that Garrisonians had established in their dealings with Free Soilers and Free Democrats. Similarities existed as well to the much earlier relationships between abolitionists and

Garrisonian abolitionist and writer Lydia Maria Child (1802–1880), while always critical of antislavery politicians, became friendlier to Republicans during the 1850s and 1860s. (Library of Congress Prints and Photographs Division)

antislavery politicians during the late 1820s. Garrisonians most often praised and expressed affection for individual politicians. In February 1855 Lydia Maria Child complimented Sumner on his "true nobility of talent and character." She compared him to second-generation immediatist Higginson, as each worked "gloriously for humanity . . . in his own way." Garrison and Phillips praised Henry Wilson, who in January 1855 joined Sumner in representing Massachusetts in the U.S. Senate, for moving the northern wing of the nativist American Party toward antislavery. And Garrisonians continued to encourage Giddings's moralistic approach to politics. Henry C. Wright in 1857 commended Giddings for his "bold & manly assertions of . . . [his] views in Congress in [response] to Southern . . . Bullyism." Wright assured Giddings, "Of all politicians, you are the most consecrated & respected in the hearts of those who have been tried in the *moral* conflict with oppression."[20]

Simultaneously Garrisonians criticized Radical Republicans for portraying denationalization as a step toward emancipation in the South *and* prodded the Radicals toward disunionism. In January 1855, at the MASS annual meeting, Stephen S. Foster described Sumner as "a proslavery man" because Sumner supported the U.S. Constitution. To end slavery, Foster asserted, abolitionists had to rebuke Republicans for upholding "the American Government." In July 1855 Chase, in a Dartmouth College speech, called for "no Slavery . . . outside the slave States." In response, at an "August First" celebration of emancipation in the British West Indies, Phillips declared, "Slavery is too strong for half-way measures." Chase, Phillips charged, would "do nothing with that [denationalization] principle"—or "nothing at present." In 1856 Garrison questioned Seward's, Hale's, Sumner's, Wilson's, and Giddings's "manhood—their self-respect—their love of liberty" because they promised to "stand by the Union to the last!"[21]

As they had earlier, those who became Radical Republicans usually ignored, rejected, or qualified Garrisonian criticism. What Garrisonians sometimes called timidity, the Radicals regarded as prudence. In October 1855 Samuel Joseph May wrote to Seward expressing fear that attempts to end slavery peacefully had failed and that "the intolerable evil cannot now be extirpated without a commotion that will tare the very joints and marrow of our body politic asunder." May hoped the nation could "avert the catastrophe of civil war." But he urged Seward to avoid "the timid spirit of compromise" and to declare "the North's intention to destroy slavery" through rapid denationalization. Seward responded to May that his advice was neither "well directed [n]or wisely conceived."[22]

RPAs also interacted positively and negatively with Radical Republicans. Gerrit Smith influenced Sumner and Chase. In March 1856 Smith sent a copy of Giddings's *Speeches in Congress* to Sumner, who called them an "arsenal of truth." But when Smith asked Chase to express his views concerning the RPA doctrine that Congress had power to end slavery in the southern states, Chase rejected it. Smith then informed Chase that he expected the Republican Party to "take a very low ground in regard to slavery." It would, Smith predicted, nominate a presidential candidate who was by "a very wide margin" not "an abolitionist."[23]

Nevertheless Chase sought to influence and use Smith and other RPAs. In one strategy Chase hoped to lure Smith and his associates into the Republican Party. Disregarding Smith's involvement in the underground railroad, Chase urged him to cease concentrating on "the abstract quality of slavery." Instead Chase suggested that Smith should join Republicans "in practical measures for combating the Slave Power," such as "denationalizing slavery." If Smith would do so, Chase promised to join him "in calling Slavery *a piracy* and an *outlaw.*" In an alternate strategy Chase hoped Smith's Radical Abolition Party would nominate a presidential candidate on a slavery illegal everywhere platform. That, Chase believed, would encourage the Republican Party to consolidate its position as the moderate antislavery party by nominating a candidate identified with denationalization—such as himself.[24]

Meanwhile, although Theodore Parker's health declined during the mid- to late 1850s and he represented no abolitionist organization, his published writings and massive private correspondence continued to have impact. His exchanges with Sumner, Wilson, and Chase reveal respectful, encouraging, and cooperative, as well as critical, relationships. In January 1855 Parker wrote to Sumner, "You stand up in Congress as the man with a conscience which reflects the natural law of God written in the human heart." When Parker called on Sumner for action in Congress regarding Kansas Territory, Sumner urged Parker to help him by organizing a Massachusetts petitioning campaign and public meetings.[25]

A month later Parker noted Henry Wilson's ties to the nativist American Party and urged him to become a "champion of justice to all men." Parker held up Sumner as an example of "one . . . who has grown morally as well as intellectually by his position in Congress." Wilson, who had just begun his U.S. Senate term, re-read this advice several times and assured Parker that he hoped "to be better and wiser for it." Later Wilson suggested that Parker had a major role in his decision to move the northern wing of the American Party toward "a moderate but positive anti-slavery position" within the Republican Party. Yet, as was generally the case with abolitionists, Parker's influence had limits. In 1856 Wilson worked to discourage moralism within the Republican Party and distance it from abolitionists. He stressed economic issues, all the while assuring Parker that he would, if he could, "overthrow slavery in the states."[26]

In July 1856 Parker praised Chase, who had been elected governor of Ohio, as "a great man and great statesman," and sent Chase copies of his sermons and speeches. But Parker also suggested that racism contributed to Chase's disinclination to advocate direct U.S. government action on behalf of immediate emancipation in the southern states. As had Gerrit Smith, Parker pushed Chase to move away from denationalization. Chase replied, "There is no spot on earth in which I would sanction slavery." Denying racial bias, he defended denationalization as a "practical" and "fundamental" step toward ending slavery in the states. Noting that he worked "in the political field," Chase claimed that "such thoughts as [Parker's] writings inspire" would promote denationalization.[27]

In regard to the Republican Party as a political organization, some abolitionists emphasized a portrayal of it as more deserving of support than the Free Soil Party had been in 1848. Other abolitionists emphasized the party's shortcomings. Tension among Garrisonians regarding these alternative views of the party arose in 1856 before that year's national election campaign began. At the MASS meeting in January, Phillips praised conservative Massachusetts Republican Nathaniel P. Banks's candidacy for Speaker of the U.S. House of Representatives. Phillips had also praised the earlier elections of Radical Republicans Sumner and Wilson to the Senate. Garrison, in contrast, said that while he thought "as well as he could of the Republicans," he had to "denounce them" for centering on the "single paltry issue of Free Soil" and proclaiming "their love of the Union."[28]

The following month Republican delegates met in Pittsburgh to form a national organization. In the process they defeated an anti-nativist resolution, elected Maryland slaveholder Francis P. Blair chairman, and limited a proposed party platform to "repeal of all laws allowing the introduction of Slavery into Territories once consecrated to Freedom, and the resistance by Constitutional means of the existence of Slavery in any Territory." The *Liberator* referred to this platform as "milk-and-water." Church-oriented RPA Lewis Tappan called it "the weakest anti Slavery platform that has been adopted by any national convention professing to be anti Slavery."[29]

The circumstances in which antislavery politicians acted on behalf of the Republican Party and abolitionists sought to shape those actions changed during the succeeding months as a result of a half-dozen events. First, shortly after the Republican's Pittsburgh convention, the American Party nominated former Whig president Millard Fillmore for president on a platform that avoided the slavery issue. Second, on May 21, proslavery forces attacked the Free Stater center of Lawrence, Kansas Territory. Third, a day later, South Carolina congressman Preston Brooks physically assaulted Sumner in the U.S. Senate. Fourth, during the same weeks, black and white northerners continued to resist enforcement of the Fugitive Slave Law of 1850. Fifth, in early June, the Democratic national convention nominated James Buchanan of Pennsylvania for president on a proslavery platform.

Sixth, while meeting in Philadelphia from June 17–19, the Republican national convention rejected formal alliance with northern wing of the American Party, nominated military hero John C. Frémont for president, and adopted a much stronger platform than had the Pittsburgh gathering. Although the Philadelphia platform fell far short of denationalization, it recognized the duty of Congress to prohibit slavery in all territories and demanded that Kansas be admitted as a free-labor state. It affirmed the party's commitment to equal rights principles imbedded in the Declaration of Independence and upheld the "liberty of conscience and equality of rights among citizens."[30]

The chance that all these developments could be used to further broad-based northern opposition to slavery led to a tactical division among abolitionist leaders. Despite the changing national circumstances regarding the slavery issue and Republican progress, Garrison and most of his associates did not immediately relent in their criticism of the Republican Party. In an Independence Day address, Garrison said he would not support the Republicans because they vowed "fealty to the Union, come what may." He also noted that the Philadelphia platform did not oppose slavery in the District of Columbia, the interstate slave trade, or the Fugitive Slave Law. He objected to racist boasts that *"Republicanism is the white man's party."* He stood, he said, "outside the tyrannical government, a seceder on principle, a revolutionist." He called for disunion, for supporting "neither . . . Fremont, nor Buchanan, nor Fillmore."[31]

But as the campaign progressed, Garrison returned to the tactic of balancing criticism with praise. In September he referred to the Republican Party as "the only political party that remains true to the original [constitutional] compact." He declared that "the Democratic and American parties [were] with the Slave Power to the utmost extent of its usurpations." Therefore, he wrote, "the sympathy of every genuine friend of freedom must be with the Republican party, in spite of its lamentable short-comings." In October, in a letter to the Pennsylvania Anti-Slavery Society annual meeting, Garrison went so far as to characterize that party as "the legitimate product of the *moral* agitation of the subject of slavery for the last quarter century." It was, he asserted, "incomparably better" than the American and Democratic Parties.[32]

A minority of Garrison's associates moved more quickly than he toward openly expressing such favorable views of the Republican Party. In August 1856 Samuel Joseph May, expecting sectional war and valuing Frémont's military experience, called on abolitionists to "back" him. May claimed that Republicans hated slavery as much as abolitionists did. Lydia Maria Child admitted that the Republican Party had only a "halfhearted" commitment to abolition and black rights. Nevertheless she wrote of Frémont, "He has pledged himself to oppose the extension of slavery. . . . That is enough for *me.*" Writing to Sumner, Child criticized the AASS for becoming "narrow and intolerant."[33]

RPAs had joined in Garrison's initially negative view of the Republican Party. In late May 1856 the tiny Radical Abolitionist Party had held its nominating convention at Syracuse, New York. There William Goodell, Lewis Tappan, and Frederick Douglass led the party in unanimously nominating Gerrit Smith for the presidency on a slavery illegal everywhere platform. In accepting the nomination Smith admitted that the Republicans were far superior to the Americans and Democrats in regard to slavery. But he charged that the Republicans conceded too much to slavery's legitimacy in the North, U.S. territories, and southern states. More forthrightly than Samuel Joseph May had a year earlier, Smith looked to sectional disruptions to push the U.S. government toward adopting a policy of general emancipation. He predicted that bloodshed in Kansas would eventually lead northerners to elect an abolitionist president and a Congress willing to use "brute force" to "kill" slavery. RPA constitutional theorist Lysander Spooner went further, suggesting that a Democratic, rather than Republican, victory in the 1856 election would "do most . . . for Freedom." Such a victory, Spooner correctly predicted, would lead Democrats to "sufficiently outrage the rights and feelings of the north[erners], to incite them to get up on their hind legs, and declare that they are men."[34]

By August, however, RPA support of the Republican Party exceeded that of most Garrisonians. Smith in a public letter to Goodell pledged not to vote for Frémont because the candidate held that "slavery is law." But Smith went on to write that he hoped Frémont would be elected. In regard to his own presidential campaign, Smith complained that he was "tired of being laughed at." Frederick Douglass went beyond Smith by announcing that he supported Frémont "as the best thing I can do *now*—but without loosing sight of the great doctrines and measures inseparable from [Smith's] great name and character." In a manner similar to Radical Republicans, Douglass claimed a Republican victory in the election would "prevent the establishment of slavery in Kansas, overthrow Slave Rule in the Republic, protect Liberty of Speech and of the Press." It would, according to Douglass, "give ascendency to Northern civilization over the bludgeon and blood-hound civilization of the South, and [put] the mark of national condemnation on Slavery." Soon after the election Tappan assumed that "most" RPAs voted for Frémont because "the Republican party was the first large party in this country that ever directly arraigned itself against Slavery, in any form."[35]

Among abolitionist leaders Parker and Whittier drew closest to the Republican Party in hopes of influencing its principles and tactics. In early 1856 Parker had urged Sumner to consider the formation of a northern antislavery coalition that included abolitionists. In May he favored Seward, Chase, and Hale as Republican presidential candidates and asked Sumner about Frémont's reliability. Shortly after the Republican nominating convention, Parker, writing as if he *were* a Republican, advised Horace Mann, "I take it we can elect Fremont; if so the battle is fought and the worst part of the contest is over." If Buchanan won, Parker predicted, with considerable accuracy, "the Union holds out for three years." But Parker also wanted more than denationalization, and after Frémont's defeat, he returned to criticizing Republicans. Their "hands," he advised Quaker abolitionist Sarah Hunt, "were not yet clean enough to be trusted with power." This outlook contributed to Parker's advocacy of antislavery violence in Kansas and elsewhere along the North-South border.[36]

Whittier by 1856 acted in politics as a Republican and simply favored electing a "Free State President." He went so far as to criticize Giddings for blocking a formal union between Republicans and the American Party's northern wing. After Frémont's defeat, Whittier remained more optimistic than Parker concerning the Republican Party's future, declaring to Sumner, "If we can hold what we have gained, our victory is only delayed four years." Whittier further claimed that "Divine Providence" had given him "a glimpse of the Canaan of Freedom." Both naive regarding "the Canaan of Freedom" and accurate regarding Republican victory in 1860, Whittier's prediction anticipated one side of the abolitionist relationship to the Republican Party during the next four years.[37]

Following the Democratic victory in the 1856 election, conservative forces within the Republican Party, comprising former Whigs, former Democrats, and former Americans, worked to turn the party away from the slavery issue. They emphasized economic development, colonization of African Americans, and restriction of foreign immigration, and they engaged in anti-Catholic bigotry.[38] This trend led some Garrisonians, second-generation abolitionists, RPAs, and black abolitionists (in contrast to Parker and Whittier) to believe they must vigorously push Republicans beyond denationalization.

When Thomas Wentworth Higginson invited Radical Republicans to a Massachusetts disunion convention at Worcester in January 1857, the Radicals responded variously. Henry Wilson and Charles Francis Adams bluntly rejected disunion and opposed holding the convention. Wilson wrote, "Impotent for good, this movement can only be productive of evil." Adams wrote, "I am willing to live indefinitely with slaveholders, even though some of them should trench a little on my rights." Giddings and Amasa Walker, a Massachusetts resident and former Liberty abolitionist, upheld denationalization while conceding that northern withdrawal from the Union "should well be considered." Giddings, sounding a bit like a pre-1842 Garrisonian, emphasized maintaining "the Union *as it is now*" while seeking a nonviolent end to slavery by changing white southern "moral and religious sentiment." Walker expressed the friendliest feelings toward the convention. He declared himself to be "a Union man, with all my heart and soul." He then added that the Union "certainly" should not continue unless "the great ideas of the Declaration of Independence can be fully realized."[39]

A few Garrisonians, including AASS field agents Parker Pillsbury, Abigail Kelley Foster, and Stephen S. Foster, confronted the Radical Republicans. They rejected cooperation with any Republican and hoped for the Republican Party's defeat in future elections. But most Garrisonians, including Garrison, Phillips, Samuel Joseph May, and Lydia Maria Child, continued to regard the party as a progressive force that should be encouraged as well as criticized. At the 1857 Massachusetts Garrisonian Independence Day celebration—four months after the U.S. Supreme Court's *Dred Scott* decision that appeared to legalize slavery everywhere in the country outside the free-labor states—Phillips asserted that abolitionists to be influential had to maintain their moral egalitarian principles while working with Republicans. Centering on Wilson, who attended the gathering, Phillips said that a politician "must count noses, to find where his majority is, and . . . must keep back half his purposes, and must express himself to suit the present." Therefore abolitionists had to regard Radical Republicans such as Wilson and Sumner differently than they regarded Conservative Republicans such as Massachusetts gubernatorial candidate Nathaniel P. Banks. Phillips warned Abigail Kelley Foster against "calling the Republican party the enemy of the cause" because that would repeal rather than influence Republican leaders. Similarly Child objected to Stephen S. Foster calling Sumner and Wilson "villains." She supported Garrison's contention that criticism of Republicans must be serious and dignified. She refused to attend meetings that Stephen S. Foster attended.[40]

As 1858 began Parker strengthened his advocacy of political action and, like increasing numbers of abolitionists, advocated physical force on behalf of African Americans. In a speech to the annual MASS meeting, Parker declared that the "moral wrong" of slavery could not be "put down . . . by ethical preaching." Rather it had to be "put down politically or militarily." As earlier, he called for U.S. government action to end slavery in the southern states. But in other respects, Parker continued to sound like a Republican. He advocated an end to slavery in the territories, admitting no more slave-labor states, and electing an antislavery president in 1860. He hoped such a policy would bring about an end to slavery in the United States by 1876.[41]

Parker also sounded like a Republican in his frequent calls for protecting white northerners' rights. He warned against Slave Power plans to establish slavery in the North, annex Mexico and central America, and revive the Atlantic slave trade. He regarded as allies Massachusetts Republican Eli Thayer (who organized free-state migration to Kansas), conservative border slave state Republicans, and northern Democrats who opposed the Lecompton Constitution, which in September 1857 proposed to admit Kansas Territory to the Union as a slave-labor state. Increasingly Parker advised Radical Republicans to adopt forceful measures in Kansas, maintain *their* principles, and develop a prudent campaign strategy for 1860. Parker assumed that abolishing slavery would lead to "an industrial democracy" commanded by those of "Anglo-Saxon blood."[42]

A year after Parker addressed the MASS, the issue of how abolitionists should deal with the Republican Party came up again. Pillsbury and Abigail Kelley Foster (this time joined by Higginson) portrayed the party as a threat to abolitionism, "stealthily sucking the very blood from our veins." Garrison replied, "There is a good deal of pro-slavery in the [Republican] party, perhaps, but [also] a great deal of warm and genuine anti-slavery—sympathy, kindness, pity

Abigail Kelley Foster (1811–1887), along with her husband, Stephen S. Foster, and Parker Pillsbury, led those abolitionists who were most critical of antislavery politicians during the Civil War years. (Library of Congress Prints and Photographs Division)

for the slave." He hoped the party in its 1860 platform would go beyond non-extension to address slavery's existence throughout the United States. But he reminded abolitionists that they, like Republicans, wanted to keep slavery out of the western territories.[43]

By the summer of 1859 most abolitionists shared Parker's and Garrison's hopeful but reserved approach to the Republican Party. Resolutions adopted by black abolitionists at a Tremont Temple August First celebration praised Republican leaders who "exerted themselves in favor of the colored men's equality" while regretting that many other Republicans failed to do so. Prosperous New York City caterer George T. Downing, who addressed the gathering, credited Republicans with "service rendered in the cause of Freedom." He urged them to nominate a presidential candidate in 1860 for "whom we can, to some degree of consistency, cast our ballots."[44]

Ten weeks after Downing spoke, abolitionist influence surged to impact not only the Republican Party but also southern politics, the national party system, and the following year's presidential election. Many commentators at the time portrayed John Brown and his tiny band's raid on the undefended federal arsenal at Harpers Ferry, Virginia, on October 16, 1859, as an isolated act of monomania. But the raid, which Brown hoped would be a step toward slave rebellion, rested on long-term developments within the abolition movement.[45]

Individuals associated with the RPA faction had since the late 1830s engaged in physical action against slavery on its northern border (see chapter 6). During the 1840s faction leaders Gerrit Smith and Henry Highland Garnet had each presented an "Address to the Slaves." Smith's address rhetorically urged slaves to escape and abolitionists to help them. Garnet's rhetorically called on slaves to demand pay from their masters. Brown, a long-term participant in the underground railroad, read these addresses. He knew about Charles T. Torrey's action in the Chesapeake and other aggressive abolitionist action in the South, and had met with Smith and Garnet to discuss such undertakings. As early as November 1847, Brown told Frederick Douglass he hoped to lead a band of men into Virginia, recruit slaves, and send other slaves "to the north by the underground railroad." During the mid-1850s Brown had joined the Free State side in the fighting in Kansas Territory. His experience fighting proslavery forces there encouraged him to change his emphasis from going south to help slaves escape to going south to lead a revolt.[46]

In addition to Douglass, Brown informed black abolitionists Lewis Hayden, Jermaine Wesley Loguen, and Harriet Tubman about his plans. Prominent white abolitionists, including Smith, Theodore Parker, Thomas Wentworth Higginson, and Samuel Gridley Howe, provided Brown with financial support. Nevertheless a remaining commitment to nonviolence, doubts about Brown's rationality, and fear of arrest as conspirators influenced these and other abolitionists. As a result some of them reacted ambivalently to news of Brown's arrest, subsequent trial for treason against Virginia, and execution on December 2, 1859. Smith had a nervous breakdown. Douglass and others left the country. The *Liberator* called the raid "well-intended but sadly misguided."[47]

Yet Brown's bravery and self-possession during his capture, trial, and imprisonment, during the last of which he appealed to a northern conscience on the slaves' behalf, allowed abolitionists to use him to affect northern politics. In anticipation of Brown's execution, the AASS executive committee called for "public moral demonstration[s] . . . in all the principal cities and towns of the North." Garrison expressed a desire "to increase the uneasiness of the oppressor, and to strengthen the hands of the friends of freedom." Following the execution, Garrison declared before a large and approving Boston crowd, "Success to every slave insurrection in the South. . . . Give me, as a non resistant, Bunker Hill, and Lexington, and Concord, rather than the cowardice and servility of a Southern slave-plantation."[48]

As Brown had intended, his raid's impact on politics went well beyond abolitionist use of it. The raid directly influenced Republicans, Democrats, the two parties' respective chances for victory in the 1860 elections, and the political balance of power in the South. A few Republicans knew Brown personally and shared the abolitionists' ambivalence toward him. Chase met Brown in early 1857, donated money toward Brown's Kansas activities, and then backed off after Brown murdered proslavery men at Pottawatomie. Other Radical Republicans, including Giddings, Henry Wilson, Charles Francis Adams,

Benjamin Wade, and George W. Julian, had attended meetings at which Brown raised money for combat in Kansas. With few exceptions, such Radicals condemned the raid more firmly than abolitionists while joining abolitionists in praising Brown's motives. Chase referred to Brown as "rash," "mad," and "criminal." Then he praised Brown's "bravery" and "unselfish desire to set free the oppressed." John A. Andrew, who became Massachusetts governor in 1861, described "John Brown and his companions" as "martyrs" in a struggle between right and wrong.[49]

Following Brown's raid Radical Republicans continued to locate the root of intersectional violence in proslavery aggression in Kansas, southern lynch law, and "slavery itself." Perhaps more significantly the raid did not weaken Moderate Republicans' antislavery resolve. Abraham Lincoln, in his Cooper Union speech of February 27, 1860, declared that "John Brown was no Republican," and that Republicans would leave slavery alone in the southern states. Lincoln, however, continued to oppose extension of slavery into U.S. territories. Some Republicans "muted their remarks" during a two-month struggle to elect a Speaker of the House that began in December 1859. But among major Republican leaders, only William Henry Seward pulled back after Brown's raid. Rather than emphasize "irrepressible conflict," as he had in his famous 1858 Senate speech, he began to reject "aggression against slavery in the states." And when in March 1860 Harrison Blake, a Republican representative from Ohio, presented a denationalization bill designed to free all slaves under Congress's exclusive jurisdiction, 59 out of 73 Republicans in the House of Representatives voted for it.[50]

Conservative Republicans initially believed that Brown's raid, by causing a reaction against extremist violence, would strengthen them and make, in historian Richard H. Sewell's words, "fusing with the Southern opposition party more advantageous." However, as proslavery politicians and journalists blamed the Republican Party for the raid, what chance there was for a Republican coalition with the American Party and remaining southern Whigs ended. This in turn discouraged efforts among Conservative and some Moderate Republicans to move away from the slavery issue. Also the raid, by increasing southern white fear of northern aggression, discouraged efforts to reconstruct a conservative national Whig Party.[51] These negative effects on conservatism within and without the Republican Party helped keep the party open to abolitionists' influence.

Meanwhile recognition that other abolitionists shared Brown's desire to provoke slave revolt encouraged southern proslavery disunionism. Fear of revolt had long been an issue in southern politics, and many white southerners regarded abolitionist-assisted slave escapes as encouraging it. One month before the Harpers Ferry raid, Virginia secessionist Edmund Ruffin had published a pamphlet portraying the "two great evils" his state faced. They were the existence of free African Americans and northern abolitionists' "seducing our slaves to abscond." Following the raid, newspapers in such cities as New Orleans; Augusta, Georgia; and Charleston, South Carolina, claimed that an abolitionist threat to the border slave states and the likelihood of slave revolt demanded white southern unity, revival of the Atlantic slave trade, and preparation for secession.[52]

It followed that during the winter of 1859–60, southern congressmen became even more unyielding in their defense of slavery. As these congressmen demanded an investigation into Brown's raid, they enjoyed the help of some prominent northern Democrats who portrayed Republicans and abolitionists as indistinguishable. Stephen A. Douglas tied Republicans to Brown. Similarly, at a Democratic meeting in Newark, New Jersey, Colonel James W. Wall charged that Republicans supported "secret organizations . . . engaged in running off thousands of slaves into Canada." Wall also charged that Republican-controlled state legislatures had effectively repealed the Fugitive Slave Law. In turn increased physical attacks in the South on free African Americans, suspected abolitionists, and tradesmen from the North encouraged abolitionists to further demonize the white South. Clearly politicians of all persuasions used Brown's raid to advance their agendas. But the greatest political impact of Brown's raid was on the Democratic Party, which in 1860 split into separate southern and northern organizations, thereby guaranteeing the election of a Republican president.[53]

8

Political Success and Failure

AN AMBIGUOUS DENOUEMENT, 1860–1870

From the 1860 national election campaign through secession, Civil War, and into Reconstruction abolitionists continued their long effort to influence politics and government. During these years they maintained their tactic of combining criticism with encouragement of antislavery politicians. In particular they denounced, ridiculed, and praised Abraham Lincoln as Republican presidential candidate in 1860, president-elect during the secession winter, and during his presidency. They criticized Lincoln mainly because of his moderate and vague antislavery commitment. And, as Radical Republicans engaged in similar criticism, most abolitionist leaders became less distinguishable from the Radicals. To a greater degree than Theodore Parker and John G. Whittier had during the late 1850s, most abolitionists after 1860 embraced the Republican Party as providing the best path toward universal emancipation. By 1863 they had become more consistent in their praise and less likely to criticize. At the same time a minority of abolitionists became more consistently critical of Lincoln and his party. At the Civil War's end and for several years thereafter, as formal emancipation became reality through political and military means, the issue of what black freedom *meant* further divided abolitionists in their political tactics. By 1870, however, even those abolitionists who were most critical of the Republicans' imperfect attempts to protect black civil and voting rights claimed victory.

Abolitionist John Brown, through his Harpers Ferry raid, helped shape the 1860 national election. But as in 1856, abolitionists in 1860 had no direct role in the Republican Party's nominating process or in drafting its platform. The great majority of Republican politicians continued to fear being linked to abolitionists. Conversely Garrisonians and radical political abolitionists (RPAs) remained distrustful of the Republican commitment to denationalization as (at best) a means toward gradually ending slavery. Abolitionists recalled that during the late 1850s, many Republicans had deemphasized the slavery issue as they appealed to northern economic interests, rejected black rights, embraced nativism, and sought to attract northern conservatives. Prior to the May 1860 Republican national convention, *National Anti-Slavery Standard* editor Oliver Johnson declared, "The Republican Party not merely disclaims . . . any design to interfere with slavery in the States . . . but accepts all the villainies incorporated into law as accomplished facts, not to be disturbed." Johnson, a longtime Garrisonian, warned against voting for a party that did not favor expunging all support for slavery from the U.S. Constitution.[1]

Yet when the Republican convention, held in Chicago, nominated Lincoln for president on a platform similar to the one the party had adopted in 1856, most abolitionists once again acknowledged the party's antislavery character while criticizing it for not going far enough. During the convention elderly Radical Republican Joshua R. Giddings successfully demanded that the delegates insert the specific equal rights doctrines of the Declaration of Independence into its platform. When Giddings reported this success to Gerrit Smith, the RPA leader responded, "I am very glad you went to Chicago. Had you not gone then the best thing in the platform would not have been in it." When at an abolitionist Independence Day celebration in Framingham, Massachusetts, Republican U.S. senator Henry Wilson denied that his party was an antislavery party, William Lloyd Garrison reprimanded him.[2]

As the 1860 presidential campaign progressed, some abolitionists engaged actively on behalf of the Republican Party and its presidential candidate. Sidney Howard Gay, David Lee Child, rising young abolitionist Theodore Tilton, and Kentucky abolitionists John G. Fee and William S. Bailey campaigned for Lincoln. Frederick Douglass did not go so far. But in June he praised Lincoln as "a man of unblemished private character; . . . and one of the most frank, honest men in political life." Even when in August Douglass endorsed RPA presidential nominee Gerrit Smith, he advised abolitionists that, although the Republican Party did not deserve their support, "great good will have been gained to the cause of the slave by its elevation to power." While the Republican Party only weakly opposed slavery and even more weakly supported black rights, Douglass emphasized, it far surpassed the Democratic Party in both regards. Smith expressed views similar to Douglass's. Although Smith would not vote for Lincoln, he characterized Lincoln as at "heart an abolitionist." Smith correctly predicted that the white South would react to Lincoln's election as if it were "an Abolitionist victory."[3]

On the other abolitionist extreme, Stephen S. Foster and Parker Pillsbury described the Republican Party as irredeemably proslavery and ridiculed Lincoln. Pillsbury believed that for abolitionists to preserve their "mighty moral power," they had to remain outside Republican political campaigns. They had to utter "stern and important truths" rather than issue "congratulatory resolutions." The similarly oriented Western Anti-Slavery Society deemed Lincoln to be the "most 'dangerous obstacle' to the antislavery movement." Black abolitionist H. Ford Douglas early in the campaign criticized Lincoln for supporting the Fugitive Slave Law. Douglas, who lived in Chicago, also charged that if black parents in Illinois sent their "children to school, Abraham Lincoln would kick them out, in the name of Republicanism and anti-slavery." Similarly Wendell Phillips, moving away from Garrison's combination of praise and criticism, scorned Lincoln as a "huckster in politics" and "the Slavehound of Illinois" because of Lincoln's support for the Fugitive Slave Law.[4]

As the election neared, however, most abolitionists became more certain that a Republican victory would be a major step in the right direction. Oliver Johnson, ignoring his earlier negative remarks, asserted that it would be "the beginning of a new and better era." John G. Whittier informed Salmon P. Chase, "For the first time in my life, I shall vote, I suppose, for a successful candidate for the presidency." Other independent abolitionists, including Richard J. Hinton, John Wallace Hutchinson, Elizur Wright Jr., and John Jay, expressed the same intention. By November H. Ford Douglas had become friendly to Lincoln and the Republican Party. "I love everything the South hates," he wrote, "and since they have evidenced their dislike of Mr. Lincoln, I am bound to love you Republicans with all your faults."[5]

When Lincoln won, Whittier naively characterized the victory as "the triumph of our principles—so long delayed." Other abolitionists expressed more qualified views. Frederick Douglass hoped that a Lincoln presidency would end attempts to revive the external slave trade and that it would reduce enforcement of the Fugitive Slave Law. He asserted that the election had broken the Slave Power's rule and "demonstrated the possibility of electing, if not an Abolitionist, at least an *anti-slavery* reputation to the Presidency of the United States." Douglass nevertheless worried that Lincoln's election could hurt "more thoroughgoing abolitionism." Phillips recognized value in the victory while characterizing it as one for John Brown and Garrison rather than for Lincoln.[6]

During the months following the election, as the Lower South states seceded and formed the Confederate States of America, Garrisonians feared Congress would pass a proslavery compromise to save the Union. RPAs shared this fear, with Smith advising Chase that he believed breaking the Union was "infinitely better" than "concessions to Slavery." Both groups of abolitionists changed their minds after the Confederate attack on Fort Sumter on April 12, 1861. They joined the great majority of their colleagues, regardless of their prewar views, in supporting a war to save the Union, end slavery, and secure black rights. Based on John Quincy Adams's reasoning of two decades earlier, the Church Anti-Slavery Society and the American Missionary Association (AMA) urged Radical Republicans to favor immediate emancipation under the war power as a "military necessity." Garrisonians soon adopted the same position.[7]

The abolitionist-Radical relationship strengthened as did abolitionist links to the entire Republican Party. Historian James Schouler, in the seventh volume of his *History of the United States* (1899), contends that abolitionists thereby became part of a Republican coalition. More recently historian James M. McPherson points out that such Radicals as Charles Sumner, John Andrew, George W. Julian, Thaddeus Stevens, and Owen Lovejoy adhered "to a set of principles that fell short of genuine abolitionism." But many abolitionists modified their principles, so that, in historian Hans L. Trefousse's words, "the difference between abolitionism and radical Republicanism became ever more blurred." At the 1861 Garrisonian Independence Day celebration at Framingham, Massachusetts, Edmund Quincy observed that "whether willingly or unwillingly [Republicans were] doing the work of the Abolitionists." In September Garrison suggested to his associate Henry T. Cheever that abolitionists should "merge ourselves, as far as we can without compromise of principle, in the onward sweeping current of Northern sentiment."[8]

Abolitionist-Radical interaction increased when Lincoln revoked General John C. Frémont's August 30, 1861, decree providing for freedom of slaves owned by Missourians in rebellion against the United States. That November abolitionists Oliver Johnson, George B. Cheever, William Goodell, and Theodore Tilton sat on the platform at the Young Men's Republican Association meeting at New York's Cooper Union as Sumner presented a pro-emancipation speech. That December the abolitionist-backed Boston Emancipation League also brought abolitionists and Radicals together. Samuel Gridley Howe chaired the league's meeting. Republican George S. Boutwell addressed it. And other Republicans joined in the league's debates and received copies of its publications.[9]

As time passed, abolitionists expanded their interactions with Republicans. When Garrison spoke at Cooper Union in February 1862, he addressed a Republican audience. That September second-generation abolitionists Samuel Gridley Howe and George L. Stearns established the *Boston Commonwealth* in part to advocate Sumner's reelection to the U.S. Senate. In September 1862 Garrison advised Oliver Johnson that abolitionists should moderate their language in order to influence a broader spectrum of Republicans. Two months later, when Republican candidates fared poorly in congressional elections,

Lydia Maria Child declared, "I think *we* shall now go ahead in earnest . . . *we* shall at last rely upon principle." When Republicans organized Union League clubs in 1863 to energize voters, abolitionists such as John Jay participated. Garrison, Phillips, Tilton, and Frederick Douglass joined with New York City Republicans in May 1863 for a series of meetings and speeches. Moncure Conway, a reinvigorated Theodore Weld, and young abolitionist sensation Anna Dickinson campaigned that year in New England for Republican candidates. Tilton did the same in New York City, New Jersey, and Pennsylvania.[10]

Other abolitionists provided advice to and joined Lincoln's presidential administration. In January 1861 Charles Dexter Cleveland, vice president of the AMA, advised Lincoln concerning cabinet appointments. Zebina Eastman of Chicago became U.S. consul at Bristol, England. Cassius M. Clay served as ambassador to Russia. In December 1862 Massachusetts abolitionist William Whiting joined the War Department as solicitor and became friends with Lincoln and Secretary of War Edwin M. Stanton. Secretary of the Treasury Chase appointed abolitionists to serve in his department. One of them declared in January 1862, "All I can do to advance the cause of *God* & Humanity shall be done free of charge as I have an appointment in the Treasury Department under Sec. Chase."[11]

Reversals in northern attitudes had much to do with developments in abolitionist-Republican relationships. During the 1850s many Conservative Republicans, most Whigs, and nearly all Democrats had portrayed abolitionists as dangerous extremists. During the 1860–61 secession winter, pro-compromise northern newspapers had aroused popular sentiment among merchants and workingmen against abolitionists and African Americans. Across the North mobs disrupted abolitionist meetings and assaulted abolitionist speakers. Claims that abolitionists were, like secessionists, threats to the Union continued among Conservative Republicans throughout the war. Racist charges that abolitionists favored amalgamation with African Americans persisted longer.[12]

But except for a mobbing of Phillips in Cincinnati in March 1862, anti-abolitionist violence in the North had ended by mid-1861, and abolitionists began to be popular there. In April of that year Garrison noticed the change in opinion. By the following December Goodell could write, "Never has there been a time when Abolitionists were as much respected and as high in favor with the community as at present. Never has there been a time in which their strongest and most radical utterances, both of principles and measures, were as readily received by the people." Garrison, Frederick Douglass, Samuel Joseph May, Samuel May Jr., Stephen S. Foster, and Abigail Kelley Foster attracted large and enthusiastic audiences. Phillips's biographer James Brewer Stewart contends that "after 1862, no Radical Republican, in Congress or out, brought more pervasive political influence to the cause of emancipation than did Phillips." In early 1862 Anna Dickinson emerged as an abolitionist speaker nearly as prominent as Phillips.[13]

Abolitionist popularity in the North during the Civil War did not bring unlimited political influence. Abolitionists had little impact on the North's conduct of the war. They did not rapidly achieve their fundamental goals. And popularity diminished their autonomy. In May 1863 Garrison observed, "Our distinctive movement is nearly swallowed up in the great revolution in Northern sentiment which has been going on against slavery and slavedom since the bombardment of Sumter." The swallowing up became especially evident in regard to abolitionist journalism. In December 1861 Tilton affiliated with the *New York Independent,* under nonabolitionist Henry Ward Beecher. In March 1862 Sydney Howard Gay became managing editor of Radical Republican Horace Greeley's *New York Tribune.* Other abolitionists found outlets for their essays and speeches in these and other high-circulation Republican weeklies and dailies. The *Anti-Slavery Bugle* ceased publication, and the *Liberator's* and *National Anti-Slavery Standard's* circulation declined. Reaction against these losses of abolitionist independence had a major role in Pillsbury's, Stephen and Abby Fosters', and (less consistently) Phillips's opposition to Republican measures and candidates.[14]

As most abolitionists' relationship to the Republican Party grew closer, their relationship to emancipation and black rights became more complicated. Early on prominent abolitionists and Radical Republicans believed the war would inevitably lead to general emancipation. Goodell claimed a few weeks after the attack on Fort Sumter that a "Second American Revolution," aimed at "a National Abolition of Slavery," had begun. But northern support for ending slavery grew based on opposition to slaveholders and military necessity, rather than on an abolitionist emphasis on black rights. The Union armies' early battlefield failures (such as at Bull Run on July 21, 1861), combined with African American actions (especially those of slaves), rather than organized abolitionism, led in transforming a war to save the Union into one for emancipation. Major events, rather than abolitionist tactics and popularity, shaped the future.[15]

In several respects the abolitionists' relationship with Lincoln was more complicated and divisive than their relationship with the Republican Party. Lincoln's policies often lowered abolitionist perceptions of his character and discouraged their hopes of influencing him. His commitment in 1861 to return to their masters those slaves who reached Union lines had this effect. So did his countermanding Frémont's Missouri emancipation order. In regard to the latter, moderate abolitionist Whittier declared, "If the present terrible struggle does not involve emancipation, partial or complete, it is at once the most wicked and the most ludicrous war ever waged." Even more moderate Lydia Maria Child described Lincoln as "narrow-minded, shortsighted, and obstinate." When Lincoln in his December 1861 annual message recommended colonization of former slaves and assured masters he did not threaten slavery in the southern states, Garrison denounced him as "a man of very small caliber." In early 1862 Frederick Douglass asserted that Lincoln had revealed himself "to be about as destitute of any anti-slavery principle or feeling as . . . James Buchanan, his [proslavery] predecessor." The following August Moncure Conway declared, in regard to progress toward emancipation, that if Lincoln were "not a tortoise than never was one made by God."[16]

To counteract what they perceived to be Lincoln's weakness and lack of principle, abolitionists relied on their established tactics of personal contacts and visits to Washington. George B. Cheever, Lydia Maria Child, Garrison, and Gerrit Smith corresponded with Indiana Radical Republican congressman (and Giddings's son-in-law) George W. Julian. Cheever also corresponded with Ohio Radical Republican James M. Ashley, a candidate for election to the House of Representative. Garrison exchanged letters with Sumner, Wilson, and Andrew. Child, Conway, Smith, and Whittier corresponded with Sumner.[17] More strikingly the abolitionist presence in Washington during the war exceeded that of the abolition lobbyists during the late 1830s and early 1840s. During the war they spoke in major venues in the city to large, enthusiastic, and influential audiences. They rarely missed a chance to lobby in Congress. And they lobbied Lincoln and members of this administration—the first time they had done so with a sitting U.S. president. This lobbying in turn complicated their impression of Lincoln as president.

Radical Republicans in Chase's Treasury Department facilitated abolitionist addresses in the capital by organizing the Washington Lecture Association, designed to bring antislavery orators to the Smithsonian Institution. Despite resistance from the institution's proslavery secretary, Joseph Henry, abolitionists George B. Cheever, Conway, Phillips, and Goodell addressed audiences there during the early months of 1862, with Radicals regularly in attendance and Lincoln occasionally. On January 10 Cheever, the older brother of Henry T. Cheever, called for "immediate military emancipation," enlisting former slaves into the Union armies, and a presidential proclamation under the war power that would declare slaves "forever FREE." On January 17 Conway described emancipation as the means of ending the war. On January 12 and 26

George B. Cheever, during Sunday sermons at the House of Representative, repeated his earlier calls. During a return visit to the Smithsonian on February 14, he called for repeal of the Fugitive Slave Law of 1850 and abolition in the District of Columbia. More controversially, Phillips on March 14 and 16, while calling on Lincoln to fight the Civil War for emancipation, praised John Brown's raid and Frémont's Missouri emancipation order. Phillips also praised Toussaint Louverture, leader of Haiti's successful black revolution during the 1790s. Later in March Goodell discussed the RPA doctrine that the Constitution authorized the federal government to abolish slavery in peace as well as in war. Republican politicians warmly greeted all of these abolitionist speakers.[18]

The abolitionist speakers also lobbied. During his twelve days in Washington, Goodell met with congressmen, "most" of whom greeted him "cordially . . . with discourtesy by none." Following Conway's lecture Sumner arranged a meeting for him with Lincoln at the White House. There Conway urged the president to end slavery during the war. Lincoln replied that more time would be required. During Phillips's visit to Washington, Sumner introduced him in the U.S. Senate, and he too visited Lincoln at the White House. Before his lecture Goodell met with Lincoln, who had read more than one of Goodell's writings. Although Goodell criticized the Lincoln's slow progress toward emancipation, he reported that the president had an air of "serious thoughtfulness."[19]

After Gerrit Smith spoke at the Capitol that March he reported, "A great change has taken place in that city. The most radical abolitionist is now applauded by a Washington audience for his most radical utterances." Later Frederick Douglass, Anna Dickinson, George Thompson, Garrison, and Phillips (again) visited Washington, the Capitol, and Lincoln. At George L. Stearns's request, Douglass came in August 1863 to lobby Congress, the War Department, and Lincoln on behalf of continued recruitment of and equal pay for black Union soldiers.[20]

Abolitionists also continued to rely on petitions to counteract what they regarded as Lincoln's and other Republicans' proslavery tendencies. During the fall of 1861, under Emancipation League auspices, they had circulated petitions calling for "total abolition" of slavery under the war power, with compensation to "such [slaveholders] as are loyal to the government." That December, as Goodell published a list of petitions, he declared, "The men and women of the North are aroused; and from thousands of firesides . . . there goes forth the prayer—*let the oppressed go free.*" He believed "petitions for emancipation" influenced both houses of Congress. In early 1862 George B. Cheever, Tilton, and Goodell led another effort to petition Congress for emancipation. This became the largest abolitionist petitioning campaign since the one that took place decades earlier against the gag rule. Radical Republican congressmen responded with seven emancipation and/or confiscation bills. On June 20 a delegation of Quakers presented Lincoln with a petition, written by Garrison, calling again (and ironically, considering Quaker pacifism) for general emancipation under the war power. Oliver Johnson, who accompanied the delegation, read the petition to Lincoln, who responded equivocally.[21]

In March 1862 Lincoln presented a gradual, compensated emancipation plan for border slave states. Conway portrayed it as "wedge," and Garrison as a weak but positive response to the petitions. Similarly a wide range of abolitionists, including Phillips, Elihu Burritt, Maria Weston Chapman, Lydia Maria Child, and Samuel Gridley Howe joined Radical Republicans in characterizing the plan as a step in the right direction. And when in April Congress passed and Lincoln signed Henry Wilson's bill for immediate compensated emancipation in the District of Columbia, Henry Highland Garnet led an African American meeting at Cooper Union in offering "three cheers for the Union." Despite the compensation for masters, Frederick Douglass called the act the "first great step towards that righteousness which exalts a nation." Child predicted that the effects of the act would be "of more importance than the act itself." But no straight path toward universal emancipation appeared. On May 19 Lincoln countermanded Union general David Hunter's emancipation decree affecting parts of Florida, Georgia, and South Carolina. Slave catching continued in the District of Columbia. On May 26 Congress failed to pass a measure designed to free slaves owned by rebels and prohibit Union soldiers from returning fugitive slaves.[22]

In response abolitionists contacted Radical Republican congressmen, organized public meetings and speaking tours, and appealed to Lincoln. Phillips concisely described abolitionist tactics when he advised Sumner, "I think the Cabinet [is] as likely to respond to *criticism* as to value support." Through such tactics abolitionists had a role in Lincoln's decision to submit a draft of a general emancipation decree, based on the war power, to his cabinet on July 22. But once again, the *degree* of abolitionist impact on Lincoln's evolving commitment to emancipation is debatable. Slaves escaped to Union lines. The Union suffered battlefield defeats. Lincoln came to appreciate the importance of gaining black enlistees in the Union armies. Radical Republicans pushed Lincoln to act. And the border slave-labor states refused to implement Lincoln's gradual emancipation plan. All of these factors had more impact than abolitionists on Lincoln's decision, following the Union military victory at Antietam, to issue on September 22, 1862, his Preliminary Emancipation Proclamation. So did the necessity of keeping Great Britain and France (which decades earlier had ended slavery within their empires) from recognizing the Confederacy. Debate continues among historians regarding Lincoln's motives in issuing the Preliminary Proclamation, which technically allowed seceded states to adopt gradual, compensated emancipation plans if they returned to the Union before January 1, 1863. The Final Proclamation, issued on that day, declared slaves to be free in areas under Confederate control, but left slavery alone in the border slave states and portions of the Confederacy occupied by the Union armies.[23]

Although encouraged by the Final Proclamation, most abolitionists wished it had gone further. They also wondered whether Lincoln would or could fulfill its emancipatory commitment. His annual message the previous December had disheartened them, as it suggested passing a constitutional amendment providing for gradual, compensated emancipation of slaves not freed under the proclamation. Like a growing number of other abolitionists, Lydia Maria Child had come to doubt the sustainability of emancipation as a "war measure" rather than one based on "principles of justice and humanity." The day before Lincoln issued the Final Proclamation, George B. Cheever, William Goodell, and church-oriented abolitionist Nathan Brown of New Hampshire delivered a memorial to the president at the White House calling for "universal and immediate emancipation."[24]

Later that January a group of Massachusetts abolitionists including Conway, Phillips, George L. Stearns, Samuel Gridley Howe, Elizur Wright Jr., and John Hubbard Stevenson traveled to Washington in hopes of influencing Congress and Lincoln to insure full emancipation in the postwar South. Conway spoke in the Senate, and that evening the delegation (accompanied by Henry Wilson) met with Lincoln, who asserted that "he knew perfectly" who the delegation members were. During the meeting Phillips praised the Emancipation Proclamation while expressing concerns to Lincoln that it would not be "honestly carried out." Lincoln responded that while he believed the proclamation had "knocked the bottom out of slavery," he did not expect "sudden results." Abolitionists also pressed their Radical Republican allies for further public abolitionist-Radical interaction. Prompted by Boston abolitionist John Murray Forbes, Sumner read to Lincoln a petition urging the president to stand by his proclamation. In April 1863 Garrison, hoping to counteract the influence of proslavery northern Peace Democrats ("Copperheads"), called on Massachusetts's Radical governor John A. Andrew to lead the state legislature to endorse the proclamation.[25]

When in July 1863 Union battlefield victories at Gettysburg and Vicksburg appeared to open the way for a negotiated peace settlement, abolitionists feared that such a settlement would, despite the proclamation, leave slavery

Elizabeth Cady Stanton (1815–
1902), an immediate abolitionist and
feminist leader since the 1830s, became
increasingly involved in politics during the
1860s. (Library of Congress Prints and
Photographs Division)

in existence. Abolitionists also recognized that "the spirit of colorphobia" remained powerful in northern politics. That fall Garrison worried that "a considerable portion of the Republican party" might "join the Copperheads in
making peace on a slaveholding basis." In December Henry C. Wright begged
Lincoln to pledge in writing: "I shall not attempt to retract or modify the
emancipation proclamation; nor shall I return to slavery any person, who
is free by the terms of the proclamation, or by any of the acts of Congress."
Other abolitionist leaders used their political contacts to press Congress for
a constitutional amendment providing for universal emancipation. All abolitionist petitions to Congress after December 1863 included pleas for such an
amendment.[26]

Abolitionist women had a prominent role in this petitioning. During the
spring of 1863 Elizabeth Cady Stanton and Susan B. Anthony organized
the Women's National Loyal League to advocate congressional action in support of Lincoln's proclamation and to widen its scope to include all slaves. In
December 1863 the league joined the American Anti-Slavery Society (AASS)
and Sumner in demanding a constitutional amendment. On February 9, 1864,
in a manner reminiscent of the huge roll of petitions placed twenty years earlier on John Quincy Adams's desk in the House of Representatives, two black
men carried a roll with 100,000 signatures to Sumner's Senate desk. By the
time Congress adjourned that July, three more petition installments had arrived
with a total of 400,000 signatures—the largest number of signees to that time.
Other factors contributed to the Senate's passage on April 8 of what became
the Thirteenth Amendment. Nevertheless, as Garrison biographer Henry
Mayer observes, the league's effort "demonstrated both the continued vitality

of the [abolitionist] movement and the fresh imperative of a feminist political participation."[27]

During the 1864 presidential election campaign abolitionists became more absorbed into Republican politics. In contrast to 1860 abolitionists joined in the pre-election struggle as they worked with and sought to lead Republicans in either supporting Lincoln's renomination or finding an alternative to him. Among the alternatives, Chase and Frémont had the greatest éclat. As early as April 1862 abolitionists helped further Chase's presidential aspirations. In August of that year Frémont's speech at Boston's Tremont Temple drew abolitionist support. During the autumn of 1863 both Chase and Frémont sought abolitionist backing, and Wendell Phillips began promoting Frémont's candidacy. In an address to New York Republicans at Cooper Union, Phillips suggested that Frémont was better suited than Lincoln to carry out military occupation of and land redistribution in the South. When Chase withdrew in March 1864, after his home-state Ohio legislature supported Lincoln, Goodell's *Principia* endorsed Frémont, and George B. Cheever, Parker Pillsbury, and RPA David Plumb helped organize a Frémont club in New York City. In the process these three abolitionists criticized Lincoln's cautious policies regarding black rights and called for "absolute equality of all men before the law."[28]

Anticipation of Union victory on the battlefield, concern for the status of African Americans in what became known as Reconstruction, and divisions among themselves had much to do with abolitionist involvement in the 1864 campaign. Phillips and Garrison epitomized the divisions. Phillips, in resolutions he presented to the Massachusetts Anti-Slavery Society (MASS) in January 1864, criticized Lincoln for not recognizing "the negro as a man." He demanded thorough reorganization of southern society based on free-labor principles and racial equality. In contrast Garrison defended Lincoln's character and criticized Frémont for failing to endorse the Emancipation Proclamation. When later in January Anna Dickinson spoke in the House of Representatives, she exemplified the abolitionists' internal divide. With Abraham and Mary Todd Lincoln in attendance, Dickinson criticized the president's willingness to compromise with the South. *And* she called on the Republican Party to renominate him for president.[29]

In mid-March Garrison urged Republicans to unite behind Lincoln as the only means of defeating "Copperheads." He praised Lincoln for having through his Emancipation Proclamation "virtually" abolished "the whole slave system." In May another confrontation between Phillips and Garrison occurred at the annual AASS meeting. As Garrison defended Lincoln, Phillips contended that the president had interfered "as lightly as possible" with slavery. Phillips again charged that Lincoln "never yet acknowledged the manhood of the negro." And, as had been the case in January, Phillips's position prevailed. A week later the Church Anti-Slavery Society opposed Lincoln, claiming he tended "to drift with events," rather than act against slavery.[30]

Most prominent abolitionists, especially among the Foster-Pillsbury faction, joined in criticizing Lincoln. Goodell, George B. Cheever, August Wattles, Lydia Maria Child, and Elizabeth Cady Stanton emphasized Lincoln's inconsistency, incoherence, and lack of passion. Child claimed he had a "slow mind . . . incapable of large, comprehensive views." And in April Dickinson denounced Lincoln in person during a visit to the White House. She recalled telling the president that his policies regarding race were "all wrong; as radically bad as can be." In May, while speaking at Grover's Theater in Washington, she criticized Lincoln and praised Frémont.[31]

Abolitionist anti-Lincoln politics peaked during late May as about a dozen of them joined Radical Republicans and those northern Democrats who supported the war effort (War Democrats) in calling for a "Radical Democratic Party" mass convention in Cleveland. Leading initiators of the convention included Radical Republican B. Gratz Brown of Missouri and War Democrats John Cochrane and Lucius Robinson of New York. Abolitionists who signed one or another of the calls for the convention included Stephen S. Foster and James Redpath, both of Massachusetts, and David Plumb and church-oriented abolitionist Edward Gilbert, both of New York. Phillips, Stanton, George B. Cheever, and Frederick Douglass wrote letters in favor of holding the convention. All of these abolitionists hoped the convention would spur Congress to enact legislation providing for immediate general emancipation, "absolute equality" of all men before the law, disfranchisement of Confederates, and confiscation of rebel property.[32]

When the Cleveland convention met on May 31, Stephen S. Foster, Goodell, Pillsbury, Gilbert, and two other members of the Church Anti-Slavery Society attended. Gilbert read a letter from Phillips criticizing Lincoln and praising Frémont. Goodell and Pillsbury served on the platform committee, which produced resolutions calling for preservation of the Union by military force and a constitutional amendment prohibiting slavery. They also called for establishing "absolute equality before the law" for "all men" and confiscating rebel lands. But War Democrats and German Americans dominated the convention. When Goodell and Pillsbury tried to make the platform more specific regarding slavery as the cause of the war, and enfranchisement and land for black men, they failed. When the convention nominated Frémont for president, it also nominated War Democrat Cochrane for vice president. All of this drew abolitionist criticism. So did a platform resolution defending freedom of speech and press and writs of habeas corpus, which appeared aimed at protecting Peace Democrats. Frémont's acceptance letter seemed to appeal to the same group.[33]

As a result of these actions at Cleveland, pro-Lincoln Garrisonian Oliver Johnson berated George B. Cheever, Henry T. Cheever, and Goodell for having been drawn into a movement allied with "Jeff. Davis." Thereafter Johnson, Garrison, Henry C. Wright, Franklin B. Sanborn, J. Miller McKim, and Theodore Tilton joined in actively promoting Lincoln's reelection. So did black abolitionists John Mercer Langston and James W. C. Pennington. Their efforts won the gratitude of Conservative and Moderate Republicans and contributed to strengthening ties between the Republican Party and those abolitionists who supported Lincoln. They also contributed to Republican attempts to coopt the abolitionists. This became clear when Garrison visited the Republican/Union national convention, held at Baltimore's Front Street Theatre in June. Garrison, seated with Tilton in a gallery, applauded Lincoln's unanimous renomination, speeches describing slavery as a "curse to be extirpated," and resolutions favoring a constitutional amendment abolishing slavery. Abolitionist support for the Cleveland convention's call for such an amendment *and* abolitionist support for Lincoln encouraged the Baltimore convention's actions.[34]

From Baltimore Garrison, Tilton, and Tilton's wife, Elizabeth, proceeded to Washington. There Garrison and Tilton met with Secretary of War Edwin Stanton, whose "thoroughgoing anti-slavery spirit and purpose" impressed Garrison. The two abolitionists then went on to the Senate, where its members received Garrison at least as respectfully as they had other abolitionists who visited during the war. Sumner and Wilson joined Garrison in the lobby, escorted him to the chamber's floor, seated him in absent John P. Hale's chair, and introduced him to Republican senators William Pitt Fessenden, Benjamin F. Wade, Morton S. Wilkinson, and Edwin D. Morgan. The following day Garrison and Tilton met with Lincoln for an hour during which time Garrison noted the central role of the Emancipation Proclamation in changing his mind about Lincoln. The president in turn emphasized his commitment to an emancipation amendment and "fair play to the emancipated." He credited Garrison with a significant role in his renomination. After this meeting Garrison declared in regard to the U.S. government's agenda, "The abolition of slavery is first in order." He refused to join other abolitionists and Radicals in criticizing Lincoln for not demanding that black men immediately gain the right to vote.[35]

Phillips, Elizabeth Cady Stanton, George B. Cheever, Goodell, Dickinson, Conway, Lydia Maria Child, and Franklin B. Sanborn continued to support Frémont. Then in August the Frémont candidacy disintegrated as the general tried to get the Democratic nomination in addition to the Cleveland convention's. This spread fear that Frémont's campaign risked, in Sanborn's words, "throwing power into the hands of the Peace Democrats." Therefore most of those abolitionists who had supported Frémont concluded that Lincoln, despite his flaws, was the better candidate.[36]

When on August 9 Phillips, Stearns, and Elizur Wright Jr. met with Frémont and several Radicals, Frémont confirmed that he hoped the Democrats at their August 29 national convention in Chicago would nominate him and form an alliance with the Radicals. Instead it soon became certain that the Democrats would nominate former Union commanding general George B. McClellan on a peace platform. As a result George B. Cheever and Tilton joined with another group of Radicals to suggest that Frémont *and* Lincoln withdraw so that the Republicans might nominate a new candidate.[37]

Shortly thereafter news reached the North that Union general William Tecumseh Sherman's army had on September 3 captured Atlanta, striking a potentially fatal blow to the Confederacy. This led most prominent abolitionists who had believed Lincoln should not or could not be reelected to change their minds. Some such as Douglass and Dickinson, who had criticized Lincoln, now urged his reelection. Gerrit Smith, Howe, and Wright asked Frémont to withdraw unilaterally. After consulting several other abolitionists (including Phillips, who urged him to continue, and Whittier, who advised the opposite), the general ended his campaign on September 22. Even so the Foster-Pillsbury faction, Phillips, Elizabeth Cady Stanton, Anthony, George B. Cheever, and Stearns still refused to support Lincoln. Stearns wrote, "Mr. Lincoln is unfitted by nature and education to carry on the government for the next four years." Stearns added that only the capture of Atlanta had kept "leaders of the Republican party" from urging Lincoln's withdrawal from the presidential race. On the other abolitionist extreme, Marius R. Robinson, Theodore D. Weld, Ichabod Codding, Calvin Fairbank, Sallie Hollie, John R. Rogers, Dickinson, Tilton, Henry C. Wright, William Burleigh, and Gerrit Smith campaigned for Lincoln.[38]

Nearly all abolitionists reacted positively when Lincoln and the Republican Party won a major victory in the November elections over McClellan and the Democratic Party. Abolitionists recognized that Lincoln, though flawed and resistant to their vision for emancipation and black rights, was far better than the Democratic alternative. That December Phillips privately asserted that abolitionists had a "common duty" to make sure Republicans carried out their pledge to amend the Constitution so as to abolish slavery—and establish black equality before the law. He and Elizabeth Cady Stanton feared, however, that they might have to do this without the assistance of Garrison, Smith, and (increasingly) Douglass, who identified with the Lincoln administration.[39]

Much abolitionist criticism of Lincoln during the 1864 national campaign had derived from the conservative plan for the postwar South he had announced on December 8, 1863, in his Proclamation of Amnesty and Reconstruction. Through this plan Lincoln sought to undermine the Confederacy by offering seceded states a quick return to the Union. Excepting only the highest Confederate civil and military leaders, the plan offered amnesty to rebels. As a precondition for readmission, it required only 10 percent of voters in each state to swear future loyalty to the Union. States also had to recognize the abolition of slavery but could determine the issue of black rights within their bounds. Lincoln implied that this might include semi-slavery for most African Americans.[40]

Some abolitionists (and some Radical Republicans) believed Lincoln's plan would leave masters in political power and provide insufficient protection for black freedom. Douglass had charged that, by failing to endorse suffrage for black men, the plan betrayed African Americans who had served in Union armies. Phillips had called Lincoln's proposal a "mere sham." The plan had also encouraged abolitionists and Radicals to continue to demand passage of a constitutional amendment abolishing slavery throughout the country. During the 1864 campaign Lincoln endorsed such an amendment. But he simultaneously expressed willingness to submit "our remaining dispute about slavery . . . to the peaceful tribunals of courts and votes." In August 1864 he finessed this contradiction at a meeting in the White House with Douglass during which he asked Douglass to devise a plan to help slaves escape "should peace be concluded while they remain within Rebel Lines."[41]

Since the beginning of the war, Lewis Tappan's AMA, working with Boston's Port Royal Education Commission, Philadelphia's Port Royal Relief Commission, and a variety of freedmen's aid societies, had sought to provide direct aid to former slaves. As Union military victory over the Confederacy approached, these nongovernmental efforts encouraged other abolitionists to employ their traditional political tactics to promote institutionalized federal action on behalf of black rights and education.[42]

In early 1862 the abolitionist-controlled Emancipation League had advocated formation of a federal agency dedicated to gaining freedom for slaves, finding employment for former slaves, guaranteeing equal protection under the law, and helping the various freedmen's aid societies. In support of the league's effort, Samuel Gridley Howe in September 1862 had gone to Washington to lobby Chase and other officials. That December J. Miller McKim had undertaken a similar journey to lobby Representatives Thaddeus Stevens and John Bingham, Senator Sumner, and Secretary of War Henry Stanton. In January 1863 Henry Wilson had presented the league's petition in the U.S. Senate. These initiatives contributed materially to the War Department's creation in March 1863 of the American Freedmen's Inquiry Commission, authorized to investigate the condition of African Americans freed under Lincoln's Emancipation Proclamation. Howe, New York abolitionist James M. McKay, and nonabolitionist social reformer Robert Dale Owen of Indiana served as commissioners.[43]

Meanwhile abolitionists continued to push for creation of a federal agency dedicated to aiding former slaves. In December 1863 four northern freedmen's aid societies cooperated in sending a delegation to meet with Lincoln. That same month the New York–based National Freedmen's Relief Association (NFRA) petitioned Lincoln, pleading that he urge Congress to act in this regard. When Lincoln complied, McKim, Francis George Shaw (the abolitionist father of Colonel Robert Gould Shaw, who had died the previous July while leading black Union troops in an attack on Confederate Fort Wagner in South Carolina), and Levi Coffin (abolitionist founder of the Western Freedman's Aid Society) lobbied cabinet members and Congress on behalf of such an agency. At about the same time, Josephine S. Griffing, a Garrisonian from Ohio employed in Washington by the NFRA, approached Lincoln, Henry Stanton, and Sumner. In May 1864 the Freedmen's Inquiry Commission's report endorsed immediate emancipation without apprenticeship, equal rights for African Americans, and creation of a federal freedmen's bureau to provide physical protection for both. Internal Republican disagreements concerning the nature of the bureau and whether it should be placed in the War Department or the Treasury Department delayed initiation of the Freedmen's Bureau until March 1865.[44]

Abolitionists also worked with Radical Republicans in Congress who continued to seek, in Elizabeth Cady Stanton's words, congressional legislation on behalf of "unconditional emancipation," "justice and equality," and the right to vote for black men in the postwar South. Phillips went to Washington in December 1864 to discuss ways of counteracting southern state-level apprenticeship systems aimed a perpetuating slavery in all but name. As 1865 began Radicals in Congress blocked readmission of Louisiana under Lincoln's Amnesty and Reconstruction plan. Abolitionist observers, including Elizur Wright Jr., Douglass, and Phillips gave Sumner much of the credit for this. They believed Sumner had become a firmer advocate of black rights than Garrison and Gerrit Smith.[45]

Within these volatile circumstances the Lincoln administration worked covertly to have the House of Representatives, on January 31, 1865, pass the Thirteenth Amendment, which the Senate had approved the previous April. Shortly after the House's action, Garrison, in a speech at Boston's Music Hall, credited Lincoln in achieving this longstanding abolitionist goal. Two weeks later Lincoln and several Republican congressmen arranged for black abolitionist Henry Highland Garnet, who had sat in the House gallery when the amendment passed, to present a sermon in the same chamber. In this sermon Garnet celebrated the amendment and pressed for black voting rights and education. Lincoln, however, continued to contemplate postponing emancipation. Garrison may not have been aware of this when he wrote to the president, "I have the utmost faith in the benevolence of your heart, the purity of your motives, and the integrity of your spirit. . . . I am sure you will consent to no compromise that will leave the slave in his fetters." Garrison, along with Frederick Douglass and Gerrit Smith, believed Lincoln's conservative scenario for Reconstruction would produce black freedom and civil rights. Other abolitionists continued to doubt this would be the case.[46]

The Lincoln administration recognized the importance of abolitionist support—especially Garrison's. Secretary of War Edwin M. Stanton included Garrison among dignitaries attending a Union victory celebration at Fort Sumter on April 14. Tilton, Joshua Leavitt, and English abolitionist George Thompson also attended, as did Garrison's son George, a Union soldier for whom Stanton provided leave. Years later former Union Army officer Daniel H. Chamberlain recalled Lincoln saying that April, "I have only been an instrument. The logic and moral power of Garrison, and the anti-slavery people of the country and the army have done all." Yet Garrison, before Lincoln's assassination on April 15, had concluded that with the Republican Party in power, the nation no longer required an independent abolition movement to advocate black rights. Several Radical Republicans, including Sumner, disagreed. They aligned with Phillips as they sought to maintain the AASS during Reconstruction.[47]

How to deal with the Republican Party had been an issue among abolitionists ever since the party organized in 1854. In January 1862 the Foster-Pillsbury faction had objected to expressions of support for the Republican-controlled Union government. At the other extreme Maria Weston Chapman and J. Miller McKim had, well before Garrison, expressed confidence in the Lincoln administration's dedication to abolitionist goals, and they called for dissolving the AASS. In January 1863 Garrison had argued that the Emancipation Proclamation had achieved abolition. Phillips, Pillsbury, the Fosters, and Charles L. Remond objected that the other abolitionist goal of equal rights remained.[48] This division had much to do with how abolitionists had engaged in the presidential election campaign of 1864.

The division widened with the House's passage of the Thirteenth Amendment in January 1865 and Confederate general Robert E. Lee's surrender the following April at Appomattox. That May at the AASS annual meeting, Garrison's motion to dissolve the organization lost by a 118–48 vote. Garrison then withdrew from the AASS, and Phillips became its president. Oliver Johnson resigned as editor of the *National Anti-Slavery Standard,* and in December 1865, when the required number of states ratified the Thirteenth Amendment, Garrison ceased publication of the *Liberator.* The Foster-Pillsbury faction, nearly all black abolitionists, feminist abolitionists, as well as Gerrit Smith, George B. Cheever, and Whittier remained active in the AASS. Phillips promised that the organization would promote "absolute equality before the law—absolute civil equality for the freedmen," and the right to vote for black men. Those abolitionists who remained in the AASS regarded voting rights as a moral issue. Garrison in contrast held it to be a *political* issue best dealt with by the Republican Party. Both groups continued to petition, contact sympathetic politicians, and lobby in Congress and the White House.[49]

With Vice President Andrew Johnson's ascendency to the presidency on Lincoln's death, abolitionists associated with both Garrison and Phillips hoped they could influence Johnson on behalf of black rights. But the Phillips group in particular feared Johnson would continue Lincoln's tendency to allow white southerners to decide the former slaves' future. During the summer of 1865 Johnson put his lenient "Restoration" plan into effect. As former Confederate states enacted discriminatory "Black Codes," and as anti-black violence spread, Phillips and some other abolitionists sought to rally Republicans against Johnson. In July Phillips demanded that representatives from the former Confederate states not be seated in Congress that December. In October, in a widely reported speech entitled "The South Victorious," he blamed Johnson and the Republican Party for white southerners' intransigent opposition to black rights.[50]

Other abolitionists had not yet given up on Johnson. When during the summer of 1865 Sumner reported to Phillips, Howe, and Stearns that he had no success with the president in regard to black rights, Stearns decided to visit Johnson at the White House to discuss black suffrage. At this meeting Johnson told Stearns that Congress had no power over voting rights in the states and that immediate suffrage for black men would lead to race-based violence. Johnson nevertheless assured Stearns that he supported gradual extension of the right to vote to black men. And, although Philips and Sumner doubted Johnson's sincerity, Stearns, some other abolitionists, and many Republicans believed the president.[51]

In December 1865 abolitionists petitioned Congress in support of granting black men the right to vote in the District of Columbia. In January 1866 the

House of Representatives passed a bill that would do so. A year later the Senate passed that bill, Johnson vetoed it, and on January 8, 1867, Congress overrode this veto. Also in December 1865 McKim, who had left the AASS, led the American Freedmen's Aid Commission in petitioning Congress to strengthen the Freedmen's Bureau's authority to protect black civil rights against southern state legislation. The Freedman's Aid petition anticipated Moderate Republican Lyman Trumbull's Freedmen's Bureau bill, introduced in February 1866, and his Civil Rights bill, introduced in March. Johnson vetoed both bills, and within months Congress overrode the vetoes. Meanwhile abolitionist groups, encouraged by Gerrit Smith and Sumner, pressed Congress on behalf of adding a guarantee for black voting rights to what became the Fourteenth Amendment, designed to place the Civil Rights Act in the Constitution. Radicals rejected this advice.[52]

In February 1866 a visit to the White House by a thirteen-member black delegation helped end lingering abolitionist belief that they could positively influence Johnson. Led by Frederick Douglass and George T. Downing, the delegation faced a more agitated and intransigent president than Stearns had. In response to Douglass's and Downing's respectful pleas for voting rights, Johnson asserted that African Americans were lucky simply to be free. He accused the delegates of contributing to race hatred in the South. He charged that they overlooked the rights and interests of nonslaveholding white southerners and disregarded state power to set voting standards. He suggested that colonization remained the best and safest avenue toward black advancement. After the meeting Johnson reportedly denounced Douglass in explicitly racist terms. Nevertheless Johnson recognized Douglass's political stature and later offered to appoint him commissioner of the Freedmen's Bureau. Douglass declined, as did John Mercer Langston and Robert Purvis.[53]

When McKim and Garrison visited Washington shortly after the black delegation, they hoped to meet with and influence such Radicals as Sumner, Chase, Wilson, George W. Julian, William D. Kelley, and Stevens, as well as President Johnson and General Oliver O. Howard of the Freedmen's Bureau. According to Garrison biographer Walter M. Merrill this visit converted Garrison from "a Lincoln moderate" to "a Radical Republican." Conversing with the Radicals, listening to the reading of Johnson's message vetoing the Freedmen's Bureau Bill, and hearing Johnson denounce Stevens, Sumner, and Phillips as traitors precipitated this transformation.[54]

As historian James Brewer Stewart points out, abolitionists depended on Republicans to put their vision of postslavery America into effect. Therefore abolitionists continued to urge the Radicals not to compromise regarding black civil and voting rights. But many Republicans, including some Radicals, worried that issues concerning black rights might hurt their party. Republican candidates often avoided the suffrage issue as they presented the Fourteenth Amendment as the *final* requirement for former Confederate states seeking readmission to the Union. During the first half of 1866 Gerrit Smith, David Plumb, Thomas Wentworth Higginson, Phillips, Stearns, and Tilton praised and prodded Sumner regarding suffrage. In June Sumner assured Phillips, "I shall never vote to receive any State [into the Union] until it establishes impartial suffrage or this is established by Congress."[55]

Later in 1866 abolitionists used their standing with northern voters to influence the congressional election campaign. But as during the 1864 campaign, abolitionists split—this time over the proposed Fourteenth Amendment. George B. Cheever, Frederick Douglass, Phillips, Robert Purvis, Gerrit Smith, and Tilton objected to the amendment's failure to provide guarantees for the right of black men to vote. Garrison, Oliver Johnson, J. Miller McKim, and Stearns regarded the amendment as a first step that should be praised rather than criticized. When antiblack violence increased in the South, those abolitionists who advocated congressional action regarding black voting rights became more active. In September Tilton, Dickinson, and Douglass led a Republican-backed Southern Loyalists Convention in Philadelphia to adopt resolutions favoring black suffrage. Phillips and Tilton interpreted the great Republican electoral victory that November, which produced a veto-proof Congress, as an opportunity to press for continued military occupation of the South and black suffrage.[56]

Historian James M. McPherson contends that Phillips's political influence reached "new heights" during the months following the 1866 election. It is true that resurgent states' rights and white supremacism in the South had more influence than abolitionists in leading Republicans in Congress to institute Military Reconstruction, beginning on March 2, 1867. Nevertheless, speaking tours undertaken by Phillips, Dickinson, Douglass, and Tilton, and petition campaigns led by George B. and Henry T. Cheever, rallied popular support for the measure. It divided the former Confederate states (except Tennessee, which had gained readmission to the Union in July 1866) into five military districts. It required that black men be allowed to vote and serve in state constitutional conventions. It instituted an "iron-clad" loyalty oath to the Union that prevented many white men from engaging in politics. And it provided for readmission to the Union when a former Confederate state ratified the Fourteenth Amendment.[57]

Abolitionists quibbled about the act's provisions and those of supplementary acts. They pointed out that once a state rejoined the Union it could disenfranchise black men. Phillips noted a predisposition among most Republican politicians toward compromising black rights. But he and other abolitionists applauded black suffrage during the Reconstruction process, and, in historian McPherson's words, trusted "that additional measures necessary to safeguard the Negro's freedom would be enacted in the future." Phillips declared, "There is no hope for the people politically . . . [other] than the triumph of the Republican party."[58]

Abolitionists had earlier joined Radicals James M. Ashley, Benjamin Butler, Thaddeus Stevens, and Zachariah Chandler in calling on the House of Representatives to impeach Andrew Johnson. On February 24, 1868, the House did so, charging Johnson with violating the Tenure of Office Act in his dismissal of Secretary of War Edwin M. Stanton. During Johnson's Senate trial, which extended from early March to late May, Tilton, church-oriented abolitionist Gilbert Haven, British-born Richard J. Hinton (who had supported John Brown in Kansas Territory), and Edmund Quincy traveled to Washington to lobby for conviction. According to conservative Secretary of the Navy Gideon Welles, Tilton had a major role in stiffening Radical resolve. When the Senate failed by one vote to convict Johnson, abolitionists joined Radicals in political defeat.[59]

Meanwhile Phillips and other abolitionists encouraged Republicans to pass what became the Fifteenth Amendment guaranteeing the right to vote to black men throughout the country. In this context they resisted Republican plans to nominate former Union commanding general Ulysses S. Grant for president, pointing out that Grant lacked a reliable political record. Abolitionists also criticized the 1868 Republican platform for not supporting black suffrage in the North. But in a manner similar to their reaction to Lincoln's victory in 1860, abolitionists portrayed Grant's election as a step toward protection for former slaves' equal rights. The *National Anti-Slavery Standard* hoped Grant would support a constitutional amendment protecting "impartial suffrage" and thereby "immortalize his administration." In a public letter Gerrit Smith urged Grant to work for "recognition of the equal rights of all races of men." More reservedly, Phillips heralded Grant's election as "reason for deep gratitude to God," then added, "in Grant himself we place no confidence."[60]

That December the Republican-controlled Congress, with Grant's enthusiastic support, began to produce a black suffrage constitutional amendment. Most abolitionists favored the version Henry Wilson unsuccessfully urged the Senate to pass on February 9, 1869. It would have banned state and federal denial of the right to vote based on "race, color, nativity, property, education, or religious beliefs." Abolitionists accommodated themselves, however, to the less comprehensive ban of denying the right to vote based on "race, color, or previous condition of servitude" that went into the Fifteenth Amendment. Surprisingly

Phillips contended that the amendment's original wording had been too strong. In addition many abolitionists (black and white, men and women) accepted not including suffrage rights for women in the proposed amendment. This further weakened the abolitionists as women's rights activists among them, led by Elizabeth Cady Stanton and Susan B. Anthony, objected and organized.[61]

Sumner demonstrated once again that he had become more radical than nearly all abolitionists when he refused on February 26, 1896, to vote for what became the Fifteenth Amendment because it failed to ban poll taxes and literacy tests. The amendment gained ratification on March 30, 1870. At that point Frederick Douglass, although aware of rising antiblack violence in the South, wondered what might be left to "be said at the [upcoming] annual meeting of the American Antislavery Society." The AASS, Douglass suggested, was no longer necessary because the "Fifteenth amendment is on its passage and in a fair way to become part of the organic law of the land." Phillips agreed, declaring, "Our long work is sealed at last!" Abigail Kelly, Stephen S. Foster, and Pillsbury dissented from this optimism. Other abolitionists recognized that racial discrimination would continue. Nevertheless the AASS and other abolitionist organizations dissolved during April 1870. What political influence abolitionists continued to wield would be through the Republican Party.[62]

Conclusion

During the two decades following the Civil War, surviving members of the last generation of abolitionists congratulated themselves. They claimed to have led the U.S. government to end slavery and establish equal rights for African Americans. They pioneered the argument, later endorsed by many historians, that their movement had achieved its objectives. Then they had second thoughts. Several of them lamented that they and their colleagues had failed to end white racism. As a result, effective enforcement of the Thirteenth, Fourteenth, and Fifteenth Amendments became impossible.[1] The absorption of most abolitionists into the Republican Party during the Civil War and Reconstruction contributed to this perception of failure.

As this book's description of abolitionists' long-term direct engagement with politics and government indicates, the truth regarding abolitionist impact lies between full success and complete failure. Abolitionist political efforts, stretching over 150 years from the colonial era through the early national period into the Civil War made universal legal emancipation possible at the war's conclusion. This would not have happened had abolitionists confined their efforts only to changing popular opinion through moral suasion or independent engagement in electoral politics. It was the abolitionists' longstanding tactics of petitioning, lobbying, direct personal contacts with antislavery politicians, and physical action that profoundly influenced the course American history. From the early eighteenth century through the Civil War era, no prominent abolitionist relied solely on propaganda and agitation.

Direct abolitionist influence on and actions within northeastern colonial and state governments led to gradual and immediate emancipation in that region between 1780 and 1804. Had this "first emancipation" not occurred, the history of slavery in the United States would have been quite different.[2] Beginning during the early national period with abolitionist engagement with the first Congress, the resulting sectional tensions set a pattern that continued through the Civil War. During the 1810s and 1820s, abolitionists directly encouraged northern political opposition to slavery expansion and interacted with anti-slavery politicians who were at times abolitionists themselves. During the same decades, abolitionists helped defeat a political effort to legalize slavery in Illinois. And they initiated a petitioning campaign that produced decades of debate in Congress concerning slavery and the slave trade in the District of Columbia.

Historians often portray the immediate abolitionists of the late 1820s and 1830s as opposed to engagement with major political parties and government. Instead such historians describe immediatists as devoted to moral suasion as a means of promoting individual conversion in favor of freeing slaves and recognizing their rights. Yet the immediatists' direct engagement with politics and government exceeded that of their predecessors. Garrisonian abolitionists, from the 1830s through the Civil War, recognized they could not rely on propaganda and meetings alone to reach an essentially political goal. Similarly church-oriented abolitionists could not depend merely on their religious affiliations and missionary efforts in the South to reach goals that could only be achieved through congressional action. Radical political abolitionists (RPAs) recognized the limits of independent participation in electoral politics. They joined Garrisonians and church-oriented abolitionists in petitioning, lobbying, and developing personal relationships with antislavery politicians, some of whom had been the RPAs' more moderate colleagues in the Liberty Party during the early to mid-1840s.

Throughout the antebellum years, the Civil War years, and the early Reconstruction period, all abolitionists engaged in the direct political strategies developed by their predecessors during the eighteenth and early nineteenth centuries. During the 1850s they worked to move antislavery politicians beyond nonextensionism and denationalization toward emancipation throughout the United States and governmental protections for black rights. Their encouragement of antislavery congressmen to criticize the Slave Power, slavery expansion, and on occasion slavery itself had a major role in proslavery defensiveness and increased sectional tensions.

Physical abolitionist action against slavery also directly impacted sectional politics and government. Such action contributed to white southern reactions and the passage of personal liberty laws by northern state legislatures. It sharpened sectional divisions in Congress and led by 1850 to a new, stronger fugitive slave law that, in turn, promoted increased abolitionist-led physical resistance across the North to slave catching. John Brown's raid at Harpers Ferry carried such physical action to a new level and had an enormous impact on antislavery and proslavery politics.

During the Civil War and early years of Reconstruction, abolitionists continued to petition, lobby, and interact with politicians to move the Union government toward universal emancipation. Their efforts in regard to Abraham
Lincoln are particularly noteworthy. But the long sectional war, black resistance
during the war, the realization by Lincoln and members of Congress that fighting against slavery was bound to weaken the Confederacy, and the need for
black Union troops had more impact than abolitionists in shaping U.S. emancipation policy. As elderly immediatists recognized in retrospect, their wartime
political tactics and deepening relationship to the Republican Party had a role
in their failure fully to achieve their goals.

Acknowledgments

For years I concentrated my research and writing on the physical, often violent clashes between antislavery and proslavery forces on both sides of the North-South sectional border. I enjoyed doing so because it was a relatively unexplored part of antebellum American history and because there were many dramatic confrontations. I came to appreciate how those involved in these confrontations, including escaping slaves, black and white abolitionists who encouraged and aided the escapees, and defensive white southerners who pursued the escapees and clashed with abolitionists, influenced the sectional politics that led to the Civil War. But my focus was on a restricted region and on a relatively brief time period. Therefore I began to wonder about other ways that abolitionists directly impacted American politics and government over a much more extended period.

As I undertook a wider study of that direct influence which led to this book, informed advice became very important. Therefore I deeply appreciate the help I have received from Manisha Sinha, Matt Mason, Hugh Davis, Jim Huston, Caleb McDaniel, Richard Blackett, Nichol Etcheson, Diane Barnes, and Bill Hine.

Manisha and Matt provided much needed critiques of this book's fist two chapters. Hugh gave me extremely insightful advice concerning the years from 1831 to 1843. Jim, Richard, and Caleb helped me clarify my approach to the abolitionists' political role between 1840 and 1852. Nichole, Diane, and Bill provided insightful suggestions for chapters on the 1850s and 1860s. In addition to these scholars and friends, I thank another friend, Doug Egerton, for his close reading (for the University of Virginia Press) of my entire manuscript and his very helpful suggestions.

Earlier I enjoyed excellent assistance in my research from a large number of archivists and librarians associated with a variety of institutions. They include in alphabetical order: Jennifer Brathovde, librarian, Manuscript Division, Library of Congress; Alison Clemens, Beinecke Rare Books and Manuscript Library, Yale University; Malia Ebel, reference librarian/archivist, New Hampshire Historical Society; Heather Furnas, American Studies librarian, Division of Rare Books and Manuscript Collections, Carl A. Kroch Library, Cornell University; Eva Garcelon-Hart, Stewart-Swift Research Center Archivist, Henry Sheldon

Museum; Susan Halpert, Department of Public Services, Houghton Library, Harvard University; David Haugaard, director of research services, Pennsylvania Historical Society; Dan Hinchen, assistant reference librarian, Massachusetts Historical Society; Marybeth Kavanagh, reference librarian, New-York Historical Society; Thomas Knoles, Marcus A. McCorison Librarian and Curator of Manuscripts, American Antiquarian Society; Tracey Kry, reading room manager and assistant curator of manuscripts, American Antiquarian Society; Julia Lipkins, reference archivist, New-York Historical Society; Kimberly Reynolds, curator of manuscripts, Boston Public Library; Salesa Richards, reference archivist/interlibrary loan, Ohio History Connection; Morgan Swan, special collections education and outreach librarian, Rauner Special Collections Library, Dartmouth College; Melinda Wallington, public services library assistant, Department of Rare Books and Special Collections, Rush Rhees Library, University of Rochester; Emily Walhout, library assistant, Department of Public Services, Houghton Library, Harvard University; Hilary Dorsh Wong, reference coordinator, Rare Books and Manuscripts, Cornell University.

In carrying out my research and writing I benefited from receiving a National Endowment for the Humanities Award for Faculty, which allowed me to work on this book without interruption during the 2013–14 academic year. In regard to the process toward publication, I thank several people associated with the University of Virginia Press. Series editors Vernon Burton and Liz Varon provided very helpful advice and encouragement, as did the press's senior executive editor for history and social science, Dick Holway. I also thank acquisitions assistant Helen Chandler and copy editor Margaret Hogan for their careful work in preparing my manuscript for publication.

Closer to home, I thank Beverly Pott, Bill Sudduth, Ross Taylor, and Crystal Williams of the Government Information and Maps Department at the University of South Carolina's Thomas Cooper Library. For many years they have helped me locate microfilm copies of newspapers and helped me figure out how to use the machine to read these newspapers and microfilmed documents.

Finally, as usual, I thank Judy Harrold and Emily Harrold for their essential help and support.

Notes

Introduction

1. Clausewitz, *On War,* 87.

2. Drake, *Quakers and Slavery;* Soderlund, *Quakers and Slavery;* Essig, *Bonds of Wickedness;* Kaplan and Kaplan, *Black Presence;* Melish, *Disowning Slavery;* Larson, *Market Revolution in America;* Stampp, *Peculiar Institution;* Foner, *Free Soil, Free Labor, Free Men;* Richards, *Slave Power.*

3. McPherson, *Struggle for Equality,* 3.

4. Mason, *Slavery and Politics,* 10–11.

5. Adams, *Neglected Period of Anti-Slavery.* Manisha Sinha both accepts "waning" of abolitionism beginning during the 1790s and rejects the idea. See Sinha, *Slave's Cause,* 97, 160.

6. U.S. Congress, *Annals,* 1st Cong., 2nd sess. (February 11–12, 1790), cols. 1224, 1239–42; Davis, *Jefferson Davis, Constitutionalist,* 1:479–80; Publicola, "Present Aspects of Abolitionism," 430; Ruffin, "Consequences of Abolitionist Agitation"; Hammond, *Selections from the Letters and Speeches,* 350; Channing, *Crisis of Fear.*

7. On denationalization as a political strategy to achieve "ultimate extinction" of slavery, see Oakes, *Freedom National,* 4–32. See also Oakes, *Scorpion's Sting.*

8. Clarke, *Anti-Slavery Days;* Garrison and Garrison, *William Lloyd Garrison;* Johnson, *Garrison and His Times;* May, *Some Recollections of Our Anti-Slavery Conflict;* Pillsbury, *Acts of the Anti-Slavery Apostles;* Stanton, *Random Recollections.*

9. Rhodes, *History of the United States,* 1:63.

10. Hart, *Slavery and Abolition,* 173–75.

11. Owsley, "Fundamental Cause of the Civil War," 16–18 (1st–2nd quotations); Craven, "The South in American History," 106 (3rd quotation); Randall, *Civil War and Reconstruction,* 146 (4th–5th quotations).

12. Barnes, *Antislavery Impulse,* 197 (1st quotation); Dumond, *Antislavery Origins of the Civil War,* 107 (2nd quotation).

13. Dillon, "The Failure of the American Abolitionists" (1st–2nd quotation); Fladeland, "Who Were the Abolitionists?" 109 (3rd quotation); Stampp, *Causes of the Civil War,* 2 (4th quotation).

14. Sewell, *Ballots for Freedom,* ix (1st–2nd quotations); Beard and Beard, *Rise of American Civilization,* 1:667, 698–700, 710, 2:40, 53–54 (3rd–4th quotations).

15. Martin B. Duberman, "The Northern Response to Slavery," in Duberman, ed., *Antislavery Vanguard,* 395 (1st quotation); Gara, "Slavery and the Slave Power," 18 (2nd

quotation). Eric Foner in his book on northern free-labor ideology follows the Beards in stressing economic and class interests. But he also maintains that "the religiously oriented abolitionism of the 1830's . . . had a profound influence on many radical [Republican] leaders." See Foner, *Free Soil, Free Labor, Free Men,* 109–10, 302–3.

16. Dillon, *Abolitionists,* 265 (1st quotation); Stewart, *Holy Warriors,* 200–203 (2nd–3rd quotations).

17. Pierson, *Free Hearts and Free Homes,* 4–5 (1st–2nd quotations); Blue, *No Taint of Compromise,* ix–x, 1–3, 270 (3rd quotation).

18. Huston, "Experiential Basis," 615; Walters, *Antislavery Appeal,* xiv–xvii (1st quotation), 54, 60–61, 70–87, 95, 111–28. On abolitionism as a surrogate religion, see Formisano, "Political Character, Antipartyism and the Second Party System," 704–6; Donald M. Scott, "Abolition as a Sacred Vocation," in Perry and Fellman, eds., *Antislavery Reconsidered,* 72 (2nd quotation); and Friedman, "'Historical Topics Sometimes Run Dry,'" 194 (3rd quotation). See also McKivigan, "The Antislavery 'Comeouter' Sects"; Walters, "The Erotic South"; Howard Temperly, "Antislavery as a Form of Cultural Imperialism," in Bolt and Drescher, eds., *Anti-Slavery Religion, and Reform,* 335–50; and Davis, *Joshua Leavitt,* 39–40, 99–100.

19. McCarthy and Stauffer, *Prophets of Protest,* back cover (quotation); Stewart, *Abolitionist Politics,* 206 (2nd quotation); Sinha, *Slave's Cause;* McDaniel, *Problem of Democracy.* Shortly after *Prophets of Protest* appeared, James Brewer Stewart lamented the "apparent irrelevance" of current "abolitionist studies" to "political historians." But at that time he suggested that in contrast to "political historians," those who studied the abolitionists "usually" recognized their impact on northern voters. See Stewart, "Reconsidering the Abolitionists in an Age of Fundamentalist Politics," 3–4.

20. Strong, *Perfectionist Politics,* 139, 156 (1st quotation); Earle, *Jacksonian Antislavery;* Laurie, *Beyond Garrison,* 272 (2nd quotation).

21. Brooks, *Liberty Power.*

22. Sinha, *Slave's Cause,* 5 (quotation). Other books that take a long view include Hart, *Slavery and Abolition,* 152–69; Filler, *Crusade against Slavery,* 10–17; Dumond, *Antislavery: The Crusade,* 16–141; Drake, *Quakers and Slavery;* and Soderlund, *Quakers and Slavery.*

1. Direct Abolitionist Engagement in Politics, 1688–1807

1. Jordan, *White over Black,* 44–100; Berlin, *Many Thousands Gone,* 1–216.

2. Simmons, *American Colonies,* 86–92; Berlin, *Many Thousands Gone,* 64–71, 142–47.

3. Simmons, *American Colonies,* 86–92; Berlin, *Many Thousands Gone,* 64–71, 142–47.

4. Horton and Horton, *In Hope of Liberty,* 5–8, 10; Berlin, *Many Thousands Gone,* 48–51, 185–94. Massachusetts legalized slavery in 1641.

5. Stewart, *Holy Warriors,* 22–23; Nash, *Race and Revolution,* 11; Foner, *History of Black Americans,* 1:345–46, 359; Nash and Soderlund, *Freedom by Degrees,* 91–98; McManus, *Black Bondage in the North,* 166–67, 169, 175–76; Egerton, *Death or Liberty,* 95–97. Historians have also portrayed white fear of slave revolt as having a determining role. See McManus, *Black Bondage in the North,* 126–42.

6. Foner, *History of Black Americans,* 1:345–46; Berlin, *Many Thousands Gone,* 228, 231, 233, 235–36; Nash and Soderlund, *Freedom by Degrees,* xiv–xv, 75, 137–38; Essig, *Bonds of Wickedness,* 20–26, 37–49, 53, 72; McManus, *History of Negro Slavery in New York,* 117–18; McManus, *Black Bondage in the North,* 160–79.

7. Sinha, *Slave's Cause,* 9–129. The Enlightenment is also known as the Age of Reason.

8. Essig, *Bonds of Wickedness,* 4–5, 10–14.

9. John Woolman, "Correspondence on the Keeping of Negroes . . . 1762," in Woolman, *Works,* 324–27; Fladeland, *Men and Brothers,* 15–16; Soderlund, *Quakers and Slavery;* Drake, *Quakers and Slavery,* 1–85; Bauman, *For the Reputation of Truth,* 66–67; Cary, *From Peace to Freedom.*

10. Mark, "The Vestigial Constitution," 2154, 2163–74 (quotations); Higginson, "Short History of the Right to Petition." Some twentieth- and twenty-first-century historians regard abolitionist petitioning during the nineteenth century as a means of affecting popular opinion rather than a narrowly political tactic. See Dillon, *Abolitionists,* 106; Stewart, *Holy Warriors,* 81–82, 87–88; Miller, *Arguing about Slavery,* 303–4; and Newman, *Transformation of American Abolitionism,* 132–34.

11. Cadbury, "Another Early Quaker Anti-Slavery Document"; Keith, *An Exhortation and Caution,* 3 (quotation); Cary, *From Peace to Freedom,* 106–10; Higginson, "Short History of the Right to Petition," 141–42; Carroll, "William Southeby," 423–24; [Pennsylvania], "Votes and Proceedings of the House of Representatives."

12. Drake, *Quakers and Slavery,* 43–47, 51–71; Soderlund, *Quakers and Slavery,* 15–53, 174–75; Nash and Soderlund, *Freedom by Degrees,* 49–46; Jackson, *Let This Voice Be Heard.*

13. Bauman, *For the Reputation of Truth,* 9–11, 66–67; Zilversmit, *First Emancipation,* 75–83.

14. Nash and Soderlund, *Freedom by Degrees,* xi–xii, 71–73; Sinha, *Slave's Cause,* 20–33; Dillon, *Abolitionists,* 9–10; Horton and Horton, *In Hope of Liberty,* 57–58.

15. Berlin, *Many Thousands Gone,* 233; Newman, *Transformation of American Abolitionism,* 17–18; Nash and Soderlund, *Freedom by Degrees,* 71–73, 86–87; Essig, *Bonds of Wickedness,* 21–26, 37–42, 44, 53, 71–72 (1st quotation); Locke, *Antislavery,* 66–69 (2nd–3rd quotations); Nash, *Race and Revolution,* 8–9.

16. Countryman, *American Revolution,* 53–204.

17. Berlin, *Many Thousands Gone,* 230–32; Dillon, *Slavery Attacked,* 28–29; Mullin, *Flight and Rebellion,* 124–36; Egerton, *Death or Liberty,* 68–75; McManus, *Black Bondage in the North,* 150–53, 160–61, 164, 171; Scott, *Black Revolts,* 99.

18. Essig, *Bonds of Wickedness,* 21–24, 26, 37–42; Horton and Horton, *In Hope of Liberty,* 73 (1st quotation); Zilversmit, *First Emancipation,* 124–25; Newman,

Transformation of American Abolitionism, 24–25, 40 (2nd–3rd quotations). The PAS from the 1780s through the 1820s sometimes used petitions as a means of spreading antislavery sentiment among the white population. But it usually had narrowly political objectives. Paul J. Polger argues that the PAS and other abolitionist organizations during the early national period were based on an enlightened commitment to black equality. But he overlooks efforts toward immediate emancipation during that time. See Polger, "'To Raise Them.'"

19. Zilversmit, *First Emancipation,* 124–26; Locke, *Antislavery,* 77–78; Nash and Soderlund, *Freedom by Degrees,* 100–108; Foner, *History of Black Americans,* 1:359–63; Konkle, *George Bryan,* 169–70, 182–83, 189–98; McManus, *Black Bondage in the North,* 161–62. Burton Alva Konkle calls Bryan "the father of legal emancipation in America" (198).

20. Allegro, "'Increasing and Strengthening the Country.'"

21. Locke, *Antislavery,* 68–70; Brown, *Moral Capital,* 138–39; Zilversmit, *First Emancipation,* 101–2, 110; Egerton, *Death or Liberty,* 58–60; Jay Coughton, "Holbrook, Felix," in Miller and Smith, eds., *Dictionary of Afro-American Slavery,* 336–37; Davis, "Emancipation Rhetoric," 254–57; freedom petition, April 20, 1773, New-York Historical Society, Columbia American History Online, text.cc.columbia.edu/dbq/11016.html#A; Quarles, *Negro in the American Revolution,* 39–40, 43–44, 47. Mary Staughton Locke speculates that Samuel Adams orchestrated both sets of petitions. Christopher Leslie Brown contends that the town's effort aimed more at embarrassing Hutchinson than changing the colony's laws.

22. Foner, *History of Black Americans,* 1:352–53; Scott, *Black Revolts,* 98–99. Massachusetts black abolitionists John and Paul Cuffe petitioned successfully in 1780 for the right to vote. They thereby had an influence on the state's supreme court. See Horton and Horton, *In Hope of Liberty,* 70–71.

23. Zilversmit, *First Emancipation,* 105–6, 116–17, 122–23; Locke, *Antislavery,* 85; Egerton, *Death or Liberty,* 59–60; Foner, *History of Black Americans,* 1:248–49, 348–49; Ebenezer Baldwin and Jonathan Edwards Jr., "Some Observations upon the Slavery of Negroes," *Connecticut Journal and New-Haven Post-Boy,* October 8, 15, December 17, 31, 1773, in Bruns, *Am I Not a Man and a Brother,* 293–302; Horton and Horton, *In Hope of Liberty,* 72–73. Gary B. Nash prints the May 1779 Hartford petition. See Nash, *Race and Revolution,* 174–76.

24. Horton and Horton, *In Hope of Liberty,* 57–58; Zilversmit, *First Emancipation,* 106 (quotation). On Newport, see Locke, *Antislavery,* 40. On Osborn, see Hambrick-Stowe, "The Spiritual Pilgrimage of Sarah Osborn," and Brekus, *Sarah Osborn's World.*

25. Egerton, *Death or Liberty,* 109–10; Foner, *History of Black Americans,* 1:350; Zilversmit, *First Emancipation,* 119–22; McManus, *Black Bondage in the North,* 168–69, 197, 182; Clark-Pujara, "Slavery, Emancipation, and Black Freedom in Rhode Island," 134. The bill exempted masters from paying for their former slaves' education and support. A 1785 act restored this responsibility.

26. Horton and Horton, *In Hope of Liberty,* 72; Berlin, *Many Thousands Gone,*

229; Hammond, "Slavery in New Hampshire," 63 (first quotation); Zilversmit, *First Emancipation*, 116–17; Foner, *History of Black Americans*, 1:347–49; Anonymous, "Portsmouth Slaves Petitioning for Freedom in 1779," History Blog, October 3, 2011, www.thehistoryblog.com/archives/13054 (2nd quotation); Egerton, *Death or Liberty*, 111; Locke, *Antislavery*, 116–17. The *New Hampshire Gazette* (Portsmouth), July 15, 1780, and *State Journal and General Advertiser* (Rockingham, N.H.), July 15, 1780, published the petition.

27. Horton and Horton, *In Hope of Liberty*, 73–74; McManus, *History of Negro Slavery in New York*, 41–43, 47–57, 194–95; Berlin, *Many Thousands Gone*, 180, 233–36.

28. Allinson to Patrick Henry, October 17, 1774, in Gerlach, *New Jersey in the American Revolution*, 88–89; Zilversmit, *First Emancipation*, 140–53; Foner, *History of Black Americans*, 1:370–72; Egerton, *Death or Liberty*, 118–20; Cooley, *A Study of Slavery in New Jersey*, 18. Allinson's surname is also spelled Allison. He freed his slaves and joined the PAS in September 1787. See Pennsylvania Abolition Society, *Centennial Anniversary*, 43, and Adelberg, *American Revolution in Monmouth County*, 92. On Cooper, see De-Brusk, "An Ordinary Man in Extraordinary Times."

29. McManus, *History of Negro Slavery in New York*, 161; Locke, *Antislavery*, 79; Zilversmit, *First Emancipation*, 139–40. Jay purchased slaves but claimed he did so in order to prepare them for manumission. See Jay to Egbert Benson, September 18, 1780, Papers of John Jay.

30. Zilversmit, *First Emancipation*, 147–48; McManus, *History of Negro Slavery in New York*, 168–71; Gellman, *Emancipating New York*, 56–60; Locke, *Antislavery*, 99; Davis, *Problem of Slavery in the Age of Revolution*, 216–17, 240–41. Arthur Zilversmit writes that James Pemberton, a Philadelphia Quaker, urged the NYMS to seek anti-slave-trade legislation and that Matthew Clarkson, vice president of the NYMS, introduced such a bill in the state assembly in 1788. Zilversmit, *First Emancipation*, 160–61. Members of Hamilton's family owned slaves, and he may have as well. Historians debate the degree of his commitment to ending slavery. See Chernow, *Hamilton*, 210, and DuRoss, "Somewhere in Between."

31. Foner, *History of Black Americans*, 1:367; Horton and Horton, *In Hope of Liberty*, 73–74; Zilversmit, *First Emancipation*, 147–49, 150.

32. Finkelman, *Slavery and the Founders*, 3–10; Zilversmit, *First Emancipation*, 148; Nash, *Race and Revolution*, 25–55.

33. Thomas Jefferson, "Notes on Virginia," in Koch and Peden, eds., *Life and Selected Writings of Thomas Jefferson*, 256–62, 262 (quotation). Paul J. Polger notes abolitionist efforts during the late 1700s and early 1800s to counter this prejudice. See Polger, "'To Raise Them,'" 240, 250–54.

34. Essig, *Bonds of Wickedness*, 73–74, 81–86; Dumond, *Antislavery: The Crusade*, 47, 61–62; Zilversmit, *First Emancipation*, 190–91, 153–55; Locke, *Antislavery*, 92–93, 97, 99, 103–4, 106; Newman, *Transformation of American Abolitionism*, 21. In New Jersey these politicians included Joseph Bloomfield and Elias Boudinot; in Pennsylvania, Benjamin Franklin and Benjamin Rush; in Connecticut, Zephaniah Swift and Noah Webster.

35. Foner, *History of Black Americans,* 1:355–56 (quotation); Zilversmit, *First Emancipation,* 153–57; Thompson, *Moses Brown,* 188, 195; *United States Chronicle,* February 26, 1789. According to Mack Thompson, James Pemberton of the PAS and NYMS influenced Brown in 1784. See also Newman, *Transformation of American Abolitionism,* 25–26.

36. Foner, *History of Black Americans,* 1:357–58; Belknap, *Life of Jeremy Belknap,* 159–70; Locke, *Antislavery,* 41; Zilversmit, *First Emancipation,* 157. Belknap, though cautious, had favored abolition since the mid-1770s and had been in contact with Brown since 1786.

37. Foner, *History of Black Americans,* 1:349, 358–59; Saillant, "'Some Thoughts on the Subject of Freeing the Negro Slaves'"; Essig, *Bonds of Wickedness,* 112–13; Locke, *Antislavery,* 126; Zilversmit, *First Emancipation,* 201–2; "Dwight, Theodore," in Johnson and Malone, *Dictionary of American Biography,* 3:569–70. James D. Essig describes the society as "ineffective" (107–12) and mistakenly claims it ceased to exist after 1796. The society influenced the legislature in 1797 to lower the age of freedom for those "held in servitude" from twenty-five to twenty-one.

38. Nash and Soderlund, *Freedom by Degrees,* 113, 127–28; Foner, *History of Black Americans,* 1:363, 365; Zilversmit, *First Emancipation,* 133; Newman, *Transformation of American Abolitionism,* 25. The PAS expanded its membership among non-Quakers in 1787, chose Benjamin Franklin as its president, and encouraged abolitionist organizations in other states. Society members chose Franklin because they wanted leaders "of high political visibility." They also chose Thomas Paine and Benjamin Rush as society officers. See Nash and Soderlund, *Freedom by Degrees,* 124–25. In 1791 the PAS contributed to the defeat of a bill to allow federal officials to hold slaves in the state. See Zilversmit, *First Emancipation,* 164.

39. McManus, *History of Negro Slavery in New York,* 166–67; McManus, *Black Bondage in the North,* 172; Zilversmit, *First Emancipation,* 147–51. Edgar J. McManus in *Negro Slavery* mistakenly dates manumission legislation to 1788.

40. Gellman, *Emancipating New York,* 131–35, 165; Zilversmit, *First Emancipation,* 176, 180–82; Foner, *History of Black Americans,* 1:368; Locke, *Antislavery,* 123; McManus, *History of Negro Slavery in New York,* 174–75; McManus, *Black Bondage in the North,* 177–78.

41. Zilversmit, *First Emancipation,* 159–61, 175; Wright, "New Jersey Laws," 175–78 (1st quotation); Cooley, *A Study of Slavery in New Jersey,* 25–26 (2nd quotation); Locke, *Antislavery,* 124. The law against importing slaves also required masters to teach slaves to read. On David Cooper, see Zilversmit, *First Emancipation,* 152.

42. Paul Finkelman, "State Constitutional Protections of Liberty and the Antebellum New Jersey Supreme Court: Chief Justice Hornblower and the Fugitive Slave Law," in McKivigan, ed., *History of the American Abolitionist Movement,* 758–59.

43. Wright, "New Jersey Laws," 175–76; Zilversmit, *First Emancipation,* 173–76, 184–95; Cooley, *A Study of Slavery in New Jersey,* 23–24, 26–27; Locke, *Antislavery,* 86;

Dumond, *Antislavery: The Crusade*, 50–51. Some historians place the formation of the society in 1792. Also historians disagree concerning the competence of the society.

44. Zilversmit, *First Emancipation*, 88–90, 97; "To the Honorable Members of the Continental Congress," [1776], in Hopkins, *Works of Samuel Hopkins*, 2:549–50. In 1783 New Jersey Quaker abolitionist David Cooper sent a similar pamphlet to Congress. See Sinha, *Slave's Cause*, 35, 38–39.

45. Ohline, "Slavery, Economics, and Congressional Politics," 336; Locke, *Antislavery*, 94, 136–37; Justice, *Life and Ancestry of Warner Mifflin;* Nash, *Warner Mifflin;* Finkelman, *Slavery and the Founders*, 3–10, 36. Mifflin also addressed the Delaware legislature regarding emancipation. The PAS did not submit the memorial because it feared the memorial would spark a counterproductive southern reaction.

46. Ohline, "Slavery, Economics, and Congressional Politics," 336–37, 340; Dumond, *Antislavery: The Crusade*, 53; Bordewich, *First Congress*, 198. Fergus M. Bordewich calls the 1790 lobbying effort "the first systematic lobbying campaign in American history." This is true only in regard to the national government.

47. Newman, *Transformation of American Abolitionism*, 39–44; Ohline, "Slavery, Economics, and Congressional Politics," 338, 341, 358–59; Essig, *Bonds of Wickedness*, 113–14; Locke, *Antislavery*, 96; Bordewich, *First Congress*, 198–203; U.S. Congress, *Annals*, 1st Cong., 2nd sess. (February 11, 1790), cols. 1224–25 (1st–3rd quotations), (February 12, 1790), cols. 1239–40 (4th–5th quotations). James Wilson had earlier raised the issue at the Constitutional Convention.

48. U.S. Congress, *Annals*, 1st Cong., 2nd sess. (February 12, 1790), cols. 1240 (4th–5th quotations), 1242 (1st quotation), (March 17, 1790), col. 1503 (2nd–3rd quotations); Foner, *History of Black Americans*, 1:412; Ohline, "Slavery, Economics, and Congressional Politics," 340–44; Locke, *Antislavery*, 115; Robert G. Parkinson, "'Manifest Signs of Passion': The First Federal Congress, Antislavery, and Legacies of the Revolutionary War," in Hammond and Mason, eds., *Contesting Slavery*, 49–52. Tucker declared, "Do these men expect a general emancipation of the slaves by law? This would not be submitted to by the Southern States without a civil war." U.S. Congress, *Annals*, 1st Cong., 2nd sess. (February 12, 1790), col. 1240.

49. U.S. Congress, *Annals*, 1st Cong., 2nd sess. (February 12, 1790), col. 1242; (February 15, 1790), cols. 1246–47; (February 11–12, 1790), cols. 1230 (1st quotation), 1246–47; (March 22, 1790), 1518–21 (2nd–3rd quotations).

50. Ohline, "Slavery, Economics, and Congressional Politics," 341; U.S. Congress, *Annals*, 1st Cong., 2nd sess. (March 8, 1790), cols., 1465–66 (1st–3rd quotations), (March 23, 1790), cols. 1523–24; Nash, *Race and Revolution*, 40–42; Locke, *Antislavery*, 114–15, 140–42; Benton, *Abridgement of the Debates of Congress*, 1:239 (4th quotation). William Smith of South Carolina and other extreme defenders of slavery voted against the amendment because it upheld taxing the trade.

51. Dumond, *Antislavery: The Crusade*, 57; U.S. Congress, *Annals*, 2nd Cong., 2nd sess., appendix (February 12, 1793), cols. 1414–15, (February 22, 1793), cols. 888–89.

52. Zilversmit, *First Emancipation*, 173; Locke, *Antislavery*, 101; Foner, *History of*

Black Americans, 1:414–15; Miller, *Federalist Era,* 99–125. During the fall of 1792, the NYMS called for a national gathering in Philadelphia.

53. Locke, *Antislavery,* 101, 141–43, 146–47; U.S. Congress, *Annals,* 3rd Cong., 1st sess., appendix (March 22, 1794), cols. 1425–26; Foner, *History of Black Americans,* 1:414–16. In 1795 the AC reported that Congress had passed "palliative legislation." See Zilversmit, *First Emancipation,* 173. For a description of the bill, see Foner, *History of Black Americans,* 1:414–16.

54. Zilversmit, *First Emancipation,* 226.

55. Foner, *History of Black Americans,* 1:377–78 (1st quotation), 416–17 (4th–6th quotations); Essig, *Bonds of Wickedness,* 113–14 (2nd–3rd quotations); Filler, *Crusade against Slavery,* 99; Newman, *Transformation of American Abolitionism,* 25; Sinha, *Slave's Cause,* 97, 172–73. See also Nash and Soderlund, *Freedom by Degrees,* 136, and Polger, "'To Raise Them.'"

56. Foner, *History of Black Americans,* 1:329, 378 (2nd quotation), 417 (1st quotation); Clavin, *Toussaint Louverture;* Egerton, *Gabriel's Rebellion;* Locke, *Antislavery,* 110, 165; Zilversmit, *First Emancipation,* 200 (3rd quotation); McManus, *Black Bondage in the North,* 179; Freehling, "The Founding Fathers and Slavery," 86 (4th quotation).

2. Continuity and Transition, 1807–1830

1. Locke, *Antislavery,* 2–7.

2. Adams, *Neglected Period of Anti-Slavery,* iii–iv, 249–52.

3. Dillon, *Abolitionists,* 18–23; Stewart, *Holy Warriors,* 211; American Convention, *American Convention for Promoting the Abolition of Slavery,* 16th sess. (November 10, 1819), 2:678 (quotation) (hereafter AC, *Minutes).* See also AC, *Minutes,* 18th sess. (October 7, 1823), 3:19.

4. Dillon, *Abolitionists,* 23–30; Stewart, *Holy Warriors,* 28–32; Newman, *Transformation of American Abolitionism,* 107–14 (quotation); Sinha, *Slave's Cause,* 160–61; Mason, *Slavery and Politics,* 176–81; John Craig Hammond, "'Uncontrollable Necessity': The Local Politics, Geopolitics, and Sectional Politics of Slavery Expansion," in Hammond and Mason, eds., *Contesting Slavery,* 138–39, 149–51. In *American Abolitionists,* I oversimplify in writing that the old gradual abolition societies "withered" as a new generation of black and white abolitionists favored immediatism. See Harrold, *American Abolitionists,* 24–33.

5. Dillon, *Benjamin Lundy,* 2 (1st–2nd quotations); AC, *Minutes,* 16th sess. (November 10, 1819), 2:685, 708 (3rd quotation), 709; AC, *Minutes,* 18th sess. (October 7, 1823), 3:819; AC, *Minutes,* 19th sess. (October 4, 1825), 3:872 (4th quotation); AC, *Minutes,* 20th sess. (November 3, 1828), 3:1027, 1029–31. See also Adams, *Neglected Period of Anti-Slavery,* 170–71, 177–78, 181–84.

6. Larson, *Market Revolution in America;* Murray, *Revival and Revivalism,* 116–19, 193–22; Walters, *American Reformers;* Griffin, *Their Brothers' Keepers.*

7. Moore, *Missouri Controversy,* 33; Forbes, *Missouri Compromise,* 51.

8. AC, *Minutes,* 15th sess. (December 10, 1818), 2:644–45 (quotation); Moore, *Missouri Controversy,* 34, 74–75; Locke, *Antislavery,* 93, 126.

9. U.S. Congress, *Annals,* 15th Cong., 2nd sess. (February 15, 1819), cols. 1191–93.

10. Moore, *Missouri Controversy,* 35 (1st quotation); U.S. Congress, *Annals,* 15th Cong., 2nd sess. (November 23, 1818), col. 307 (2nd–3rd quotations); Carter and Stone, *Reports of the Proceedings and Debates of the Convention of 1821,* 172 (4th quotation), 485–86. The motion to admit Illinois passed 117–34. The Manumission Society of the City of New York published Tallmadge's speech. See Tallmadge, *Speech of the Honorable James Tallmadge Jr. . . . on Slavery.*

11. Ress, *Governor Edward Coles,* 80–81 (1st quotation); Tallmadge, *Speech of the Honorable James Tallmadge Jr. . . . on Slavery,* 9, 10, 11–13 (2nd–4th quotations), 22.

12. Tallmadge, *Speech of the Honorable James Tallmadge Jr. . . . on Slavery,* 18, 21. On abolitionists before and after Tallmadge, see Torrey, *Portraiture of Domestic Slavery,* 63–64, and Huston, "Experiential Basis," 620–24.

13. U.S. Congress, *Annals,* 15th Cong., 1st sess. (February 15, 1819), cols. 1170–84; King, *Life and Correspondence of Rufus King,* 6:690–703. See also *Niles Register,* December 4, 1819, 215–21; King to John B. Coles and John T. Irving, November 22, 1819, *Niles Register,* December 4, 1819, 215. Fuller maintained that the Declaration of Independence recognized black natural rights. *Annals of Congress* did not record King's speech. See King, *Life and Correspondence of Rufus King,* 6:217. See also King to Charles Gore, February 20, 1820, in King, *Life and Correspondence of Rufus King,* 6:276–78.

14. Moore, *Missouri Controversy,* 74–75 (1st quotation); *New York Daily Advertiser,* February 20, 1819; Ely to Roberts Vaux, March 26, 1819, Vaux Family Papers; Tallmadge, *Speech of the Hon. James Tallmadge Jr. . . . on Slavery,* 23–24 (2nd–5th quotations); Peters to King, November 23, 1819, in King, *Life and Correspondence of Rufus King,* 6:234–35 (6th quotation); Chapman-Smith, "Philadelphia and the Slave Trade." On Ketchum, see his obituary in the *New York Times,* September 17, 1870. For Burrill's remarks, see U.S. Congress, *Annals,* 15th Cong., 1st sess. (January 2, 1818), cols. 74, 76.

15. Dillon, *Benjamin Lundy,* 35–42, 48; *Genius of Universal Emancipation,* April 1822, 150 (quotation).

16. U.S. Congress, *Annals,* 15th Cong., 2nd sess. (March 2, 1819), cols., 273, 279, 1214–15.

17. Moore, *Missouri Controversy,* 65–66 (quotation); Forbes, *Missouri Compromise,* 54.

18. Boyd, *Elias Boudinot; National Gazette and Literary Register,* September 2, 1820; Moore, *Missouri Controversy,* 68–69; Pennsylvania Abolition Society, *Centennial Anniversary,* 54, 60; Konkle, *Joseph Hopkinson.*

19. *Friend,* August 28, 1828, 360 (quotation); *National Gazette and Literary Register,* September 2, 1820; Peters, "Trying to Track Down Sources"; William Newbold to George Newbold, May 6, 1823, Quaker and Special Collections; PAS incorporation

document, December 8, 1789, in Pennsylvania, *Statutes at Large,* 13:426; Moore, *Missouri Controversy,* 69. Newbold invited Hopkinson to the meeting. On Boudinot's and Newbold's respective roles, see Moore, *Missouri Controversy,* 68, and Forbes, *Missouri Compromise,* 301n69. On the Newbolds, see Willian Newbold to George Newbold, May 6, 1823, Quaker and Special Collections.

20. Moore, *Missouri Controversy,* 70–71; *True American* (Trenton), November 1, 1819 (1st quotation); *Niles Register,* November 20, 1819, 189 (2nd quotation). Once again, Newbold initiated the call. See *Friend,* August 23, 1828, 360, and *True American,* September 6, 1819. Griffith had been one of John Adams's "midnight justices" in 1801. See Hills, *History of the Church in Burlington,* 396–97. Earlier in 1819, Griffith had formed a new state abolition society dedicated to protecting African Americans from kidnapping.

21. *New York Daily Advertiser,* November 10, 13, 1819; Moore, *Missouri Controversy,* 78–79; *New York Evening Post,* November, 17, 1819, reprinted in *Niles Register,* November 27, 1819, 199–200 (quotations). On abolitionists at the meeting, see also Adams, *Neglected Period of Anti-Slavery,* 255, 257, and American Convention, *Minutes of the Sixteenth Session of the American Convention,* 6–8.

22. Needles, *Historical Memoir,* 42; Locke, *Antislavery,* 127; Allen, *Life, Experiences,* 14; Adams, *Neglected Period of Anti-Slavery,* 254; *Genius of Universal Emancipation,* quoted in *Freedom's Journal,* February 1, 1828; Birney, *James G. Birney,* 409; *Niles Register,* December 11, 1819, 241 (quotations). Of the twenty-three identifiable men mentioned in a local newspaper's report on the meeting, ten were abolitionists. That constituted a slightly smaller abolitionist percentage than at the New York meeting. See Adams, *Neglected Period of Anti-Slavery,* 254–55, 258–59, and Pennsylvania Abolition Society, *Centennial Anniversary,* 53. In 1826 Horace Binney wrote that slavery "ought to be regarded as an evil and a sin." See Binney, *Life of Horace Binney,* 82.

23. *Niles Register,* December 11, 1819, 241–42 (quotations); Moore, *Missouri Controversy,* 28n, 81–82; *A Memorial to the Congress of the United States.* On Gallison, see William E. Channing, "Memoir of John Gallison," in Channing, *Works,* 618–25; "John Gallison" in Wilson and Fiske, eds., *Appleton's Cyclopedia of American Biography,* 2:580; John Gallison Diaries. Gallison, a Unitarian who studied law with John Quincy Adams, had ties to future immediate abolitionists Arthur Tappan, Lewis Tappan, and Samuel J. May. Black opposed antislavery measures, and Austin later became an anti-abolitionist. See Moore, *Missouri Controversy,* 81–82.

24. AC, *Minutes,* 16th sess. (October 5, 1819), 2:686, 707–8 (1st quotation), 727, 734–36 (2nd quotation); U.S. Congress, *Annals,* 16th Cong., 1st sess. (December 15, 1819), col. 24, (December 16, 1819), cols. 736–37, (February 9, 1820), cols. 1206 (3rd quotation), 1211–12, 1215–16; Moore, *Missouri Controversy,* 107; Forbes, *Missouri Compromise,* 71, 75–78; List of PAS Counselors, 1815, Pennsylvania Abolition Society Papers (hereafter PAS Papers). On Rawle, see "Penn Biographies." The AC also arranged to publish King's speech along with one by Rhode Island senator James Burrill. See Richard Peters Jr. to King, November 23, 1819, in King, *Life and Correspondence of Rufus*

King, 6:234–35. Roberts on January 5, 1820, presented the Pennsylvania legislature's moderate anti-extensionist resolutions to the Senate. He also called for total abolition in Pennsylvania. See U.S. Congress, *Annals*, 16th Cong., 1st sess. (January 6, 1820), cols. 70–71; *Niles Register*, January 1, 1820, 296–97; and Needles, *Historical Memoir*, 70–71.

25. U.S. Congress, *Annals*, 16th Cong., 1st sess. (February 8, 1820), cols. 1174 (1st and 2nd quotations), 1188 (3rd quotation).

26. U.S. Congress, *Annals*, 16th Cong., 1st sess. (January 5, 1820), col. 69; (January 10, 1820), col. 75; (January 12, 1820), col. 81; (January 18, 1820), col. 157; (January 27, 1820), col. 276; (February 3, 1820), col. 361 (quotation).

27. *New York Daily Advertiser*, March 28, 1820 (1st quotation); Moore, *Missouri Controversy*, 131; PAS, "Protest against the Extension of Slavery," *Poulson's American Daily Advertiser*, April 28, 1820 (2nd quotation); *Richmond Enquirer*, April 18, 1820 (3rd quotation). Walsh, a Quaker of Irish descent, advocated gradual abolition and a version of black colonization. His writings on slavery are variously interpreted. Yet he had written the previous December that proslavery attitudes among the founders constituted "a gross anomaly and incongruity, giving to their revolutionary creed . . . an air of imposture or infatuated selfishness." He asserted, "Our negro-slavery presented itself . . . as a fixed contradiction and solecism disfiguring both our juridical and political codes." See Lochemes, *Robert Walsh*, 114–17, and [Walsh,] *Free Remarks*, 4–5. Larry Tise includes Walsh among northern proslavery writers. See Tise, *Proslavery*, 47–52.

28. Forbes, *Missouri Compromise*, 148 (1st quotation); Dillon, *Abolitionists*, 23 (2nd quotation); *Genius of Universal Emancipation*, February 1822, 117 (3rd quotation); AC, *Minutes*, 17th sess. (October 3, 1821), 2:750, 764–65; Dillon, *Benjamin Lundy*, 41. The same historians note that twenty years later, a younger abolitionist generation regarded the prohibition of territorial slavery north of the 36° 30′ line of latitude to have been an antislavery victory. AC and PAS leaders thought of themselves as discreet and diplomatic. See AC, *Minutes*, 20th sess. (October 2, 1827), 2:764–65.

29. *Genius of Universal Emancipation*, February 1822, 117; AC, *Minutes*, 20th sess. (October 2, 1827), 2:967–68. Merton L. Dillon characterizes the outcome in Illinois as the abolitionists' last victory during the 1820s. He also contends that it was their last victory based on "moderate means" (meaning "peaceful rational persuasion and conventional political action"). But abolitionists also won a victory in 1826, and the struggle in Illinois was not always peaceful. See Dillon, *Abolitionists*, 24, Morris, *Free Men All*, 52; and Harrold, *Border War*, 19–20.

30. Ress, *Governor Edward Coles*, 49–176, 100 (quotation); Dumond, *Antislavery: The Crusade*, 101; Dillon, *Abolitionists*, 23; Coles to Nicholas Biddle, April 22, 1823, in Washburne, *Sketch of Edward Coles*, 148. On the impact of the Missouri crisis, see J. M. Peck to H. Warren, March 27, 1855, in Coles, *Governor Edward Coles*, 333, and Locke, *Antislavery*, 159n. See also Guasco, *Confronting Slavery*, and Ress, *Governor Edward Coles*.

31. J. M. Peck to H. Warren, March 27, 1855, in Coles, *Governor Edward Coles*, 334–36; Dillon, *Abolitionists*, 23–24; Dillon, *Benjamin Lundy*, 73–74; *Genius of Universal Emancipation*, April 10, 30, 1823, 135, 140, 145–46. On Illinois anticonventionists and their

abolitionist views, see Washburne, *Sketch of Edward Coles,* 167–76, 182, 186, 196, and Ress, *Governor Edward Coles,* 17, 48, 104–7, 124–25.

32. Coles to Biddle, April 22, 1823; Biddle to Coles, May 20, 26 (2), 1823; Vaux to Coles, May 27, December 11, 1823, January 21, 1824, in Washburne, *Sketch of Edward Coles,* 147–49, 152–55 (quotation), 163–64, 205. Biddle worked on behalf of the Missouri Compromise. See Forbes, *Missouri Compromise,* 118, 123.

33. Coles to Vaux, June 27, 1823; Coles to Nicholas Biddle, September 18, 1823; Vaux to Coles, July 14, 1824, in Washburne, *Sketch of Edward Coles,* 155–56 (1st quotation), 159–60 (5th quotation), 211 (2nd–3rd quotations); Governor's Message, November 16, 1824, in Coles, *Governor Edward Coles,* 270–71 (4th quotation); Ress, *Governor Edward Coles,* 129–32.

34. Coles to Nicholas Biddle, September 18, 1823; Coles to John Rutherford, July 5, 1826, in Washburne, *Sketch of Edward Coles,* 159–60 (1st quotation), 225–28 (2nd–3rd quotations); Ress, *Governor Edward Coles,* 167–69.

35. Leslie, "Pennsylvania Fugitive Slave Act of 1826," 429–45, 445 (quotation).

36. Ibid., 436–37; *National Gazette and Literary Register,* January 26, February 7, 1826; George Stroud to Meredith, February 10, 1826; Vaux to Stephen Duncan and Meredith, February 9, 1826 (quotation), Meredith Family Papers.

37. Morris, *Free Men All,* 48; "Minutes of the Pennsylvania Society for Promoting the Abolition of Slavery, 1825–1847," February 10, 1826, 3:28–29 (1st quotation); March 29, 1826, 35–36; J.B. to William Duncan, January 25, 1826, PAS Papers; Leslie, "Pennsylvania Fugitive Slave Act of 1826," 438, 443–44 (3rd quotation). An eye disease prevented William Rawle from accompanying Shipley and Vaux to Harrisburg. See Rawle to PAS, February 10, 1826, PAS Papers. A Shipley obituary is in the *Liberator,* October 22, 1836. African Americans and Quakers sent remonstrances to the Pennsylvania legislature. See Leslie, "Pennsylvania Fugitive Slave Act of 1826," 440.

38. Morris, *Free Men All,* 45, 50–53; Shipley to Isaac Barton, February 15, 1826; "Minutes of the Pennsylvania Society for Promoting the Abolition of Slavery, 1825–1847," March 29, 1826, 3:35–36, PAS Papers; Leslie, "Pennsylvania Fugitive Slave Act of 1826," 440–41, 443; Pennsylvania Abolition Society, Acting Committee Minutes, 3:35–36, PAS Papers; *National Gazette and Literary Register,* February 23, 1826.

39. Tremain, *Slavery in the District of Columbia,* 58; Locke, *Antislavery,* 163; Bendler, "James Sloan," 1–3, 8–9.

40. U.S. Congress, *Annals,* 14th Cong., 1st sess. (March 1, 1816), cols. 1115–17; Newman, *Transformation of American Abolitionism,* 25, 49–50; Torrey, *Portraiture of Domestic Slavery;* AC, *Minutes,* 16th sess. (November 10, 1819), 2:684; AC, *Minutes,* 15th sess. (December 10, 1818), 2:657, 659. Mary Tremain perceives coordination between Randolph and Torrey. See Tremain, *Slavery in the District of Columbia,* 58–59. Charles F. Richardson and Elizabeth Miner Richardson believe nothing resulted from Randolph's effort. See Richardson and Richardson, *Charles Miner,* 95. Matthew Mason speculates that Randolph was disingenuous in his resolutions as he sought to shore up an image of benevolence among slaveholders. See Mason, *Slavery and Politics,* 168–69, 284n58.

Merton L. Dillon observes that before 1827, the abolitionist petitioning effort against slavery in the District of Columbia "had been rather desultory and not very well organized." See Dillon, *Benjamin Lundy,* 121.

41. AC, *Minutes,* 15th sess. (December 10, 1818), 2:658–61 (quotations); AC, *Minutes,* 16th sess. (November 10, 1819), 2:706–7, 718, 755, 781–82; *Genius of Universal Emancipation,* February 1822, 117; March 1822, 142–43.

42. AC, *Minutes,* 18th sess. (October 7, 1823), 2:825, 837 (quotation); Newman, *Transformation of American Abolitionism,* 54–55; *Genius of Universal Emancipation,* January 1824, 97–99; Needles, *Historical Memoir,* 80–81; AC, *Minutes,* adjourned [19th] sess. (October 25, 1826), 3:947, 949. A sympathetic congressman urged Lundy to be cautious. See Unknown to Lundy, May 3, 1824, *Genius of Universal Emancipation,* June 1824, 181–82. Abolitionist conservatism and fear of sectional discord is a major theme in Newman's book. Mary Tremain concludes that the effort "did not gather much force until 1826." See Tremain, *Slavery in the District of Columbia,* 60–61. Alice Dana Adams underestimates when she contends that none of this had "any real effect." See Adams, *Neglected Period of Anti-Slavery,* 170.

43. Lundy, *Life, Travels, and Opinions of Benjamin Lundy,* 23, 191 (1st quotation); Newman, *Transformation of American Abolitionism,* 30 (2nd quotation); U.S. Congress, *Register of Debates,* 19th Cong., 2nd sess. (December 27, 1826), 563–64.

44. AC, *Minutes,* 19th sess. (October 4, 1825), 3:892 (1st quotation); *Genius of Universal Emancipation,* September 24, 1825, 5; October 1, 1825, 44–45; November 5, 1825, 86. Raymond led a similar effort in 1826. See AC, *Minutes,* adjourned [19th] sess. (October 25, 1826), 3:911; *Genius of Universal Emancipation,* December 10, 1825, 116 (2nd quotation); March 4, 1826, 213 (3rd–4th quotations); Tremain, *Slavery in the District of Columbia,* 60–61 (5th quotation); Richardson and Richardson, *Charles Miner,* 91–93; and U.S. Congress, *Register of Debates,* 91st Cong., 2nd sess. (December 27, 1826), col. 559 (6th quotation).

45. Richardson and Richardson, *Charles Miner,* 94; Tuckerman, *William Jay,* 29–31 (quotation). For the Westchester resolutions, see *Niles Register,* September 9, 1826, 25.

46. Tuckerman, *William Jay,* 31–34; Wilson, *Freedom at Risk,* 73–74; AC, *Minutes,* adjourned [19th] sess. (October 25, 1826), 3:949 (quotations). Jay told Miner that he did not think Congress would favorably receive the petition but that the effort against slavery in the district would "finally succeed." As Merton L. Dillon puts it, slavery in the district "remained a constantly live issue." During the mid-1820s "petitions became more numerous and more insistent." See Dillon, *Benjamin Lundy,* 122.

47. U.S. Congress, *Register of Debates,* 19th Cong., 2nd sess. (December 26–27, 1826), 555–562 (1st–2nd quotations); Tuckerman, *William Jay,* 34–36 (3rd quotation).

48. Dillon, *Benjamin Lundy,* 122–23; *Genius of Universal Emancipation,* December 23, 1826, 103; January 27, 1827, 133; U.S. Congress, *Register of Debates,* 19th Cong., 2nd sess. (February 10, 1827), 1099–1101 (quotations).

49. AC, *Minutes,* 20th sess. (October 2, 1827), 3:961–62 (1st–2nd quotations), 981–82, 986 (3rd–4th quotations).

50. Richardson and Richardson, *Charles Miner,* 99–100 (1st–3rd quotations); Dillon, *Benjamin Lundy,* 125; Tremain, *Slavery in the District of Columbia,* 62–64 (4th–5th quotations). As early as October 2, 1827, AC members knew about the D.C. petition effort. See AC, *Minutes,* 20th sess. (October 2, 1827), 3:990. Mary Tremain notes that the petition was reread in the House in 1834 and 1835. The latter reading came at William Slade's request.

51. AC, *Minutes,* adjourned [20th] sess. (November [n.d.], 1828), 3:1018–19, 1027–32, 1029 (1st quotation), 1040–41, 1046 (2nd–3rd quotations).

52. *Niles Register,* January 31, 1829, 363–64; February 21, 1829, 433–34; Newman, *Transformation of American Abolitionism,* 51–52; Rawle to Miner, January 14, 1829, in Richardson and Richardson, *Charles Miner,* 105. Richard S. Newman, without documentary support, asserts that the PAS "helped Miner prepare his controversial proposals for submission to the House." See Newman, *Transformation of American Abolitionism,* 51.

53. U.S. Congress, *Register of Debate,* 20th Cong., 2nd sess. (January 6–7, 1829), 167 (1st quotation), 180 (2nd quotation), 177 (3rd quotation), 181 (4th quotation).

54. Ibid. (January 7, 1829), 181–87; [John Compton Weems], "Will of John Crompton Weems, Anne Arundel County, Md., February 5, 1858," Ancestry.com, http//boards.ancestry.com/surname.weems/20/mb.ashx?pnt+1.

55. U.S. Congress, *Register of Debate,* 20th Cong., 2nd sess. (January 9, 1829), 191–92; Tremain, *Slavery in the District of Columbia,* 66–67; *National Intelligencer,* February 7, 1829 (quotations). William Rawle expressed pleasure that Miner's effort had "so far succeeded as to get to committee." See Rawle to Miner, January 14, 1829, in Richardson and Richardson, *Charles Miner,* 105. Richard S. Newman writes that the response to Miner's resolutions seemed to give abolitionism a "bright . . . future." See Newman, *Transformation of American Abolitionism,* 52–53.

56. Needles, *Historical Memoir,* 87–88; AC, *Minutes,* 21st sess. (December 8–12, 1829), 3:1090 (1st quotation), 1101–7 (2nd–4th quotations).

57. AC, *Minutes,* 21st sess. (December 8–12, 1829), 3;1107 (quotations); Tremain, *Slavery in the District of Columbia,* 65. Mary Tremain writes that the effort "flagged in 1829."

3. Escalation, 1831–1840

1. *Liberator,* January 1, 1831; Stewart, *Holy Warriors,* 45–46; Newman, *Transformation of American Abolitionism,* 6–7, 107–14; Abzug, *Cosmos Crumbling,* 145. Richard S. Newman notes the immediatists' debt to earlier abolitionist organizations and to African Americans. See Newman, *Transformation of American Abolitionism,* 1, 86–87.

2. Harrold, *American Abolitionists,* 25 (quotation), 28–29, 44, 46–47, 51; Dillon, *Abolitionists,* 23–30, 49–51, 56–60; Stewart, *Holy Warriors,* 28–32, 44, 46–50; Miller, *Arguing about Slavery,* 66–67; Davis, *Joshua Leavitt,* 49–103; Wyatt-Brown, *Lewis Tappan,* 78–148; Zaeske, *Signatures of Citizenship,* 2–3, 11–13; Deborah Bingham Van

Broekhoven, "'Let Your Names Be Enrolled': Method and Ideology in Women's Anti-slavery Petitioning," in Yellin and Van Horne, eds., *Abolitionist Sisterhood*, 179–99. Although she stresses 1835, Susan Zaeske is not clear concerning when women became active petitioners. Earlier involvement existed.

3. McCormick, *Second American Party System;* Vaughan, *Antimasonic Party.* See also Wilentz, *Rise of American Democracy*, 181–520, and Holt, *Rise and Fall of the American Whig Party*, 1–59.

4. Dillon, *Abolitionists*, 39; Stewart, *William Lloyd Garrison*, 26–28; Stewart, *Holy Warriors*, 48–50; Harrold, *American Abolitionists*, 31–34.

5. Sewell, *Ballots for Freedom*, 7 (1st quotation); Fladeland, *Men and Brothers*, 224–28; Barnes, *Antislavery Impulse*, 120; Dillon, *Abolitionists*, 44 (2nd quotation), 106; Stewart, *Holy Warriors*, 81–82, 87–88; Miller, *Arguing about Slavery*, 107–8, 303–4; Nye, *Fettered Freedom*, 59–60 (3rd quotation).

6. Filler, *Crusade against Slavery*, 99; Sewell, *Ballots for Freedom*, 7; Nye, *Fettered Freedom*, 42–44; Merrill, *Against Wind and Tide*, 21–23 (quotation), 201; *Liberator*, January 1, 1831. Garrison erred in claiming that only a "few struggling petitions, relative to this subject, ha[d previously] gone to Congress." See *Liberator*, January 1, 1831.

7. *Liberator*, February 5 (1st–2nd quotations), June 18, 1831 (3rd–5th quotations); *Extra Globe*, September 4, 1840; Merrill, *Against Wind and Tide*, 201; Goodman, *Of One Blood*, 165–66. Gilbert H. Barnes credits western "moderate . . . abolitionists" for the petitioning campaign. This is, to say the least, an overgeneralization. See Barnes, *Antislavery Impulse*, 131.

8. *Liberator*, December 17, 1831 (1st–2nd quotations); Jay to Henry D. Sedgewick, 1831, in Tuckerman, *William Jay*, 37 (3rd–4th quotations). In 1837 Congressman John Quincy Adams wrote, "The abolition of Slavery in the District of Columbia is viewed by the Abolitionists themselves, as well as by their opponents, as a mere stepping stone to that of Slavery in the States." See Adams to Gerrit Smith, April 5, 1837, Gilder Lehrman Institute of American History, New-York Historical Society, https://gilderlehrman.org/collections/a6f50fl09aa.

9. Bemis, *John Quincy Adams and the Union*, 327.

10. U.S. Congress, *Register of Debates*, 22nd Cong., 1st sess. (December 12, 1831), 1425–26; *Liberator*, December 24, 1831 (1st quotation); *Advocate of Truth*, quoted in *Liberator*, December 24, 1831 (2nd quotation).

11. U.S. Congress, *Register of Debates*, 22nd Cong., 2nd sess. (February 4, 1833), cols. 1584–85. In November 1832, black abolitionist James G. Barbadoes led a Boston meeting of the Massachusetts Colored Associates to initiate a similar petition drive. See *Liberator*, November 17, 24, 1832.

12. U.S. Congress, *Register of Debates*, 22nd Cong., 2nd sess. (February 4, 1833), cols. 1584–85.

13. Barnes, *Antislavery Impulse*, 130–31; Woodwell, *John Greenleaf Whittier;* Thomas, *Theodore Weld*, 3–132. Gilbert H. Barnes portrays the AASS as reluctant to support petitioning. He claims the organization was not "serious" about it until December 1834

and that it acted out of "duty" rather than "hope." This interpretation contradicts what abolitionists wrote at the time.

14. *Emancipator,* June 24, December 16, 1834; Barnes, *Antislavery Impulse,* 131; Merrill, *Against Wind and Tide,* 114.

15. Barnes, *Antislavery Impulse,* 110; Miller, *Arguing about Slavery,* 27, 111–12, 297; Sewell, *Ballots for Freedom,* 7–8; Stewart, *Holy Warriors,* 81–82; *Liberator,* February 21, 1835 (quotation).

16. U.S. Congress, *Register of Debates,* 23rd Cong., 2nd (February 2, 1835), 1131–40.

17. Ibid. (February 2, 1835), 1141–42; (February 16, 1835), 1393–1401 (quotation). Phillips, a Whig, presented a petition signed by 1,249 "male citizens" and 2,643 "ladies" from Massachusetts's Essex County. The *Liberator* noted the increase in such petitions. See *Liberator,* March 7, 1835.

18. Barnes, *Antislavery Impulse,* 131–32, 311; *Liberator,* February 21 (1st–3rd quotations), March 3 (4th quotation), May 16, 1835; Miller, *Arguing about Slavery,* 111–12 (5th quotation). The PAS sent one of the petitions. See Needles, *Historical Memoir,* 91–92.

19. Lovejoy, "Racism in Antebellum Vermont," 63; *Vermont Chronicle,* February 14, 1834; *Middlebury Telegraph,* quoted in *United States Telegraph,* September 21, 1836. Contrary to historian Russell B. Nye, Slade was not an abolitionist in 1835. See Nye, *Fettered Freedom,* 44.

20. *Liberator,* January 2, 1836; U.S. Congress, *Register of Debates,* 24th Cong., 1st sess. (December 16, 1835), 1961–63 (1st and 3rd quotations); Burgess, *Middle Period,* 257–58 (2nd and 4th quotations); Miller, *Arguing about Slavery,* 29–36; Nye, *Fettered Freedom,* 44–45. See also Lovejoy, "Racism in Antebellum Vermont," 54–55. Slade said he had petitions that "contained the names of many individuals who had no connection with abolition societies, and who did not harmonize with their views."

21. Nye, *Fettered Freedom,* 44–45; U.S. Congress, *Register of Debates,* 24th Cong., 1st sess. (December 21, 1835), cols. 2000–2002; *Liberator,* January 2, 1836 (1st–2nd quotations); John Quincy Adams to Solomon Lincoln, April 4, 1836, Gilder Lehrman Institute of American History—Primary Sources, https://www.gilderlehrman.org/content/solomon-lincoln-esq (3rd quotations).

22. Nye, *Fettered Freedom,* 46; *Niles Register,* June 4, 1836, 241 (quotations); Dumond, *Antislavery: The Crusade,* 237–38; Stewart, *Holy Warriors,* 81–84.

23. American Anti-Slavery Society, *Third Annual Report,* 84–88. In addition Henry Stanton, Theodore D. Weld, and John G. Whittier boasted that it was the "exercise of the right of petition" that aroused the North.

24. Bemis, *John Quincy Adams and the Union,* 416, 420–22 (1st quotation); Stewart, *Holy Warriors,* 87–88 (2nd–3rd quotations; emphasis added); Dillon, *Abolitionists,* 99; Burgess, *Middle Period,* 274 (4th–5th quotations); Nye, *Fettered Freedom,* 65 (6th quotation); Laurie, *Beyond Garrison,* 41 (7th–8th quotations); Edward Magdol, "A Window on the Abolitionist Constituency: Antislavery Petitions, 1836–1839," in Kraut, ed., *Crusaders and Compromisers,* 46–47 (9th–10th quotations).

25. Bemis, *John Quincy Adams and the Union,* 331, 334, 343–45; Kaplan,

Adams, 482–85; Filler, *Crusade against Slavery* 98–99; Miller, *Arguing about Slavery,* 214–73.

26. *Liberator,* January 2, February 2, 1837; "Fifth Annual Meeting of the Massachusetts Anti-Slavery Society, January 27, 1837," *Liberator,* February 11, 1837 (quotation). In January 1838 the *Liberator* published Adams's December 1837 speech on the unconstitutionality of the gag rule. See *Liberator,* January 5, 1838, and Bemis, *John Quincy Adams and the Union,* 331, 336–40. In 1839 the black abolitionist newspaper *Colored American* portrayed Adams's opposition to abolition in the District of Columbia as based on a belief that ending slavery there would "be but a 'partial, ineffective plaister for a great elemental evil.'" See *Colored American,* February 9, 1839.

27. Stanton, *Remarks of Henry B. Stanton,* 24–25 (quotations). Stanton also demanded "no tests" for the right to vote "on account of color."

28. Barnes, *Antislavery Impulse,* 133–37, 133 (quotation), 144–45; Weld, *Power of Congress;* Miller, *Arguing about Slavery,* 277, 303; Dumond, *Antislavery: The Crusade,* 245–46; Magdol, "Window on the Abolitionist Constituency," 45–46.

29. Neuenschwander, "Senator Thomas Morris," 123–28.

30. Smith, *Liberty and Free Soil Parties,* 24; Neuenschwander, "Senator Thomas Morris," 128–29; Morris, *Life of Thomas Morris,* 77–79, 79 (1st quotation), 91 (2nd quotation).

31. *Cincinnati Daily Gazette,* January 5, 1838; Morris, *Life of Thomas Morris,* 83, 85–86 (2nd–4th quotations), 93 (1st quotation). The Brown County petition came from white residents, not black.

32. Stewart, *Joshua R. Giddings,* 11–33, 35–36; Julian, *Life of Joshua R. Giddings,* 45; Barnes, *Antislavery Impulse,* 82; Thomas, *Theodore Weld,* 102, 35–36; Price, "The Ohio Anti-Slavery Convention of 1836," 182; Ohio Anti-Slavery Society, *Report of the Second Anniversary,* 9. James Brewer Stewart denies that Weld converted Giddings to immediatism. Stewart also denies that Giddings and his law partner, Benjamin F. Wade, established the Ashtabula Anti-Slavery Society. George W. Julian does not claim the latter.

33. Miller, *Arguing about Slavery,* 339–42, 450–51 (quotation); Julian, *Life of Joshua R. Giddings,* 64–65.

34. Julian, *Life of Joshua R. Giddings,* 61–62, 65–70 (quotations); U.S. Congress, *Congressional Globe,* 25th Cong., 3rd sess. (February 13, 1839), 181.

35. Slade, *Speech of Mr. Slade of Vermont on the Abolition of Slavery;* U.S. Congress, *Congressional Globe,* 25th Cong., 2nd sess. (December 20,1837), 41 (1st–2nd quotations); *Daily Ohio Statesman,* December 25, 1837; *Baltimore Patriot,* quoted in *Daily Herald and Gazette,* December 26, 1837 (3rd quotation); *Pennsylvania Freeman,* April 11, 1839 (4th quotation); *Emancipator,* October 6, 1838 (5th quotation); "Hillsboro' County [N.H.] Anti-Slavery Society," *Liberator,* February 2, 1838 (6th quotation); Julian, *Life of Joshua R. Giddings,* 61 (7th quotation).

36. Slade to Young Men's Anti-Slavery Society of Philadelphia, March 18, 1836, in *Liberator,* July 16, 1836; *Vermont Chronicle,* November 15, 1837; *Emancipator,* October 6, 1836; Slade to Editor of the *National Intelligencer,* February 15, 1837, in *Vermont*

Watchman and State Journal, March 28, 1837 (quotation). Along with moderation, Slade called for "firmness" in conveying "truth" to white southerners.

37. Slade to Jackson, n.d., in *Liberator,* June 22, 1838; Slade to Leavitt, August 7, 1838, in *Liberator,* September 7, 1838 (1st quotation); Thome and Kimball, *Emancipation in the West Indies;* Slade to A. Libolt, January 25, 1839, in *Pennsylvania Freeman,* April 11, 1839 (2nd–3rd quotations).

38. Slade to Editor of the *Emancipator,* October 12, 1838, in *Pennsylvania Freeman,* November 1, 1838 (1st quotation); Slade to Editor of the *Emancipator,* February 18, 1839, in *Pennsylvania Freeman,* March 14, 1839 (2nd–3rd quotations); Adams, *Memoirs,* 10:63; Slade to Editors of the Colored American, February 12, 1839, in *Colored American,* February 16, 1839; Oliver Johnson to Isaac Knapp, October 2, 1838, in *Liberator,* October 5, 1838; Slade to Oliver Johnson, September 20, 1838, in *Liberator,* October 12, 1838; Slade to A. Libolt, January 25, 1839, in *Pennsylvania Freeman,* April 11, 1839.

39. Neuenschwander, "Senator Thomas Morris," 130 (quotation); Stanton to Birney, June [January?] 25, 1837, in Birney, *Letters,* 2:388–89; Morris to Samuel Webb, J. M. Truman, and William McKee, January 30, 1838, in Morris, *Life of Thomas Morris,* 209.

40. Morris to Webb, Truman, and McKee, May 11, 1838, in Morris, *Life of Thomas Morris,* 210–22.

41. Morris to the Legislature and People of Ohio, November 23, 1838, in *Cincinnati Daily Gazette,* November 26, 1838. In a response to a speech by Henry Clay (just before he opposed racial prejudice), Morris portrayed slavery as causing "amalgamation of the races" and "licentiousness." See U.S. Congress, *Congressional Globe,* 25th Cong., 3rd sess. (February 9, 1839), appendix 172.

42. U.S. Congress, *Congressional Globe,* 25th Cong., 3rd sess. (February 9, 1839), appendix 167–75 (quotations); Dumond, *Antislavery: The Crusade,* 286; Harrold, *Gamaliel Bailey,* 39–40, 49, 63–67; Neuenschwander, "Senator Thomas Morris," 137.

43. Harrold, *Gamaliel Bailey,* 12–69; Bailey to Giddings, February 7, 12, 1839, Joshua R. Giddings–George W. Julian Papers (hereafter Giddings-Julian Papers) (quotations).

44. Stewart, *Joshua R. Giddings,* 39; Bemis, *John Quincy Adams and the Union,* 2:334, 336; Adams to Joshua Leavitt and Henry B. Stanton, July 11, 1839; Adams to Gerrit Smith, July 31, 1839, Adams Papers; Joshua R. Giddings, journal, January 21, 1839, in Julian, *Life of Joshua R. Giddings,* 61 (quotation). See also Barnes, *Antislavery Impulse,* 127–28; Parsons, *John Quincy Adams,* 224; Remini, *John Quincy Adams,* 139; Richards, *Life and Times,* 105–6.

45. Adams to Brown, December 9, 1833, Adams Papers.

46. Lewis Tappan to Adams, February 15, 1837; Adams to Samuel Webb, April 23, 1839; Adams to Joshua Leavitt and Henry B. Stanton, July 11, 1839; Adams to Gerrit Smith, July 31, 1839, Adams Papers; Merrill, *Against Wind and Tide,* 154; Barnes, *Antislavery Impulse,* 122–26; U.S. Congress, *Register of Debates,* 24th Cong., 2nd sess. (January 9, 1837), cols. 1314–19 (1st–2nd quotations); *Niles Register,* May 25, 1836, 277–78 (3rd–4th quotations).

47. Bemis, *John Quincy Adams and the Union*, 355–56; Adams to Lundy, May 12, 20, 1836, Adams Papers.

48. Adams, *Memoirs*, 9:302–3 (1st quotation); Lundy to Adams, January 21, 1837; Adams to Lundy, February 1, (2nd quotation), December 29, 1837, Adams Papers; Bemis, *John Quincy Adams and the Union*, 356, 361–67, 370. Adams commiserated with Lundy and other abolitionists concerning the May 1838 burning of Pennsylvania Hall. He corresponded with Lundy regarding evangelical abolitionist Elijah P. Lovejoy's death in November 1838 while fighting a proslavery mob at Alton, Illinois. Adams later wrote the introduction for the *Memoir of Elijah P. Lovejoy*. See Adams to Lundy, May 22, 1838, Adams Papers; Adams, *Memoirs*, 9:536 (diary entry, May 19, 1838); and Bemis, *John Quincy Adams and the Union*, 366–67.

49. Miller, *Arguing about Slavery*, 214–22; Whittier to Adams, January 23, 1837 (1st–2nd quotations); Garrison to Adams, February 1, 1837; Smith to Adams, February 3, 1837 (3rd quotation); Stanton to Adams, February 15, 1837 (4th quotation), Adams Papers.

50. Adams to John G. Whittier, January 26, 1837 (1st–4th quotations); Adams to Joshua Leavitt and Henry B. Stanton, July 11, 1839 (5th–10th quotations), Adams Papers. See also Whittier to Adams, February 9, 1837, Adams Papers, and Adams, *Memoirs*, 10:128.

51. Adams, *Memoirs*, 9:365. In 1839 Adams joined a majority of abolitionists in opposing William Lloyd Garrison's increasing radicalism. See Barnes, *Antislavery Impulse*, 165–66. Two years later Gamaliel Bailey assured Joshua Giddings that while the *Liberator* might "attack" Adams, Bailey's *Philanthropist* and Joshua Leavitt's *Emancipator* would not. Although Bailey believed Adams erred, he also believed Adams had "done much for the cause of freedom" and was "destined . . . to do still more." Bailey to Giddings, February 7, 1839, Giddings-Julian Papers.

52. Adams to Leavitt and Stanton, July 11, 1839, Adams Papers.

53. Dillon, *Abolitionists*, 99–100; Kraditor, *Means and Ends*, 240–41.

54. Grimsted, *American Mobbing*, 33–82; Mabee, *Black Freedom*, 27–50; Richards, *"Gentlemen of Property and Standing"*; Stewart, *Holy Warriors*, 63–74. See also Tomek, *Pennsylvania Hall*.

55. Sewell, *Ballots for Freedom*, 26–27; McKivigan, *War against Pro-Slavery Religion*, 64–69; Perry, *Radical Abolitionism*, 161; Garrison and Garrison, *William Lloyd Garrison*, 3:134–36. Historian Frederick J. Blue mistakenly declares, "Some abolitionists like Garrison opposed political activity of any kind." See Blue, *Free Soilers*, 2.

56. McKivigan, *War against Proslavery Religion*, 74–92; Wyatt-Brown, *Lewis Tappan*, 197–98; Friedman, *Gregarious Saints*, 68–79.

57. Friedman, *Gregarious Saints*, 96–128 (quotation); John Quincy Adams to Smith, July 31, 1839, Adams Papers; Harrold, *Rise of Aggressive Abolitionism*, 11, 92, 95–98, 120–23, 125.

58. Niven, *Salmon P. Chase*, 48–57; Harrold, *Gamaliel Bailey*, 17–69; Blue, *Salmon P. Chase*, 41–61; Chase to Gerrit Smith, May 14, 1842, in Chase, *Papers*, 2:96–99; Wiecek,

Sources of Antislavery Constitutionalism, 15–16 (1st quotation); Oakes, *Freedom National,* 2–34 (2nd quotation).

59. Harrold, *Border War,* 35–52, 116–37.

4. The Rise and Fall of the Abolition Lobby, 1836–1845

1. Leavitt to Giddings, August 7, 1842, Giddings Papers.

2. On the railroad link, see Green, *Washington,* 1:129. Recent broad interpretations of the era include Sellers, *Market Revolution;* Wilentz, *Rise of American Democracy;* and Howe, *What God Hath Wrought.*

3. Torrey, *Portraiture of Domestic Slavery,* 63–64 (quotation); U.S. Congress, *Register of Debates,* 19th Cong., 2nd sess. (December 17, 1826), cols. 563–64; Davis, *Joshua Leavitt,* 60–61; Jay, *Miscellaneous Writings on Slavery,* 157–58; Harrold, *Subversives,* 34–63. Between fall 1830 and October 1833 Benjamin Lundy published the *Genius of Universal Emancipation* in Washington. But Lundy was rarely in the city. In 1830 Leavitt had lobbied at the Capitol on behalf of the American Seaman's Friend Society.

4. Barnes, *Antislavery Impulse,* 180; Miller, *Arguing about Slavery,* 404; Joshua R. Giddings to Laura Waters Giddings, February 18, 1842, in Barnes and Dumond, *Letters of Weld, Grimké,* 2:883n (quotation; hereafter *Weld-Grimké Letters);* Adams, *Memoirs,* 9:39–40.

5. Barnes, *Antislavery Impulse,* 128, 177; Adams, *Memoirs,* 8:316; Brooks, *Liberty Power,* 51–52; Joshua Leavitt to Weld, [November 16, 1837], in Barnes and Dumond, *Weld-Grimké Letters,* 1:478; McPherson, "Fight against the Gag Rule," 178–79; Emerson, *Richard Hildreth,* 57; Johnson, *Liberty Party,* 227, 348.

6. Stanton, *Random Recollections,* 60; "CHA'S L*****" to William Goodell, n.d., in *Friend of Man,* March 22, 1838 (1st quotation); *Pennsylvania Freeman,* March 11, 1838 (2nd quotation). Stanton suggested that he influenced Adams's argument in favor of abolition by constitutional amendment.

7. Adams to Samuel May, January 7, 1838; Adams to Samuel Webb and William H. Scott, January 19, 1838; Adams to A. Bronson, July 30, 1838; Adams to Oliver Johnson, December 13, 1838; Adams to Webb, April 23, 1839; Adams to American Anti-Slavery Society Committee of Arrangements, July 11, 1839; Adams to Gerrit Smith, July 31, 1839, Adams Papers; Barnes, *Antislavery Impulse,* 148; Sewell, *Ballots for Freedom,* 37; Whittier to the secretary of the Philadelphia County Anti-Slavery Society, August 27, 1839, in Whittier, *Letters,* 1:368 (quotations).

8. Stewart, *Joshua R. Giddings,* 51; "Ann Sprigg," Bytes of History, http://bytesofhistory. com/Collections/UGRR/spriggann/SpriggAnn_Biography.html; Theodore Weld to Angelina Grimké Weld, January 1, December 27, 1842, in Barnes and Dumond, *Weld-Grimké Letters,* 2:883, 947; Johnson, *Liberty Party,* 343; American Anti-Slavery Society, *Fifth Annual Report,* 38; Gates, *Hon. Seth M. Gates on Freemasonry;* Gates to T. Allen, January 30, 1840, in *National Intelligencer,* February 5, 1840; Whittier to Adams,

December 12, 1839, in Whittier, *Letters,* 1:381–82; *Signal of Liberty,* September 25, 1847. Weld suggested that Slade did not board at Sprigg's until December 1842. By 1847 Calhoun viewed Liberty "principle and policy" favorably.

9. Smith to Gates, December 21, 1839, letterbook, Smith Papers (1st–2nd quotations); *Emancipator,* December 26, 1839 (3rd–4th quotations); Stewart, *Joshua R. Giddings,* 67–68; Holt, *Rise and Fall of the American Whig Party,* 126; Giddings to unknown, December 28, 1839, Giddings Papers (5th–6th quotations); Davis, *Joshua Leavitt,* 155. Leavitt described Gates as "an intelligent and zealous abolitionist" before clashing with him. See *Emancipator,* December 26, 1839. James Brewer Stewart notes that House committee appointments also had a role in the congressmen's loyalty to the Whig Party.

10. Slade, *Speech of Mr. Slade of Vermont on the Right of Petition,* 21–22 (2nd–7th quotations), 33–34 (1st quotation, 8th–9th quotations). William Lee Miller calls Slade's speech the "most advanced antislavery speech made in the House so far." See Miller, *Arguing about Slavery,* 361–62.

11. Adams, *Memoirs,* 10:198 (1st quotation); Slade, *Speech of Mr. Slade of Vermont on the Right of Petition,* 40–41 (2nd quotation).

12. Whittier to *Essex Transcript,* October 30, 1843, in Whittier, *Letters,* 1:610–15; Adams, *Memoirs,* 10:206 (quotation); Mordell, *Quaker Militant,* 108; Miller, *Arguing about Slavery,* 362–72; McPherson, "Fight against the Gag Rule," 180. While in Washington, Whittier also spoke with Caleb Cushing (whom Whittier thought had antislavery potential), Henry Clay, and other "Southern as well as Northern members." He hoped he had "some effect," and after he returned to Philadelphia, Whittier sent Adams a "memorial" opposing the new gag. See Whittier to Caleb Cushing, February 5, 1840; Whittier to *Essex Transcript,* October 30, 1843, in Whittier, *Letters,* 1:382–83, 382n, 610–15.

13. Bemis, *John Quincy Adams and the Union,* 422; *Colored American,* November 14, December 19, 1840; Barnes, *Antislavery Impulse,* 177–78; McPherson, "Fight against the Gag Rule," 180, 185; Davis, *Joshua Leavitt,* 176–80. In effect, Leavitt sent himself.

14. McPherson, "Fight against the Gag Rule," 182–83; Miller, *Arguing about Slavery,* 381–82; Stewart, *Joshua R. Giddings,* 63–65 (1st quotation); Gates to Smith, February 1, 25, 1841, Smith Papers (2nd quotation); Adams, *Memoirs,* 10:439–40.

15. Slade to Leavitt, April 29, 1841, in *Emancipator,* May 6, 1841 (1st–2nd quotations); Gates to James G. Birney, June 7, 1841, in Birney, *Letters,* 2:630–31 (3rd quotation); Gates to Leavitt, n.d., in *Emancipator,* May 6, 1841 (4th–5th quotations).

16. Gates to James G. Birney, June 7, 1841, in Birney, *Letters,* 2:630–31 (1st quotation); McPherson, "Fight against the Gag Rule," 184–86; *Emancipator,* June 24, 1841 (2nd–3rd quotations).

17. Leavitt to Piercy and Reed, June 26, 1841, in *Emancipator,* July 1, 1841 (1st–2nd quotations); *Emancipator,* July 8 (3rd, 5th–6th quotations), 15, 1841 (4th quotation). Leavitt had again returned to New York City when he made these comments.

18. Slade to Leavitt, July 10, 1841, in ibid., July 15, 1841 (1st quotation); Giddings to

Leavitt, July 10, 1841, in ibid. See also Davis, *Joshua Leavitt,* 183, 189, and McPherson, "Fight against the Gag Rule," 185–86.

19. Tappan to Giddings, July 24, 1841, Giddings Papers (1st–2nd quotations); Gates to James G. Birney, December 11, 1841, in Birney, *Letters,* 2:642–43 (3rd quotation). In contrast to the approach here, Gilbert H. Barnes and James M. McPherson credit Leavitt for independent action among antislavery Whig congressmen. Hugh Davis is relatively neutral. See Barnes, *Antislavery Impulse,* 179; McPherson, "Fight against the Gag Rule," 194–95; and Davis, *Joshua Leavitt,* 183–84, 189.

20. *Emancipator,* September 16 (1st quotation), October 28, 1841 (2nd quotation). Also in September 1841, the AFASS named Seth Gates to be its congressional coordinator for petitions. See U.S. Congress, *Congressional Globe,* 27th Cong., 2nd sess. (January 25, 1842), 172. Leavitt had worried about raising funds to pay for the trip. See Leavitt to James G. Birney, October 12, 1841, in Birney, *Letters,* 2:639–40.

21. Leavitt to Giddings, October 29, 1841, Giddings Papers (quotations); Barnes, *Antislavery Impulse,* 178; Davis, *Joshua Leavitt,* 183–84, 187. Leavitt regretted the weak response to the AFASS's plan to have, in his words, "a number of known abolitionists visit Washington for the purpose of sustaining by their continence, those of our representatives who are disposed to do right." Leavitt to "Readers," December 4, 1841, in *Emancipator,* December 10, 1841. Leavitt expected that in December "recognition of Texas" would come up. He wrote, "I hope to see, during my stay here many of our friends who can afford it, coming up to stay for a few days or weeks."

22. Davis, *Joshua Leavitt,* 187–88; Gates to James G. Birney, December 11, 1841, in Birney, *Letters,* 2:642–43; Theodore Weld to Lewis Tappan, December 14, 1841; Theodore Weld to Angelina Grimké Weld, January 1, 1842, in Barnes and Dumond, *Weld-Grimké Letters,* 2:879–81, 883; "Cleveland's Freedmen's Aid Society"; Cheek and Cheek, *John Mercer Langston,* 132; Ken Champlin, [untitled], *Standard-Times,* February 12, 1998; "Nathaniel Briggs Borden," in [White], ed., *Memorial Biographies,* 6:94–95; Grover, *Fugitive's Gibraltar,* 140; Champlin, "Fall River Underground," *Standard-Times,* June 25, 1997; Brooks, *Liberty Power,* 86. Kathryn Grover contends that by 1839, Borden had become "Fall River's most prominent white abolitionist." Mattocks had favored black rights in state courts. He supported congressional action against slavery in the District of Columbia. See "Vermont" to Preston Blair, September 7, 1840 (quoting a *Voice of Freedom,* August 22, 1840, article), in *Extra Globe,* September 8, 1840.

23. Leavitt to "Readers," December 4, 1841, in *Emancipator,* December 10, 1841 (1st–3rd quotations); [Charles Torrey] to Mary Torrey, December 13, 1841, in Lovejoy, *Memoir of Rev. Charles T. Torrey,* 88 (4th quotation); Theodore Weld to Angelina Grimké Weld, January 18, 1842, in Barnes and Dumond, *Weld-Grimké Letters,* 2:895–96; Pacheco, *Pearl,* 44. See also Torrey, *Martyrdom of Abolitionist Charles Torrey.*

24. Theodore Weld to Lewis Tappan, December 14, 1841; Theodore Weld to Angelina Grimké Weld, January 2, 1842, in Barnes and Dumond, *Weld-Grimké Letters,* 2:879–82 (1st–2nd quotations), 879–80 (3rd–4th quotations), 886. Gilbert H. Barnes and Dwight L. Dumond, in *Weld-Grimké Letters,* credit Leavitt as the developer of this

plan. So does Benjamin Platt Thomas in *Theodore Weld,* 195. But Barnes in a later work does not. See Barnes, *Antislavery Impulse,* 180–83, 191–95. Weld asked Tappan to pay for work at Weld's New Jersey farm during Weld's absence in Washington. Hugh Davis gives Leavitt credit for inviting Weld to Washington, D.C. See Davis, *Joshua Leavitt,* 188.

25. Theodore Weld to Tappan, December 14, 1841, in Barnes and Dumond, *Weld-Grimké Letters,* 2:879–82. Weld sometimes became a bit more ambivalent concerning the Liberty Party. See Weld to James G. Birney, January 22, 1841, in Birney, *Letters,* 2:662–63. Personality conflicts also led Weld to distrust Torrey. See Theodore Weld to Angelina Grimké Weld, January 18, 1842, in Barnes and Dumond, *Weld-Grimké Letters,* 2:986.

26. Theodore Weld to Angelina Grimké Weld, January 1, 2, 9, 1842, in Barnes and Dumond, *Weld-Grimké Letters,* 2:882–83, 285–86, 889 (1st–2nd quotations); Barnes, *Antislavery Impulse,* 181–84; McPherson, "Fight against the Gag Rule," 188; Stanley Harrold, "Romanticizing Slave Revolt: Madison Washington, the *Creole* Mutiny, and Abolitionist Celebration of Violent Means," in McKivigan and Harrold, eds., *Antislavery Violence,* 89–107. Gates, Giddings, and Leavitt had been waiting for Weld. Sherlock Andrews and John Mattocks arrived soon after Weld. Barnes and Dumond suggest without proof that Adams at the salon joined Giddings's "select committee." See Barnes, *Antislavery Impulse,* 184–85, and Barnes and Dumond, *Weld-Grimké Letters,* 2:889n.

27. Harrold, *Subversives,* 71–72 (quotation); Theodore Weld to Angelina Grimké Weld, January 18, 1842, in Barnes and Dumond, *Weld-Grimké Letters,* 2:895–97; Lovejoy, *Memoir of Rev. Charles T. Torrey,* 97, 100.

28. Gates to James G. Birney, January 24, 1842, in Birney, *Letters,* 2:667; McPherson, "Fight against the Gag Rule," 188–91; Editorial Correspondence, January 28, 1842, in *Emancipator,* February 4, 1842; Theodore Weld to Angelina Grimké Weld, January [23], 1842, in Barnes and Dumond, *Weld-Grimké Letters,* 2:899 (quotation). Mattocks dramatically declined to make additional presentations in what he called "Slavery's Hall." None of this is reported in the *Congressional Globe.*

29. Editorial Correspondence, January 28, 1842, in *Emancipator,* February 4, 1842 (1st quotation); Theodore Weld to Angelina Grimké Weld, January [23], 25, 30, February 6, 1842, in Barnes and Dumond, *Weld-Grimké Letters,* 2:897–906 (2nd quotation), 911–13 (3rd quotation); Bemis, *John Quincy Adams and the Union,* 425–39; U.S. Congress, *Congressional Globe,* 27th Cong., 2nd sess. (January 25, 1842), 168–70, 202–7; (February 7, 1842), 215; McPherson, "Fight against the Gag Rule," 190–91; *Emancipator,* March 31, 1842. Gilmer was a Democrat by November 1842. In early February Washington newspapers stopped publishing Adams's remarks, as he turned his southern accusers' rhetoric against them.

30. Editorial Correspondence, January 29, 1842, in *Emancipator,* February 4, 1842 (quotation); Weld to James G. Birney, January [30], 1842, in Birney, *Letters,* 2:664 (2nd quotation); Whittier to Adams, January 31, 1842, in Whittier, *Letters,* 1:541 (2nd quotation); Edward Wade to Joshua R. Giddings, January 26, 1842, Giddings Papers.

31. Joshua R. Giddings to Laura Giddings, February 2, 1842, in Julian, *Life of*

Joshua R. Giddings, 111 (1st quotation); Joshua R. Giddings to Laura Maria Giddings, February 8, 1842 (2nd quotation), Giddings-Julian Papers; Theodore Weld to Angelina Grimké Weld, February [7], 1842, in Barnes and Dumond, *Weld-Grimké Letters,* 2:913 (3rd quotation); Brooks, *Liberty Power,* 66–67; Bemis, *John Quincy Adams and the Union,* 425 (4th quotation); Thomas, *Theodore Weld,* 208–12 (5th–6th quotations); McPherson, "Fight against the Gag Rule," 191–92 (7th–8th quotations); Nye, *Fettered Freedom,* 53 (9th quotation). Giddings added in his letter to his daughter, Laura Maria Giddings, "They call me an *abolitionist."* Benjamin P. Thomas notes limits to Weld's optimism but contends Weld "helped to bring slavery's demise." See Thomas, *Theodore Weld,* 211.

32. Theodore Weld to Angelina Grimké Weld, February 17, 1842, in Barnes and Dumond, *Weld-Grimké Letters,* 2:923–24 (1st–2nd quotations); Bemis, *John Quincy Adams and the Union,* 443 (3rd–4th quotations).

33. Theodore Weld to Angelina Grimké Weld, January 2, 9, 15?, 25, February 9, 20, 1842, in Barnes and Dumond, *Weld-Grimké Letters,* 2:887, 889, 893 (1st quotation), 901, 903–4, 906, 915, 922–28; Barnes, *Antislavery Impulse,* 183–84, 289n; Bemis, *John Quincy Adams and the Union,* 425; Stewart, *Joshua R. Giddings,* 70–71, 73–76; Wiecek, *Sources of Antislavery Constitutionalism,* 39, 213–19; Foner, *Free Soil, Free Labor, Free Men,* 73–102; U.S. Congress, *Journal of the House of Representatives,* 28th Cong., 2nd sess. (March 22, 1842), 567–80 (2nd–4th quotations); U.S. Congress, *Congressional Globe,* 27th Cong., 2nd sess. (March 22, 1842), 344–46; McPherson, "Fight against the Gag Rule," 192–93. Samuel Flagg Bemis and James Brewer Stewart give Weld credit for drafting Giddings's *Creole* resolutions. William M. Wiecek suggests otherwise. Giddings on February 21, 1842, visited Weld in Weld's room at Sprigg's boardinghouse. See Theodore Weld to Angelina Grimké Weld, February 20, 1842, in Barnes and Dumond, *Weld-Grimké Letters,* 2:927–28.

34. Gates to James G. Birney, April 4, 1842, in Birney, *Letters,* 2:687–88 (1st–2nd quotations); Phelps to Joseph Sturge, April 30, 1842, Antislavery Collection/Garrison Papers (3rd quotation). Gilbert H. Barnes regards Adams's victory as helping the northern Whigs. Barnes, *Antislavery Impulse,* 189–90. See also Brooks, *Liberty Power,* 68.

35. Barnes, *Antislavery Impulse,* 188–90 (1st–3rd quotations); McPherson, "Fight against the Gag Rule," 194–95; Thomas, *Theodore Weld,* 211; Seth M. Gates to Gerrit Smith, March 14, 1842, Smith Papers; Gates to James G. Birney, March 23, 1842, in Birney, *Letters,* 2:684–85; *Emancipator,* March 31, 1842; Torrey to "Alden," March 19, 1842, in *Emancipator,* March 31, 1842; Torrey to *Emancipator,* n.d., in *Spirit of Liberty,* April 16, 1842 (4th quotation). Benjamin Platt Thomas writes, "Insofar as Weld was instrumental in implementing the insurgent assault, he helped to bring slavery's demise." See Thomas, *Theodore Weld,* 211. Barnes contends that Seth M. Gates failed in an attempt to organize a northern Whig caucus on Giddings's behalf. See Barnes, *Antislavery Impulse,* 188.

36. Gates to James G. Birney, March 23, 24, 1842, in Birney, *Letters,* 2:684–86.

37. U.S. Congress, *Congressional Globe,* 27th Cong., 2nd sess. (April 22, 1842), 439; Leavitt to *Emancipator,* April 28, 30, May 12, 1842, in *Emancipator,* May 5, 12, 19, 1842;

Adams, diary, July 20, 1842, quoted in Davis, *Joshua Leavitt,* 192 (quotation); Leavitt to Giddings, August 7, 1842, Giddings Papers. See also McPherson, "Fight against the Gag Rule," 193, and Davis, *Joshua Leavitt,* 193–94. Hugh Davis suggests that Leavitt relished Botts's charges.

38. Barnes, *Antislavery Impulse,* 193–94; Theodore Weld to Angelina Grimké Weld, December 27, 1842, in Barnes and Dumond, *Weld-Grimké Letters,* 2:947; *Liberator,* December 16, 1842 (quotations).

39. Barnes, *Antislavery Impulse,* 193–94; Theodore Weld to Angelina Grimké Weld, January 1, 4, 16, February 1, 1843, in Barnes and Dumond, *Weld-Grimké Letters,* 2:953–56 (3rd quotation), 964, 973 (1st–2nd quotations); *Emancipator,* January 5, 1843 (4th quotation). Weld reported that John Quincy Adams, Winfield Scott, and William S. Archer of Virginia attended Mott's lecture.

40. Theodore Weld to Angelina Grimké Weld, December 27, 1842, January 1, 1843, in Barnes and Dumond, *Weld-Grimké Letters,* 2:948–49, 953 (quotation). Adams thought he could still "battle for liberty" even as slaveholders lay low. Historians have similarly misjudged the impact of "dispirited" southern congressmen on the effectiveness of the abolition lobby. See McPherson, "Fight against the Gag Rule," 194, and Davis, *Joshua Leavitt,* 194. See also Seth M. Gates to James G. Birney, March 24, 1842, in Birney, *Letters,* 2:686. James McPherson points out that the Whig Party adopted a policy of not confronting Joshua R. Giddings after his return to Congress in May 1842. But McPherson does not link this to a decline of the lobby/caucus. Also Gilbert H. Barnes and Dwight L. Dumond suggest that Whig Party leaders restrained slaveholders out of fear of losses in northern elections. See Barnes and Dumond, *Weld-Grimké Letters,* 2:953n.

41. Theodore Weld to Angelina Grimké Weld, January 9, 12, 14, 22, February 1, 3, 1843; Theodore Weld to Tappan, January 23, February 3, 1843; Leavitt to Angelina Grimké Weld, February 7, 1843, in Barnes and Dumond, *Weld-Grimké Letters,* 2:959, 962–65 (3rd quotation), 971, 973–75 (1st, 4th, 5th–6th quotations); U.S. Congress, *Congressional Globe,* 27th Cong., 3rd sess. (January 14, 19, 1843), 161, 176; D. L. C[hild] to *[Liberator],* March 14, 1843, in *Liberator,* March 17, 1843 (2nd quotation); Giddings, *Speeches in Congress,* 32–51; Barnes, *Antislavery Impulse,* 194; Leavitt to James G. Birney, February 10, 1843, in Birney, *Letters,* 2:715–16. After April 1844 Weld essentially retired from the movement. See Thomas, *Theodore Weld,* 218. In his letter to Birney, Leavitt also charged that Gates, Giddings, and Slade "risked everything" for "the Whig Party, with a bigotry and devotion worthy of monkdom."

42. Joshua Giddings to Theodore Weld, February 21, 1843, in Barnes and Dumond, *Weld-Grimké Letters,* 2:975–76; D. L. C[hild] to *[Liberator],* March 13, 1842, in *Liberator,* March 17, 1842; Leavitt to *Emancipator,* February 21, 1843, in *Emancipator,* March 9, 1843.

43. Theodore Weld to Angelina Grimké Weld, December 27, 1842, in Barnes and Dumond, *Weld-Grimké Letters,* 2:947–48; Barnes, *Antislavery Impulse,* 193; Davis, *Joshua Leavitt,* 211; Gates to James G. Birney, December 11, 1841, in Birney, *Letters,* 2:642–43; Gates to Gerrit Smith, March 14, 1842, Smith Papers; Miller, *Arguing about Slavery,*

471–75; U.S. Congress, *Congressional Globe,* 28th Cong., 1st sess. (February 28, 1844), 335. See also *Emancipator,* January 11, 18, 25, 1844. Other antislavery Whig congressmen who did not return included William B. Calhoun, William W. Irwin, and Samuel C. Crofts. Along with Gates, Slade, Andrews, and Mattocks, none of them served in the House after March 1843.

44. Leavitt to Joshua R. Giddings, April 22, 1842; Joshua R. Giddings to Laura Waters Giddings, December 10, 1843, Giddings Papers (1st–2nd quotations); Editorial Correspondence, January 4, 1844, in *Emancipator,* January 11, 1844; Editorial Correspondence, January 15, 1844, in *Emancipator,* January 25, 1844; Davis, *Joshua Leavitt,* 211–12; Theodore Weld to Tappan, [January 11, 1844], in Barnes and Dumond, *Weld-Grimké Letters,* 2:990 (3rd quotation); Harrold, *Subversives,* 81–84; Thomas, *Theodore Weld,* 217. Weld expected Torrey to return in February as correspondent of the *Tocsin of Liberty,* the newspaper Torrey edited. See Theodore Weld to Angelina Grimké Weld, December 27, 1842, in Barnes and Dumond, *Weld-Grimké Letters,* 2:947–48, and *Emancipator,* January 5, 1843.

45. Giddings to Weld, January 28, 1844, in Barnes and Dumond, *Weld-Grimké Letters,* 2:990–91.

46. Harrold, *Subversives,* 84–85; Davis, *Joshua Leavitt,* 221–22; Freehling, *Road to Disunion,* 1:351.

47. Miller, *Arguing about Slavery,* 476–85; Freehling, *Road to Disunion,* 1:351.

48. Adams, *Memoirs,* 9:29 (1st quotation); *Liberator,* December 20, 1844 (2nd quotation); Bemis, *John Quincy Adams and the Union,* 447–48 (3rd quotation); Miller, *Arguing about Slavery,* 486 (4th quotation); Freehling, *Road to Disunion,* 1:308, 312. Bemis claims repeal of the gag rule constituted the "first clear victory over the Slave Power." William Freehling also notes the gag rule struggle's importance. See Freehling, *Road to Disunion,* 1:334, 352.

49. *Emancipator,* December 11, 1844.

50. Ibid. (1st–2nd quotations); Leavitt to James G. Birney, December 18, 1844, in Birney, *Letters,* 2:890 (3rd–5th quotations).

51. Davis, *Joshua Leavitt,* 223–24. Historian Corey M. Brooks mistakenly portrays the lobby Gamaliel Bailey began in 1847 as "a permanent abolitionist congressional lobby." It was in fact a nonabolitionist Liberty Party/Free Soil Party lobby. See Brooks, *Liberty Power,* 72.

5. Discord, Relationships, and Free Soil, 1840–1848

1. Pickard, *Life and Letters of John Greenleaf Whittier,* 1:171–72; Sewell, *Ballots for Freedom,* 11–20; Barnes, *Antislavery Impulse,* 147–48.

2. Johnson, *Liberty Party,* 10–16; Sewell, *Ballots for Freedom,* 45, 51–71; Whittier to Elizur Wright Jr., March 25, 1840, in Albree, *Whittier Correspondence,* 274–75 (quotation).

3. Johnson, *Liberty Party,* 3, 19–20, 76 (3rd–4th quotations); Sewell, *Ballots for Freedom,* 74–79, 164; Roosevelt, *Thomas Hart Benton,* 260 (1st quotation); Dillon, *Abolitionists,* 135 (2nd quotation); Friedman, *Gregarious Saints,* 179–81, 225–29 (5th quotation); Alan M. Kraut, "Partisanship and Principles: The Liberty Party in Antebellum Political Culture," in Kraut, ed., *Crusaders and Compromisers,* 72 (6th quotation). Gilbert Barnes labels the Liberty Party "the most pathetic residue of antislavery organization." See Barnes, *Antislavery Impulse,* 176. Johnson notes historians' negative views of the Liberty Party. See Johnson, *Liberty Party,* 303–4. John Mayfield regards the Liberty Party mission as primarily educational. See Mayfield, *Rehearsal for Republicanism,* 63. Ronald G. Walters perceives Liberty aims as similar to Garrisonian: to use propaganda to influence public sentiment. RPAs in particular adopted this point of view, and some who joined the Liberty Party sought only to save themselves from complicity in a sinful, proslavery, two-party system. See Walters, *Antislavery Appeal,* 14–16; Perry, *Radical Abolitionism,* 185; and Massachusetts Anti-Slavery Society, *Twelfth Annual Report,* 93–94.

4. Kraut, "Partisanship and Principles," 4 (quotation), 73; Brooks, *Liberty Power;* Stewart, *Holy Warriors,* 97–104. Kraut also contends that the Liberty Party "shifted the issue of slavery from the pulpit to the stump" (92). Richard H. Sewell notes the "upward swing of political abolitionism" beginning in 1843. See Sewell, *John P. Hale,* 27–28. Julie Roy Jeffrey makes virtually the same remark as Kraut concerning the Liberty Party impact. See Jeffrey, *Great Silent Army,* 163.

5. *Emancipator,* February 28, 1839; *Philanthropist,* December 30, 1836; Leavitt to James G. Birney, October 12, 1841, in Birney, *Letters,* 2:639–40; Wyatt-Brown, *Lewis Tappan,* 275–76; Harrold, *Gamaliel Bailey,* 74–76; Johnson, *Liberty Party,* 30–32; Blue, *Free Soilers,* 6. See also Whittier to the chairman of the Liberty Party Committee, August 10, 1841; Henry B. Stanton to Whittier, February 3, July 20, 1844, in Albree, *Whittier Correspondence,* 79–80, 86–87, 91–93.

6. Johnson, *Liberty Party,* 32–34, 292–301; Rayback, *Free Soil,* 105–6; "The Address of the Southern and Western Liberty Convention, Held at Cincinnati, June 11 and 12, 1845," in Chase and Cleveland, *Anti-Slavery Addresses,* 76–125; Massachusetts Anti-Slavery Society, *Twelfth Annual Report,* 34–38, 53–57; Kraditor, *Means and Ends,* 29–34; William Lloyd Garrison to Henry C. Wright, October 1, 1844, in Garrison, *Letters,* 3:265 (quotation).

7. *Herald of Freedom,* quoted in *Liberator,* July 26, 1839 (1st quotation); Stewart, *Joshua R. Giddings,* 95–98; James G. Birney to Leicester King, January 1, 1844, in Birney, *Letters,* 2:772 (2nd–4th quotations). "Abolitionists," Birney asserted, had "contributed more than any other class of persons to swell the tide of [Adams's] influence."

8. Yacovone, *Samuel Joseph May,* 76–78.

9. Mabee, *Black Freedom,* 260; Adams, *Memoirs,* 11:285–86; Karcher, *First Woman of the Republic,* 291–93; Gamble, "Joshua Giddings," 39; Yacovone, *Samuel Joseph May,* 132. On January 3, 1843, Adams wrote that Mott was a "distinguished abolitionist" and that her views were "little" different from his. But considering how "obnoxious" he was in the House of Representatives, he believed her request would be more likely accepted

if another congressman presented it. In 1843, despite David Lee Child's Whig Party ties, he succeeded Lydia Maria Child as the *Standard*'s editor.

10. Goldfarb, "Life of Gamaliel Bailey," 219–20. Chase denied being an abolitionist. But as late as 1849 he served on the board of Tappan's church-oriented AFASS. See Niven, *Salmon P. Chase*, 48–57, and American and Foreign Anti-Slavery Society, *[9th] Annual Report*, 11, 154–55.

11. Massachusetts Anti-Slavery Society, *Annual Report and Proceedings*, 10th report, appendix, 9; Frederick Douglass, "I Have Come to Tell You Something about Slavery: An Address Delivered in Lynn, Massachusetts, in October 1841," in Douglass, *Frederick Douglass Papers. Series One*, 1:4 (1st–2nd quotations); Tappan to Salmon P. Chase, March 18, 1842, in Chase, *Papers*, 2:93 (3rd quotation); Leavitt to James G. Birney, February 10, 1843, in Birney, *Letters*, 2:715–16 (4th quotation).

12. Tappan to Giddings, February 1, 1840, in Julian, *Life of Joshua R. Giddings*, 90 (quotation); Harrold, *Gamaliel Bailey*, 33, 51; Johnson, *Liberty Party*, 181; Mabee, *Black Freedom*, 261; Salmon P. Chase to Giddings, December 30, 1841, in Chase, *Papers*, 2:81–82. In 1844 Giddings's former House colleague Seth M. Gates, who had joined the Liberty Party, advised Giddings to cut his ties with Henry Clay. Gates to Giddings, October 2, 1844, Giddings Papers; Harrold, *Gamaliel Bailey*, 51–52, 73.

13. Massachusetts Anti-Slavery Society, *Annual Reports and Proceedings*, 10th report, 28 (quotation); Gamble, "Joshua Giddings," 38–46. For examples of Garrisonian criticism of Giddings and rhetorical use of his position to advance their agenda, see *Anti-Slavery Bugle*, September 19, 1845; September 18, 1846.

14. *Pennsylvania Freeman*, January 16, 1840 (1st–2nd quotations); *Louisville Journal*, January 13, 1842; Smith to John Price and Daniel Sullivan, March 9, 1842, in *Globe*, December 10, 1842; *Albany Weekly Patriot*, January 26, 1843; Smith to Seward, February 19, March 5, 1842; Tappan to Seward, March 18, 1842; Seward to Smith, February 23, March 19, 1842, Seward Papers; Tappan to Chase, March 1, 1842, in Chase, *Papers*, 2:93; Chase to Tappan, September 15, 1842, Chase Papers, Library of Congress; Seward to Chase, Samuel Lewis, and others, May 25, 1845, in Seward, *Works*, 440–43 (3rd–7th quotations). Chase worked with abolitionist Jonathan Blanchard in attempts to draw rising antislavery Whig Thaddeus Stevens of Pennsylvania into the Liberty Party. Blanchard had a lasting influence on Stevens's antislavery views. See Trefousse, *Thaddeus Stevens*, 50, 67–68, 77, 83.

15. See James L. Huston's brief but illuminating discussion of forces, events, and contingency in Civil War causation, "Interpreting the Causation Sequence," 329–30.

16. American Anti-Slavery Society, *Fourth Annual Report*, 24–25; Massachusetts Anti-Slavery Society, *Fifth Annual Report*, 42–51; *Liberator*, February 11, 1837; Miller, *Arguing about Slavery*, 297; Massachusetts, *Massachusetts General Court Joint Committee on the Annexation of Texas;* U.S. Congress, *Senate Executive Documents*, 48th Cong., 1st, 2nd, and special sess.; Birney to Salmon P. Chase, June 5, 1837, in Chase, *Papers*, 2:63–66 (1st quotation); Whittier to William James Allinson, June 17, 1837; Whittier to Clay, July 5, 1837, in Whittier, *Letters*, 1:238–39 (2nd quotation), 241–42.

17. Smith, *Annexation of Texas,* 54–55, 63–65; Curtis, *Fox at Bay, 152–566;* Wilson, *Presidency of Martin Van Buren;* Miller, *Arguing about Slavery,* 297–98. William Lee Miller claims, "Adams and the anti-Texas resolutions had unsettled the administration sufficiently for it to call off any scheme to annex Texas, and had unsettled the Texas government sufficiently for it to withdraw its proposal . . . for the time being." See Miller, *Arguing about Slavery,* 297–98.

18. Miller, *Arguing about Slavery,* 297–98 (1st quotation); Dumond, *Antislavery: The Crusade,* 246; Theodore Weld to Angelina Grimké Weld, February 17, 20, 1842, in Barnes and Dumond, *Weld-Grimké Letters,* 2:922–23, 926; Torrey to *Emancipator,* n.d., in *Spirit of Liberty,* April 16, 1842 (2nd quotation)

19. Seth M. Gates, "Address to the People of the Free States of the Union, Washington, March 3, 1843," *National Intelligencer,* May 4, 1843 (1st–3rd quotations); Greeley, *History of the Struggle for Slavery Extension or Restriction,* 33–36; *Emancipator,* May 18, 1843; Tappan to John Scoble, April 24, 1850, in Abel and Kingberg, *Side-Light on Anglo-American Relations,* 239–40 (4th quotation).

20. Freehling, *Road to Disunion,* 1:376–87, 394–95; Green to John Tyler, July 3, 1843; Green to Upshur, August 3, 1843, in Merk, *Slavery and the Annexation of Texas,* 221–24. On Andrews, see Stern, "Stephen Pearl Andrews."

21. *Liberator,* April 19, May 10, 1844; Child, *Letters of Lydia Maria Child,* viii (quotations); *Lowell Journal,* quoted in *Liberator,* July 5, 1844; *Signal of Liberty,* July 15, 1844; Stewart, *Joshua R. Giddings,* 93–98; McKay, *Henry Wilson,* 30–31. Biographer Walter M. Merrill exaggerates when he contends that William Lloyd Garrison, in contrast to Lewis Tappan, had by the mid-1840s less interest in Texas than "in the Free Church controversy in Scotland." See Merrill, *Against Wind and Tide,* 221.

22. Smith, *Annexation of Texas,* 322–45; Holt, *Rise and Fall of the American Whig Party,* 195; Mayer, *All on Fire,* 277.

23. Brauer, *Cotton Versus Conscience,* 1.

24. Donald, *Charles Sumner and the Coming of the Civil War,* 16, 131; Martyn, *Wendell Phillips,* 34, 39, 49; Sumner to Francis Leiber, January 9, 1836; Sumner to Cornelius Felton, April 9, 1850, in Sumner, *Selected Letters,* 1:18 (1st quotation), 290; Sumner to Joseph Story, February 5, 1845, in Pierce, *Memoir and Letters of Charles Sumner,* 2:331 (2nd–3rd quotations), 364–76; Sumner to Whittier, January 5, [1848], in Albree, *Whittier Correspondence,* 96; Garrison to Sumner, August 23, 1846, in Garrison, *Letters,* 3:319; Parker to Sumner, August 17, 1845, Sumner Papers; Weiss, *Life and Correspondence of Theodore Parker,* 1:26 (4th–6th quotations), 3; Pickard, *Life and Letters of John Greenleaf Whittier,* 1:308. Sumner resisted Maria Weston Chapman's suggestion that he work more closely with the Garrisonians. See Pierce, *Memoir and Letters of Charles Sumner,* 2:195.

25. Garrison and Garrison, *William Lloyd Garrison,* 3:136–38 (quotations); Charles Sumner to Wendell Phillips, February 4, 1845, in Sumner, *Selected Letters,* 1:145; Mayer, *All on Fire,* 338–44; McKay, *Henry Wilson,* 34. Sumner also opposed interference in the South. See Donald, *Charles Sumner and the Coming of the Civil War,* 139–40, and

Schwartz, *Samuel Gridley Howe,* 154–56n. In regard to the anti-Texas convention, historian John Mayfield asserts incorrectly that Garrisonians were only in the "balconies." See Mayfield, *Rehearsal for Republicanism,* 36–37. Charles Francis Adams especially disliked disunionism. Adams also objected to abolitionist criticism of northern Whigs. Historian Martin B. Duberman suggests that threats to white civil liberties and "aggressive behavior of the ultra-Southern leaders in Congress," rather than sympathy for slaves, motivated Adams. See Duberman, *Charles Francis Adams,* 61–64, 104–6.

26. Garrison and Garrison, *William Lloyd Garrison,* 3:140–42 (quotation); Stewart, *Wendell Phillips,* 140; Duberman, *Charles Francis Adams,* 106–7. Henry Stanton represented the Liberty Party at the same gathering.

27. Schwartz, *Samuel Gridley Howe,* 155; McKay, *Henry Wilson,* 34–35; Mordell, *Quaker Militant,* 143; Mayer, *All on Fire,* 138, 344; Duberman, *Charles Francis Adams,* 109 (quotation).

28. Calarco, *People of the Underground Railroad,* 88–89; McNeal, "Antimasonic Party in Lancaster County, Pennsylvania"; Earle, *Jacksonian Antislavery,* 3; U.S. Congress, *Congressional Globe,* 29th Cong., 2nd sess. (February 15, 1847), 424–25; Richards, *Slave Power,* 152–53. David M. Potter reports that the original version of the proviso passed 80–64. Earle reports 77–58. See Potter, *Impending Crisis,* 22, and Earle, *Jacksonian Antislavery,* 3.

29. Going, *David Wilmot,* 34 (1st quotation), 116 (2nd quotation), 174 (3rd quotation); Earle, *Jacksonian Antislavery,* 134; Harrold, *Gamaliel Bailey,* 29–30; Sewell, *Ballots for Freedom,* 52; Foner, *Free Soil, Free Labor, Free Men,* 60; Stewart, *Holy Warriors,* 119–20. As historian Jonathan H. Earle points out, the Barnburners did not condone "slavery in the South" or wish "for African Americans' perpetual enslavement." They vaguely believed that preventing slavery expansion would lead to its termination. See Earle, *Jacksonian Antislavery,* 133, 136.

30. Garrison to Henry C. Wright, March 1, 1847, in Garrison, *Letters,* 3:473 (quotation); *Emancipator,* June 16, October 13, 1847.

31. Whittier to Elizur Wright Jr., October 19, 1845, in Pickard, *Whittier as a Politician,* 37–39; Whittier to Elizabeth Smith, November [?] 1845, in Pickard, *Life and Letters of John Greenleaf Whittier,* 1:310 (1st–2nd quotations); Friedman, *Gregarious Saints,* 242–43; Goodheart, *Abolitionist, Actuary,* 132–33; Whittier to Joshua Leavitt, January 24, 1846; Whittier to Henry I. Bowditch, January 26, 1846; Whittier to John G. Palfrey, September 21, 1846, in Whittier, *Letters,* 2:9–12 (2nd–4th quotations), 36–37 (5th quotation). Whittier specifically sought cooperation regarding the anti-annexation petition drive. The Anti-Texas Committee had issued the call before it disbanded on December 30, 1845. Salmon P. Chase had similar ideas concerning antislavery union. See Chase to Preston King, July 15, [1847], in Chase, "Diary and Correspondence," 120–22. That summer Whittier worked with Giddings in Maine "to carry . . . [that state] for freedom." See Whittier to Bowditch, July 31, 1846, in Whittier, *Letters,* 2:28.

32. Sewell, *John P. Hale,* 31–34, 43–47; Parkman to Hale, December 12, 1843, Hale Papers; Earle, *Jacksonian Antislavery,* 80, 84–85, 101; Pillsbury to Hale, January 10, 1844, Hale-Chandler Papers. Parkman had been a vice president of the MASS.

33. "Letter of the Hon. John P. Hale of N.H. to His Constituents on the Annexation of Texas," *Liberator,* January 24, 1845 (1st quotation); Sewell, *John P. Hale,* 57–59, 62–65 (2nd quotation); *Liberator,* January 24, 1845 (3rd–4th quotations); Wilson, *History of the Rise and Fall of the Slave Power,* 1:625; Whittier to Hale, January 24, 1845, in Pickard, *Life and Letters of John Greenleaf Whittier,* 1:306–7; Whittier to Elizur Wright Jr., October 19, 1845, in Pickard, *Whittier as a Politician,* 38–39 (5th–6th quotations). New Hampshire Garrisonian Stephen S. Foster had disrupted the Democratic convention that dropped Hale's candidacy.

34. Whittier to Elizur Wright Jr., October 19, 1845, in Pickard, *Whittier as a Politician,* 38–39; Whittier to "Dear Cousin," September 7, [1846], Cartland Papers. The coalition aimed to elect Joseph Cilley, a Whiggish Liberty candidate, to a short Senate term and Hale to a full one. See Sewell, *John P. Hale,* 82, and Mordell, *Quaker Militant,* 146–47. On the other candidates, see Sewell, *Ballots for Freedom,* 128–29. Whittier hoped the New Hampshire victory would push northern Democrats toward "the side of Liberty." See Whittier to "Independent Democrats of New Hampshire," March 18, 1846, in Whittier, *Letters,* 2:13–14. In June 1848 Hale presented a resolution calling for abolition in the District of Columbia. See Sewell, *John P. Hale,* 118–19.

35. Sewell, *Ballots for Freedom,* 129 (1st quotation); Whittier to Hale, September 16, 1846; Whittier to *Essex Transcript,* September 17, 1846, in Whittier, *Letters,* 2:33–36 (3rd quotation); Hale to Bowditch, October 9, 1846, in Bowditch, *Life and Correspondence of Henry Ingersoll Bowditch,* 1:185 (2nd quotation). Whittier made a similar plea to Conscience Whig John G. Palfrey. See Whittier to Palfrey, September 21, 1846, in Whittier, *Letters,* 2:36–37.

36. Whittier to Fessenden, July 26, [1847]; Whittier to Hale, July 30, November 2, 8, 1847, in Whittier, *Letters,* 2:93–97; Whittier to Hale, August 11, 1847, in Pickard, *Life and Letters of John Greenleaf Whittier,* 1:323–24; Stanton to Hale, July 6, 1847, Hale Papers; Sewell, *Ballots for Freedom,* 134; Sewell, *John P. Hale,* 91–92, 258n; *Emancipator,* September 1, 15, 1847; Harrold, *Gamaliel Bailey,* 115–23; Earle, *Jacksonian Antislavery,* 101. In September 1846 Whittier invited Charles Sumner and George S. Hilliard to a "mass meeting" at New Market, New Hampshire, that had been called by "united parties." Whittier suggested that the two Massachusetts Whigs meet with Hale there in regard to a trip to Boston. The result was that Hale lectured at Faneuil Hall at the invitation of Conscience Whigs. See Whittier to Sumner, September 8, [1846]; Whittier to Hale, September 16, 1846, in Whittier, *Letters,* 2:34, and Sewell, *John P. Hale,* 86.

37. Sewell, *Ballots for Freedom,* 136–37.

38. Whittier to Hale, [November] 2, 1847, in Whittier, *Letters,* 2:95; Sewell, *Ballots for Freedom,* 133–34. Hale reluctantly accepted the Liberty nomination on January 1, 1848, by which time he had entered the U.S. Senate. See Sewell, *Ballots for Freedom,* 138.

39. Wendell Phillips to Elizabeth Pease, August 29, 1847, in Garrison and Garrison, *William Lloyd Garrison,* 3:212–13 (1st–2nd quotations); *Liberator,* December 17, 1847 (3rd–4th quotations); Smith to Stephen C. Phillips, October 23, 1846, in Smith, "Gerrit Smith Broadside and Pamphlet Collection"; "Call for a National Nominating

Convention," in William Goodell to James G. Birney, April 1, 1847, in Birney, *Letters,*
2:1047; Fladeland, *James Gillespie Birney,* 262–63; Brooks, *Liberty Power,* 135–36; Goodell, *Address of the Macedon Convention,* 13. In contrast to Quincy, Garrison believed
Hale performed "softly, cautiously, almost weakly" in the Senate. See Garrison to Sidney
Howard Gay, April 7, 1848, in Garrison, *Letters,* 3:553. The RPAs had nominated Smith
in June 1847.

40. *Albany Weekly Patriot,* December 25, 1845 (1st–3rd quotations); *Constitution,* quoted in *Liberty Herald,* January 23, 1846 (4th quotation). See also *New York
Herald,* quoted in *Liberator,* January 17, 1845.

41. *Albany Weekly Patriot,* January 8, February 12, 1845; J.L., editorial correspondence, January 2, 1845, in *Liberty Herald,* January 23, 1845; *Emancipator,* August 19,
1846; *Cincinnati Weekly Herald and Philanthropist,* August 26, 1846; Smith, *Liberty and
Free Soil Parties,* 89; Hamlin to Salmon P. Chase, February 19, 1850, Chase Papers,
Microfilm Edition; Hamlin to Joshua Leavitt, February 12, 1847 (quotation); Leavitt to
Hamlin, February 24, 1847, in *Emancipator,* March 10, 1847. Assuming that such a con-
vention would also endorse immediate emancipation, John Whittier supported Hamlin.
See Whittier to Joseph Sturge, August 28, 1846, in Whittier, *Letters,* 2:31.

42. *Albany Weekly Patriot,* December 18, 1844 (quotation); Whittier to Elizur Wright Jr.,
December 15, 1845, in Pickard, *Whittier as a Politician,* 39–41; Tappan to Salmon P. Chase,
March 9, 1846, Chase Papers, Historical Society of Pennsylvania; Tappan to Bigelow, Jan-
uary 7, 1848; Tappan to Charles B. Boyton, October 11, 1847, letterbook, Tappan Papers;
Tappan to Joshua Leavitt, February 28, 1847, in *Emancipator,* March 10, 1847.

43. Tappan to Gerrit Smith, August 24, 1846, Smith Papers; Harrold, *Gamaliel Bailey,* 84; *Emancipator,* November 4, 1846 (1st quotation); Whittier to John P. Hale, December 18, 1846, in Pickard, *Life and Letters of John Greenleaf Whittier,* 1:317–18 (2nd
quotation). Phelps died in September 1847.

44. U.S. Congress, *Congressional Globe,* 30th Cong., 1st sess. (April 25, 1848), 666
(quotation); Whittier to John Quincy Adams, December 19, 1846, in Whittier, *Letters,*
2:46; Harrold, *Gamaliel Bailey,* 127–28, 132–34.

45. Lewis Tappan to Amos A. Phelps, February 27, 1847, letterbook, Tappan Papers;
Mordell, *Quaker Militant,* 149–50; Harrold, *Gamaliel Bailey,* 127–28.

46. Harrold, *Gamaliel Bailey,* 84–85, 127, 133; Whittier to Bailey, [December 7,
1847]; Whittier to Charles Sumner, February 23, 1848; Whittier to Tappan, July 14,
1849, in Whittier, *Letters,* 2:97, 99, 140–41; Wyatt-Brown, *Lewis Tappan,* 329; Salmon
P. Chase to Sarah Belle Dunlop Ludlow Chase, June 4, 1850, in Chase, *Papers,* 2:297–
98. Whittier met with John Quincy Adams in Washington shortly before Adams died.
Bertram Wyatt-Brown regards "Free Soilers and abolitionists [as] more united than ever
before" in this period.

47. Sewell, *Ballots for Freedom,* 133–34, 148–50 (quotation); Niven, *Salmon P. Chase,*
100–101; Chase to John P. Hale, May 12, 1847, in Chase, *Papers,* 2:151–54. The Barnburner was Jacob Bigelow.

48. McKee, *National Conventions and Platforms,* 66–69 (quotations); Blue, *Free*

Soilers, 118–19; Schor, *Henry Highland Garnet,* 97; Dyer, *Phonographic Report,* 21, 24; Blue, *Salmon P. Chase,* 64; Earle, *Jacksonian Antislavery,* 167; Yacovone, *Samuel Joseph May,* 137.

49. Dyer, *Phonographic Report,* 60–61 (1st quotation); Leavitt to Salmon P. Chase, August 21, 1848, in Chase, *Papers,* 2:181 (2nd quotation); Goodheart, *Abolitionist, Actuary,* 134–37; Whittier to Henry I. Bowditch, July 31, 1848, in Whittier, *Letters,* 2:112 (3rd–5th quotations). In June Whittier had encouraged Conscience Whigs to merge into what he called "the great party of Christian Democracy." He hoped John P. Hale would be its presidential candidate and (with considerable exaggeration) called Hale "a thorough hearty abolitionist." See Whittier to Charles Sumner, June 20, 1848, in Whittier, *Letters,* 2:103–4, and Whittier to Sumner, June 28, 1848, in Albree, *Whittier Correspondence,* 97–99.

50. Mayer, *All on Fire,* 383–84, 427–28; *Liberator,* August 11 (1st quotation), 18, 1848 (2nd–4th quotations). The MASS later published this and Quincy's similar editorial of August 18, 1848, in its *Annual Reports and Proceedings,* 17th report, 18–31. "Men whose purity of purpose and personal honor are above suspicion," Quincy claimed, led the Free Soil Party. See *Liberator,* August 11, 1848.

51. Yacovone, *Samuel Joseph May,* 132–33 (1st–2nd quotations); Mayer, *All on Fire,* 382–84; *North Star,* August 18 (3rd quotation), September 1, 1848. Donald Yacovone contends that calls for Giddings and the presence of black delegates misled May regarding the character of the gathering.

52. Sewell, *Ballots for Freedom,* 163–64; Harrold, *Rise of Aggressive Abolitionism,* 95, 124, 134; Gerrit Smith to John W. Norton, January 9, 1849, letterbook, Smith Papers (1st quotation); Smith to editor of the *Rams Horn,* October 2, 1848, in *Pennsylvania Freeman,* October 26, 1848 (2nd–3rd quotations); Wright to James Haughton, August 31, 1848, in *Liberator,* October 13, 1848.

53. Sewell, *Ballots for Freedom,* 163–64; Harrold, *Rise of Aggressive Abolitionism,* 95, 124, 134; Smith to John W. Norton, January 9, 1849, letterbook, Smith Papers (1st quotation); Smith to Editor of the *Rams Horn,* October 2, 1848, in *Pennsylvania Freeman,* October 26, 1848 (2nd–3rd quotations); Goodell, *Slavery and Anti-Slavery,* 484 (4th–5th quotations). Historian William M. Wiecek follows Goodell in describing the Free Soil Party as "antislavery at its most ambivalent." The Wilmot Proviso, Wiecek points out, "furnished common ground on which Liberty moderates could join hands with nonabolitionists from the regular parties." See Wiecek, *Sources of Antislavery Constitutionalism,* 221–22.

54. Samuel Ringgold Ward, "Address to the Four Thousand Colored Voters of the State of New York," in *North Star,* September 1, 1848 (1st–2nd quotations); *Report of the Proceedings of the Colored National Convention* (3rd–5th quotations); Arthur Tappan et al. to "Friends of Liberty," July 1, 1848, in *National Era,* July 6, 1848 (6th quotation); Lewis Tappan to Salmon P. Chase, June 14, 1848, in Chase, *Papers,* 2:169; Lewis Tappan to John G. Whittier, August 22, 1848, in Albree, *Whittier Correspondence,* 108–10 (7th quotation); Wyatt-Brown, *Lewis Tappan,* 280–18; Sewell, *Ballots for Freedom,* 163–64;

Blue, *Free Soilers,* 107. Lewis Tappan complained bitterly when Hale withdrew. See Sewell, *John P. Hale,* 103–4.

55. Blue, *Free Soilers,* 137–39, 144–51.

56. Whittier to Tappan, July 14, 1849, in Whittier, *Letters,* 2:140–41.

57. Stewart, *Joshua R. Giddings,* 157 (1st quotation); Douglass to "Dear Readers," November 11, 1848, in *North Star,* November 17, 1848 (2nd quotation).

58. Garrison to Sumner, July 27, 1849, in Garrison, *Letters,* 3:642–43; Palfrey to Samuel May Jr., July 27, 1849 (1st quotation); Sumner to Garrison, August 1, 1849, in *Liberator,* August 10, 1848; Sewell, *John P. Hale,* 105, 108, 119; Stanton, *Random Recollections,* 127–28; Douglass to Chase, May 30, 1850, in Chase, *Papers,* 2:296–97; Douglass to Seward, [July] 31, 1850, April 23, 1853 (3rd–5th quotations), Seward Papers; Sumner to Whittier, December 6, 1848, in Albree, *Whittier Correspondence,* 111 (2nd quotation). Whittier continued to advise Sumner concerning Massachusetts politics. See Sumner to Whittier, December 3, 1850; Whittier to Sumner, October 7, 1851, Sumner, *Selected Letters,* 1:315–16, 339.

6. Physical Action, Fugitive Slave Laws, and the Free Democratic Party, 1845–1852

1. Gara, *Liberty Line,* 156–60; Potter, *Impending Crisis,* 478; McPherson, *Ordeal by Fire,* 121; Barney, *Secession Impulse,* 178; Davis, *Slave Power Conspiracy,* 38–39; Virginia, "Decisions of the General Court," 236–37; Berlin, *Many Thousands Gone,* 67; Bordewich, *Bound for Canaan,* 111–12, 123–24.

2. Harrold, *Border War,* 21, 23, 30–31; Isaac Hopper to Elisha Tyson, July 10, 1811; Tyson to R. Ridgeway, July 25, 1811; Tyson to William Masters, December 12, 1811, April 9, August 20, November 11, 1812, PAS Papers; Fehrenbacher, *Slaveholding Republic,* 209; Finkelman, *Slavery and the Founders,* 85; Palmer and McRae, *Calendar of Virginia State Papers,* 5:320, 396–98, 402–3; Leslie, "Study of the Origins of Interstate Rendition," 67–73; Mifflin to Pennsylvania Assembly, August 24, 1791, in Reed, *Pennsylvania Archives,* 179–81.

3. Finkelman, *Slavery and the Founders,* 98–99; Fehrenbacher, *Slaveholding Republic,* 212–15. In 1822 Congressman Thomas L. Moore of Fauquier County, Virginia, declared the law "inadequate to the object it proposed to effect," thereby forcing Virginia to strengthen its defensive measures. See U.S. Congress, *Annals,* 17th Cong., 1st sess. (March 27, 1822), col. 1380.

4. *Niles Register,* February 25, 1826, 419; *Maryland Gazette and State Register,* January 12, 1826 (quotation); *National Gazette and Literary Register,* February 4, 10, 1826; Leslie, "Pennsylvania Fugitive Slave Act of 1826," 438–40, 443–45; Harrold, *Border War,* 75–77; Wiecek, *Sources of Antislavery Constitutionalism,* 99; Morris, *Free Men All,* 84–88, 221. One member of the Maryland delegation described the law as "worse for the Slave holders than no Law at all." Thomas Shipley to Isaac Barton, February 15, 1826, PAS

Papers. In 1847 the Pennsylvania legislature passed an act that prevented state officials from aiding in renditions.

5. Morris, *Free Men All,* 71–129; *Liberator,* April 21, 1836 (1st quotation); Whittier to Abijah Wyman Thayer, March 31, 1837, in Whittier, *Letters,* 1:229 (2nd quotation). According to Whittier, other abolitionist lobbyists included Gardner B. Perry of Bradford, Dr. Amos Farnsworth of Groton, and historian George Bancroft of Springfield.

6. Morris, *Free Men All,* 79–80, 82–84; Harrold, *Border War,* 78–79; Van Deusen, *William Henry Seward,* 65–67.

7. Mayer, *All on Fire,* 316–20 (1st quotation); Duberman, *Charles Francis Adams,* 80–85; Stewart, *Wendell Phillips,* 140–41 (2nd quotation); Commager, *Theodore Parker,* 217–18.

8. Hagedorn, *Beyond the River,* 27–57, 87–89, 144–65, 186–87; Coffin, *Reminiscences,* 106–16; Birney, *James G. Birney,* 166; *Maysville Eagle,* November 21, 1838.

9. James Clark, "Annual Message," in *Maysville Eagle,* December 5, 1838 (1st quotation); *Cincinnati Daily Gazette,* October 6, 11, 24, 1838; *Pennsylvania Freeman,* October 11, 1838; *Maysville Eagle,* November 14, 1838; *Ohio Statesman,* quoted in *Pennsylvania Freeman,* October 11, 1838; Harrold, *Border War,* 82–93 (2nd quotation); "Speech of Mr. Wade, on the Bill Relating to Fugitives from Labor," *Philanthropist,* April 30, 1839. Clark also recommended a death penalty for those convicted of helping slaves escape. Kentucky journalists and politicians had pressured the legislature to act. See *Ohio State Journal,* October 26, 1838; *Maysville Eagle,* November 14, 1838; *Maysville Monitor,* quoted in *Philanthropist,* January 1, 1839; and James Byers to "Citizens of Mason and Bracken Counties," February 1, 1839, in *Maysville Eagle,* February 13, 1839. Kentucky, Wade claimed in his speech, threatened civil war, which if it came would result in immediate emancipation. Wade said he was not unreservedly committed to the Union.

10. Harrold, *Abolitionists and the South,* 68; Thompson, *Prison Life and Reflections;* Alvan Stewart to *Friend of Man,* n.d., in *Pennsylvania Freeman,* December 15, 1851; *St. Louis Republican,* quoted in *Liberator,* August 27, 1841; Harrold, "Nonfiction Madison Washington," 8–20.

11. Wise, *Life of Henry A. Wise,* 50 (1st quotation); *Louisville Public Advertiser,* February 29, 1840 (2nd quotation); *Globe,* quoted in *Pennsylvania Freeman,* September 3, 1840; Stewart, *Joshua R. Giddings,* 70–74; Downey, Creole *Affair.*

12. Harrold, *Subversives,* 33, 52–53; *Pennsylvania Freeman,* February 28, 1839 (quotation). Arrested in the district and convicted in Virginia, Grimes served two years at Richmond State Prison before moving to Boston. Since the 1790s, free African Americans and white abolitionists in and about Washington had supported freedom suits, some of which succeeded. See Harrold, *Subversives,* 24–25, 52.

13. Harrold, *Subversives,* 83–86; Torrey, *Martyrdom of Abolitionist Charles Torrey,* 125–26; *Tocsin of Liberty,* October 27, 1844; Torrey to Gerrit Smith, November 16, 1844, Smith Papers. The most complete account of Torrey's arrest, trial, imprisonment, and death is Torrey, *Martyrdom of Abolitionist Charles Torrey,* 104–66. Two other aggressive abolitionist actions in 1844 fortified proslavery perceptions. That July a northern

abolitionist helped seven slaves attempt to escape from Pensacola, Florida Territory. That September a Kentucky posse arrested two northern abolitionists after they had helped future black leader Lewis Hayden, his wife, and child escape to Ohio. See "Trial and Imprisonment of Jonathan Walker," *Liberator,* August 29, 1845; Jonathan Walker to Horace Mann, February 5, 1849, Mann Papers; Fairbank, *Rev. Calvin Fairbank,* 1–57; Coffin, *Reminiscences,* 719–21; and Coleman, "Delia Webster and Calvin Fairbank," 130–32.

14. Harrold, *Border War,* 130, 137, 139, 143; Giddings, *Speeches in Congress,* 116–17 (1st quotation); *Liberator,* February 14, 1845 (2nd quotation). Giddings served as defense attorney for John Bush, the black man from whose home Torrey and Smallwood planned to depart with the escapees. See Joshua R. Giddings to C. P. Giddings, December 24, 1843, Giddings Papers, and Lovejoy, *Memoir of Rev. Charles T. Torrey,* 105. John Dawson of Louisiana vowed to shoot Giddings.

15. Wyatt-Brown, *Southern Honor,* 407, 414–16, 452–53; Harrold, *Border War,* 38–39, 129–31 (quotation).

16. Harrold, *Border War,* 132; Chaplin to Joseph C. Jackson, January 3, 1845, in *Albany Weekly Patriot,* January 8, 1845 (quotation).

17. Harrold, *Subversives,* 97–116, 121.

18. U.S. Congress, *Congressional Globe,* 30th Cong., 1st sess. (April 18, 1848), 641; (April 20, 1848), 654 (quotations); Harrold, *Border War,* 132–33.

19. U.S. Congress, *Congressional Globe,* 30th Cong., 1st sess. (April 18, 1848), 641, 653 (quotations), appendix 501–3, 505, 508; *Daily Union,* April 21, 1848; Harrold, *Subversives,* 142–43. See also Sewell, *John P. Hale,* 114–18, and Pacheco, *Pearl,* 167–69.

20. U.S. Congress, *Congressional Globe,* 30th Cong., 1st sess. (April 20, 1848), appendix 506 (2nd quotation); (April 25, 1848), 670–73 (1st quotation).

21. Chase to John P. Hale, April 29, 1848, Hale Papers (1st–2nd quotations); Wade to Giddings, April 25, 1848 (3rd quotation); Sumner to Giddings, May 6, 1848 (4th quotation), Giddings Papers.

22. *Liberator,* May 5, 12, 1848; *Pennsylvania Freeman,* May 18, 24, June 1, 1848; *Albany Weekly Patriot,* April 26, June 14, 1848; Douglass, *Frederick Douglass Papers. Series One,* 2:119–20; *North Star,* May 5, 1848 (quotation). Hale's abolitionist pastor, John Parkman, complimented Hale for "the admirable way" he conducted himself in the Senate. See Parkman to Hale, July 10, 1848, Hale Papers. At first sounding like an immediatist, Charles Sumner announced to Joshua R. Giddings his hope that Hale would move "forward" with "some *aggressive* measures on Slavery." Then Sumner calmed down, suggesting only a bill "for the Abolition of the *Slave-trade* in the District." See Sumner to Giddings, May 6, 1848, Giddings Papers.

23. Potter, *Impending Crisis,* 1–89; Sewell, *Ballots for Freedom,* 131–69; Blue, *Free Soilers,* 137–43; [Kentucky], "Resolutions of the Legislature of Kentucky"; John C. Calhoun, "Address of Southern Delegates," in Calhoun, *Papers,* 26:230–32, 232 (quotation). The issue of slavery and the slave trade in the District of Columbia remained a point of sectional contention in Congress, as abolitionists sent petitions for emancipation and northern congressmen presented them.

24. John C. Calhoun, "Address of Southern Delegates in Congress," January 22, 1849, in Calhoun, *Papers,* 26:232 (1st quotation); Virginia, General Assembly, House of Delegates, *Report of the Select Committee,* 19 (2nd quotation); U.S. Congress, *Congressional Globe,* 31st Cong., 1st sess. (January 3–28, 1850), 99, 103, 171, 220, 233–37; "An Act to Amend . . . the Act Entitled 'An Act Respecting Fugitives from Justice, and Persons Escaping from the Service of Their Masters,'" in United States, *Statutes at Large,* 9:462–65.

25. U.S. Congress, *Congressional Globe,* 31st Cong., 1st sess. (January 29, 1850), 244–47.

26. Harrold, *Border War,* 143; *Baltimore Sun,* August 22 (quotation), 26, 27, 28, 1850.

27. Harrold, *Subversives,* 146–47; Harrold, *Rise of Aggressive Abolitionism,* 123–35, 189–96 (quotation). The young women's freedom had been purchased.

28. *Liberator,* August 30, 1850; *Baltimore Sun,* August 26, 1850 (1st quotation); *Republic,* quoted in *Louisville Observer and Reporter,* September 9, 1850 (2nd quotation). The *Daily Missouri Republican* predicted on October 19–20, 1850, that the new, stronger fugitive slave law would ease renditions.

29. Hamilton, *Prologue to Conflict,* 133–65.

30. May to *North Star,* October 2, 1850, in *Liberator,* October 25, 1850. On confrontations over enforcement of the Fugitive Slave Law of 1850, see Mayfield, *Rehearsal for Republicanism,* 175–76, and Harrold, *Border War,* 147–49. Campbell, *Slave Catchers,* 148–69, underestimates the number of confrontations.

31. *Liberator,* October 18 (quotation), 25, 1850; Harlow, *Gerrit Smith,* 295–96; Messerli, *Horace Mann,* 531–32. At the Faneuil Hall meeting abolitionist women had to sit in the galleries.

32. Commager, *Theodore Parker,* 219–21; Collins, *Shadrach Minkins;* Shapiro, *Richard Henry Dana Jr.,* 61–63; Sumner to Parker, April 19, 1851, in Pierce, *Memoir and Letters of Charles Sumner,* 3:246 (quotations); Stewart, *Wendell Phillips,* 152–54; Tuttleton, *Thomas Wentworth Higginson,* 32–36. A federal judge indicted Hayden and Free Soiler bystander Elizur Wright. See Goodheart, *Abolitionist, Actuary,* 135–36.

33. "Seventh Annual Meeting of the Western New York Anti-Slavery Society," January 16–19, 1851, in *North Star,* January 23, 1851 (quotation); Campbell, *Slave Catchers,* 154–57; Yacovone, *Samuel Joseph May,* 143–49. Frederick Douglass, Abby Kelly Foster, Stephen S. Foster, Hiram Wilson, and Samuel Joseph May had prominent roles at the meeting. Estimates of the number involved vary.

34. Van Deusen, *William Henry Seward,* 149; Yacovone, *Samuel Joseph May,* 149; Chase to R. R. Raymond, September 27, 1852 (1st–2nd quotations); Lewis to May, September 29, 1852 (3rd–5th quotations); Adams to May, September 30, 1852 (6th–9th quotations), in *Liberator,* October 15, 1852; Giddings to James Fuller, September 22, 1853, in *Liberator,* October 10, 1853 (10th quotation). William Lloyd Garrison advised May that Hale was even less likely than the others to attend the meeting or take a clear stand on resistance to the Fugitive Slave Law. See Garrison to May, September 17, 1852,

in Garrison, *Letters,* 4:219. As it turned out, May's meeting brought together RPAs and Garrisonians rather than either group and politicians. The resolutions emphasized RPA contentions that slavery could not be legalized anywhere and that the Fugitive Slave Law must be treated "as no law." See "Jerry Rescue Celebration," *Liberator,* October 8, 1852. Abolitionists and antislavery politicians came together in court. Richard Henry Dana, Samuel Sewell, Robert Rantoul, and Ellis Gray Loring served on Lewis Hayden's defense team. Antislavery Whig Thaddeus Stevens defended two Quaker abolitionists, Caster Hanway and Elijah Lewis, who had been charged in connection with the violent death of a Maryland master at Christiana, Pennsylvania, in September 1851 as he attempted to recapture a slave. Roscoe Conkiling served as a defense attorney for the Jerry Rescuers. See Morris, *Free Men All,* 151–52; Trefousse, *Thaddeus Stevens,* 84–85; and Harlow, *Gerrit Smith,* 300.

35. Harrold, *Gamaliel Bailey,* 138; Mayer, *All on Fire,* 397–98; Dillon, *Abolitionists,* 212–13; Stewart, *Holy Warriors,* 151–52; Mayfield, *Rehearsal for Republicanism,* 167–72, 175; Blue, *Free Soilers,* 152–87.

36. Blue, *Salmon P. Chase,* 70–73; Blue, *Free Soilers,* 202–3; Mayfield, *Rehearsal for Republicanism,* 173–74; Goodell, *Slavery and Anti-Slavery,* 485 (quotation). Former abolitionist Henry B. Stanton also joined the Democratic Party. As John Mayfield notes, "by the spring of 1851 there was very little left of the Free Soil party in New York."

37. Blue, *Free Soilers,* 207–31.

38. Whittier to Charles Sumner, September 14, 1851; Whittier to Gamaliel Bailey, December 8, [1852], in Whittier, *Letters,* 2:181, 183, 202; *Anti-Slavery Bugle,* September 20, 1851 (1st quotation); Tappan to F. Julius LeMoyne, December 26, 1849, Woodson Collection (2nd quotation); *Frederick Douglass' Paper,* April 5, 1852 (3rd–4th quotations). Albert A. Guthrie of Ohio, a former Liberty abolitionist and Free Soiler, suggested that rather than standing for "the non-extension of slavery," the party should have made a "bold push for the *abolition* of slavery." But when Guthrie wrote "abolition," he meant "denationalization." See Goodell, *Slavery and Anti-Slavery,* 482–85.

39. Massachusetts Anti-Slavery Society, *Annual Reports and Proceedings,* 18th report, 35–37.

40. Ibid., 37 (quotation); Blue, *Free Soilers,* 134–37, 155, 166–68, 184, 217–23. Although Seward was a Whig, he was elected in March 1849 because Barnburners had defected from the Democratic Party to the Free Soil Party. Wade was elected in December 1851 by a Free Soil–Whig coalition in the Ohio legislature.

41. Sumner to John G. Whittier, January 5, [1848], in Albree, *Whittier Correspondence,* 96; William Lloyd Garrison to Sumner, July 27, 1849, in Garrison, *Letters,* 3:642–43; Whittier to Sumner, January 16, March 28, 1851; Whittier to Grace Greenwood, May 18, 1851, in Whittier, *Letters,* 2:171–72, 174–75, 177; Mordell, *Quaker Militant,* 161–64; Donald, *Charles Sumner and the Coming of the Civil War,* 187, 191–204; Parker to Sumner, April 26, July 11, 1851, in Weiss, *Life and Correspondence of Theodore Parker,* 2:111–13 (1st–3rd quotations); Whittier to Sumner, [December 1851], in Pickard, *Life and Letters of John Greenleaf Whittier,* 1:363–64 (4th quotation). Free Soil politician

Henry Wilson had more influence than abolitionists in persuading the state legislature to elect Sumner to the Senate on April 24, 1851.

42. Phillips to Sumner, March 15, April 27, 1852 (quotations), Sumner Papers; Stewart, *Wendell Phillips,* 163–64; *Liberator,* March 19, April 23, June 18, August 13, 1852. Phillips had congratulated Sumner on his conduct in Washington before turning to criticism. See Bartlett, *Wendell Phillips,* 61–63.

43. Donald, *Charles Sumner and the Coming of the Civil War,* 223–26; Sumner to John Greenleaf Whittier, August 13, 1852, in Pickard, *Life and Letters of John Greenleaf Whittier,* 1:365; Sumner to Parker, August 11, 1852, in Sumner, *Selected Letters,* 1:368–69; Parker to Sumner, August 4, 1852, Sumner Papers (1st quotation); Sumner to Parker, "Saturday evening," in Weiss, *Life and Correspondence of Theodore Parker,* 2:215 (2nd–3rd quotations); Sumner, *Freedom National.* In March, Sumner and William Seward presented anti–Fugitive Slave Law petitions, which the Senate discussed briefly then tabled. See Sewell, *Ballots for Freedom,* 299. When on July 27 Sumner moved "immediate repeal," the Senate, by a 32–10 vote, kept him from speaking on the issue. See Donald, *Charles Sumner and the Coming of the Civil War,* 224–25. Parker advised Sumner that the delay had "already excited some considerable distrust & suspicion" among abolitionists and Free Soilers. Pioneered by Theodore Weld, Thomas Morris, and Salmon P. Chase, the freedom national argument had become common among the more antislavery Free Soilers. See Foner, *Free Soil, Free Labor, Free Men,* 74, 80–83, and Oakes, *Freedom National,* 16–19, 21–23.

44. Parker to Sumner, September 6, 1852, in Weiss, *Life and Correspondence of Theodore Parker,* 2:215 (1st–3rd quotations); Child to Frances Shaw, September 5, 1852, in Child, *Lydia Maria Child,* 265 (4th quotation); *Frederick Douglass' Paper,* October 1, 1852 (5th quotation); Phillips to Sumner, September 3, [1852], Sumner Papers (6th–10th quotations); Massachusetts Anti-Slavery Society, *Annual Reports and Proceedings,* 21st report, 9–14 (11th quotation). In January 1853, the MASS praised the speech's power. See Massachusetts Anti-Slavery Society, *Annual Reports and Proceedings,* 21st report, 8–9. The MASS also praised speeches by Massachusetts Democrat Robert Rantoul and Whiggish Free Democrat Horace Mann. Parker Pillsbury and Stephen S. Foster criticized Sumner and Mann more harshly at the MASS meeting. See Massachusetts Anti-Slavery Society, *Annual Reports and Proceedings,* 21st report, 85–87.

45. Sumner to Phillips, [January 30, 1853], in Sumner, *Selected Letters,* 1:383 (1st quotation); Massachusetts Anti-Slavery Society, *Annual Reports and Proceedings,* 21st report, 12 (2nd–4th quotations); Phillips to Sumner, April 27, 1852, Sumner Papers (5th quotation). Sumner recognized that his and Phillips's "system . . . differed," but he believed they were "friends."

46. Harrold, *Rise of Aggressive Abolitionism,* 123–31; Harlow, *Gerrit Smith,* 295–97; Mayfield, *Rehearsal for Republicanism,* 171–72; Harrold, *Gamaliel Bailey,* 146–51; Blue, *Free Soilers,* 234; Stewart, *Joshua R. Giddings,* 176–79. By August 1851, Giddings had come to share the goal of uniting "the entire antislavery force" in the Free Democratic Party. See Giddings to Tappan, August 27, 1851, Giddings-Julian Papers. Smith

had invited abolitionists of all types to attend the Cazenovia meeting of August 1850. He also hosted the AASS annual meeting at Syracuse in May 1851. Giddings agreed with RPAs in regarding an independent antislavery party as a vehicle for shaping popular opinion rather than directly setting government policy.

47. Mayfield, *Rehearsal for Republicanism,* 172; Harrold, *Gamaliel Bailey,* 147–50; Stewart, *Joshua R. Giddings,* 203–5; "Convention of the Friends of Freedom," *National Era,* October 9, 1851 (quotations); Wyatt-Brown, *Lewis Tappan,* 331. On LeMoyne presiding, see Marshall, "Free Democratic Convention," 149.

48. Harrold, *Gamaliel Bailey,* 149 (1st quotation); Charles Francis Adams, diary, December 6, 1851, Adams Papers (2nd quotation); *Frederick Douglass' Paper,* April 8, 1852 (3rd quotation).

49. "Democratic Party Platform of 1852," June 1, 1852; "Whig Party Platform of 1852," June 17, 1852, in Peters and Woolley, *American Presidency Project;* Tappan to Joshua R. Giddings, June 17, 1852, Giddings Papers (quotation); Blue, *Free Soilers,* 239–40; Lewis, *Biography of Samuel Lewis,* 395–9; Marshall, "Free Democratic Convention," 149–51; LeMoyne to editor, July 1, 1852, in *National Era,* July 8, 1852.

50. Mayfield, *Rehearsal for Republicanism,* 179–80; Frederick Douglass, "Let All Soil Be Free Soil: An Address Delivered in Pittsburgh, Pennsylvania, on 11 August 1852," in Douglass, *Frederick Douglass Papers. Series One,* 2:389–90 (1st quotation); Marshall, "Free Democratic Convention," 154–59 (2nd–5th quotations); McKee, *National Conventions and Platforms,* 80–84. Tappan offered a substitute similar to Smith's that pronounced slavery to be "invalid, illegal, not law." See Marshall, "Free Democratic Convention," 157.

51. "Free Democratic National Convention," *National Era,* August 19, 1852 (1st quotation); Smith et al. to Hale, September 2, 1852, in *National Anti-Slavery Standard,* September 23, 1852 (2nd quotation); Smith to Julian, September 2, 1852, Giddings-Julian Papers. Lewis Tappan did not join the National Liberty Party but provided little support for Hale and Julian. See Wyatt-Brown, *Lewis Tappan,* 331–32.

52. *Frederick Douglass' Paper,* September 10, 1852; Frederick Douglass, "Northern Ballots and the Election of 1852: An Address Delivered in Ithaca, New York, on 14 October 1852," in Douglass, *Frederick Douglass Papers. Series One,* 2:414–15 (quotations).

53. Massachusetts Anti-Slavery Society, *Annual Reports and Proceedings,* 21st report, 25–26 (1st quotation); "Annual Meeting of the Pennsylvania Anti-Slavery Society," October 25–27, 1852, in *Liberator,* November 12, 1852 (2nd quotation). The MASS defined denationalization as "separating the General Government from slavery, and leaving it and the matter of rendition of Slaves to the States in their Sovereign capacity."

54. Marshall, "Free Democratic Convention," 166; Blue, *Free Soilers,* 263.

55. Stewart, *Joshua R. Giddings,* 215–16; Yacovone, *Samuel Joseph May,* 159; Harlow, *Gerrit Smith,* 313–14; Frederick Douglass to Smith, October 21, [1851], in Douglass, *Frederick Douglass Papers. Series Three,* 1:550–55.

56. Tappan to editor of the *Reporter,* November 20, 1852, in Abel and Kingberg, *Side-Light on Anglo-American Relations,* 303 (1st–3rd quotations); *Liberator,* November 12,

1852 (4th–5th quotations); Reynolds, *Mightier Than the Sword*, 128–30. Gamaliel Bailey's *National Era* published *Uncle Tom's Cabin* as a serial in 1851. The novel appeared as a book in 1852.

57. Massachusetts Anti-Slavery Society, *Annual Reports and Proceedings*, 21st report, 25–26.

7. Abolitionists and Republicans, 1852–1860

1. Stewart, *Holy Warriors*, 151–53; Dillon, *Abolitionists*, 189–90, 213; Massachusetts Anti-Slavery Society, *Annual Reports and Proceedings*, 21st report, 87 (1st–2nd quotations); Massachusetts Anti-Slavery Society, *Proceedings of the . . . Annual Meetings; Anti-Slavery Bugle*, May 4, 1861; William Lloyd Garrison to Oliver Johnson, July 3, 1861, December 14, 1862, in Garrison, *Letters*, 5:29, 129; Clifford, *Crusader for Freedom*, 229–30 (3rd quotation).

2. Theodore Parker to "Old Lady," June 17, 1852, in Frothingham, *Theodore Parker*, 309–10; "Speech of Theodore Parker," July 5, 1852, in *Liberator*, July 30, 1852; J.T., "What Next?" *Frederick Douglass' Paper*, November 12, 1852; Friedman, *Gregarious Saints*, 220–22; Harrold, *Abolitionists and the South*, 119–20; Massachusetts Anti-Slavery Society, *Annual Reports and Proceedings*, 21st report, 96 (1st quotation); Whittier to McKim, November 30, 1853, in Whittier, *Letters*, 2:241–42 (2nd–3rd quotations).

3. Holt, *Rise and Fall of the American Whig Party*, 726–64, 953, 959.

4. "Speech of Theodore Parker," July 5, 1852, in *Liberator*, July 30, 1852 (1st–2nd quotations); J.T., "What Next?" *Frederick Douglass' Paper*, November 12, 1852 (3rd quotation); Phillips to Elizabeth Pease, November 21, 1852, Antislavery Collection/Garrison Papers (4th–5th quotations); *Liberator*, July 30, 1852; *Frederick Douglass' Paper*, November 5, 1852. That December Gamaliel Bailey, writing as a Free Democrat, agreed implicitly with J.T. The Free Democrats, Bailey suggested, had to keep their organization as a rallying point for antislavery Democrats and Whigs, who to defeat slavery had to leave their parties. See *National Era*, December 2, 9, 16, 1852. Phillips "rejoice[d] beyond measure with the election of Gerrit Smith to Congress." Phillips declared, "His presence will be itself an advancement."

5. Douglass to Seward, April 23, 1853, Seward Papers (1st–3rd quotations); Whittier to Sumner, November 15, 1853, in Whittier, *Letters*, 2:238–39 (4th–5th quotations).

6. Trefousse, *Radical Republicans*, 15; Commager, *Theodore Parker*, 200–201; Garrison and Garrison, *William Lloyd Garrison*, 3:380–81 (quotations). Shared interests beyond the slavery issue drew abolitionists and antislavery politicians together during the early 1850s. In 1853 Horace Greeley and Joshua R. Giddings joined Garrisonians to promote a world temperance convention that would include women. Theodore Parker and Horace Mann discussed literature. Garrison and Giddings had similar religious views, and when Garrison traveled west in October 1853 to attend abolitionist events in Michigan and Ohio, he lodged at Giddings's home during his return journey. See also Garrison, *Letters*,

4:249–50n; Parker to Mann, October 19, 1853, in Weiss, *Life and Correspondence of Theodore Parker,* 2:222–23; and Garrison and Garrison, *William Lloyd Garrison,* 3:395.

7. Massachusetts Anti-Slavery Society, *Annual Reports and Proceedings,* 21st report, 86–87 (quotations), 96–98.

8. Phillips, *Speeches, Lectures,* 98 (1st quotation); Massachusetts Anti-Slavery Society, *Annual Reports and Proceedings,* 21st report, 108–10 (2nd–4th quotations), 114, 124–27 (5th–7th quotations). Phillips noted that Giddings and Sumner, in contrast to how they spoke in Congress, spoke more like abolitionists on the Western Reserve and in Boston. But, Phillips added, when they did so, "their associates on the platform are sure they are wrecking the [Free Democratic] party."

9. Sumner to Phillips, January 30, 1853, in Sumner, *Selected Letters,* 1:383–84 (1st–2nd quotations); Pilgrim Society, *An Account of the Pilgrim Celebration at Plymouth,* 85 (3rd–5th quotations); Seward to Parker, September 14, 1853, in Seward, *Seward at Washington,* 2:208 (6th–8th quotations); Mann to William Lloyd Garrison, February 21, 1853, in *Liberator,* March 4, 1853; Messerli, *Horace Mann,* 539–44 (9th–10th quotations).

10. Sumner to Cornelius C. Fenton, April 9, 1850; Sumner to Parker, March 28, 1853, in Sumner, *Selected Letters,* 1:290 (1st quotation), 386–87 (2nd–4th quotations); Van Deusen, *William Henry Seward,* 149.

11. Nevins, *Ordeal of the Union,* 2:82–100; Potter, *Impending Crisis,* 146–62; Etcheson, *Bleeding Kansas,* 14–21.

12. U.S. Congress, *Congressional Globe,* 33rd Cong., 1st sess. (January 30, 1854), 281–82. In separate speeches, Giddings, Smith, and Wade advocated black rights.

13. Chase to Parker, March 12, April 5, 1854; Parker to Chase, March 16, 1854, in Weiss, *Life and Correspondence of Theodore Parker,* 2:517 (1st–5th quotations), 226 (6th–8th quotations); Sumner to Parker, March 9, 1854; Parker to Sumner, March 3, 1854, in Sumner, *Selected Letters,* 1:405, 405n (9th quotation). On February 14 at New York City's Broadway Tabernacle, William Lloyd Garrison dealt summarily with the Nebraska bill while discussing slavery in the South, black rights, and disunion. See Garrison, *No Compromise with Slaveholders.* The *Liberator* publicized the Massachusetts legislature's protest against the bill. See *Liberator,* February 24, 1854. On Parker's sermon, see Parker, *Nebraska Question.*

14. Glickstein, "Chattelization of Northern Whites," 48 (1st–3rd quotations); Bancroft, *Life of William H. Seward,* 381 (4th quotation); Parker to Seward, May 19, 1854, in Weiss, *Life and Correspondence of Theodore Parker,* 2:206 (5th–6th quotations); Van Deusen, *William Henry Seward,* 151–52 (7th quotation), 154–55 (8th quotation); Nevins, *Ordeal of the Union,* 2:78. Beyond abolitionists, John Quincy Adams in 1832 had questioned whether a nation divided between "freemen" and "masters and slaves" could long exist. See Adams, *Memoirs,* 8:510.

15. Griffiths to Douglass, February 18, 25, 1854, in *Frederick Douglass' Paper,* February 24 (1st–5th quotations), March 17, 1854; Douglas, "A Cherished Friendship"; Douglass to Sumner, February 27, 1854, in Linden, *Voices from the Gathering Storm,* 103 (6th

quotation); Sewell, *Ballots for Freedom,* 254–65; Gienapp, *Origins of the Republican Party,* 69–91; Potter, *Impending Crisis,* 154–67; Etcheson, *Bleeding Kansas,* 1–38. Griffiths also met with another abolitionist visitor to the city, Sarah Grimké. See Griffiths to Douglass, February 22, 1854, in *Frederick Douglass' Paper,* March 3, 1854.

16. Parker to Seward, May 19, 1854, in Weiss, *Life and Correspondence of Theodore Parker,* 2:207 (quotation); Seward, *Seward at Washington,* 1:231–32; Gienapp, *Origins of the Republican Party,* 103–237; *Ohio State Journal,* March 23, 24, 1854; Newton, *Lincoln and Herndon,* 61–62, 71.

17. Campbell, *Slave Catchers,* 124–28; Stewart, *Wendell Phillips,* 168–72; Frothingham, *Theodore Parker,* 422–29; Pierce, *Memoir and Letters of Charles Sumner,* 3:364–65, 374–75; Sumner to Parker, June 12, 1854, in Pierce, *Memoir and Letters of Charles Sumner,* 3:376–77.

18. Jones, *Speech of Hon. James C. Jones of Tenn.,* 4 (1st quotation); Pierce, *Memoir and Letters of Charles Sumner,* 3:380–86 (2nd quotation); Donald, *Charles Sumner and the Coming of the Civil War,* 262–66. According to David Herbert Donald, the proslavery senators blamed the events in Boston on Sumner's speech against the Nebraska bill. See Donald, *Charles Sumner,* 261–62.

19. Pierce, *Memoir and Letters of Charles Sumner,* 3:378–88; Garrison to Sumner, June 27, 1854, in Garrison, *Letters,* 4:301 (1st quotation); McDaniel, *Problem of Democracy,* 204–5; Filler, *Crusade against Slavery,* 215–16 (2nd–3rd quotations). See also Whittier to Sumner, July 3, 1854, in Whittier, *Letters,* 2:265–66 (4th quotation).

20. Child to Sumner, February 12, 1855, in Pierce, *Memoir and Letters of Charles Sumner,* 3:414 (1st–2nd quotations); Abbott, *Cobbler in Congress,* 75; Wright to Giddings, February 4, 1857, Giddings Papers (3rd–4th quotations). See also Gamble, "Joshua Giddings," 52–54, and Stewart *Joshua R. Giddings,* 256–59. Abolitionist-Republican relations have confused historians. Historian Eric Foner asserts that Garrisonians "wasted little enthusiasm on Republicans." But he also observes that "considerable debate occurred" among abolitionists concerning what should be their "attitude toward Republicanism." See Foner, *Free Soil, Free Labor, Free Men,* 302–3. Historian James Brewer Stewart notes that, despite "abolitionist vehemence toward the Republican party," they were *not* "hostile" to it. See Stewart, *Joshua R. Giddings,* 265n34. In 1857 Child wrote of Sumner, "I never received such an impression of holiness from a mortal man." See Lydia Maria Child to David Lee Child, January 7, 1857, in Child, *Letters of Lydia Maria Child,* 88. No politician during the mid- to late 1850s responded more positively to abolitionist contacts than Giddings. By 1858 these contacts and Giddings's moralistic exhortations for action against the Slave Power had alienated many Republicans throughout the North *and* many of his constituents. When Giddings failed to gain renomination to Congress that year, he intensified his efforts to keep the Republican Party from becoming more conservative. See Stewart, *Joshua R. Giddings,* 255–61.

21. "Twenty-Third Annual Report," in Massachusetts Anti-Slavery Society, *Proceedings of the . . . Annual Meetings,* 38 (1st–2nd quotations); "Celebration at Abingdon, August First," *Liberator,* August 10, 1855 (3rd–7th quotations); Garrison to J. Miller

McKim, October 14, 1856, in Garrison, *Letters,* 4:410 (8th–9th quotations). The previous January Phillips had allowed that, as an alternative to disunionism, Republicans could adopt the RPAs' "view of the Constitution." See Massachusetts Anti-Slavery Society, *Proceedings of the . . . Annual Meetings,* 38. Garrison's letter to McKim appeared in the *National Anti-Slavery Standard,* October 25, 1856.

22. May to Seward, October 17, 1855 (1st–4th quotations); Seward to May, November 9, 1855 (5th quotation), Seward Papers.

23. Sumner to Smith, March 18, 1856, in Pierce, *Memoir and Letters of Charles Sumner,* 3:433 (1st quotation); Trefousse, *Radical Republicans,* 16; Lewis Tappan to Sumner, September 29, 1855; Smith to Sumner, March 2, 1856, Sumner Papers; Chase to Smith, February 15, 1856; Smith to Chase, April 20, 1856, Chase Papers, Microfilm Edition (2nd–4th quotations). Smith asked Sumner, "How long, my dear friend, shall we delay having an Abolition party?" The previous fall Smith had declined an invitation from Sumner to speak in Boston. See Sumner to Smith, October 16, 1855, in Sumner, *Selected Letters,* 1:431–32.

24. Chase to Smith, December 15, 1854; Chase to Edward L. Pierce, April 14, 1856, in Chase, *Papers,* 2:390–91 (quotations), 433; Chase to Smith, February 15, 1856; Smith to Chase, April 20, 1856, Chase Papers, Microfilm Edition. Chase also informed Smith that he regretted Smith's resignation from Congress.

25. Parker to Sumner, January 1855, January 14, May 21, 1856; Sumner to Parker, March 26, 1856, in Weiss, *Life and Correspondence of Theodore Parker,* 2:157–58 (quotation), 178–180.

26. Parker to Wilson, February 15, 1855 (1st–2nd quotations); Wilson to Parker, February 28, July 23, 1855 (3rd quotation), in ibid., 2:209–11; Abbott, *Cobbler in Congress,* 88–91 (4th quotation).

27. Parker to Chase, July 25, 1856 (1st quotation); Chase to Parker, June 23, July 17, 1856, March 25, 1858, in Weiss, *Life and Correspondence of Theodore Parker,* 2:227–28, 518–20 (2nd–6th quotations); Niven, *Salmon P. Chase,* 169–75. Parker himself demonstrated blatant racial prejudice. See Parker to Chase, August 30, 1858, in Weiss, *Life and Correspondence of Theodore Parker,* 2:230–31, and Fredrickson, *Black Image in the White Mind,* 119–21. Parker also maintained a correspondence with John P. Hale in 1856. He lectured Hale about Republican "timidity" and dealt with practical matters. See Parker to Hale, October 21, December 19, 1856; Hale to Parker, December 23, 1856, in Weiss, *Life and Correspondence of Theodore Parker,* 2:187 (quotation), 223–24.

28. Massachusetts Anti-Slavery Society, *Proceedings of the . . . Annual Meetings,* 61–62. Historian Richard H. Sewell oversimplifies when he writes that Garrison began "a drift toward political reinvolvement" during the 1856 national election campaign. As this book points out, Garrison had always been politically involved. Some of his associates had been more so. See Sewell, *Ballots for Freedom,* 288.

29. *Liberator,* March 7, 1856 (1st–2nd quotations); Tappan to John G. Fee, February 29, 1856 (3rd quotation); Tappan to Daniel R. Goodloe, H. L. Brown, and Lewis Clephane, March 6, 1856, letterbook, Tappan Papers.

30. [Greeley], *Proceedings of the First Three Republican National Conventions,* 15–82.

31. *Liberator,* July 7, 1856. In September Garrison added that the Republican Party did not oppose the U.S. Constitution's three-fifths clause or the North's constitutional obligation to help put down slave revolts. See *Liberator,* September 5, 1856.

32. *Liberator,* September 5, 1856 (1st–3rd quotations); Garrison to J. Miller McKim, October 14, 1856, in Garrison, *Letters,* 4:405–10 (4th–5th quotations). Garrison continued to argue that abolitionists should not vote. Historian Richard H. Sewell summarizes the abolitionist political outlook in 1856. He writes, "Many [abolitionists] shared a growing appreciation of [the Republican Party's] accomplishments and principles and a conviction that whatever their shortcomings, the Republicans were infinitely preferable to the 'pro-slavery,' negrophobic Democrats." See Sewell, *Ballots for Freedom,* 336.

33. Yacovone, *Samuel Joseph May,* 161–65 (1st quotation); Sewell, *Ballots for Freedom,* 287; Clifford, *Crusader for Freedom,* 229–31 (2nd quotation); Child to Sumner, July 7, 1857; Child to Sarah Shaw, September 14, 1856, in Child, *Lydia Maria Child,* 285 (3rd quotation), 293 (2nd quotation). May only temporarily rejected disunion. He attended a disunion convention held in Cleveland in 1857.

34. *New York Herald,* May 29 (2nd quotation), May 30, 1856 (1st quotation); Spooner to George Bradburn, May 25, 1856, Spooner Papers (3rd–4th quotations). The words in the first two quotations may be the newspaper's correspondent, rather than Smith's.

35. Smith to Goodell, August 15, 1856, in *National Anti-Slavery Standard,* September 6, 1856 (1st–2nd quotations); Douglass to Smith, August 31, 1856 (3rd quotation), September 6, 1856, Smith Papers; *Frederick Douglass' Paper,* August 15, 1856 (4th–5th quotations); Tappan to L. A. Camerovzow, December 10, 1856, letterbook, Tappan Papers (6th–7th quotations). Not all RPAs became more supportive of the Republican Party as the campaign progressed. Kentucky abolitionist John G. Fee remained very critical of the Republican Party throughout 1856. See Fee to Cassius M. Clay, May 10, 1856, Fee-Clay Correspondence, and Fee to Simeon S. Jocelyn, August 18, 1856; Fee to Smith, October 10, 1856, American Missionary Association Archives. Tappan denied he had voted for any presidential candidate. The RPA tendency toward advocating violence kept him from voting for Smith. The Republican devotion to what Tappan called "white man's" interests kept him from voting for Frémont. Rather than influence the Republican Party directly, Tappan believed the RPA mission would be "to elevate the principles of citizens in the free States."

36. Parker to Sumner, January 14, May 21, 1856; Parker to Mann, June 27, 1856; Parker to Hale, October 21, December 19, 1856, in Weiss, *Life and Correspondence of Theodore Parker,* 2:159–60, 179–80, 182, 188 (1st–2nd quotations), 223; Commager, *Theodore Parker,* 261 (3rd–4th quotations); Parker to Hunt, November 16, 1856; Parker to "Mrs. Apthorp," December 29, 1856, in Frothingham, *Theodore Parker,* 439–40. In October 1855 Parker mentioned Frémont to Nathaniel P. Banks. See Parker to Banks, October 23, 1855, in Weiss, *Life and Correspondence of Theodore Parker,* 2:206. Parker advised Mann that the fall 1856 election would be "the beginning of the end!"

In September he wrote, "The wrath of God [would be] too hot to allow a permanent Union." See Parker to Hunt, September 4, 1856, in Frothingham, *Theodore Parker,* 436–37. After the 1856 presidential election, Sumner reported to Whittier that he saw the "beginning of the end of our great struggle. The North seems to have assumed an attitude which it cannot abandon." See Sumner to Whittier, December 28, 1856, in Albree, *Whittier Correspondence,* 128. Cassius M. Clay influenced Sumner by inviting him to Kentucky in May 1855. William Jay and his son John Jay corresponded with Sumner. See Pierce, *Memoir and Letters of Charles Sumner,* 3:417–19; Donald, *Charles Sumner and the Coming of the Civil War,* 272; Sumner to William Jay, October 7, [1855?]; Sumner to John Jay, October 18, [1855], in Pierce, *Memoir and Letters of Charles Sumner,* 3:420; and Trefousse, *Radical Republicans,* 106.

37. Whittier to Sumner, March 29, 1855; June 13, November 12, 1856; January 11, 1858; Whittier to unknown, June 20, 1856; Whittier to Henry B. Stanton, January 10, 1858, in Whittier, *Letters,* 2:275–76, 297–99 (1st quotation), 317–20, 354–55; Whittier to Sumner, November 12, 1856, in Albree, *Whittier Correspondence,* 280–81 (2nd–5th quotations); Sewell, *Ballots for Freedom,* 336. Whittier's mother's death in late 1857 and his devotion to writing for the *Atlantic Monthly* limited his antislavery activities.

38. Sewell, *Ballots for Freedom,* 321–36; Foner, *Free Soil, Free Labor, Free Men,* 250–60; Harrold, *Gamaliel Bailey,* 205–7.

39. Giddings to Higginson, January 7, 1857; Walker to [Higginson], January 10, 1857; Wilson to Higginson, January 10, 1857, in *Liberator,* January 23, 1857 (1st, 3rd–8th quotations); Garrison and Garrison, *William Lloyd Garrison,* 3:451 (2nd quotation). According to Glyndon G. Van Deusen, Seward wrote a letter to Higginson denouncing the convention, but fearing that it would hurt him among antislavery voters, did not send the letter. See Van Deusen, *William Henry Seward,* 188, and Friedman, *Gregarious Saints,* 244–77.

40. Sewell, *Ballots for Freedom,* 339–40; Stewart, *Wendell Phillips,* 197–98; Robertson, *Parker Pillsbury,* 119–20; Mayer, *All on Fire,* 491; *Liberator,* July 10, 1857; Phillips to Abigail Kelley Foster, June 30, 1859, Foster Papers; Child to Sarah Shaw, July 7, 1857; Child to Maria W. Chapman, July 26, [1857?], in Child, *Lydia Maria Child,* 310–11 (quotation).

41. Parker, *Present Aspect of Slavery,* 41–42, 44 (quotations). Parker called the Republican Party "cowardly," "a little deceitful," and the "best party we have." Parker based his call for direct U.S. government action against slavery in the southern states on the principles of the Declaration of Independence and the U.S. Constitution's clause guaranteeing each state a republican form of government.

42. *Liberator,* February 19, 1858; Parker to Thayer, February 26, April 5, 1858, Thayer Papers; Parker to Charles Sumner, March 28, May 6, 1858; Parker to Salmon P. Chase, March 29, 1858; Parker to John P. Hale, May 12 1858, in Weiss, *Life and Correspondence of Theodore Parker,* 2:220–21, 225, 229–30 (quotations), 240–43.

43. "Annual Meeting of the Massachusetts Anti-Slavery Society," January 27, 1859, in *Liberator,* February 4, 1859 (quotations). These exchanges caused resentment between

Pillsbury, Foster, and Higginson on one side and Garrison on the other. See Garrison to Pillsbury, June 3, 1859, Garrison, *Letters,* 4:627–30.

44. *Liberator,* August 19, 1859.

45. Oates, *To Purge This Land with Blood,* 360; Reynolds, *John Brown,* 97–101, 362–63, 413; Filler, *Crusade against Slavery,* 273; Nevins, *Ordeal of the Union,* 3:11; Boyer, *Legend of John Brown,* 87–88; Harrold, *Abolitionists and the South,* 64–83; Harrold, *Rise of Aggressive Abolitionism,* 138–39, 142–45.

46. Harrold, *Rise of Aggressive Abolitionism,* 142–44. William Lloyd Garrison also rhetorically addressed slaves.

47. Oates, *To Purge This Land with Blood,* 224, 233, 241–42; Quarles, *Allies for Freedom,* 73–80; Rossbach, *Ambivalent Conspirators,* 205–14; *Liberator,* October 28, 1859 (quotation). In May 1857 Garrisonians Henry C. Wright and Wendell Phillips advocated providing arms for slave revolt. See Stewart, *Holy Warriors,* 169. On July 12, 1858, Parker hoped for slave revolt. See Frothingham, *Theodore Parker,* 475.

48. *Liberator,* October 28, November 4 (1st quotation), December 16, 1859 (3rd quotation); Garrison to Oliver Johnson, November 1, 1859, in Garrison, *Letters,* 4:660–61 (2nd quotation).

49. Niven, *Salmon P. Chase,* 192, 211; Stewart, *Holy Warriors,* 175; Sewell, *Ballots for Freedom,* 355–57; Chase to H. H. Barrett, October 29, 1859, in Chase, *Papers,* 3:22–23 (1st–5th quotations); Andrew, *Speeches of John A. Andrew,* 8 (6th–7th quotations). Giddings and John P. Hale publicly denied involvement in the raid. See Trefousse, *Radical Republicans,* 130.

50. Sewell, *Ballots for Freedom,* 355–57, 358–59 (3rd–5th quotations); Salmon P. Chase to H. H. Barrett, October 29, 1855, in Chase, *Papers,* 3:22–23 (1st quotation); Abraham Lincoln, "Address at Cooper Institute, New York City," February 27, 1860, in Lincoln, *Collected Works,* 3:538 (2nd quotation), 549–50, 358.

51. Sewell, *Ballots for Freedom,* 335, 354–55 (quotation); Trefousse, *Radical Republicans,* 129–30.

52. Reynolds, *John Brown,* 419–24; Schwartz, *Slave Laws in Virginia,* 134–35, 137–40, 143–45 (quotations); Harrold, *Border War,* 121–22, 137, 185–87; *Daily Delta* (New Orleans), February 1, 1860, *New Orleans Bee,* February 9, March 5, 1860, *Charleston Mercury,* October 11, 1860, all in Dumond, ed., *Southern Editorials on Secession,* 21–24, 30–32, 48–55, 178–79.

53. Donald, *Charles Sumner and the Coming of the Civil War,* 348–51; Trefousse, *Radical Republicans,* 131; Reynolds, *John Brown,* 424–26; Sewell, *Ballots for Freedom,* 355; *Richmond Enquirer,* January 6, 1860 (quotations); Garrison, *New Reign of Terror.*

8. Political Success and Failure

1. Sewell, *Ballots for Freedom,* 339–40, 358–62; Reynolds, *John Brown,* 425–29; Mayer, *All on Fire,* 509; *Liberator,* January 26, February 3, 1860; *Anti-Slavery Bugle,*

March 3, 1860; John G. Fee to S. S. Jocelyn, January 18, 1860, American Missionary Association Archives; *National Anti-Slavery Standard,* March 3 (quotation), June 2, 1860.

2. Republican Party, *Proceedings of the Republican National Convention Held at Chicago,* 33–88; Giddings to Smith, May 24, 1860, Smith Papers; Smith to Giddings, June 2, 1860, Giddings Papers; *Liberator,* July 20, 1860; Mayer, *All on Fire,* 507–9. On the similarities of the two platforms regarding slavery, see Foner, *Free Soil, Free Labor, Free Men,* 132–33.

3. McPherson, *Struggle for Equality,* 14; Johnson, "American Missionary Association," 218–19; *Douglass Monthly,* June 1860, 276 (1st quotation); August 1860, 306 (2nd quotation); Douglass, *Frederick Douglass: Selected Speeches and Writings,* 493; Smith to Joshua R. Giddings, June 2, 1860, Giddings Papers (3rd quotation). Tilton served as assistant editor, and by 1863 editor, of the influential *New York Independent.* Both Douglass and Smith charged that Lincoln favored white supremacy. See McPherson, *Struggle for Equality,* 24–25, 87–88.

4. Stewart, *Wendell Phillips,* 210; Robertson, *Parker Pillsbury,* 119–23 (1st–3rd quotations); Mayer, *All on Fire,* 525; *National Anti-Slavery Standard,* October 13, 1860 (4th quotation); Douglas, speech at Framingham, Massachusetts, July 4, 1860, in McPherson, *Negro's Civil War,* 5–7 (5th quotation); Garrison and Garrison, *William Lloyd Garrison,* 3:503 (6th quotation); *Liberator,* June 22, 1860 (7th quotation). In November 1861 Foster proposed an abolitionist political party to oppose the Republican Party. See Stewart, *Wendell Phillips,* 226. The *National Anti-Slavery Standard,* June 2, 1860, urged abolitionists not to support any candidate who claimed the U.S. Constitution recognized slavery.

5. Sewell, *Ballots for Freedom,* 341–42; Johnson to J. Miller McKim, October 11, 1860, May Anti-Slavery Collection (1st quotation); Whittier to Chase, October 30, 1860, in Whittier, *Letters,* 2:474 (2nd quotation); McPherson, *Struggle for Equality,* 19–23; Quarles, *Lincoln and the Negro,* 56 (3rd–5th quotations).

6. Whittier to Salmon P. Chase, November 9, 1860, Chase Papers, Microfilm Edition (1st quotation); *Douglass Monthly,* December 1860, 360 (3rd quotation), 370–71 (2nd quotation); Phillips, *Speeches, Lectures,* 294–318. Abolitionists may be characterized as a "loyal opposition" to Lincoln and the Republican Party. See Stewart, *Wendell Phillips,* 226–27.

7. Mayer, *All on Fire,* 35–36, 515–16; *Liberator,* February 15, 1861; McPherson, *Struggle for Equality,* 29–38, 52, 62–66; Smith to Chase, December 18, 1860, Smith Papers (1st–2nd quotations); McKivigan, *War against Proslavery Religion,* 188–89; Howard, *Religion and the Radical Republican Movement,* 18–19 (3rd quotation); Wendell Phillips, "Under the Flag," [April 21, 1861], in Phillips, *Speeches, Lectures,* 407–14; William Lloyd Garrison to Henry T. Cheever, September 9, 1861; Garrison to Charles Sumner, December 20, 1861; Garrison to George W. Julian, April 13, 1862, in Garrison, *Letters,* 5:35–36, 53, 90–91. Lincoln, for example, endorsed a constitutional amendment to protect slavery in the southern states. On Garrison and disunionism in early 1861, see McDaniel, *Problem of Democracy,* 212–14. Throughout the war RPAs held that the Constitution, without amendment, prohibited slavery. See *Principia,* April 21, 1864.

8. Sumner to Lewis Tappan, June 25, 1860, American Missionary Association Archives; Schouler, *History of the United States of America under the Constitution,* 6:19; McPherson, *Struggle for Equality,* 3 (1st quotation); Trefousse, *Radical Republicans,* 204 (2nd quotation), 339; *Liberator,* July 12, 1861 (3rd quotation); Garrison to Cheever, September 9, 1861; Garrison to Sumner, December 20, 1861, in Garrison, *Letters,* 35–36 (4th quotation), 53. For years many historians have confused abolitionists and Radical Republicans. For examples, see Sewell, *Ballots for Freedom,* 362, 365, and Burlingame, *Abraham Lincoln,* 2:424.

9. *Principia,* December 7, 1861; *Liberator,* December 20, 27, 1861. See also Gerrit Smith to Lincoln, August 31, 1861, in *Liberator,* September 13, 1861, and John G. Fee to Lincoln, October 3, 1861, Lincoln Papers. Shortly after the Cooper Union meeting, Garrison approved Johnson's plan to send copies of the *National Anti-Slavery Standard* to U.S. senators and representatives. See Garrison to Johnson, December 6, 1861, in Garrison, *Letters,* 5:46–47.

10. Mayer, *All on Fire,* 532; Stearns, *Life and Public Service of George Luther Stearns,* 263, 268–69; *Commonwealth,* September 6, 1862; January 24, 1863; McPherson, *Struggle for Equality,* 123; Child to Sarah Shaw, November 11, 1862, in Melzer and Holland, *Lydia Maria Child,* 420 (quotation; emphasis added); William Lloyd Garrison to Helen E. Garrison, May 14, 1863, in Garrison, *Letters,* 5:152–53; Howard, *Religion and the Radical Republican Movement,* 57–58; Gallman, *America's Joan of Arc,* 24–30, 36.

11. Cleveland to Lincoln, January 5, 1861, Lincoln Papers; Burlingame, *Abraham Lincoln,* 2:92; Smiley, *Lion of White Hall,* 173–75; McPherson, *Struggle for Equality,* 68–69; C. R. Vaughan to George Whipple, January 25, 1862, American Missionary Association Archives (quotation).

12. McPherson, *Struggle for Equality,* 40–45; Mayer, *All on Fire,* 514–15; Stewart, *Wendell Phillips,* 213–15; McFeely, *Frederick Douglass,* 208–11; William Lloyd Garrison to Oliver Johnson, January 19, April 19, 1861, in Garrison, *Letters,* 5:5–6, 16–18; James W. White to Charles Sumner, February 19, 1863, Sumner Papers; Donald, *Charles Sumner and the Rights of Man,* 2:104–5; Blair, *Speech of the Hon. Montgomery Blair,* 3–7. As late as October 1861 Garrison recommended postponing the PAS convention to avoid violence. See Garrison to J. Miller McKim, October 13, 1861, in Garrison, *Letters,* 5:39–40.

13. McPherson, *Struggle for Equality,* 81–82, 85–86, 128; Garrison to James Gibbons, April 28, 1861, in Garrison, *Letters,* 5:19–20; *Principia,* December 21, 1861 (1st quotation); Stewart, *Wendell Phillips,* 228, 238–39 (2nd quotation); Mayer, *All on Fire,* 532. James McPherson calls the evidence for abolitionist popularity "overwhelming."

14. Stewart, *Wendell Phillips,* 228, 239; Stewart, *Holy Warriors,* 187–89; William Lloyd Garrison to Oliver Johnson, May 9, July 3, 1861; William Lloyd Garrison to Helen E. Garrison, May 14, 1863, in Garrison, *Letters,* 5:21–22, 29, 152–53 (quotation); McPherson, *Struggle for Equality,* 86–88, 91–92; *Anti-Slavery Bugle,* May 4, 1861; Robertson, *Parker Pillsbury,* 119–20, 123–25; Mayer, *All on Fire,* 560–61.

15. Aptheker, *Abolitionism,* 143; McPherson, *Struggle for Equality,* 55–57, 70–71, 90–91, 133; Joshua R. Giddings to Gerrit Smith, June 17, December 20, 1861, in Stewart,

Joshua R. Giddings, 275; *Principia,* May 4, 1861 (quotations); Stewart, *Holy Warriors,* 184–89.

16. Burlingame, *Abraham Lincoln,* 2:55–60, 200–205; Whittier to George L. Stearns, September 19, 1861, in Pickard, *Life and Letters of John Greenleaf Whittier,* 2:467 (1st quotation); Child to Whittier, January 21, 1862, Child Papers (2nd quotation); Garrison to Oliver Johnson, December 8, 1861, in Garrison, *Letters,* 5:47 (3rd quotation); *Douglass Monthly,* January 1862, 577 (4th quotation); *Liberator,* August 8, 1862 (5th quotation). Child described Secretary of State William H. Seward as "utterly selfish and unprincipled."

17. McPherson, *Struggle for Equality,* 95n; Smith to J. A. Gurley, December 16, 1861, in *Liberator,* January 3, 1862; Child to Julian, April 8, 1865, in Child, *Letters of Lydia Maria Child,* 187–88; Cheever to Ashley, December 23, 1862, Cheever Family Papers; Garrison, *Letters,* 5:xix–xxiv; Child, *Lydia Maria Child,* 283, 340, 353, 387, 411, 416, 479, 493; Conway to Sumner, September 17, December 12, 1861, Sumner Papers; 35 letters from Sumner in Smith Papers; Whittier, *Letters,* 3:6–7, 13–17, 30–31, 73, 98; Holmes, "Whittier and Sumner," 58–72.

18. Conlin, "Smithsonian Abolition Lecture Controversy," 301–10, 313–14, 317; Croffut, *American Procession,* 56–81; *Principia,* January 30 (quotations), April 10, 1862; Howard, *Religion and the Radical Republican Movement,* 23–24; D'Entremont, *Southern Emancipator,* 161–62. Elderly former Massachusetts Liberty and Free Soil Party activist John Pierpont led in creating the Washington Lecture Association. See also Conway, *Golden Hour,* 11–13.

19. *Principia,* April 10, 1862 (quotations); Conway, *Autobiography,* 1:306–8; Stewart, *Wendell Phillips,* 236; McPherson, *Struggle for Equality,* 85–86. That April Smithsonian Institution secretary Joseph Henry blocked invitations to Frederick Douglass and William Lloyd Garrison to join the lecture series. See Conlin, "Smithsonian Abolition Lecture Controversy," 320, and Garrison to George W. Julian, April 13, 1862, in Garrison, *Letters,* 90–91.

20. Smith to Richard Webb, March 15, 1862, Antislavery Collection/Garrison Papers (quotation); Douglass to Stearns, August 12, 1863, in Simpson, *Civil War,* 3:457–60; McFeely, *Frederick Douglass,* 228–30.

21. *Liberator,* September 27, 1861 (1st–2nd quotations); March 14, 1862; *National Anti-Slavery Standard,* October 5, 1861; Garrison to Charles Sumner, December 20, 1861, in Garrison, *Letters,* 5:53; *Principia,* December 28, 1861 (3rd quotation). Other abolitionist petitions did not mention compensation. Victor B. Howard notes Cheever's ineffective plan to hold a convention in Washington and his testimonials to state legislatures. Garrison claimed that "multitudes of petitions from all the free States, signed by tens of thousands of estimable citizens . . . asking for the immediate abolition of slavery under the war power" had reached Congress. See Howard, *Religion and the Radical Republican Movement,* 24–25, and *Liberator,* March 14, 1862.

22. Howard, *Religion and the Radical Republican Movement,* 24–26 (1st quotation), 27–28; Garrison and Garrison, *William Lloyd Garrison,* 4:48–49; *New York Tribune,*

June 21, 1862; Burlingame, *Abraham Lincoln,* 2:347–50; Howe to F. W. Bird, March 5, 1862, in Howe, *Letters and Journals,* 2:500–501; *Liberator,* March 14, 1862; Child to Horace Greeley, March 9, 1862, in Child, *Lydia Maria Child,* 407; Burlingame, *Abraham Lincoln,* 2:344–45 (2nd–4th quotations), 354; McPherson, *Struggle for Equality,* 106–12.

23. McPherson, *Struggle for Equality,* 109–12; Phillips to Sumner, June 7, 29, 1862, Sumner Papers (quotation); Harrold, "Dramatic Turning Point or *Points?"* 11–12; Burlingame, *Abraham Lincoln,* 2:407–10. James M. McPherson emphasizes the effectiveness of these abolitionist tactics during the summer of 1862.

24. McPherson, *Struggle for Equality,* 119–20; Howard, *Religion and the Radical Republican Movement,* 36–37, 47, 49, 52–56; Child to Mrs. S. B. Shaw, 1863, in Child, *Letters of Lydia Maria Child,* 171 (quotations). Cheever, Goodell, and James Freeman Clark criticized the Preliminary Emancipation Proclamation as insufficient. Victor B. Howard notes that there were rumors after the message that Lincoln would withdraw the proclamation. Child charged that Lincoln acted "reluctantly and stintedly."

25. Conway, *Autobiography,* 1:377–81 (quotations); *Liberator,* January 30, 1863; *National Anti-Slavery Standard,* February 28, 1863; Sumner to John Murray Forbes, December 28, 1862, in Sumner, *Selected Letters,* 2:135–36; Garrison to Andrew, April 6, 1863, in Garrison, *Letters,* 5:141–42.

26. Garrison to Samuel Joseph May, April 6, 1863; Garrison to Gerrit Smith, October 31, 1863; Garrison to Henry Wilson, February 2, 1864, in Garrison, *Letters,* 5:142–43 (1st quotation), 170–71 (2nd–3rd quotations), 191; Wright to Lincoln, December 16, 1863, Lincoln Papers (4th quotation); McPherson, *Struggle for Equality,* 125–26.

27. McPherson, *Struggle for Equality,* 125–26; Mayer, *All on Fire,* 257–58 (quotation); Donald, *Charles Sumner and the Rights of Man,* 147–50.

28. McPherson, *Struggle for Equality,* 262; Stewart, *Wendell Phillips,* 234–35, 246–49, 251; B. Rush Plumbly to Chase, April 21, 1862, Chase Papers, Microfilm Edition; *Liberator,* September 5, 12, 1862; March 25, 1864 (quotation); Burlingame, *Abraham Lincoln,* 2:609–13, 637–38; Howard, *Religion and the Radical Republican Movement,* 70; Mayer, *All on Fire,* 562; Blue, *Salmon P. Chase,* 221–26; *Principia,* March 24, 1864. Phillips recognized the importance of the Emancipation Proclamation, but he accused the Lincoln administration of seeking a "sham peace" that would betray "civil rights." In December 1863 Radicals had formed a Chase-for-president organization, and Chase had formally announced his candidacy in January 1864. James Freeman Clarke, assuming a Republican identity, wrote to Chase in February to dissuade him from running on the grounds that "unless some change takes place, Lincoln is sure to be reelected. . . . We cannot afford to try any experiment." See Clarke to Chase, February 26, 1864, Chase Papers, Microfilm Edition. In contrast Goodell declared, "Henceforth, the *Principia* goes for JOHN C. FREMONT, for president."

29. *Liberator,* February 5, 1865 (quotation); Mayer, *All on Fire,* 562–63; Giraud, *Embattled Maiden,* 6–7, 74–78; Young, "Anna Elizabeth Dickinson," 68–70. State legislatures and city governments also invited Dickinson to address them.

30. *Liberator,* March 18 (1st–3rd quotations), May 20 (4th–5th quotations), 27,

1864; McKivigan, *War against Proslavery Religion,* 193; *Principia,* June 16, 1864 (6th quotation); McPherson, *Struggle for Equality,* 268–69.

31. Wattles to Horace Greeley, February 6, 1864, Greeley Papers; Child to Gerrit Smith, July 23, 1864, in Child, *Lydia Maria Child,* 446 (1st quotation); Stanton to Caroline Healey Dall, ca. April 22, 1864, in Gordon, *Selected Papers of Elizabeth Cady Stanton and Susan B. Anthony,* 1:514–15; Giraud, *Embattled Maiden,* 80–81 (2nd quotation); Burlingame, *Abraham Lincoln,* 2:634–35; Howard, *Religion and the Radical Republican Movement,* 76–77. Michael Burlingame notes that Dickinson's reconstruction of her meeting with Lincoln contrasts that with that of a witness. Elizabeth Cady Stanton wrote to Caroline Healey Dall that William Lloyd Garrison was no "better than an admirer & adulator of Abraham with the foul serpent of slavery coiled up in his bosom." See Burlingame, *Abraham Lincoln,* 2:634–35, and Stanton to Dall, ca. April 22, 1864, in Gordon, *Selected Papers of Elizabeth Cady Stanton and Susan B. Anthony,* 1:514–15.

32. McPherson, *Political History of the United States of America, during the Great Rebellion,* 410–13; McGuire, *Democratic Party of the State of New York,* 391. In a parallel strategy, Phillips sought to influence the Republican national convention (known as the National Union Convention) to be held in Baltimore in June. See Stewart, *Wendell Phillips,* 251–52.

33. *Harper's Weekly,* June 18, 1864, 386; *New York Tribune,* June 1, 1864; McPherson, *Political History of the United States of America, during the Great Rebellion,* 412–14; *Liberator,* June 3, 1864; Frémont to Worthington G. Snethen et al., June 4, 1864, in *Principia,* June 9, 1864; Oliver Johnson to Henry T. Cheever, June 16, 1864, Cheever Family Papers.

34. Johnson to Henry T. Cheever, June 16, 1864, Cheever Family Papers (1st quotation); Garrison and Garrison, *William Lloyd Garrison,* 4:122–24; Stewart, *Wendell Phillips,* 253; Burlingame, *Abraham Lincoln,* 2:643–44, 638; Howard, *Religion and the Radical Republican Movement,* 77–78; Cheek and Cheek, *John Mercer Langston,* 424–25; Pennington to [Robert Hamilton], editor, June 9, 1864, in *Weekly Anglo-African,* June 25, 1864; McPherson, *Struggle for Equality,* 265–66; William Lloyd Garrison to Henry Wilson, February 20, 1864; William Lloyd Garrison to Helen E. Garrison, June 6, 8, 1864, in Garrison, *Letters,* 5:190–93, 204–9 (2nd quotation), 212; Mayer, *All on Fire,* 567; *Liberator,* June 24, 1864; Wendell Phillips to Elizabeth Cady Stanton, August 22, 1864, in Stanton and Blatch, *Stanton as Revealed,* 2:98n. Langston based his support of Lincoln on continued proslavery sentiment within the Democratic Party, his belief that Lincoln's "head and . . . heart were right," and his desire for "vigorous prosecution of the war."

35. William Lloyd Garrison to Helen E. Garrison, June 9, 11, 1864, in Garrison, *Letters,* 5:209–10 (1st quotation), 512 (2nd quotation); *Liberator,* June 24, 1864; Garrison and Garrison, *William Lloyd Garrison,* 4:117; William Lloyd Garrison to Francis W. Newman, [n.d.], in *Liberator,* July 22, 1864.

36. Burlingame, *Abraham Lincoln,* 2:634, 637–38, 686–87; Howard, *Religion and the Radical Republican Movement,* 78–79; *Principia,* June 9, 1864; Garrison to Oliver

Johnson, June 16, 1864, in Garrison, *Letters,* 5:213–14; D'Entremont, *Southern Emancipator,* 209–10; Child to John Greenleaf Whittier, June 19, 1864, in Albree, *Whittier Correspondence,* 147–49; Child to Gerrit Smith, July 23, 1864, in Child, *Letters of Lydia Maria Child,* 445; Child to Whittier, November 1864, in Baer, *Heart Is Like Heaven,* 280; Sanborn to Conway, July 10, 1864, Conway Papers (quotations).

37. McPherson, *Struggle for Equality,* 279–82; Burlingame, *Abraham Lincoln,* 2:665, 974.

38. McPherson, *Struggle for Equality,* 282–85; Phillips to Stanton, September 27, 1864, in Stanton and Blatch, *Stanton as Revealed,* 2:100–101n; Dickinson to "My Dear Friend," September 3, 1864, in *Independent,* September 8, 1864; Frederick Douglass to William Lloyd Garrison, September 17, 1864, in *Liberator,* September 23, 1864; Garrison to Samuel J. May, September 9, 1864, in Garrison, *Letters,* 2:235; Burlingame, *Abraham Lincoln,* 2:691–92; Whittier to Harriet McEwen Kimball, December 20, 1864, in Pickard, *Life and Letters of John Greenleaf Whittier,* 2:486–87 (quoting Jesse Frémont); Nevins, *Frémont,* 579; Stearns to Garrison, September 12, 1864, in *Commonwealth,* September 23, 1864 (quotations); Howard, *Religion and the Radical Republican Movement,* 76–78.

39. Burlingame, *Abraham Lincoln,* 2:728, 986; Mayer, *All on Fire,* 571; Stewart, *Wendell Phillips,* 254; Phillips to Stanton, November 20, 1864, Stanton Papers (quotation); Stanton to Susan B. Anthony, December 29, 1864, in Stanton and Blatch, *Stanton as Revealed,* 2:104; Douglass, *Life and Times,* 439–45. In March 1865 Douglass attended Lincoln's second inauguration.

40. Foner, *Reconstruction,* 35–37; "Proclamation of Amnesty and Reconstruction," December 8, 1863, in Lincoln, *Collected Works,* 7:55.

41. Burlingame, *Abraham Lincoln,* 2:600; Donald, *Charles Sumner and the Rights of Man,* 2:178–79; Phillips to Benjamin F. Butler, December 13, 1862, in Butler, *Private and Official Correspondence,* 3:207 (1st quotation); Howard, *Religion and the Radical Republican Movement,* 69, 74–76, 92; Lincoln to Charles D. Robinson, August 16, 1864 (2nd quotation); Douglass to Lincoln, August 29, 1864 (2nd quotation), Lincoln Papers. Abolitionists influenced Lincoln's decision to favor such an amendment. He in turn influenced the Republican/Union national convention. See Trefousse, *Radical Republicans,* 292.

42. Wyatt-Brown, *Lewis Tappan,* 339; Rose, *Rehearsal for Reconstruction,* 13–14, 36–37, 75–77; Stewart, *Wendell Phillips,* 255–56; McPherson, *Struggle for Equality,* 239–40. J. Miller McKim established Philadelphia's Port Royal Relief Commission.

43. Howe to Frank Bird, September 17, 1862, in Howe, *Letters and Journals,* 2:502; Wilson, *History of the Antislavery Measures,* 328; McPherson, *Struggle for Equality,* 182–83.

44. McPherson, *Struggle for Equality,* 183–89; Stanton et al., *History of Woman Suffrage,* 2:26–30; Griffing to William Lloyd Garrison, August 19, 1864, in *Liberator,* August 26, 1864; Harrold, *Subversives,* 235–36; Donald, *Charles Sumner and the Rights of Man,* 174–78. Abolitionist Griffing later worked for the Freedmen's Bureau.

45. Stanton to Susan B. Anthony, December 29, 1864, in Stanton and Batch, *Stanton as Revealed*, 103–4 (quotation); 308–9; McPherson, *Struggle for Equality*, 309–11; Donald, *Charles Sumner and the Rights of Man*, 2:192–205. James McPherson places Phillips's visit in January or February 1865. See McPherson, *Struggle for Equality*, 309n.

46. Burlingame, *Abraham Lincoln*, 2:749–51; Garnet, *A Memorial Discourse*, 69–91; Guelzo, *Abraham Lincoln Redeemer President*, 339, 408; Garrison to Lincoln, February 13, 1865, Lincoln Papers (quotation); Elizabeth Cady Stanton to Susan B. Anthony, December 29, 1864, in Stanton and Blatch, *Stanton as Revealed*, 104.

47. William Lloyd Garrison to Helen Garrison, April 7, 9, 1865; William Lloyd Garrison to Henry B. Stanton, September 15, 1865, in Garrison, *Letters*, 5:263–70, 295–97; Mayer, *All on Fire*, 577–84; Chamberlain to editor, September 22, 1883, in *New York Tribune*, November 4, 1883 (quotation); Donald, *Charles Sumner and the Rights of Man*, 228, 232–33; McPherson, *Struggle for Equality*, 299. In 1883 Chamberlain was responding to former colonizationist Leonard Bacon's claim that Garrison and the AASS "never succeeded in anything."

48. McPherson, *Struggle for Equality*, 100–103, 109, 287–99; Friedman, *Gregarious Saints*, 260–61; Stewart, *Wendell Phillips*, 244.

49. McPherson, *Struggle for Equality*, 289–99, 305–6, 336–37; Stewart, *Wendell Phillips*, 265–66 (quotation); Mayer, *All on Fire*, 587–88; Garrison to George W. Julian, February 11, 1866; Garrison to Fanny Garrison Villard, February 11, March 3, 1866; Garrison to Theodore Tilton, [March 8, 1866], in Garrison, *Letters*, 5:382, 384–86, 394–400; Oakes, *Radical and the Republican*, 249–55; Howard, *Religion and the Radical Republican Movement*, 109.

50. Mayer, *All on Fire*, 591–92; Stewart, *Wendell Phillips*, 266–67, 269; McPherson, *Struggle for Equality*, 329–33; "'The South Victorious.' The Speech of Wendell Phillips . . . Oct. 17 [1865]," *National Anti-Slavery Standard*, October 28, 1865. In June 1865 Horace Greeley urged Gerrit Smith to go to Washington in hopes of influencing Johnson. See Howard, *Religion and the Radical Republican Movement*, 95. James M. McPherson and James Brewer Stewart give abolitionists credit for shaping political events. On wide press comment of Phillips's speech, see "North" to editor, October 22, 1866, in *National Anti-Slavery Standard*, October 27, 1866.

51. Moncure Conway to Sumner, October 16, 1865, Sumner Papers; Stearns, *Life and Public Service of George Luther Stearns*, 358–60.

52. McPherson, *Struggle for Equality*, 342; Masur, *An Example for All the Land*, 131–46; *Liberator*, December 22, 1865; White, *Life of Lyman Trumbull*, 257–62; Smith, *Gerrit Smith to Senator Sumner; Gerrit Smith's Reply to Henry Wilson March 26, 1866* (Peterboro, N.Y.: Smith, 1866), in Smith, "Gerrit Smith Broadside and Pamphlet Collection"; Trefousse, *Radical Republicans*, 339–40, 345–48, 416–19. The Fourteenth Amendment provided that states that denied black men the right to vote would have their representation in Congress proportionally reduced. Radicals and abolitionists wanted a stronger guarantee for black suffrage.

53. Oakes, *Radical and the Republican*, 249–55; McPherson, *Political History of the*

United States of America during the Period of Reconstruction, 52–56; Bentley, *History of the Freedmen's Bureau,* 196; Bacon, *But One Race,* 169–70. James Oakes quotes Johnson's alleged remark that Douglass was "just like any nigger" (255).

54. McKim to Joseph Simpson, February 28, 1866, American Freedman's Union Commission Letter Books; Merrill, *Against Wind and Tide,* 313–14 (quotations); Garrison to Julian, February 11, 1866, in Garrison, *Letters,* 5:382; Donald, *Charles Sumner and the Rights of Man,* 2:256–57. Biographer Henry Mayer emphasizes that it was during the summer of 1865 that Garrison "blended in" with Radical Republicans, and abolitionists generally opposed Johnson within a context established by the Radicals. See Mayer, *All on Fire,* 592, 602–4. As late as his letter to Julian, Garrison believed Johnson was "sincere" in his view of Reconstruction and wondered why Johnson did "not see his error." A month later, injuries Garrison suffered in a fall limited his political role. See Merrill, *Against Wind and Tide,* 313.

55. Stewart, *Wendell Phillips,* 271; Smith to Sumner, February 8, 1866; Sumner to Phillips, June 7, 1866, in Sumner, *Selected Letters,* 2:357n, 370 (quotation); Higginson to Sumner, February 18, 1866; Phillips to Sumner, April 23, 1866, Sumner Papers; Howard, *Religion and the Radical Republican Movement,* 122–23.

56. Cheever, "The Robbery and Moral Assassination of the Colored Race by Legislation," *National Anti-Slavery Standard,* June 23, 1866; Douglass to John T. Sargent, n.d., in *National Anti-Slavery Standard,* July 7, 1866; Stewart, *Wendell Phillips,* 271–73; Bacon, *But One Race;* McPherson, *Struggle for Equality,* 351, 354–56, 358–68; Johnson to William Lloyd Garrison, June 16, 1866, Antislavery Collection/Garrison Papers; Howard, *Religion and the Radical Republican Movement,* 130–38, 142–43. When the convention ended Tilton, Dickinson, and Douglass organized a mass meeting on behalf of black suffrage.

57. McPherson, *Struggle for Equality,* 360–63 (1st quotation); Foner, *Reconstruction,* 3–79; Howard, *Religion and the Radical Republican Movement,* 149–50; Trefousse, *Radical Republicans,* 353–61 (2nd quotation). See also Stewart, *Wendell Phillips,* 278–79, 281.

58. McPherson, *Struggle for Equality,* 375–76 (1st quotation); Stewart, *Wendell Phillips,* 283–86 (2nd quotation).

59. Trefousse, *Radical Republicans,* 367–68; McPherson, *Struggle for Equality,* 369, 384–85; Foner, *Reconstruction,* 333–36; Trefousse, *Impeachment of a President,* 44–50, 96–112; Welles, *Diary of Gideon Welles,* 3:357. Ashley introduced impeachment resolutions in the House of Representatives in January 1867. On Haven, see Gravely, *Gilbert Haven.*

60. McPherson, *Struggle for Equality,* 418–19; *Independent,* November 5, 12, 19, 1868; William Lloyd Garrison to Charles Sumner, January 20, 1869, in Garrison, *Letters,* 6:100; *National Anti-Slavery Standard,* November 14 (4th–5th quotations), 21, 1868 (1st–2nd quotations); Smith to Grant, November 4, 1868, in *National Anti-Slavery Standard,* December 12, 1868 (3rd quotation). Garrison wrote to Sumner, "I have strong confidence in the integrity, patriotism, and fidelity to the cause of freedom of General

Grant. . . . I believe he will sustain Congress in all necessary measures for the protection of our colored population in the possession and exercise of all the rights of American citizenship." Smith had favored voting rights for black soldiers in April 1863. That May, the AASS supported black suffrage. Theodore Tilton called for "universal suffrage" in late 1864. During the summer of 1865, Sumner called for a suffrage amendment. Tilton called for one in April 1867. See Howard, *Religion and the Radical Republican Movement,* 165–70. On Frederick Douglass's support for Grant and the Republican Party, see Barnes, *Frederick Douglass,* 109–10.

61. *National Anti-Slavery Standard,* December 12, 1868, February 6, 1869; McPherson, *Political History of the United States during the Period of Reconstruction,* 401 (1st quotation); McPherson, *Struggle for Equality,* 377–79 (2nd quotation); Stewart, *Wendell Phillips,* 293–94.

62. McPherson, *Struggle for Equality,* 426–29; Franklin, *Reconstruction,* 82–83; Douglass to Theodore Tilton, April 24, 1869, Miscellaneous American Collection (1st–2nd quotations); Phillips to John F. Sargent, May 12, 1869, in Martyn, *Wendell Phillips,* 371 (3rd quotation); Stewart, *Wendell Phillips,* 293–94; Robertson, *Parker Pillsbury,* 150; Abbott, *Cobbler in Congress,* 207–8; Stewart, *Holy Warriors,* 203–4. Stacey M. Robertson emphasizes that Pillsbury dissented because the amendment did not include woman suffrage.

Conclusion

1. Harrold, "Morality, Violence, and Perceptions of Abolitionist Failure," 10–12.
2. Zilversmit, *First Emancipation.*

Bibliography

Primary Sources

Manuscripts Collections

Adams Papers, Massachusetts Historical Society, Boston

American Freedmen's Union Commission Letter Books, 1815–68, Department of Rare Books and Manuscripts, Cornell University Library, Ithaca, N.Y.

American Missionary Association Archives, Amistad Research Center, Tulane University, New Orleans

Antislavery Collection/Garrison Papers, Rare Books and Manuscripts, Boston Public Library

Moses A. Cartland Papers, Houghton Library, Harvard University, Cambridge, Mass.

Salmon P. Chase Papers, Historical Society of Pennsylvania, Philadelphia

Salmon P. Chase Papers, Library of Congress, Washington, D.C.

Salmon P. Chase Papers, Microfilm Edition, John Niven, ed., University Publications of America

Cheever Family Papers, American Antiquarian Society, Worcester, Mass.

Lydia Maria Child Papers, Library of Congress, Washington, D.C.

Moncure Conway Papers, Rare Books and Manuscripts, Columbia University, New York

John G. Fee–Cassius M. Clay Correspondence, Berea College Library, Berea, Ky.

Abby Kelley Foster Papers, American Antiquarian Society, Worcester, Mass.

John Gallison Diaries, Massachusetts Historical Society, Boston

Joshua R. Giddings Papers, Ohio History Connection, Columbus

Joshua R. Giddings–George W. Julian Papers, Library of Congress, Washington, D.C.

Horace Greeley Papers, Manuscript and Archives Division, New York Public Library

John P. Hale Papers, New Hampshire Historical Society, Concord

Hale-Chandler Papers, Rayner Special Collections Library, Dartmouth College, Hanover, N.H.

John Jay Papers, Butler Library, Columbia University, New York

Abraham Lincoln Papers, Library of Congress, Washington, D.C.

Horace Mann Papers, Massachusetts Historical Society, Boston

Samuel J. May Anti-Slavery Collection, Division of Rare Books and Manuscripts Collection, Cornell University Library, Ithaca, N.Y.

Meredith Family Papers, Historical Society of Pennsylvania, Philadelphia

Miscellaneous American Collection, Pierpont Morgan Library, New York

Pennsylvania Abolition Society Papers, Historical Society of Pennsylvania, Philadelphia

Quaker and Special Collections, Haverford College Libraries, Haverford, Penn.

William H. Seward Papers, Rare Book and Special Collections, River Campus Libraries, University of Rochester, Rochester, N.Y.

Gerrit Smith Papers, Special Collections Research Center, Syracuse University Libraries, Syracuse, N.Y.

Lysander Spooner Papers, Manuscript Collections Relating to Slavery, New-York Historical Society, New York

Elizabeth Cady Stanton Papers, Library of Congress, Washington, D.C.

Charles Sumner Papers, Houghton Library, Harvard University, Cambridge, Mass.

Lewis Tappan Papers, Library of Congress, Washington, D.C.

Eli Thayer Papers, Special Collections Department, Brown University, Providence, R.I.

Vaux Family Papers, Historical Society of Pennsylvania, Philadelphia

Carter J. Woodson Collection, Library of Congress, Washington, D.C.

Published Documents, Letters, and Papers

Abel, Annie Heloise, and Frank J. Kingberg, eds. *A Side-Light on Anglo-American Relations 1839–1858*. Lancaster, Penn.: Association for the Study of Negro Life and History, 1927.

Adams, John Quincy. *Memoirs of John Quincy Adams, Comprising Portions of His Diary from 1795 to 1858*. Edited by Charles Francis Adams. 12 vols. Philadelphia: J. B. Lippincott, 1874–77.

Albree, John, ed. *Whittier Correspondence from the Oak Knoll Collections, 1830–1892*. Salem, Mass.: Essex Book and Print Club, 1911.

Allen, Richard. *The Life, Experiences, and Gospel Labors of the Rt. Rev. Richard Allen*. Philadelphia: Allen, 1833.

American and Foreign Anti-Slavery Society. *[9th] Annual Report*. New York: American and Foreign Anti-Slavery Society, 1850.

American Anti-Slavery Society. *Fifth Annual Report*. New York: American Anti-Slavery Society, 1838.

———. *Fourth Annual Report*. New York: American Anti-Slavery Society, 1837.

———. *Third Annual Report*. New York: American Anti-Slavery Society, 1836.

American Convention. *American Convention for Promoting the Abolition of Slavery and Improving the Condition of the African Race: Minutes, Constitution, Addresses, Memorials, Resolutions*. 3 vols. New York: Bergman, 1969.

———. *Minutes of the Sixteenth Session of the American Convention—Special Meeting December 1819*. Philadelphia: American Convention, 1819.

Andrew, John A. *Speeches of John A. Andrew at Hingham and Boston*. N.p.: Republican State Committee, [1860].

Barnes, Gilbert H., and Dwight L. Dumond, eds. *Letters of Theodore Weld, Angelina Grimké Weld, and Sarah Grimké*. 2 vols. 1934; reprint New York: Da Capo Press, 1970.

Belknap, Jeremy. *Life of Jeremy Belknap, D.D., the Historian of New Hampshire.* New York: Harper and Brothers, 1847.

Benton, Thomas Hart, ed. *Abridgement of the Debates of Congress from 1789 to 1865.* 16 vols. New York: D. Appleton, 1860–67.

Birney, James G. *Letters of James G. Birney.* Edited by Dwight L. Dumond. 2 vols. New York: D. Appleton-Century, 1938.

Blair, Montgomery. *Speech of the Hon. Montgomery Blair (Postmaster General), on the Revolutionary Scheme of the Ultra Abolitionists, and in Defense of the President.* New York: S. W. Lee, 1863.

Bowditch, Vincent Y., ed. *Life and Correspondence of Henry Ingersoll Bowditch.* 2 vols. Boston: Houghton Mifflin, 1902.

Bruns, Roger, ed. *Am I Not a Man and a Brother: The Antislavery Crusade in Revolutionary America.* New York: Chelsea House, 1977.

Butler, Benjamin F. *Private and Official Correspondence of Gen. Benjamin F. Butler.* Edited by Jesse Ames Marshall. 5 vols. Norwood, Mass.: Plimpton Press, 1927.

Cadbury, Henry J., ed. "Another Early Quaker Anti-Slavery Document." *Journal of Negro History* 27 (April 1942): 210–15.

Calhoun, John C. *The Papers of John C. Calhoun.* Edited by Clyde N. Wilson et al. 28 vols. Columbia, S.C.: University of South Carolina Press, 1959–2003.

Carter, Nathaniel H., and William L. Stone, eds. *Reports of the Proceedings and Debates of the Convention of 1821.* Albany, N.Y.: E. and E. Hosford, 1821.

Channing, William E. *Works of William E. Channing, D.D.* Boston: American Unitarian Association, 1891.

Chase, Salmon Portland. "Diary and Correspondence of Salmon P. Chase." In *American Historical Association Annual Report for the Year 1902,* edited by S. H. Dodson, 2:11–527. Washington, D.C.: American Historical Association, 1903.

———. *The Salmon P. Chase Papers.* Edited by John Niven. 5 vols. Kent, Ohio: Kent State University Press, 1993–99.

Chase, Salmon Portland, and Charles Dexter Cleveland. *Anti-Slavery Addresses of 1844 and 1845 by Salmon P. Chase and Charles Dexter Cleveland.* Philadelphia: J. A. Bancroft, 1867.

Child, Lydia Maria. *Letters of Lydia Maria Child, 1802–1880.* Boston: Houghton, Mifflin, 1883.

———. *Lydia Maria Child: Selected Letters.* Edited by Milton Meltzer and Patricia G. Holland. Amherst: University of Massachusetts Press, 1982.

Coffin, Levi. *Reminiscences of Levi Coffin, the Reputed President of the Underground Railroad.* 1880; reprint New York: Arno, 1968.

Coles, Edward. *Governor Edward Coles.* Edited by Clarence Walworth Alvord. Springfield: Illinois State Library, 1910.

Conway, Moncure. *Autobiography, Memoirs, and Experiences.* 2 vols. Boston: Houghton Mifflin, 1904.

———. *The Golden Hour.* Boston: Ticknor and Fields, 1862.

Davis, Jefferson. *Jefferson Davis, Constitutionalist: His Letters, Papers, and Speeches.* Edited by Dunbar Roland. 10 vols. Jackson: Mississippi Department of Archives and History, 1923.

Douglass, Frederick. *The Frederick Douglass Papers. Series One, Speeches, Debates, and Interviews.* Edited by John Blassingame et al. 5 vols. New Haven, Conn.: Yale University Press, 1979–92.

———. *The Frederick Douglass Papers. Series Three, Correspondence.* Edited by John R. McKivigan et al. 2 vols. to date. New Haven, Conn.: Yale University Press, 2009.

———. *Frederick Douglass: Selected Speeches and Writings.* Edited by Philip S. Foner. Chicago: Lawrence Hill Books, 1999.

———. *Life and Times of Frederick Douglass.* Hartford, Conn.: Park, 1881.

Dumond, Dwight L., ed. *Southern Editorials on Secession.* 1931; reprint Gloucester, Mass.: Peter Smith, 1964.

Dyer, Oliver. *Phonographic Report of the Proceedings of the National Free Soil Convention.* Buffalo: G. H. Derby, 1848.

Fairbank, Calvin. *Rev. Calvin Fairbank during Slavery Times: How He "Fought the Good Fight to Prepare the Way."* Chicago: R. R. McCabe, 1890.

Garnet, Henry Highland. *A Memorial Discourse Delivered in the House of Representatives, Washington, D.C. on Sabbath, February 12, 1865.* Philadelphia: Joseph M. Wilson, 1865.

Garrison, William Lloyd. *The Letters of William Lloyd Garrison.* Edited by Walter Mitchell Merrill and Louis Ruchames. 6 vols. Cambridge, Mass.: Harvard University Press, 1971–81.

———. *The New Reign of Terror in the Slaveholding States, for 1859–60.* 1861; reprint New York: Arno, 1959.

———. *No Compromise with Slaveholders: An Address Delivered in Broadway Tabernacle, New York, February 14, 1854.* New York: American Anti-Slavery Society, 1854.

Gates, Seth M. *Hon. Seth M. Gates on Freemasonry: Proof That the Institution That Murdered Moran I[s] Unchanged in Character.* Warsaw, New York: National Christian Association, 1873.

Gellman, David N. *Emancipating New York: The Politics of Slavery and Freedom, 1777–1827.* Baton Rouge: Louisiana State University Press, 2006.

Gerlach, Larry, ed. *New Jersey in the American Revolution.* Trenton: New Jersey Historical Society, 1975.

Giddings, Joshua R. *Speeches in Congress.* 1853; reprint New York: Negro Universities Press, 1968.

Goodell, William. *Address of the Macedon Convention.* Albany: S. W. Green, 1847.

Gordon, Ann D., ed. *Selected Papers of Elizabeth Cady Stanton and Susan B. Anthony.* 2 vols. New Brunswick, N.J.: Rutgers University Press, 1997.

[Greeley, Horace]. *Proceedings of the First Three Republican National Conventions of 1856, 1860, and 1864.* Minneapolis: Charles W. Johnson, 1893.

Hammond, James H. *Selections from the Letters and Speeches of Hon. James H. Hammond of South Carolina*. Edited by Clyde N. Wilson. 1866; reprint Spartanburg, S.C.: Reprint Company, 1977.

Hopkins, Samuel. *The Works of Samuel Hopkins, D.D.* 3 vols. Boston: Doctrinal Tract and Book Society, 1852.

Howe, Samuel Gridley. *Letters and Journals of Samuel Gridley Howe*. Edited by Laura E. Richards. 2 vols.; Boston: Dana Estes, 1909.

Jay, William. *Miscellaneous Writings on Slavery*. Boston: John P. Jewett, 1853.

Jones, James C. *Speech of Hon. James C. Jones of Tenn. on a Petition for the Repeal of the Fugitive Slave Law . . . June 26, 1854*. Washington, D.C.: Congressional Globe Office, 1854.

Keith, George. *An Exhortation and Caution to Friends, Concerning the Buying or Keeping of Negroes*. New York: William Bradford, 1693.

[Kentucky]. "Resolutions of the Legislature of Kentucky," *United States Senate Reports*, 30th Cong., 1st sess., May 3, 1848, 143. Serial Set 512.

King, Charles R., ed. *The Life and Correspondence of Rufus King: Comprising His Letters, Private and Official, His Public Documents and His Speeches*. 4 vols. New York: G. P. Putnam, 1894–1900.

Koch, Adrienne, and William Peden, eds. *The Life and Selected Writings of Thomas Jefferson*. New York: Modern Library, 1944.

Lincoln, Abraham. *Collected Works of Abraham Lincoln*. Edited by Roy P. Basler. 9 vols. New Brunswick, N.J.: Rutgers University Press, 1953.

Linden, Glenn M., comp., *Voices from the Gathering Storm: The Coming of the American Civil War*. Wilmington, Del.: Scholarly Resources, 2001.

Lundy, Benjamin. *Life, Travels, and Opinions of Benjamin Lundy*. Philadelphia: William D. Parrish, 1847.

McKee, Thomas Hudson, comp. *National Conventions and Platforms of All Political Parties, 1789–1901*. Baltimore: Frieden-Wald, 1901.

McPherson, James M. *The Negro's Civil War: How American Blacks Felt and Acted during the War for the Union*. 1991; reprint New York: Vintage Books, 2003.

Massachusetts. *Massachusetts General Court Joint Committee on the Annexation of Texas to the United States*. Boston: Commonwealth of Massachusetts, 1838.

Massachusetts Anti-Slavery Society. *Annual Reports and Proceedings*. Boston: Massachusetts Anti-Slavery Society, 1833–56.

———. *Fifth Annual Report*. Boston: Massachusetts Anti-Slavery Society, 1837.

———. *Proceedings of the . . . Annual Meetings Held in 1854, 1855, and 1856*. Boston: Massachusetts Anti-Slavery Society, 1856.

———. *Twelfth Annual Report*. 1844; reprint, Westport, Conn.: Negro Universities Press, 1970.

May, Samuel J. *Some Recollections of Our Anti-Slavery Conflict*. 1869; reprint New York: Arno, 1986.

A Memorial to the Congress of the United States, on the Subject of Restraining the

Increase of Slavery in New States to be Admitted to the Union. Boston: Sewell and Phelps, 1819.

Ohio Anti-Slavery Society. *Report of the Second Anniversary.* Cincinnati: Ohio Anti-Slavery Society, 1837.

Palmer, William P., and Sherwin McRae, eds. *Calendar of Virginia State Papers and Other Manuscripts from July 2, 1790 to August 10, 1792.* Volume 5. Richmond: Rush U. Derr, 1885.

Parker, Theodore. *The Nebraska Question: Some Thoughts on the New Assault upon Freedom in America.* Boston: B. B. Mussey, 1854.

———. *The Present Aspect of Slavery and the Immediate Duty of the North: A Speech Delivered in the Hall of the State House before the Massachusetts Anti-Slavery Convention . . . January 29, 1858.* Boston: Bela Marsh, 1856.

Pennsylvania. *Statutes at Large.* 18 vols. Harrisburg: Commonwealth of Pennsylvania, 1908.

———. "Votes and Proceedings of the House of Representatives of the Province of Pennsylvania 1681–1777." In *Pennsylvania Archives, Eighth Series,* 2:1012–13. Philadelphia: Pennsylvania, 1931–35.

Pennsylvania Abolition Society. *Centennial Anniversary of the Pennsylvania Society for Promoting the Abolition of Slavery.* Philadelphia: Pennsylvania Abolition Society, 1876.

Peters, Gerhard, and John T. Woolley, eds. *The American Presidency Project.* University of California at Santa Barbara. www.presidency.ucsb.edu.

Phelps, Amos A. *Lectures on Slavery and Its Remedy.* Boston: New England Anti-Slavery Society, 1834.

Phillips, Wendell. *Speeches, Lectures, and Letters. First Series.* 1864; reprint New York: Negro Universities Press, 1968.

Pickard, Samuel T. *Life and Letters of John Greenleaf Whittier.* 2 vols. Boston: Houghton, Mifflin, 1894.

———, ed. *Whittier as a Politician: Illustrated by His Letters to Professor Elizur Wright Jr.* Boston: C. E. Goodspeed, 1900.

Pierce, Edward L. *Memoir and Letters of Charles Sumner.* 4 vols. 1893; reprint New York: Arno, 1969.

Pilgrim Society. *An Account of the Pilgrim Celebration at Plymouth, August 1, 1853.* Boston: Crosby, Nichols, 1853.

Publicola. "Present Aspects of Abolitionism." *Southern Literary Messenger* 8 (July 1847): 429–34.

Reed, George Edward, ed. *Pennsylvania Archives, Fourth Series,* vol. 4, *Papers of the Governors.* Harrisburg: Commonwealth of Pennsylvania, 1900.

Report of the Proceedings of the Colored National Convention Held at Cleveland, Ohio, on Wednesday, September 6, 1848. Rochester: North Star, 1848.

Republican Party. *Proceedings of the Republican National Convention Held at Chicago, May 16, 17, and 18, 1860.* Albany, N.Y.: Republican Party, 1860.

Ruffin, Edmund. "Consequences of Abolitionist Agitation." *De Bow's Review* 22 (June 1857): 587–88.

Saillant, John, ed. "'Some Thoughts on the Subject of Freeing the Negro Slaves in the Colony of Connecticut' by Levi Hart, with a Reply by Samuel Hopkins." *New England Quarterly* 75 (March 2002): 107–28.

Sergeant, John. *Select Speeches of John Sergeant of Pennsylvania.* Philadelphia: E. L. Carey and A. Hart, 1832.

Seward, William H. *The Works of William H. Seward.* Edited by George E. Baker. 3 vols. New York: Redfield, 1853.

Simpson, Brooks D., ed. *The Civil War: The Third Year Told by Those Who Lived It.* 5 vols. New York: Library of America, 2013.

Slade, William. *Speech of Mr. Slade of Vermont on the Abolition of Slavery and the Slave Trade in the District of Columbia . . . December 20, 1837.* Samuel May Anti-Slavery Collection. http://ebooks.librry.cornell.edu.

———. *Speech of Mr. Slade of Vermont on the Right of Petition; Power of Congress to Abolish Slavery and the Slave Trade in the District of Columbia, and the Principles, Purpose, and Prospects of Abolition.* Washington, D.C.: Gales and Seaton, 1840.

Smith, Gerrit. "Gerrit Smith Broadside and Pamphlet Collection." Syracuse University Library, Digital Edition. http://librry.syr.edu/digitl/collections/g/GerritSmith/536.

———. *Gerrit Smith to Senator Sumner, February 5, 1866.* Peterboro, N.Y.: [Gerrit Smith], 1866.

Stampp, Kenneth M., ed. *The Causes of the Civil War.* Englewood Cliffs, N.J.: Prentice-Hall, 1965.

Stanton, Henry B. *Random Recollections.* New York: Harper, 1887.

———. *Remarks of Henry B. Stanton, in the Representatives Hall, on the 23d and 24th of February . . . 1837.* Boston: Isaac Knapp, 1837.

Stanton, Theodore, and Harriet Stanton Blatch, eds. *Elizabeth Cady Stanton as Revealed in Her Letters, Diary, and Reminiscences.* 2 vols. New York: Harper, 1922.

Sumner, Charles. *Freedom National; Slavery Sectional: Speech of Hon. Charles Sumner . . . in the Senate of the United States, August 26, 1852.* Washington, D.C.: Buell and Blanchard, 1852.

———. *The Selected Letters of Charles Sumner.* 2 vols. Edited by Beverly Wilson Palmer. Boston: Northeastern University Press, 1990.

Tallmadge, James, Jr. *Speech of the Honorable James Tallmadge Jr. . . . on Slavery to Which Is Added the Proceedings of the Manumission Society of the City of New York.* New York: Manumission Society, 1819.

Thome, James A., and J. Horace Kimball. *Emancipation in the West Indies: A Sixth Months' Tour in Antiqua, Barbadoes, and Jamaica in the Year 1837.* New York: American Anti-Slavery Society, 1838.

Thompson, George. *Prison Life and Reflections; or, A Narrative of the Arrest, Trial, Conviction, Imprisonment, Observations, Reflections, and Deliverance of Work, Burr, and Thompson.* Hartford, Conn.: A. Work, 1855.

Torrey, Jesse. *A Portraiture of Domestic Slavery in the United States.* 2nd ed. Ballston, Pa.: [Jesse Torrey], 1817.

United States. *Statutes at Large and Treaties of the United States of America.* 17 vols. Boston: Little, Brown, 1845–73.

U.S. Congress. *Annals of Congress: The Debates and Proceedings of the Congress of the United States, 1789–1824.* Washington, D.C.: Gales and Seaton, 1834–56.

———. *Congressional Globe.* Washington, D.C.: Blair and Rivers, 1834–73.

———. *Journal of the House of Representatives of the United States.* Washington, D.C.: U.S. Government Printing Office, 1789–1875.

———. *Register of Debates in Congress: Comprising the Leading Debates and Incidents of the . . . Session of the . . . Congress.* Washington: Gales and Seaton, 1825–37.

———. *Senate Executive Documents and Reports.* Washington, D.C.: Congressional Information Service, 1987.

Virginia. *Calendar of Virginia State Papers and Other Manuscripts.* 11 vols. Richmond: Virginia, 1875–93.

———. "Decisions of the General Court." *Virginia Magazine of History and Biography* 5 (January 1898): 233–41.

Virginia General Assembly, House of Delegates. *Report of the Select Committee Appointed under a Resolution of the House to Enquire into Existing Legislation of Congress upon the Subject of Fugitive Slaves, and to Suggest Such Legislation as May Be Proper.* Richmond: Virginia General Assembly, 1848–49.

[Walsh, Robert, Jr.?]. *Free Remarks on the Spirit of the Federal Constitution.* 1819; reprint London: Forgotten Books, 2013.

Weiss, John, ed. *Life and Correspondence of Theodore Parker, Minister of the Twenty-Eighth Congregational Society, Boston.* 2 vols. New York: D. Appleton, 1864.

Weld, Theodore D. *The Power of Congress over the District of Columbia.* New York: American Anti-Slavery Society, 1838.

Welles, Gideon. *Diary of Gideon Welles, Secretary of the Navy under Lincoln and Johnson.* 3 vols. Boston: Houghton Mifflin, 1911.

Whittier, John Greenleaf. *The Letters of John Greenleaf Whittier.* Edited by John B. Pickard. 3 vols. Cambridge, Mass.: Harvard University Pres, 1975.

Wise, Barton Haxall. *Life of Henry A. Wise of Virginia, 1806–1899.* New York: Macmillan, 1899.

Woolman, John. *Works of John Woolman.* Philadelphia: Joseph Cruckshank, 1775.

Wright, Marion T. "New Jersey Laws and the Negro 1776–1875." *Journal of Negro History* 28 (April 1948): 168–224.

Newspapers and Periodicals

Albany Weekly Patriot (Albany, N.Y.), 1843–48.

Anti-Slavery Bugle (Salem, Ohio), 1845–61.

Baltimore Sun, 1850.

Cincinnati Daily Gazette, 1838.

Cincinnati Weekly Herald and Philanthropist, 1846.

Colored American (New York), 1839–40.

Commonwealth (Boston), 1862–64.

Daily Herald and Gazette (Cleveland), 1837.

Daily Missouri Republican (St. Louis), 1850.

Daily Ohio Statesman (Columbus), 1837.

Daily Union (Washington, D.C.), 1848.

Douglass Monthly (Rochester, N.Y.), 1860–62.

Emancipator (New York), 1834–41; (Boston), 1836–47.

Extra Globe (Washington, D.C.), 1840.

Frederick Douglass' Paper (Rochester, N.Y.), 1852–56.

Freedom's Journal (New York), 1828.

Friend (Philadelphia), 1828.

Friend of Man (Utica, N.Y.), 1838.

Genius of Universal Emancipation (Mount Pleasant, Ohio), 1822; (Jonesboro, Tenn.), 1823; (Baltimore), 1824–26.

Globe (Washington, D.C.), 1842.

Harper's Weekly (New York), 1864.

Independent (New York), 1864–68.

Liberator (Boston), 1837–65.

Liberty Herald (Warren, Ohio), 1846.

Louisville Journal, 1842.

Louisville Observer and Reporter, 1850.

Louisville Public Advertiser, 1839–40.

Maryland Gazette and State Register (Annapolis), 1826.

Maysville Eagle (Maysville, Ky.), 1838–39.

National Anti-Slavery Standard (Philadelphia), 1852–68.

National Era (Washington, D.C.), 1848–52.

National Gazette and Literary Register (Philadelphia), 1820–26.

National Intelligencer (Washington, D.C.), 1829–43.

New York Daily Advertiser, 1819.

New York Herald, 1856.

New York Times, 1870.

New York Tribune, 1862–83.

Niles Register (Baltimore), 1819–36.

North Star (Rochester, N.Y.), 1848–51.

Ohio State Journal (Columbus), 1838, 1854.

Pennsylvania Freeman (Philadelphia), 1838–51.

Philanthropist (Cincinnati), 1836.

Poulson's American Daily Advertiser (Philadelphia), 1820.

Principia (New York), 1861–64.
Richmond Enquirer (Richmond, Va.), 1820–60.
Signal of Liberty (Ann Arbor, Mich.), 1847.
Spirit of Liberty (Pittsburgh), 1842.
Standard-Times (Fall River, Mass.), 1997–98.
Tocsin of Liberty (Albany, N.Y.), 1844.
True American (Trenton, N.J.), 1819.
United States Chronicle (Philadelphia), 1789.
United States Telegraph (Washington, D.C.), 1836.
Vermont Chronicle (Bellows Falls), 1834–37.
Vermont Watchman and State Journal (Montpelier), 1837.
Weekly Anglo-African (New York), 1864.

Secondary Sources

Abbott, Richard H. *Cobbler in Congress: Life of Henry Wilson, 1812–1875.* Lexington: University Press of Kentucky, 1972.

Abzug, Robert H. *Cosmos Crumbling: American Reform and the Religious Imagination.* Boston: Twayne, 1979.

Adams, Alice Dana. *The Neglected Period of Anti-Slavery in America (1808–1831).* 1908; reprint Gloucester, Mass.: Peter Smith, 1964.

Adams, Kevin, and Leonne Hudson, eds. *Democracy and the Civil War: Race and African Americans in the Nineteenth Century.* Kent, Ohio: Kent State University Press, 2016.

Adelberg, Michael S. *The American Revolution in Monmouth County: The Theatre of Spoil and Destruction.* Charleston, S.C.: History Press, 2010.

Allegro, James J. "'Increasing and Strengthening the Country': Law, Politics, and the Antislavery Movement in Early-Eighteenth-Century Massachusetts Bay." *New England Quarterly* 75 (March 2002): 5–23.

Aptheker, Herbert. *Abolitionism: A Revolutionary Movement.* Boston: Twayne, 1989.

Bacon, Margaret Hope. *But One Race: The Life of Robert Purvis.* Albany: State University of New York Press, 2007.

Baer, Helen C. *The Heart Is Like Heaven: The Life of Lydia Maria Child.* Philadelphia: University of Pennsylvania Press, 1964.

Bancroft, Frederick. *The Life of William H. Seward.* 1900; reprint Gloucester, Mass.: Peter Smith, 1967.

Barnes, Gilbert H. *The Antislavery Impulse, 1830–1844.* 1933; reprint Gloucester, Mass.: Peter Smith, 1973.

Barnes, L. Diane. *Frederick Douglass: Reformer and Statesman.* New York: Routledge, 2013.

Barney, William. *Secession Impulse: Alabama and Mississippi in 1860.* Princeton, N.J.: Princeton University Press, 1974.

Bartlett, Irving H. *Wendell Phillips: Brahman Radical.* Boston: Beacon, 1961.

Bauman, Richard. *For the Reputation of Truth: Politics, Religion, and Conflict among Pennsylvania Quakers, 1750–1800.* Baltimore: Johns Hopkins University Press, 1971.

Beard, Charles A., and Mary R. Beard. *The Rise of American Civilization.* 2 vols. New York: Macmillan, 1927.

Bemis, Samuel Flagg. *John Quincy Adams and the Union.* New York: Knopf, 1956.

Bendler, Bruce. "James Slone: . . . Renegade or True Republican." *New Jersey History* 125 (2010): 1–19.

Bentley, George R. *A History of the Freedmen's Bureau.* Philadelphia: University of Pennsylvania Press, 1955.

Berlin, Ira. *Many Thousands Gone: The First Two Centuries of Slavery in North America.* Cambridge, Mass.: Harvard University Press, 1998.

Binney, Charles C. *The Life of Horace Binney: With Selections from His Letters.* Philadelphia: J. B. Lippincott, 1903.

Birney, William. *James G. Birney and His Times: The Genesis of the Republican Party with Some Account of the Abolition Movement.* New York: D. Appleton, 1890.

Blight, David W. *Frederick Douglass' Civil War: Keeping Faith in Jubilee.* Baton Rouge: Louisiana State University Press, 1989.

Blue, Frederick J. *The Free Soilers: Third Party Politics, 1848–54.* Urbana: University of Illinois Press, 1973.

———. *No Taint of Compromise: Crusaders in Antislavery Politics.* Baton Rouge: Louisiana State University Press, 2005.

———. *Salmon P. Chase: A Life in Politics.* Kent, Ohio: Kent State University Press, 1987.

Bolt, Christine, and Seymour Drescher, eds. *Anti-Slavery Religion and Reform: Essays in Memory of Roger Anstey.* Folkestone, U.K.: W. Dawson, 1980.

Bordewich, Fergus M. *Bound for Canaan: The Underground Railroad and the War for the Soul of America.* New York: Amistad, 2005.

———. *The First Congress: How James Madison, George Washington, and a Group of Extraordinary Men Invented the Government.* New York: Simon and Schuster, 2016.

Boyd, George Adams. *Elias Boudinot: Patriot and Statesman, 1740–1821.* Princeton, N.J.: Princeton University Press, 1952.

Boyer, Richard O. *The Legend of John Brown: A Biography and a History.* New York: Knopf, 1973.

Brauer, Kinley. *Cotton Versus Conscience: Massachusetts Whig Politics and Southwestern Expansion, 1843–1847.* Lexington: University of Kentucky Press, 1967.

Brekus, Catherine A. *Sarah Osborn's World: The Rise of Evangelical Christianity in Early America.* New Haven, Conn.: Yale University Press, 2013.

Brooks, Corey M. *Liberty Power: Antislavery Third Parties and the Transformation of American Politics.* Chicago: University of Chicago Press, 2016.

Brown, Christopher Leslie. *Moral Capital: Foundations of British Abolitionism.* Chapel Hill: University of North Carolina Press, 2006.

Burgess, John W. *The Middle Period, 1817–1858.* New York: C. Scribner's Sons, 1898.

Burlingame, Michael. *Abraham Lincoln: A Life.* 2 vols. Baltimore: Johns Hopkins University Press, 2008.

Calarco, Tom, ed. *People of the Underground Railroad: A Bibliographical Dictionary.* Westport, Conn.: Greenwood Press, 2008.

Campbell, Stanley W. *The Slave Catchers: Enforcement of the Fugitive Slave Law, 1850–1860.* Chapel Hill: University of North Carolina Press, 1970.

Carroll, Kenneth L. "William Southeby, Early Quaker Antislavery Writer." *Pennsylvania Magazine of History and Biography* 89 (October 1965): 416–27.

Cary, Brycchan. *From Peace to Freedom: Quaker Rhetoric and the Birth of American Antislavery, 1657–1768.* New Haven, Conn.: Yale University Press, 2017.

Channing, Steven A. *Crisis of Fear: Secession in South Carolina.* New York: Norton, 1974.

Chapman-Smith, V. "Philadelphia and the Slave Trade: The Ganges African." *Pennsylvania Legacies,* November 2005. https://hsp.org/publications/pennsylvania-legacies/the-pennsylvania-abolition-society.

Cheek, William, and Aimee Lee Cheek. *John Mercer Langston and the Fight for Black Freedom.* Urbana: University of Illinois Press, 1989.

Chernow, Ron. *Alexander Hamilton.* New York: Penguin, 2004.

Clarke, James Freeman. *Anti-Slavery Days: A Sketch of the Struggle.* 1884; reprint New York: AMS Press, 1972.

Clark-Pujara, Christy Mikel. "Slavery, Emancipation, and Black Freedom in Rhode Island 1652–1842." Ph.D. dissertation, University of Iowa, 2008.

Clausewitz, Carl von. *On War.* Edited by Michael Howard and Peter Paret. Princeton, N.J.: Princeton University Press, 1976.

Clavin, Matthew. *Toussaint Louverture and the Civil War: The Promise and Peril of a Second Haitian Revolution.* Philadelphia: University of Pennsylvania Press, 2010.

"Cleveland's Freedmen's Aid Society." N.d. http://drbronsontours.com/bronsonclevelandfreedy.

Clifford, Deborah Pickman. *Crusader for Freedom: A Life of Lydia Maria Child.* Boston: Beacon Press, 1992.

Coleman, J. Winston, Jr. "Delia Webster and Calvin Fairbank—Underground Railroad Agents." *Filson Club History Quarterly* 17 (July 1943): 129–42.

Collins, Gary. *Shadrach Minkins: From Fugitive Slave to Citizen.* Cambridge, Mass.: Harvard University Press, 1998.

Commager, Henry Steele. *Theodore Parker, Yankee Crusader.* 1936; reprint Boston: Unitarian Universalist Association, 1947.

Conlin, Michael F. "The Smithsonian Abolition Lecture Controversy: The Clash of Antislavery Politics with American Science in Wartime Washington." *Civil War History* 46 (December 2000): 301–23.

Cooley, Henry Schofield. *A Study of Slavery in New Jersey.* 2 vols. Baltimore: Johns Hopkins University Press, 1896.

Countryman, Edward. *The American Revolution.* New York: Hill and Wang, 1985.

Craven, Avery O. "The South in American History." *Historical Outlook* 21 (March 1930): 105–9.

Croffut, William A. *An American Procession, 1855–1914: A Personal Chronical of Famous Men.* 1931; reprint Freeport, N.Y.: Books for Libraries, 1968.

Cromwell, Otelia. *Lucretia Mott.* Cambridge, Mass.: Harvard University Press, 1958.

Curtis, James C. *The Fox at Bay: Martin Van Buren and the Presidency, 1837–1841.* Lexington: University Press of Kentucky, 1970.

Davis, David Brion. *The Problem of Slavery in the Age of Revolution, 1770–1823.* Ithaca, N.Y.: Cornell University Press, 1975.

———. *The Slave Power Conspiracy and the Paranoid Style.* Baton Rouge: Louisiana State University Press, 1970.

Davis, Hugh. *Joshua Leavitt: Evangelical Abolitionist.* Baton Rouge: Louisiana State University Press, 1990.

Davis, Thomas J. "Emancipation Rhetoric, Natural Rights, and Revolutionary New England: A Note on Four Black Petitions in Massachusetts, 1773–1777." *New England Quarterly* 62 (June 1989): 248–63.

DeBrusk, Kristan. "An Ordinary Man in Extraordinary Times: David Cooper's Fight against Slavery." B.A. thesis, Texas Tech University, 2004.

D'Entremont, John. *Southern Emancipator: Moncure Conway, the American Years.* New York: Oxford University Press, 1987.

Dillon, Merton L. *The Abolitionists: The Growth of a Dissenting Minority.* New York: Norton, 1974.

———. *Benjamin Lundy and the Struggle for Negro Freedom.* Urbana: University of Illinois Press, 1966.

———. "The Failure of the American Abolitionists." *Journal of Southern History* 25 (May 1959): 159–77.

———. *Slavery Attacked: Southern Slaves and Their Allies, 1619–1865.* Baton Rouge: Louisiana State University Press, 1990.

Donald, David Herbert. *Charles Sumner and the Coming of the Civil War.* New York: Knopf, 1960.

———. *Charles Sumner and the Rights of Man.* New York: Knopf, 1970.

Douglas, Janet. "A Cherished Friendship: Julia Griffiths Crofts and Frederick Douglass." *Slavery and Abolition* 33 (May 2012): 265–74.

Downey, Arthur T. *The Creole Affair: The Slave Rebellion That Led the U.S. and Great Britain to the Brink of War.* Lanham, Md.: Rowman and Littlefield, 2014.

Drake, Thomas E. *Quakers and Slavery in America.* New Haven, Conn.: Yale University Press, 1950.

Duberman, Martin B., ed. *The Antislavery Vanguard: New Essays on the Abolitionists.* Princeton, N.J.: Princeton University Press, 1965.

———. *Charles Francis Adams, 1807–1886.* Stanford, Calif.: Stanford University Press, 1960.

Dumond, Dwight L. *Antislavery Origins of the Civil War in the United States.* 1939; reprint Ann Arbor: University of Michigan Press, 1959.

———. *Antislavery: The Crusade for Freedom in America.* New York: Norton, 1961.

DuRoss, Michelle. "Somewhere in Between: Alexander Hamilton and Slavery." *Early American Review* 9 (December 2010): 1–8.

Earle, Jonathan H. *Jacksonian Antislavery and the Politics of Free Soil, 1824–1854.* Chapel Hill: University of North Carolina Press, 2004.

Egerton, Douglas R. *Death or Liberty: African Americans and Revolutionary America.* New York: Oxford University Press, 2009.

———. *Gabriel's Rebellion: The Virginia Slave Conspiracies of 1800 and 1802.* Chapel Hill: University of North Carolina Press, 1993.

Emerson, Donald E. *Richard Hildreth.* Baltimore: Johns Hopkins University Press, 1946.

Essig, James D. *The Bonds of Wickedness: American Evangelicals against Slavery, 1770–1801.* Philadelphia: Temple University Press, 1982.

Etcheson, Nicole. *Bleeding Kansas: Contested Liberty in the Civil War Era.* Lawrence: University Press of Kansas, 2004.

Fehrenbacher, Don E. *The Slaveholding Republic: An Account of the United States Government's Relations to Slavery.* New York: Oxford University Press, 2001.

Filler, Louis. *The Crusade against Slavery, 1830–1860.* New York: Harper and Row, 1960.

Finkelman, Paul. *Slavery and the Founders: Race and Liberty in the Age of Jefferson.* Armonk, N.Y.: M. E. Sharpe, 1996.

Fladeland, Betty. *James Gillespie Birney: Slaveholder to Abolitionist.* Ithaca, N.Y.: Cornell University Press, 1955.

———. *Men and Brothers: Anglo-American Antislavery Cooperation.* Urbana: University of Illinois Press, 1972.

———. "Who Were the Abolitionists?" *Journal of Negro History* 49 (April 1964): 99–115.

Foner, Eric. *Free Soil, Free Labor, Free Men: The Ideology of the Republican Party before the Civil War.* New York: Oxford University Press, 1970.

———. *Reconstruction: America's Unfinished Revolution.* New York: Harper and Row, 1988.

Foner, Phillip S. *History of Black Americans.* 3 vols. Westport, Conn.: Greenwood Press, 1975.

Forbes, Robert Pierce. *The Missouri Compromise and Its Aftermath: Slavery and the Meaning of America.* Chapel Hill: University of North Carolina Press, 2007.

Formisano, Ronald P. "Political Character, Antipartyism, and the Second Party System." *American Quarterly* 21 (Winter 1969): 683–709.

Franklin, John Hope. *Reconstruction after the Civil War.* 2nd edition. Chicago: University of Chicago Press, 1994.

Fredrickson, George M. *The Black Image in the White Mind: The Debate on Afro-American Character and Destiny, 1817–1914.* New York: Harper and Row, 1977.

Freehling, William W. "The Founding Fathers and Slavery." *American Historical Review* 77 (February 1972): 81–93.

————. *The Road to Disunion.* 2 vols. New York: Oxford University Press, 1990–2007.

Frey, Sylvia. "Antislavery before the Revolutionary War." *History Now* 5 (Fall 2005). http://www.historynow.org/09-2005/historian2.html.

Friedman, Lawrence J. *Gregarious Saints: Self and Community in American Abolitionism, 1830–1870.* New Rochelle, N.Y.: Cambridge University Press, 1982.

————. "'Historical Topics Sometimes Run Dry': The State of Abolitionist Studies." *Historian* 43 (February 1981): 177–94.

Frothingham, Octavious Brooks. *Theodore Parker: A Biography.* Boston: J. R. Osgood, 1874.

Gallman, J. Matthew. *America's Joan of Arc: The Life of Anna Elizabeth Dickinson.* New York: Oxford University Press, 2006.

Gamble, Douglas A. "Joshua Giddings and the Ohio Abolitionists: A Study in Radical Politics." *Ohio History* 88 (Winter 1979): 37–56.

Gara, Larry. *The Liberty Line: The Legend of the Underground Railroad.* Lexington: University of Kentucky Press, 1961.

————. "Slavery and the Slave Power: A Crucial Distinction." *Civil War History* 15 (March 1969): 5–18.

Garrison, Wendell Phillips, and Francis Jackson Garrison. *William Lloyd Garrison, 1805–1879: The Story of His Life Told by His Children.* 4 vols. New York: Century, 1885–89.

Gellman, David N. *Emancipating New York: The Politics of Slavery and Freedom, 1777–1827.* Baton Rouge: Louisiana State University Press, 2006.

Gienapp, William E. *The Origins of the Republican Party, 1852–1856.* New York: Oxford University Press, 1986.

Giraud, Chester. *Embattled Maiden: The Life of Anna Dickinson.* New York: G. P. Putnam's Sons, 1951.

Glickstein, Jonathan A. "The Chattelization of Northern Whites: An Evolving Abolitionist Warning." *American Nineteenth Century History* 4 (2003): 25–58.

Going, Charles Buxton. *David Wilmot, Free-Soiler: A Biography of the Great Advocate of the Wilmot Proviso.* 1924; reprint Gloucester, Mass.: Peter Smith, 1966.

Goldfarb, Joel. "The Life of Gamaliel Bailey prior to the Founding of the National Era." Ph.D. dissertation, University of California, 1958.

Goodell, William. *Slavery and Anti-Slavery: A History of the Great Struggle in Both Hemispheres.* 1852; reprint New York: Negro Universities Press, 1963.

Goodheart, Lawrence B. *Abolitionist, Actuary, Atheist: Elizur Wright and the Reform Impulse.* Kent, Ohio: Kent State University Press, 1990.

Goodman, Paul. *Of One Blood: Abolitionism and the Origins of Racial Equality.* Berkeley: University of California Press, 1998.

Gravely, William B. *Gilbert Haven, Methodist Abolitionist: A Study in Race, Religion, and Reform, 1850–1880.* Nashville, Tenn.: Abingdon Press, 1973.

Greeley, Horace. *A History of the Struggle for Slavery Extension or Restriction in the United*

States from the Declaration of Independence to the Present Day. New York: Dix, Edwards, 1856.

Green, Constance M. *Washington.* 2 vols. Princeton, N.J.: Princeton University Press, 1862–63.

Griffin, Clifford S. *Their Brothers' Keepers: Moral Stewardship in the United States, 1800–1864.* New Brunswick, N.J.: Rutgers University Press, 1960.

Grimsted, David. *American Mobbing, 1828–1861: Toward Civil War.* New York: Oxford University Press, 1998.

Grover, Kathryn. *The Fugitive's Gibraltar: Escaping Slaves and Abolitionism in New Bedford, Massachusetts.* Amherst: University of Massachusetts Press, 2001.

Guasco, Suzanne Cooper. *Confronting Slavery: Edward Coles and the Rise of Antislavery Politics in Nineteenth-Century America.* DeKalb: Northern Illinois University Press, 2013.

Guelzo, Allen C. *Abraham Lincoln: Redeemer President.* Grand Rapids, Mich.: Eerdmans, 1999.

Hagedorn, Ann. *Beyond the River: The Untold Story of the Heroes of the Underground Railroad.* New York: Simon and Schuster, 2002.

Hambrick-Stowe, Charles E. "The Spiritual Pilgrimage of Sarah Osborn (1714–1796)." *Church History* 61 (December 1992): 408–21.

Hamilton, Holman. *Prologue to Conflict: The Crisis and Compromise of 1850.* Lexington: University of Kentucky Press, 1964.

Hammond, Isaac W. "Slavery in New Hampshire." *Magazine of American History* 21 (January–June 1889): 62–65.

Hammond, John Craig, and Matthew Mason, eds. *Contesting Slavery: The Politics of Bondage in the New American Nation.* Charlottesville: University of Virginia Press, 2011.

Harlow, Ralph V. *Gerrit Smith, Philanthropist and Reformer.* New York: Henry Holt, 1939.

Harrold, Stanley. *The Abolitionists and the South, 1831–1861.* Lexington: University Press of Kentucky, 1995.

———. *American Abolitionists.* New York: Longman, 2001.

———. *Border War: Fighting over Slavery before the Civil War.* Chapel Hill: University of North Carolina Press, 2010.

———. "Dramatic Turning Point or *Points?* Teaching Lincoln's Emancipation Proclamation." *OAH Magazine of History* 27 (April 2012): 11–16.

———. *Gamaliel Bailey and Antislavery Union.* Kent, Ohio: Kent State University Press, 1986.

———. "Morality, Violence, and Perceptions of Abolitionist Failure from before the Civil War to the Present." In *Democracy and the Civil War: Race and African Americans in the Nineteenth Century,* edited by Kevin Adams and Leonne Hudson, 6–26. Kent, Ohio: Kent State University Press, 2016.

———. "The Nonfiction Madison Washington Compared to the Character in Frederick

Douglass's *The Heroic Slave* and Similar Civil-War-Era Fiction." *Journal of African American History* 102 (Winter 2017): 8–20.

———. *The Rise of Aggressive Abolitionism: Addresses to the Slaves.* Lexington: University Press of Kentucky, 2004.

———. *Subversives: Antislavery Community in Washington, D.C., 1828–1865.* Baton Rouge: Louisiana State University Press, 2003.

Hart, Albert Bushnell. *Slavery and Abolition, 1831–1841.* 1906; reprint New York: Haskell House, 1968.

Higginson, Stephen A. "A Short History of the Right to Petition Government for the Redress of Grievances." *Yale Law Journal* 96 (November 1986): 142–66.

Hills, George Morgan. *History of the Church in Burlington, New Jersey.* 2nd edition. Trenton, N.J.: [Historical Society of Pennsylvania], 1885.

Holmes, J. Welfred. "Whittier and Sumner: A Political Friendship." *New England Quarterly* 30 (March 1957): 58–72.

Holt, Michael F. *The Rise and Fall of the American Whig Party: Jacksonians Politics and the Onset of the Civil War.* New York: Oxford University Press, 1999.

Horton, James Oliver, and Lois E. Horton. *In Hope of Liberty: Culture, Community, and Protest among Northern Free Blacks, 1700–1860.* New York: Oxford University Press, 1997.

Howard, Victor B. *Religion and the Radical Republican Movement, 1860–1870.* Lexington: University Press of Kentucky, 1990.

Howe, David Walker. *What God Hath Wrought: The Transformation of America, 1815–1848.* New York: Oxford University Press, 2007.

Huston, James L. "The Experiential Basis of the Northern Antislavery Impulse." *Journal of Southern History* 56 (November 1990): 609–40.

———. "Interpreting the Causation Sequence: The Meaning of Events Leading to the Civil War." *Reviews in American History* 34 (September 2006): 324–31.

Jackson, Maurice. *Let This Voice Be Heard: Anthony Benezet, Father of Atlantic Abolitionism.* Philadelphia: University of Pennsylvania Press, 2009.

Jeffrey, Julie Roy. *The Great Silent Army of Abolitionism: Ordinary Women in the Antislavery Movement.* Chapel Hill: University of North Carolina Press, 1998.

Johnson, Allen, and Dumas Malone, eds. *Dictionary of American Biography.* 3 vols. New York: Charles Scribner's Sons, 1959.

Johnson, Clifton H. "The American Missionary Association, 1846–1861: A Study of Christian Abolitionism." Ph.D. dissertation, Johns Hopkins University, 1952.

Johnson, Oliver. *William Lloyd Garrison and His Times; or, Sketches of the Anti-Slavery Movement in America.* 1881; reprint Miami: Mnemosyn, 1969.

Johnson, Reinhard O. *The Liberty Party, 1840–1848.* Baton Rouge: Louisiana State University Press, 2009.

Jordan, Winthrop D. *White over Black: Attitudes toward the Negro, 1550–1812.* New York: Norton, 1968.

Julian, George W. *The Life of Joshua R. Giddings.* Chicago: A. C. McClurg, 1892.

Justice, Hilda. *Life and Ancestry of Warner Mifflin, Friend-Philanthropist-Patriot.* Philadelphia: Ferris and Leach, 1905.

Kaplan, Fred. *John Quincy Adams: American Visionary.* New York: HarperCollins, 2014.

Kaplan, Sidney, and Emma Nogrady Kaplan. *The Black Presence in the Era of the American Revolution.* Amherst: University of Massachusetts Press, 1989.

Karcher, Carolyn L. *The First Woman of the Republic: A Cultural Biography of Lydia Maria Child.* Durham, N.C.: Duke University Press, 1994.

Konkle, Burton Alva. *George Bryan and the Constitution of Pennsylvania, 1731–1791.* Philadelphia: William J. Campbell, 1922.

———. *Joseph Hopkinson, 1770–1842, Jurist-Scholar-Inspirer of the Arts: Author of Hail Columbia.* Philadelphia: University of Pennsylvania Press, 1931.

Kraditor, Aileen S. *Means and Ends in American Abolitionism: Garrison and His Critics on Strategy and Tactics, 1834–1850.* New York: Pantheon, 1967.

Kraut, Alan M., ed. *Crusaders and Compromisers: Essays on the Relationship of the Antislavery Struggle to the Antebellum Party System.* Westport, Conn.: Greenwood Press, 1983.

Larson, John L. *The Market Revolution in America: Liberty, Ambition, and the Eclipse of the Common Good.* New York: Cambridge University Press, 2010.

Laurie, Bruce. *Beyond Garrison: Antislavery and Social Reform.* New York: Cambridge University Press, 2005.

Leslie, William R. "The Pennsylvania Fugitive Slave Act of 1826." *Journal of Southern History* 18 (November 1952): 429–45.

———. "A Study of the Origins of Interstate Rendition: The Big Beaver Creek Murders." *American Historical Review* 57 (October 1951): 63–76.

Lewis, William G. *Biography of Samuel Lewis: First Superintendent of Common Schools for the State of Ohio.* Cincinnati: William C. Lewis, 1857.

Lochemes, Mary Frederick. *Robert Walsh: His Story.* New York: American-Irish Historical Society, 1941.

Locke, Mary Staughton. *Antislavery in America from the Introduction of African Slaves to the Prohibition of the Slave Trade (1619–1808).* 1901; reprint Gloucester, Mass.: Peter Smith, 1965.

Lovejoy, John N. "Racism in Antebellum Vermont." *Vermont History* 69 (Symposium Supplement 2001): 48–65.

Lovejoy, Joseph P. *Memoir of Rev. Charles T. Torrey Who Died in the Penitentiary of Maryland Where He Was Confined for Showing Mercy to the Poor.* Boston: John P. Jewett, 1847.

Mabee, Carleton. *Black Freedom: The Nonviolent Abolitionists from 1830 through the Civil War.* New York: Macmillan, 1970.

McCarthy, Timothy Patrick, and John Stauffer, eds. *Prophets of Protest: Reconsidering the History of American Abolitionism.* New York: New Press, 2006.

McCormick, Richard P. *The Second American Party System: Party Formation in the Jacksonian Era.* Chapel Hill: University of North Carolina Press, 1966.

McDaniel, W. Caleb. *The Problem of Democracy in the Age of Slavery: Garrisonian Abolitionists and Transatlantic Reform.* Baton Rouge: Louisiana State University Press, 2013.

McFeely, William S. *Frederick Douglass.* New York: Norton, 1991.

McGuire, James K. *The Democratic Party of the State of New York.* 3 vols. New York: United States History Company, 1905.

McKay, Earnest. *Henry Wilson: Practical Radical: A Portrait of a Politician.* Port Washington, N.Y.: Kennikat Press, 1971.

McKivigan, John R. "The Antislavery 'Comeouter' Sects: A Neglected Dimension of the Abolition Movement." *Civil War History* 26 (June 1980): 142–60.

———, ed. *History of the American Abolitionist Movement: Abolitionism and American Law.* New York: Garland, 1999.

———. *The War against Pro-Slavery Religion: Abolitionism and the Northern Churches, 1830–1865.* Ithaca, N.Y.: Cornell University Press, 1984.

McKivigan, John R., and Stanley Harrold, eds. *Antislavery Violence: Sectional, Racial, and Cultural Conflict in Antebellum America.* Knoxville: University of Tennessee Press, 1999.

McManus, Edgar J. *Black Bondage in the North.* Syracuse, N.Y.: Syracuse University Press, 1973.

———. *A History of Negro Slavery in New York.* Syracuse, N.Y.: Syracuse University Press, 1966.

McNeal, John Edward. "The Antimasonic Party in Lancaster County, Pennsylvania, 1828–1843." *Journal of Lancaster County Historical Society* 69 (1965): 104–10.

McPherson, Edward. *The Political History of the United States of America, during the Great Rebellion, from November 6, 1860 to July 4, 1864.* Washington, D.C.: Philip and Solomons, 1864.

———. *The Political History of the United States of America during the Period of Reconstruction from April 15, 1866 to July 15, 1870.* Washington, D.C.: Solomons and Chapman, 1875.

McPherson, James M. "The Fight against the Gag Rule: Joshua Leavitt and the Antislavery Insurgency in the Whig Party, 1839–1842." *Journal of Negro History* 48 (July 1963): 177–95.

———. *Ordeal by Fire: The Civil War and Reconstruction.* New York: Knopf, 1982.

———. *The Struggle for Equality: Abolitionists and the Negro in the Civil War and Reconstruction.* Princeton, N.J.: Princeton University Press, 1964.

Mark, Gregory S. "The Vestigial Constitution; The History and Significance of the Right to Petition." *Fordham Law Review* 66 (1997–98): 2154–2231.

Marshall, Schuyler C. "The Free Democratic Convention of 1852." *Pennsylvania History* 22 (January 1955): 146–67.

Martyn, W. Carlos. *Wendell Phillips: The Agitator, with an Appendix Containing Three of the Orator's Masterpieces.* New York: Funk and Wagnalls, 1890.

Mason, Matthew. *Slavery and Politics in the Early American Republic.* Chapel Hill: University of North Carolina Press, 2006.

Masur, Kate. *An Example for All the Land: Emancipation and the Struggle over Equality in Washington, D.C.* Chapel Hill: University of North Carolina Press, 2010.

Mayer, Henry. *All on Fire: William Lloyd Garrison and the Abolition of Slavery.* New York: St. Martin's Press, 1998.

Mayfield, John. *Rehearsal for Republicanism: Free Soil and the Politics of Antislavery.* Port Washington, N.Y.: Kennikat Press, 1980.

Melish, Joanne Pope. *Disowning Slavery: Gradual Emancipation and "Race" in New England, 1780–1860.* Ithaca, N.Y.: Cornell University Press, 1998.

Merk, Frederick. *Slavery and the Annexation of Texas.* New York: Knopf, 1972.

Merrill, Walter M. *Against Wind and Tide: A Biography of Wm. Lloyd Garrison.* Cambridge, Mass.: Harvard University Press, 1963.

Messerli, Jonathan. *Horace Mann: A Biography.* New York: Knopf, 1972.

Miller, John C. *The Federalist Era, 1789–1801.* New York: Harper and Row, 1960.

Miller, Randall M., and John David Smith, eds. *Dictionary of Afro-American Slavery.* Westport, Conn.: Greenwood, 1988.

Miller, William Lee. *Arguing about Slavery: The Great Battle in the United States Congress.* New York: Knopf, 1996.

Moore, Glover. *The Missouri Controversy, 1819–1821.* Lexington: University of Kentucky Press, 1953.

Mordell, Albert. *Quaker Militant, John Greenleaf Whittier.* Port Washington, N.Y.: Kennikat Press, 1969.

Morris, Thomas. *The Life of Thomas Morris: Pioneer and Long a Legislator of Ohio, and U.S. Senator from 1833 to 1836.* Edited by B. F. Morris. Cincinnati: Moore, Wilstach, Keys, and Overend, 1856.

Morris, Thomas D. *Free Men All: The Personal Liberty Laws of the North, 1780–1861.* Baltimore: Johns Hopkins University Press, 1974.

Mullin, Gerald W. *Flight and Rebellion: Slave Resistance in Eighteenth-Century Virginia.* New York: Oxford University Press, 1972.

Murray, Lain Hamish. *Revival and Revivalism: The Making and Marring of American Evangelicalism, 1750–1858.* Edinburgh: Banner of Truth Trust, 1994.

Nash, Gary B. *Race and Revolution.* Revised edition. 1990; Lanham, Md.: Rowman and Littlefield, 2001.

———. *Warner Mifflin: Unflinching Quaker Abolitionist.* Philadelphia: University of Pennsylvania Press, 2017.

Nash, Gary B., and Jean R. Soderlund. *Freedom by Degrees: Emancipation in Pennsylvania and Its Aftermath.* New York: Oxford University Press, 1991.

Needles, Edward. *An Historical Memoir of the Pennsylvania Society for Promoting the Abolition of Slavery.* Philadelphia: Merrihew and Thompson, 1848.

Neuenschwander, John. "Senator Thomas Morris: Antagonist of the South." *Cincinnati Historical Society Bulletin* 32 (Fall 1974): 123–39.

Nevins, Allen. *Frémont, Path Finder of the West.* 1939; reprint Lincoln: University of Nebraska Press, 1992.

————. *Ordeal of the Union.* 4 vols. New York: Charles Scribner's Sons, 1947–59.

Newman, Richard S. *The Transformation of American Abolitionism: Fighting Slavery in the Early Republic.* Chapel Hill: University of North Carolina Press, 2002.

Newton, Joseph F. *Lincoln and Herndon.* Cedar Rapids, Iowa: Torch Press, 1910.

Niven, John. *Salmon P. Chase: A Biography.* New York: Oxford University Press, 1995.

Nye, Russell B. *Fettered Freedom: Civil Liberties and the Slavery Controversy.* East Lansing: Michigan State College Press, 1949.

Oakes, James. *Freedom National: The Destruction of Slavery in the United States, 1861–1865.* New York: Norton, 2013.

————. *The Radical and the Republican: Frederick Douglass, Abraham Lincoln, and the Triumph of Antislavery.* New York: Norton, 2007.

————. *The Scorpion's Sting: Antislavery and the Coming of the Civil War.* New York: Norton, 2014.

Oates, Stephen B. *To Purge This Land with Blood: A Biography of John Brown.* Amherst: University of Massachusetts Press, 1984.

Ohline, Howard A. "Slavery, Economics, and Congressional Politics, 1790." *Journal of Southern History* 46 (August 1980): 335–60.

Owsley, Frank L. "The Fundamental Cause of the Civil War: Egocentric Sectionalism." *Journal of Southern History* 7 (February 1941): 3–18.

Pacheco, Josephine E. *The Pearl: A Failed Slave Escape on the Potomac.* Chapel Hill: University of North Carolina Press, 2005.

Parsons, Lynn Hudson. *John Quincy Adams.* Madison, Wis.: Madison House, 1998.

"Penn Biographies." University of Pennsylvania Archives and Records Center. archives.upenn.edu/people/bioa.html.

Perry, Lewis. *Radical Abolitionism: Anarchy and the Government of God in Antislavery Thought.* Ithaca, N.Y.: Cornell University Press, 1973.

Perry, Lewis, and Michael Fellman, eds. *Antislavery Reconsidered: New Perspectives on the Abolitionists.* Baton Rouge: Louisiana State University Press, 1979.

Pierson, Michael D. *Free Hearts and Free Homes: Gender and American Antislavery Politics.* Chapel Hill: University of North Carolina Press, 2003.

Pillsbury, Parker. *Acts of the Anti-Slavery Apostles.* 1883; reprint Miami: Mnemosyne, 1969.

Polger, Paul J. "'To Raise Them to an Equal Participation': Early National Abolitionism, Gradual Emancipation, and the Promise of African American Citizenship." *Journal of the Early Republic* 31 (Summer 2011): 229–58.

Potter, David M. *The Impending Crisis, 1848–1861.* New York: Harper, 1963.

Price, Robert. "The Ohio Anti-Slavery Convention of 1836." *Ohio State Archaeological and Historical Quarterly* 45 (April 1936): 173–88.

Quarles, Benjamin. *Allies for Freedom: Blacks and John Brown.* New York: Oxford University Press, 1974.

————. *Lincoln and the Negro.* New York: Oxford University Press, 1962.

————. *The Negro in the American Revolution.* Chapel Hill: University of North Carolina Press, 1961.

Randall, James G. *The Civil War and Reconstruction.* Boston: D. C. Heath, 1937.

Rayback, Joseph G. *Free Soil: The Election of 1848.* Lexington: University Press of Kentucky, 1971.

Remini, Robert W. *John Quincy Adams.* New York: Henry Holt, 2002.

Ress, David. *Governor Edward Coles and the Vote to Forbid Slavery in Illinois, 1823–1824.* Jefferson, N.C.: McFarland, 2006.

Reynolds, David S. *John Brown, Abolitionist: The Man Who Killed Slavery, Sparked the Civil War, and Seeded Civil Rights.* New York: Knopf, 2005.

————. *Mightier Than the Sword:* Uncle Tom's Cabin *and the Battle for America.* New York: Norton, 2011.

Rhodes, James Ford. *History of the United States from the Compromise of 1850.* 9 vols. New York: Macmillan, 1894–1913.

Richards, Leonard L. *"Gentlemen of Property and Standing": Anti-Abolition Mobs in Jacksonian America.* New York: Oxford University Press, 1971.

————. *The Life and Times of Congressman John Quincy Adams.* New York: Oxford University Press, 1986.

————. *The Slave Power: The Free North and Southern Domination, 1780–1860.* Baton Rouge: Louisiana State University Press, 2000.

Richardson, Charles F., and Elizabeth Miner Richardson. *Charles Miner, a Pennsylvania Pioneer.* Wilkes-Barre, Penn.: privately published, 1916.

Robertson, Stacey M. *Parker Pillsbury: Radical Abolitionist, Male Feminist.* Ithaca, N.Y.: Cornell University Press, 2000.

Roosevelt, Theodore. *Thomas Hart Benton.* Boston: Houghton Mifflin, 1887.

Rose, Willie Lee. *Rehearsal for Reconstruction: The Port Royal Experiment.* Indianapolis: Bobs-Merrill, 1964.

Rossbach, Jeffery S. *Ambivalent Conspirators: John Brown, the Secret Six, and a Theory of Slave Violence.* Philadelphia: University of Pennsylvania Press, 1982.

Schor, Joel. *Henry Highland Garnet, a Voice of Black Radicalism in the Nineteenth Century.* Westport, Conn.: Greenwood, 1977.

Schouler, James. *History of the United States of American under the Constitution.* 7 vols. New York: Dodd, Mead, 1894–1913.

Schwartz, Harold. *Samuel Gridley Howe, Social Reformer, 1801–1876.* Cambridge, Mass.: Harvard University Press, 1956.

Schwartz, Philip J. *Slave Laws in Virginia.* Athens: University of Georgia Press, 1996.

Scott, Joseph W. *The Black Revolts: Racial Stratification in the U.S.A.* Cambridge, Mass.: Schenkman, 1967.

Sellers, Charles. *The Market Revolution: Jacksonian America, 1815–1844.* New York: Oxford University Press, 1991.

Seward, Frederick W. *Seward at Washington, as Senator and Secretary of State: A Memoir of His Life, with Selections from His Letters, 1846–1872.* 2 vols. New York: Derby and Miller, 1891.

Sewell, Richard H. *Ballots for Freedom: Antislavery Politics in the United States, 1837–1860.* New York: Oxford University Press, 1976.

———. *John P. Hale and the Politics of Abolition.* Cambridge, Mass.: Harvard University Press, 1965.

Shapiro, Samuel. *Richard Henry Dana Jr., 1815–1882.* East Lansing: Michigan State University Press, 1961.

Sheehan-Dean, Aaron, ed. *A Companion to the U.S. Civil War.* 2 vols. Malden, Mass.: Wiley Blackwell, 2014.

Simmons, Richard C. *The American Colonies from Settlement to Independence.* London: Longman, 1976.

Sinha, Manisha. *The Slave's Cause: A History of Abolition.* New Haven, Conn.: Yale University Press, 2016.

Smiley, David L. *Lion of White Hall: The Life of Cassius M. Clay.* Madison: University of Wisconsin Press, 1962.

Smith, Justin H. *Annexation of Texas.* 1919; reprint New York: AMS Press, 1971.

Smith, Theodore Clarke. *Liberty and Free Soil Parties in the Northwest.* New York: Longmans, Green, 1897.

Soderlund, Jean R. *Quakers and Slavery: A Divided Spirit.* Princeton, N.J.: Princeton University Press, 1985.

Stampp, Kenneth M. *The Peculiar Institution: Slavery in the Antebellum South.* 1956; reprint New York: Vintage, 1989.

Stanton, Elizabeth Cady, et al. *History of Woman Suffrage.* 6 vols. New York: Fowler and Wells, 1881–1922.

Stearns, Frank Preston. *The Life and Public Service of George Luther Stearns.* Philadelphia: J. B. Lippincott, 1907.

Stern, Madeleine. "Stephen Pearl Andrews, Abolitionist, and the Annexation of Texas." *Southwestern Historical Quarterly* 66 (April 1964): 491–523.

Stewart, James Brewer. *Abolitionist Politics and the Coming of the Civil War.* Amherst: University of Massachusetts Press, 2008.

———. *Holy Warriors: The Abolitionists and American Slavery.* Revised edition. 1976; New York: Hill and Wang, 1997.

———. *Joshua R. Giddings and the Tactics of Radical Politics.* Cleveland: Press of Case Western Reserve University, 1970.

———. "Reconsidering the Abolitionists in an Age of Fundamentalist Politics." *Journal of the Early Republic* 26 (Spring 2006): 1–24.

———. *Wendell Phillips, Liberty's Hero.* Baton Rouge: Louisiana State University Press, 1986.

———. *William Lloyd Garrison and the Challenge of Emancipation.* Arlington Heights, Ill.: Harland Davidson, 1992.

Strong, Douglas M. *Perfectionist Politics: Abolitionism and the Religious Tensions of American Democracy.* Syracuse, N.Y.: Syracuse University Press, 1999.

Thomas, Benjamin Platt. *Theodore Weld: Crusader for Freedom.* New Brunswick, N.J.: Rutgers University Press, 1950.

Thompson, Mack. *Moses Brown: Reluctant Reformer.* Chapel Hill: University of North Carolina Press, 1962.

Tise, Larry E. *Proslavery: A History of the Defense of Slavery in America.* Athens: University of Georgia Press, 1987.

Tomek, Beverly C. *Pennsylvania Hall: A "Legal Lynching" in the Shadow of the Liberty Bell.* New York: Oxford University Press, 2014.

Torrey, E. Fuller. *The Martyrdom of Abolitionist Charles Torrey.* Baton Rouge: Louisiana State University Press, 2013.

Trefousse, Hans L. *Impeachment of a President: Andrew Johnson, the Blacks, and Reconstruction.* Knoxville: University of Tennessee Press, 1976.

———. *The Radical Republicans: Lincoln's Vanguard for Racial Justice.* New York: Knopf, 1969.

———. *Thaddeus Stevens: Nineteenth-Century Egalitarian.* Chapel Hill: University of North Carolina Press, 1997.

Tremain, Mary. *Slavery in the District of Columbia: The Policy of Congress and the Struggle for Abolition.* New York: G. P. Putnam's Sons, 1892.

Tsesis, Alexander. *The Thirteenth Amendment and American Freedom: A Legal History.* New York: New York University Press, 2004.

Tuckerman, Bayard. *William Jay and the Constitutional Movement for the Abolition of Slavery.* New York: Dodd, Mead, 1893.

Tuttleton, James W. *Thomas Wentworth Higginson.* Boston: Twayne, 1978.

Van Deusen, Glyndon G. *William Henry Seward.* New York: Oxford University Press, 1967.

Vaughan, William Preston. *The Antimasonic Party in the United States, 1826–1843.* Lexington: University Press of Kentucky, 1983.

Walters, Ronald G. *American Reformers, 1815–1860.* New York: Hill and Wang, 1978.

———. *The Antislavery Appeal: American Abolition ism after 1830.* Baltimore: Johns Hopkins University Press, 1976.

———. "The Erotic South: Civilization and Sexuality in American Abolitionism." *American Quarterly* 25 (May 1973): 177–202.

Washburne, E. B. *Sketch of Edward Coles, Second Governor of Illinois and the Slavery Struggle, 1823–24.* 1882; reprint New York: Negro Universities Press, 1969.

White, Horace. *Life of Lyman Trumbull.* Boston: Houghton Mifflin, 1913.

[White, J. Gardner, ed.]. *Memorial Biographies of the New England Genealogical Society, 1866–1871.* 9 vols. Boston: New England Historic Genealogical Society, 1880–1908.

Wiecek, William M. *The Sources of Antislavery Constitutionalism in America, 1760–1841.* Ithaca, N.Y.: Cornell University Press, 1977.

Wilentz, Sean. *The Rise of American Democracy: Jefferson to Lincoln.* New York: Norton, 2005.

Wilson, Carol. *Freedom at Risk: The Kidnapping of Free Blacks in America, 1780–1865.* Lexington: University Press of Kentucky, 1994.

Wilson, Henry. *History of the Antislavery Measures of the Thirty-Seventh and Thirty-Eighth Congresses, 1861–1865.* Boston: Walker, Wise, 1865.

———. *History of the Rise and Fall of the Slave Power in America.* 3 vols. 1873–77; reprint New York: Negro Universities Press, 1969.

Wilson, James G., and John Fiske, eds. *Appleton's Cyclopedia of American Biography.* 6 vols. New York: D. Appleton, 1887.

Wilson, Major L. *The Presidency of Martin Van Buren.* Lawrence: University Press of Kansas, 1984.

Wise, Barton H. *The Life of Henry A. Wise of Virginia, 1806–1876.* New York: Macmillan, 1899.

Wright, Marion Thompson. "New Jersey Laws and the Negro." *Journal of Negro History* 28 (April 1943): 156–99.

Woodwell, Roland. *John Greenleaf Whittier: A Biography.* Haverhill, Mass.: Trustees of the John Greenleaf Whittier Homestead, 1985.

Wyatt-Brown, Bertram. *Lewis Tappan and the Evangelical War against Slavery.* Cleveland: Press of Case Western Reserve University, 1969.

———. *Southern Honor: Ethics and Behavior in the Old South.* New York: Oxford University Press, 1982.

Yacovone, Donald. *Samuel Joseph May and the Dilemmas of the Liberal Persuasion, 1797–1871.* Philadelphia: Temple University Press, 1991.

Yellin, Jean Fagan, and John C. Van Horne, eds. *Abolitionist Sisterhood: Women's Political Culture in Antebellum America.* Ithaca, N.Y.: Cornell University Press, 1994.

Young, James Harvey. "Anna Elizabeth Dickinson and the Civil War: For and Against Lincoln." *Mississippi Valley Historical Review* 31 (June 1944): 59–80.

Zaeske, Susan. *Signatures of Citizenship: Petitions and Women's Political Identity.* Chapel Hill: University of North Carolina Press, 2003.

Zilversmit, Arthur. *The First Emancipation: The Abolition of Slavery in the North.* Chicago: University of Chicago Press, 1967.

Index